NEW DIRECTIONS IN MEASURES AND METHODS

ADVANCES IN MOTIVATION AND ACHIEVEMENT

Series Editors: Martin L. Maehr and Paul R. Pintrich

Recent volumes:

Volume 9: Culture, Motivation and Achievement – Edited by Martin L. Maehr and Paul R. Pintrich
Volume 10: Advances in Motivation and Achievement – Edited by Martin L. Maehr and Paul R. Pintrich
Volume 11: The Role of Context – Edited by Timothy C. Urdan

ADVANCES IN MOTIVATION AND ACHIEVEMENT
VOLUME 12

NEW DIRECTIONS IN MEASURES AND METHODS

EDITED BY

PAUL R. PINTRICH
Combined Program in Education and Psychology,
The University of Michigan, Ann Arbor, USA

MARTIN L. MAEHR
Combined Program in Education and Psychology,
The University of Michigan, Ann Arbor, USA

Emerald

United Kingdom – North America – Japan
India – Malaysia – China

Emerald Group Publishing Limited
Howard House, Wagon Lane, Bingley BD16 1WA, UK

British Library Cataloguing in Publication Data
A catalogue record for this book is available from the British Library

ISBN: 978-0-7623-0819-4
ISSN: 0749-7423 (Series)

CONTENTS

LIST OF CONTRIBUTORS

Mary Ainley	University of Melbourne, Australia
Monique Boekaerts	Leiden University, The Netherlands
Harris Cooper	University of Missouri – Columbia, Columbia, Missouri, USA
Elisabeth Vialpando De Groot	University of Michigan, Ann Arbor, Michigan, USA
Suzanne Hidi	University of Toronto, Canada
Janis E. Jacobs	Pennsylvania State University, University Park, Pennsylvania, USA
Dianne Jamieson-Noel	Simon Fraser University, Burnaby, British Columbia, Canada
Sanna Järvelä	University of Oulu, Finland
Janne Lepola	University of Turku, Finland
Krista R. Muis	Simon Fraser University, Burnaby, British Columbia, Canada
Markku Niemivirta	University of Helsinki, Finland
D. Wayne Osgood	Pennsylvania State University, University Park, Pennsylvania, USA
Pekka Salonen	University of Turku, Finland
Oliver C. Schultheiss	The University of Michigan, Ann Arbor, Michigan, USA
Jeffrey C. Valentine	University of Missouri – Columbia, Columbia, Missouri, USA

Philip H. Winne	Simon Fraser University, Burnaby, British Columbia, Canada
Christopher A. Wolters	University of Houston, Houston, Texas, USA
Shirley L. Yu	University of Houston, Houston, Texas, USA

PREFACE

The study of achievement motivation began as part of a broader attempt to make the study of human motivation a truly scientific enterprise. David McClelland built upon the solid scientific, but narrow, basis established by Clark Hull and expanded this model significantly by incorporating psychodynamic perspectives and focusing on human motives. In this regard, he was no doubt influenced by the work of Henry Murray and measurement research that eventuated in the development of the TAT. Subsequently both the laboratory methods of Hull and the psychometric work of Murray framed perhaps the most important early basis for the now broad and diverse literature on motivation and achievement that exists today. Nearly six decades since the first major volume concerned with motivation research methods appeared, issues of methods remain and have re-emerged as paramount. This volume was framed in direct response to this state of affairs.

Over the last 60 or so years procedures have come and gone, but some basic issues remain and deserve focused attention and reconsideration. Questions of philosophy as well as practicality have been at issue in formulating procedures for conducting research in the social sciences generally. This has only begun to happen in the area of motivation, but doubtless there are many reasons why procedures, methods and measurement will be focal over the next several years. This volume, we believe, should contribute significantly to the dialogue. First, the chapters present a rich sample of the methods and measures that are currently employed – and suggestions relative to their strengths and limitations. Recent research in the implicit motive tradition inspired by McClelland is featured as well as observational methods and examples of the use of various self-report methods, including questionnaires, interviews, and "on line" assessment of thoughts, feelings and action employing cognitive science technology and methodology and reflecting social cognitive approaches to motivation theory. In addition, there are chapters that address issues of data analysis, a key concern given the different questions, methods, and measures that are generated by different approaches to the study of motivation.

Importantly, the range of approaches discussed and the consideration of the theoretical underpinnings for using them make this volume more than merely a compendium of motivational research methods. The issue throughout is methodology, not simply procedures – with the authors giving extensive consideration to the theoretical rationale at the root of a procedural option. However, readers searching for means and methods for pursuing motivational research will not go unsatisfied either. Rather they will, we feel, be provided both stimulation and suggestions for designing assessments and studies of their own.

A major theme that cuts across all the chapters in this book concerns the tension between person-centered or individual difference measures of motivation and those measures and methods that are more situated or contextual. It has been an axiom of psychology in general and motivational research in particular, since at least Lewin's time, that human behavior is always a function of the person and the context. However, while this assumption is always honored in the abstract, at the level of actual measures and methods, it has been far easier for researchers to rely on either more person-centered methods or ones that focus more on the context, with few attempts at integration. Of course, there is a great need for research that integrates both personal and contextual factors and examines human motivation in a much more dynamic manner, allowing for both personal construals as well as contextual shaping and scaffolding of behavior. Integration is a difficult theoretical problem as well as a thorny pragmatic one in terms of research, but it is heartening to see the authors in this volume grappling with these issues and developing some new and innovative approaches to this longstanding problem.

Schultheiss discusses the role of implicit motives in motivational dynamics and shows how TAT measures can be used, in combination with experimental methods, to generate consistent findings regarding the relations between motives and behavior. His chapter shows the importance of considering implicit motives, psychophysiological correlates, as well as more social cognitive constructs such as goals and information processing in our models. In addition, we think his chapter will increase interest in implicit motives and projective techniques among researchers studying achievement and motivation in school settings.

The next three chapters in this volume stress the importance of obtaining dynamic and situated measures of motivation and self-regulation. Ainley and Hidi describe their program of research on personal and situational interest using "on-line" computer-based methods that assess student interest as they are working on text comprehension tasks. They show how their measure can be used to generate reliable and valid measures of interest and affect and how these constructs are linked to text comprehension and learning.

Boekaerts also uses an on-line methodology to assess student appraisals of the learning situation and shows how these appraisals can vary by situation.

Her measure does not require computer technology, but still provides a dynamic and situated measure of student motivation that is contextualized. Her chapter reviews her and her colleagues program of research documenting the important variation in motivation over different contexts and how these differences are related in reliable ways with important educational outcomes.

Winne, Jamieson-Noel, and Muis focus on self-regulated learning, not just student motivation, but summarize some of the inherent difficulties in using simple self-report questionnaires to assess self-regulation and motivation. They make an important distinction between self-regulation as a general aptitude in comparison to self-regulation as a dynamic unfolding event and discuss the methodological implications of such a distinction. They offer a number of important methodological suggestions for the measurement of self-regulation and motivation as well as new methods for the analysis of both self-report and event-related measures of self-regulation.

The next chapter by De Groot focuses on self-reports, but emphasizes the use of interviews as a source of information about motivation and learning. She discusses several different uses of interviews, including highly structured individual interviews, more open-ended or ethnographic individual interviews, and group interviews or focus groups. In line with the general theme of the book, this chapter stresses how student and teacher motivation are both highly contextualized and that often these person-in-context relations are lost when simple surveys or questionnaires are used to assess motivation.

Järvelä, Salonen, and Lepola are also concerned with person-in-context relations and in issues of assessment and analysis. They emphasize the use of multiple methods including self-reports, interviews, and observations and note how these multiple sources of data can provide a much richer and detailed description of student motivation in the classroom context. The studies reported on in their chapter show the power of such multiple methods when combined with a strong theoretical framework for conceptualizing student motivation.

The remaining four chapters shift from a specific emphasis on new ways of assessing and measuring motivation to a concern with analysis issues. Niemivirta deals with the problems of integrating variable-centered and person-centered analyses in studies of motivation. Variable-centered analyses have been the traditional data analysis method in motivational research. However, if one is concerned with individuals and how they develop or learn in different contexts, then it is important to understand how the person changes over time, not how variables change over time. Person-centered analyses have usually relied on cluster analysis procedures which have some major limitations. Niemivirta discusses several new and much more powerful analysis methods that allow for person-centered analysis, but avoid the problems inherent in simple cluster analysis procedures.

Jacobs and Osgood also are concerned with the nature of development of motivation in individuals across different contexts. This is a classic problem in research on motivation as individuals are always clustered within different levels of contexts (i.e. classrooms, schools, communities). Jacobs and Osgood show how the use of multi-level modeling can be used to study individual developmental change over time as well as the independent effects of contexts on these developmental trajectories.

Valentine and Cooper discuss the use of meta-analysis in motivational research. As they point out, there is a large and well-developed corpus of studies on student motivation in various educational settings. However, research synthesis techniques are rarely used when this corpus of work is summarized. Valentine and Cooper point out the inherent scientific and logical problems with simple narrative reviews and provide a number of very important and pragmatic suggestions for implementing research synthesis techniques.

The final chapter in this volume, by Yu and Wolters, discusses both measurement and analysis issues in terms of ethnic and cultural differences. As our field becomes more interested in issues of ethnicity and the role of culture in motivation, it is very important to understand how well our motivational models can generalize to different populations and cultures. Yu and Wolters provide a very cogent and important analysis of the construct validity issues that confront motivational researchers as they attempt to build general models of motivation. They make a number of key suggestions that all motivational researchers would do well to heed in future research.

In summary, the chapters in this volume all provide important theoretical, conceptual, methodological, and pragmatic suggestions about new directions for measures and methods in motivational research. As in all scientific endeavors, a field makes progress not just because of new theoretical perspectives or ideas, but also because of the development of new methodologies. We believe that the chapters here offer the field of motivational research many new and important tools and perspectives for developing methodologies that will greatly advance our scientific understanding of motivation. We look forward to using many of these new ideas in our own research and hope the readers of this volume will do so likewise.

Paul R. Pintrich
Martin L. Maehr
Series Editors

1. AN INFORMATION PROCESSING ACCOUNT OF IMPLICIT MOTIVE AROUSAL

Oliver C. Schultheiss

When McClelland, Atkinson, Clark and Lowell published their groundbreaking monograph *The achievement motive* in 1953, scientific research on human motives such as the needs for achievement, affiliation, or power was off to a great start as a respectable, promising and flourishing branch of psychology. It generated thousands of published research reports over the next three decades and spilled over into other disciplines such as political science, economics, history, or sociology. Roughly at the beginning of the 1980s, however, the former stream of research output had dwindled down to a trickle, and this development was foreshadowed by earlier reviews critical both of the construct validity of motives and their mode of measurement (e.g. Entwisle, 1972; Fineman, 1977; Klinger, 1966). Criticisms of the Thematic Apperception Test (TAT) and its variants as being unreliable motive measures turned out to be largely unfounded and based on methodological artifacts (e.g. Lundy, 1985; Winter & Stewart, 1977; see also Kuhl, 1978) as well as the inappropriate application of classical test theory to motivational phenomena (Atkinson, 1981; Atkinson & Birch, 1970; Cramer, 1999; McClelland, 1980) and will not be further reviewed here. Criticisms leveled at the validity of the motive construct in the McClelland-Atkinson tradition, however, may be more difficult to counter and, to the extent that they reflect the frustrations of many researchers who failed to find meaningful relationships between motives and behavior in

New Directions in Measures and Methods, Volume 12, pages 1–41.

ISBN: 0-7623-0819-2

their studies, may have contributed substantially to the demise of motive research.

For instance, Klinger (1966) noted in a review of studies focusing on achievement motivation that while roughly half of the then published studies obtained significant and meaningful relationships between the achievement motive and performance measures, the other half failed to obtain such relationships. This state of affairs led Klinger to question whether TAT-based achievement motive measures actually measure anything motivational at all. Lazarus (1961) summarized research showing either no or paradoxical relationships between the achievement motive and behavior. Taking an essentially Freudian stance, he concluded that the achievement motive is expressed in primary process-like fantasy (i.e. in TAT stories) only to the extent that it is blocked from behavioral manifestations or not filtered away by ego defenses when it is too strongly aroused. According to this point of view, one should not expect to be able to predict performance and behavior from a TAT measure of the achievement motives (or any other motive) in any direct and straightforward way.

In the present chapter, I will argue that, contrary to the views of Klinger and Lazarus, motives *do* have a direct, motivating effect on behavior, and that this effect depends on the type of incentive present in a given situation. My main claim will be that motives are aroused by and respond to directly perceived and experienced incentives rather than to verbal-symbolic incentives. I will also argue that failure to present incentives in an experiential format or lack of control for features of the testing situation that cue motives experientially will produce the non-significant or sometimes even paradoxical effects cited by Klinger and Lazarus. In support of these claims, I will present an information-processing framework to account for the effects of incentives and motives on behavior, report findings from four experimental studies that support this model and illustrate a technique through which motives can be reliably aroused in experimental laboratory research, and conclude with some thoughts on the interplay between motivational systems in humans. To set the stage for these ideas, however, it might be informative to first take a look at what motives are and how previous researchers have (mis-)conceived the characteristics of motive-arousing incentives.

PREVIOUS VIEWS OF MOTIVE-AROUSING INCENTIVES

Motives like the needs for achievement, power or affiliation are inherently affect-driven: they aim at gaining pleasure from the consummation of a motive-specific incentive (McClelland, 1987). In the case of the achievement motive, the incentive is doing something better or improving on a task; in the case of the power motive, it is having impact on other people or the world at large; and in the case of the affiliation motive, it is having close, friendly contact with others. Motives are aroused by situational cues that predict the availability of a motive-specific-incentive in a given situation and subsequently recruit and fuel behavior aimed at attaining the incentive. As individual-difference variables, motives indicate to what extent a person can become motivated by such cues and eventually gain pleasure from making contact with an incentive. For instance, a person with a strong power motive will experience having an impact on somebody as more rewarding and desirable than a person with a weak power motive. This affect-amplifying function of implicit motives was recently documented by Brunstein, Schultheiss and Grässmann (1998), who found that individuals high in an implicit motive reported a greater sense of satisfaction after attaining a motive-specific incentive than individuals low in the same motive. According to McClelland (1987), individuals high in a motive will consequently strive more frequently or more intensely for a motive-specific incentive than individuals low in the same motive.

In the McClelland-Atkinson tradition, the needs for achievement, power and affiliation have also been termed *implicit motives* because they operate outside of a person's conscious awareness and cannot be validly assessed with self-report measures designed to tap these motivational domains (cf. McClelland, Koestner & Weinberger, 1989). However, they are assumed to influence imagined and real behavior after being aroused by motive-relevant situational cues. Therefore, the strength of an individual's motive can be determined by analyzing the content of fantasies she or he reports in response to motive-relevant picture cues, as used in the TAT and similar measures.

However, despite over 50 years of research on implicit motives, the exact nature of motive-arousing cues is still not understood very well. McClelland et al.'s (1953; see also McClelland, 1958) original theory of motive-arousing stimuli was couched in the language of Pavlovian conditioning and stated that initially neutral stimuli that reliably predict a positive (or negative) affective end state will become conditional stimuli that can evoke approach (or avoidance) motivation related to these end states. No further attempt was made to pinpoint what types of stimuli might or might not be suitable for such conditioning to occur and hence to arouse a motive.

McClelland (1980) essentially abandoned the 1953 model by using Skinnerian language and stating that motives influence *operant* behavior, that is, behavior that is spontaneously emitted and occurs in the absence of identifiable eliciting stimuli. He contrasted motives with the values individuals consciously endorse and which influence *respondent* behavior, that is, behavior in response to an identifiable eliciting stimulus. McClelland also proposed that the TAT is an operant measure of implicit motives: "I favor referring to these [TAT] thought samples as operant because in Skinner's sense it is not possible to identify the exact stimulus that elicits them. [. . .] the stimulus is vague [. . .]" (p. 12). Conversely, he considered the questionnaires typically used to assess how much value individuals place on achievement, power, or affiliation to be respondent measures because they present the testee with a specifiable stimulus (e.g. a self-descriptive item) and also specify the response mode (e.g. "agree" or "disagree").

These conclusions are in direct contradiction to the majority of theorizing and research on implicit motives. First, at the level of the terms used by McClelland (1980), the 1953 model of motive arousal would be that of a respondent rather than an operant process, since it explicitly takes motive-arousing stimuli into account. Second, McClelland and other motive researchers did not just use *any* TAT picture cues to collect stories from their subjects (as could be suspected on the basis of McClelland's assertion that it is impossible to determine which stimulus influences a story's content). From the outset, investigators employed pictures that were tailored to the assessment of the particular motive they were interested in measuring. For instance, in their pioneering work on the hunger motive, Atkinson and McClelland (1948) used pictures suggesting satiation, food deprivation, invitation to eat, place of eating, or food to elicit stories from food-deprived and non-deprived participants. McClelland et al. (1953) employed pictures showing people in various achievement-related situations (e.g. two men in a shop working at a machine; a boy sitting at a desk with an open book in front of him) to assess their participants' achievement motive. Moreover, these researchers carefully analyzed the "pull" different pictures had for eliciting achievement imagery and found significant and reliable differences between pictures. Similar picture cue effects on motive imagery have recently been reported by Schultheiss and Brunstein (in press) for the needs for power, achievement, and affilition. Thus, the TAT can hardly be termed an "operant measure" in the sense that it does not contain identifiable stimuli whose effects on subjects' fantasies can be measured reliably. Third and finally, researchers have relied heavily on their ability to control motive-arousing stimuli in experimental research on implicit motives. Again, two studies from McClelland et al.'s (1953) influential monograph on the achievement motive can serve as a case in point. These researchers experimentally varied participants' achievement arousal by providing no feedback, failure feedback, success feedback or success/failure feedback on a series of performance tests and then administered a TAT. They found that participants' TAT achievement motive scores varied systematically as a function of the experimental condition – a clearcut demonstration of stimulus effects on achievement motivation. In another study, participants worked on a number of tasks under neutral, task-oriented, or achievement-oriented instructions and were then interrupted before they had completed the tasks. Individuals with a strong achievement motive in the achievement-oriented condition, relative to those in the neutral or task-oriented condition, subsequently remembered more uncompleted tasks than individuals with a weak achievement motive. These results then, too, document that a motive's influence on behavior depends on the presence of identifiable motive-arousing stimuli and that researchers, including McClelland himself, have made strategic use of such stimuli in their research.

Overall, then, McClelland's (1980) distinction between "operant" motives and "respondent" values seems to be an inaccurate and misleading one in that it suggests that motive-arousing stimuli can not be identified or may not even exist. Implicit motives clearly respond differentially to specific stimuli, be they TAT picture cues or experimental conditions and instructions; if this were not the case, research on implicit motives would have been impossible from the outset.

McClelland, Koestner and Weinberger (1989; see also Koestner, Weinberger & McClelland, 1991) made another attempt to come to grips with the nature of motive-arousing stimuli by discriminating between explicit, social-extrinsic and implicit, task-intrinsic stimuli. They argued that implicit motives respond to incentives that are inherent in performing a task or an activity whereas consciously endorsed values – now called explicit or self-attributed motives –respond to explicit social expectations, demands, rewards or prompts. Although this distinction has had some heuristic value for subsequent research on the separate and conjoint effects of implicit and explicit motives on behavior (e.g. Biernat, 1989; Brunstein & Hoyer, in press; Koestner et al., 1991), it is not without problems. First and foremost, while it clearly predicts that explicit task instructions will activate a person's self-attributed motives (e.g. the instruction "It is important that you work hard and excel at this task" should trigger a person's explicit achievement motive), it fails to identify what the "inherent" activity features are that supposedly engage a person's implicit motives. Since what cannot be pinpointed cannot be manipulated, either, it comes as little surprise that in a set of experiments which Koestner et al. (1991) conducted in order to support the social-extrinsic/task-intrinsic distinction, only the presence or absence of social-extrinsic incentives was varied experimentally, but not the presence or absence of task-intrinsic incentives.

Furthermore, placing motive arousal or satisfaction into the performance of an activity itself while excluding the social context of the activity may represent an adequate description of how the relatively non-social achievement motive, which is mainly about doing well or improving on a task, works. But in all likelihood this definition falls short in capturing the essence of stimuli to which the socially oriented needs for power or affiliation respond. For these motives, crucial stimuli are those that indicate whether one has had impact on others (power) or has established rapport with others (affiliation) and the activities leading to these outcomes may not necessarily be intrinsically motive-arousing or -rewarding by themselves, but rather follow the laws of means-end instrumentality (cf. Schultheiss & Brunstein, in press).

The Koestner et al. (1991) studies also highlight another problem with the social-extrinsic/task-intrinsic distinction, namely, that the same type of instructions that are used here as a social-extrinsic incentive to activate participants' self-attributed motives have been and continue to be employed to arouse participants' implicit motives in other studies. Compare the "social-extrinsic" instructions used by Koestner et al. (1991) in Experiment 1 to engage participants' *explicit* achievement motive (top) with those used by McClelland (1995) to arouse participants' *implicit* achievement motive (bottom):

> People seem to remember words related to their personalities best. [. . .] People interested in achievement are *better* at remembering how hard people are working or how well they are doing on various tasks (Koestner et al., 1991, p. 67; italics in original).

> Let's see how many [arithmetic problems] you can do in five minutes. Work as hard and correctly as you can. Do your very best. I want to see who can do the most problems in five minutes (McClelland, 1995; p. 64).

In both studies, the effects of these instructions were compared to the effects of neutral instructions in a control group. In both studies, the interaction effect of arousal instructions with motivational dispositions on performance on a memory task was assessed. In the Koestner et al. (1991) study, higher levels of *self-attributed* achievement motivation, but not of implicit achievement motivation, predicted better recall performance in the arousal condition. Conversely, in the McClelland (1995) study, higher levels of *implicit* achievement motivation, but not of explicit achievement motivation, predicted better recall performance in the arousal condition. It is hard to see in what sense McClelland's (1995) arousal instructions are any less social-extrinsic or more task-intrinsic than Koestner et al.'s (1991) arousal instructions. At the same time, the result patterns from these studies are completely at odds with each other. This suggests either that McClelland and colleagues' social-extrinsic/task-intrinsic distinction is not a valid or accurate way to conceive of motivational arousal processes, or that other, unidentified factors account for the differences in findings from these studies, or both.

This conclusion is also supported by the paradoxical motive-behavior relationships first pointed out by Lazarus (1961). Corroborating Lazarus's observation, Spangler (1992) found in a meta-analysis of the validity of implicit and explicit achievement motive measures that in the presence of social-extrinsic incentives, the implicit achievement motive correlates negatively with behavioral outcomes. He characterized this finding as a suppressor effect, because social-extrinsic incentives did not leave motive-behavior relationships unaffected but seemed to actively drive the implicit motive "away" from its normal behavioral manifestation. Such suppressor effects are not compatible with McClelland et al.'s (1989) prediction that social-extrinsic incentives should only interact with explicit motives, but not with implicit motives, and thus cast further doubt on the usefulness of the social-extrinsic/task-intrinsic distinction.

In summary, then, previous attempts to pinpoint the properties of stimuli that reliably arouse implicit motives have not been successful. The 1953 model described a process through which stimuli can acquire motivational significance but did not further specify which stimuli are most likely to be furnished with motivational properties. The 1980 distinction between operant and respondent measures of motivation and behavior is inconsistent with the extant motive research literature in that it denies the existence of identifiable motive-arousing stimuli. And although the 1989 distinction between task-intrinsic and social-extrinsic incentives acknowledges that there must be a class or type of stimuli to which implicit motives respond, it fails to provide a convincing, valid and precise description of the properties of such stimuli. I do not deny that in many cases these attempts to come to grips with the nature of motivational incentives have had some value for thinking about and conducting research on motives. However, to the extent that these attempts have been inaccurate or even misleading, they inadvertently may have contributed to many researchers' frustration and dissatisfaction with the construct of implicit motives and thus eventually to a premature demise of research in this area.

AN INCENTIVE-REPRESENTATION ACCOUNT OF IMPLICIT MOTIVE AROUSAL

The present approach to delineate the nature of motive-arousing stimuli is based on the notion that humans are simultaneously exposed to two separate, but superimposed forms of reality, one residing in the domain of the symbols of verbal language and the other in the domain of the physical world. Following other theorists of human information processing (most notably Epstein, 1994, Paivio, 1986, 1991, Wilson, 1985, and Zajonc, 1980), I suggest that humans are equipped with two independent systems to process and respond to information originating from these two domains, namely the verbal-symbolic system (VSS) and the experiential system (ES).

The ES processes a reality that is comprised of the sights and sounds, the smells and sensations that impinge on our senses every second. Stimuli from this domain can also be termed experiential stimuli because we perceive and experience them immediately and directly, without the necessity to convert them into a different representational format. A few illustrative examples of such experiential stimuli are: the sight of a friendly, smiling face; the sight of a snake; the sound of an angry voice; the smell of a person's scent; the sensation of an insect crawling on one's skin; the taste of a strawberry. Some experiential stimuli can be directly meaningful for a limited number of needs ensuring the survival of the species and the individual, such as feeding, exploration, social bonding, dominance, sexual procreation, parental care, or harm avoidance. Their meaning for the organism is coded by specific emotional-motivational states, such as curiosity, affection, anger, joy, or fear, that these stimuli elicit unconditionally and that either aim at meeting these needs or indicate the fulfillment of a need. Other experiential stimuli may initially have no particular meaning for these needs, but become meaningful because they reliably co-occur with unconditional stimuli and thus acquire the power to elicit motivational states on their own. This process has also been termed incentive learning and is described by the laws of Pavlovian conditioning (cf. Berridge, 2001). The principles of instrumental conditioning, on the other hand, determine which behaviors the individual will use once a motivational-emotional state has been aroused. Behaviors that in the past have been instrumental in achieving a desired end state under a given set of situational conditions will be the most likely to be recruited, whereas behaviors that have failed in this regard will not be attempted. Which behaviors are instrumental for satisfying a particular need can also be learned through observational learning and imitation (cf. Mazur, 1998). In addition, the ES also hosts learning mechanisms that do not require stimuli to be emotionally significant, as the case of implicit learning demonstrates. Implicit learning, which is defined as learning without intention to learn or awareness of what is being learned, is based on the detection of covariations between stimuli in the environment, and this knowledge can be used to navigate and deal with the environment more effectively (cf. Reber, 1989).

The output of the ES results from these mechanisms of information processing and can simply be the correct prediction of stimuli in the case of implicit learning, but is typically characterized by strong motivational-emotional impulses urging the individual to engage in certain behavioral strategies or avoid others in the case of need-based learning mechanisms. These impulses can also be interpreted as the output of evolutionarily old "command" systems, because they make very strong "suggestions" as to which general course of action should be taken next or what feels "natural" to do (Panksepp, 1998). It is important to point out, though, that while the impulses, feelings, and emotions that they generate may become conscious, the stimuli giving rise to this output and the processing mechanisms that lead to it can remain completely non-conscious. For instance, Dimberg, Thunberg and Elmehed (2000) recently reported that individuals respond affectively to pictures of happy and angry faces that are presented outside of participants' conscious awareness. Öhman and Soares (1994, 1998) have repeatedly demonstrated that subliminally presented neutral stimuli that reliably predict an unconditional stimulus (shock) can acquire emotion-eliciting properties and thus become conditional stimuli without ever reaching conscious awareness. Working with an instrumental avoidance conditioning paradigm that involved an implicit learning task, Corr, Pickering and Gray (1997) found that highly anxious individuals show superior implicit learning of behavior that can stave off punishment (for other examples of non-conscious behavioral conditioning, see Corr, Pickering & Gray, 1995; Gupta & Shukla, 1989; Lieberman, Sunnucks & Kirk, 1998). Although I am not aware of studies dealing with the role of conscious awareness in observational learning in humans, the fact that observational learning can be demonstrated even in chicks makes it seem likely that this form of learning does not require high-level (i.e. self-reflective) consciousness, either (cf. Mazur, 1998).

In the aforementioned studies, psychophysiological and behavioral variables were the main and most strongly affected ES output measures and in many instances, participants themselves were not aware of any change in these variables. And in those studies in which participants consciously experienced a change in affective state in response to non-recognized stimuli, they were prone to attribute their feelings to irrelevant events (e.g. Murphy & Zajonc, 1993). But ES-based stimulus processing and response preparation can also occur in the complete absence of any conscious awareness of the stimuli involved or the motivational state elicited, as a recent study by Winkielman, Berridge, and Wilbarger (2001) shows. These researchers first measured participants' consumption of a fruit-flavored drink, then subliminally presented participants either with a happy face or with an angry face and subsequently assessed participants' drink consumption once more. Intriguingly, participants in the happy-face condition drank more and participants in the angry-face condition drank less after being exposed to the facial stimuli. Even more intriguingly, self-report measures of pleasure and arousal failed to show any change in mood as a function of experimental condition. Thus, conscious awareness of eliciting stimuli, mediating processes, or emotional and behavioral output does not seem to be a necessary requirement for the ES's operation (cf. Kihlstrom, 1999). An individual's ES can therefore process stimuli and generate emotional and behavioral responses without any participation of her or his consciousness.

In phylogenetic terms, the structures and processes constituting the ES are rather old and humans share many of them with other mammalian and non-mammalian species. Technically, they are housed mainly in the paleo-mammalian brain and parts of the reptilian brain, although neocortical structures undoubtedly play a significant role in the fine-grained analysis of stimulus information, too (cf. LeDoux, 1996; MacLean, 1987). There is also evidence that ES-based information processing may be lateralized to the right hemisphere (e.g. Springer & Deutsch, 1998). Because the ES is rooted in subcortical parts of the brain, a considerable part of its output becomes manifested in psychophysiological changes, such as the release of hormones, sweat gland activity, increases or decreases in heart rate and blood pressure, or immune system changes, which are driven by the hypothalamus, the pituitary, and associated structures. Note, however, that evolutionarily old does not mean crude and simple in this context. In fact, some argue that the ES has reached an unprecedented level of complexity, sophistication and openness to environmental influences and learning in humans (LeDoux, 1996; Panksepp, 1998) and it seems very likely that future research on the processes and structures involved in emotion and learning in humans will further add to this picture.

Ontogenetically, the structures and processes involved in the ES's operation maturate and function earlier than those involved in the VSS. For example, emotional responses to stressful and fear-eliciting stimuli can be observed in infants a few weeks after birth and probably even earlier (Kagan, 1994). Similarly, children are able to differentiate between and emotionally respond to emotional facial expressions long before they are able to verbally label those expressions (e.g. Serrano, Iglesias & Loeches, 1995). Not suprisingly, then, children start to learn at an experiential-emotional level before they acquire language, and these early learning experiences may have long-lasting effects on adult behavior, even though individuals can not verbalize or consciously remember them (Jacobs & Nadel, 1985).

Implicit motives are at home in and part of the experiential system (ES), chiefly because they operate outside of a person's conscious awareness but can manifest themselves in a person's emotions, psychophysiological responses and behavior, and are rooted in socialization experiences in preverbal childhood (e.g. McClelland, 1958, 1987, 1989). Moreover, they have been assumed to modify behavior through Pavlovian and instrumental conditioning mechanisms (McClelland, 1958; Winter, 1996), a hypothesis that has only recently found some emprical confirmation (Schultheiss & Rohde, in press), and their cross-cultural universality and limited number suggests that they are part of our evolutionary heritage. This general argument is not entirely new; McClelland (1987), McClelland et al. (1989) and Weinberger and McClelland (1990) have also proposed that implicit motives are rooted in the older, emotional reaches and functions of the brain. What is new about the position presented here is the notion that if implicit motives are part of the ES, *they should primarily be aroused by and respond to experiential stimuli.* Thus, for instance, a person's power motive should more likely be triggered by another person's threatening gestures, loud voice and angry face than by the words "I am going to sue you for this!", a person's affiliation motive should respond more strongly to another person's smiles and affectionate touches than to the words "I really like you!", and a person's achievement motive should be more easily satisfied by having some tangible proof of doing well on a task, such as increased output or quicker performance, than by the words "You have done well on this task". A similar point was made by LeDoux (1996) with reference to unconscious and emotional information processing in general:

> [Verbal stimuli] are the currency of the systems that are involved in conscious processing, which is an evolutionarily new system. Unconscious processing, on the other hand, is the stock-in-trade of evolutionarily old systems that are likely to be more readily studied with non-verbal measures (p. 308). And: "We will probably not gain an accurate picture of how the more basic unconscious systems work as long as most work on unconscious processing is done using verbal stimuli (p. 312).

Before I go into the ramifications and subtleties of my hypothesis, however, it is necessary to take a closer look at the properties of the VSS first to better understand how this system differs from the ES, why verbal stimuli and instructions may not be effective in activating implicit motives, and how the ES and VSS may interact in processing information and shaping behavior.

The reality processed by the verbal-symbolic system (VSS) is that of verbal language, of the written or spoken words that humans use to communicate with each other. One of the great advantages of language is that it frees its user from the constraints of the presently experienced situation and can refer to objects or events that happen or exist far away, or in the distant past or future, or to intangible ideas and concepts that may completely lack any direct manifestation in the experiential world (e.g. "virtue", "locus of control", "quantum"). It also provides symbolic "shortcuts" for whole classes of events, objects and situations and thus makes it possible to encapsulate very complex, rich, and extended experiences in one word or phrase (e.g. "Let's go wild-water rafting").

The VSS encodes information by translating nonverbal information into a symbolic format (i.e. naming an object or event) or directly from the verbal information received from others. This information is retained in verbal form in declarative memory and typically deals with spatial, temporal, or causal relationships between persons, objects, events or their attributes. In contrast to the learning mechanisms governing the ES, learning in the VSS does not depend on the survival value of an information or the covariation frequency of stimuli or events; rather, acquisition of new knowledge is primarily determined by its fit or lack of fit with existing knowledge in declarative memory, by its meaningfulness in the context of what is already known. Within these constraints, the contents of declarative memory are freely programmable and allow for a myriad of possible connections and associations between elements (Paivio, 1986).

As in the case of the ES, the output of information processing in the VSS can control behavior. In the simplest case, verbally represented knowledge forms the basis of choices and decisions of whether to engage in a behavior or not. Knowing that today is a Tuesday (a completely abstract, language-based concept, since the sun does not rise in the morning with a different color for every day of the week), I got up early this morning and went to my office. Had it been a Sunday, I would not have done that. In more complex cases, verbally based knowledge can help to schedule and pace elaborate behavioral sequences that are difficult or have never been executed before, such as baking a cake according to a recipe, or driving a car for the first time. It can also tell a person when to refrain from certain behaviors because they might be dangerous, even though the person may never before have actually experienced the danger or the danger itself may be completely intangible (exposing oneself to an activated X-ray machine for half an hour would be a case in point).

But this influence of the VSS on behavior immediately begs the question: Why is there a second behavior-guiding system, if there already exists one system (the ES) that can adapt the organism's behavior to the demands of the environment in complex ways? A look at some of the emerging functions of language over the course of development may suggest an answer. When children start to acquire language at age 2 to 3 years, this process greatly expands their possibilities of social interaction. At the same time, it also opens the door for parents to better regulate their childrens' behavior by verbally instructing them about do's and don'ts and the norms and standards of social conduct. Typically, these rules aim either at making children do something they are not motivated to do, or at channeling their motivational-emotional impulses into socially accepted outlets, or at inhibiting such impulses altogether. Over time, children pick up such verbally transmitted rules, expectations and norms and use them to instruct themselves and regulate their own behavior, even in the absence of their parents or other authority figures. Initially, this process is readily observable, because children are audibly talking to themselves, but it becomes more covert in middle childhood when children learn to speak to themselves silently (cf. Vygotsky, 1986; Zivin, 1979). Thus, the acquisition of language introduces self-instruction as an important tool for the regulation of behavior in the service of complex social demands, a tool that has the capacity to override the output of an individual's ES and make his or her behavior consistent with others' expectations.

Language also has a second, more indirect, socializing function on behavior by helping children to wait for a reward for a longer time than they could if their behavior were completely ES-controlled. As Mischel's (1996; Mischel, Shoda & Rodriguez, 1989) work on delay of gratification shows, language enables children to keep a representation of the desired incentive in their minds that is abstract enough to make it easy to wait for (rather than to get motivationally aroused and go for the next available substitute), but reminds them of the existence of the future incentive at the same time. The importance of this function of symbolic language can hardly be overstated as it enables humans to develop, mentally represent, and tenaciously pursue long-term goals and thus makes their social behavior more stable and dependable than it could ever be were it purely ES-driven. Not surprisingly, then, adolescents who have been particularly adept at delaying gratification in childhood are also likely to be described by others as deliberative, planful, dependable, persistent, competent and verbally skilled (Mischel, Shoda & Peake, 1988; see also Funder, Block & Block, 1983).

I suggest, however, that the VSS's very power to encapsulate a particular incentive in a string of symbols is a double-edged sword. Through the development of delay of gratification, individuals learn to use the verbal-symbolic mode of incentive representation and may grow used to the fact that goals represented in this way do not experientially arouse a strong motivational-emotional state. At the same time they may come to expect that they will experience such a state when they finally attain the incentive. Therefore, the development of gratification delay through symbolization not only enables them to pursue long-term goals, but may also make them more vulnerable to adopt and pursue goals that may not be emotionally rewarding in the end. I will present some evidence for this hypothesis below.

Verbal-symbolic language is also a necessary prerequisite of conscious thought and a sense of self, and both are closely related to each other. According to a theory presented by Jaynes (1986, 1990), one of the main reasons why language evolved in early hunter-gatherer communities was that it enabled early humans to modify other group members' behavior through commands, which in turn may have served a behavior-stabilizing function and have increased the level and complexity of social coordination within the group. That simple verbal commands can have such power over another person's behavior is still evident today in, for instance, the phenomenon of hypnosis or studies of obedience to authority (e.g. Milgram, 1963; see also Miller, Galanter & Pribram, 1960, chap. 8). Jaynes contends that early humans were not conscious and aware of themselves in the same way modern humans are, and speculates that their VSSs generated hallucinatory voices that they attributed to authority figures in their tribe or to gods and that controlled their actions when other group members were not around. He also points out that early languages did not start out with the vocabulary that would have enabled individuals to think of themselves in terms of an "I", a "Me" or as possessing a "Self". Rather, modern human consciousness and self-awareness evolved when language became more metaphorical and words that had originally been used for phenomena and processes of the outside world were applied to "spaces" and states inside a person, eventually giving rise to the metaphorical mind-space of an "I" and to a self. An example of this process is the word *comprehend* whose original literal meaning was "to get a firm grip on something", but was later used in Latin and in modern languages to denote the mental process of making sense of, grasping (!) something. Another example is the Greek word *psychein*, which originally meant "to breathe", but as a noun later was used to mean "mind" or "spirit" (this word, too, has its root in "breathing"). Thus, humans came to think about themselves and to develop a self only to the extent that they developed the necessary verbal-symbolic tools. At this point, Jaynes claims, they no longer hallucinated commanding voices that aligned their behavior with the demands of the group but could now instruct themselves about what to do.

While the specifics of Jaynes' theory (e.g. the concept of a bicameral consciousness) are often speculative and may be open to debate, its bottom line is highly compatible with developmental (cf. the previous section on the development of language) as well as social psychological (cf. Cooley, 1964; Mead, 1968) and cognitive (cf. Hunt & Agnoli, 1991; Mandelbaum, 1963; Whorf, 1971) accounts of the functions of language: symbolic language, and in its wake consciousness and the self, evolved to improve coordination within complex social groups and to represent the expectations, demands and goals of the group in the mind of the individual. It did *not* evolve to consciously represent the needs, emotions, and motivations of an individual within the individual. The ES would not require such a re-duplication of its functions and outputs on a verbal-symbolic level to control behavior adaptively and efficiently.

According to this point of view, the self is basically and inherently an agent and representative of the social group within the skin of the individual and not a structure whose primary function is to read out and represent the individual's ES. This helps to explain why people may often not be in a better position than outside observers to understand themselves and need to rely on self-observation, feedback from others, or causal theories and emotional scripts to decipher (or reconstruct) their own feelings, motivations, and behaviors (cf. Bem, 1972; Nisbett & Wilson, 1977; Wilson, 1985). As LeDoux (1987) has pointed out, the functional independence between the VSS and the ES may be due to the fact that although those parts of the neocortex that are associated with language functions (i.e. the left-hemispherical areas of Wernicke and Broca) are extensively connected with other neocortical structures (e.g. frontal and prefrontal cortices; cf. Deacon, 1997), they only have few direct connections to limbic structures involved in emotional processing of information.

Of course, inferring one's motivational-emotional states from indirect cues can be inaccurate and error-prone, especially if one is looking in the wrong place, lacking the words to identify them, or misattributing them (cf. Schachter & Singer, 1962), or only relies on general beliefs or sociocultural scripts (e.g. "I haven't slept much last night, that must be the reason why I feel crummy now"; cf. Nisbett & Wilson, 1977). Individuals may thus develop views of themselves, their ways of responding emotionally to events or their enduring motivational aspirations that can be inconcongruent with the operating characteristics and preferences of their ESs. I suggest that this is the deeper reason why self-report measures of motives typically do not correlate with measures of implicit motivation.

In summary, the ES and the VSS are dissociable systems that process different kinds of information (experiential vs. verbal-symbolic) and serve different functions: the ES is primarily driven by the motivational-emotional needs of the individual, whereas the VSS has evolved to represent the needs of the social group and the wider sociocultural context one is part of.[1] I would like to point out in passing that evidence for the existence and dissociability of these two systems comes from a diverse range of psychological research outside the area of motivation. For instance, Brewin (1989; Brewin, Dalgleish & Joseph, 1996) has pointed out that traumatic experiences split up in memory into an emotional component that is reactivated by experiential cues and a declarative component that is accessible to consciousness and can be verbalized. Importantly, the emotional component is likely to become dissociated from the verbal one and lead a life of its own, manifesting itself in spontaneous flashbacks and intrusive imagery. Bechara, Damasio and Tranel (1995) have presented an elegant study that focuses on some of the brain structures and learning processes that presumably underly such ES-VSS dissociations. They compared normal individuals with amygdala-lesioned, hippocampus-lesioned, and amygdala/hippocampus-lesioned individuals in a study in which participants could learn both verbally and experientially a contingency between a visual stimulus and a subsequent startling noise. After learning, normal participants were able to verbally report the contingency (an indicator of information processing in the VSS) and also showed an anticipatory change in skin conductance in response to the noise-predicting stimulus (an indicator of information processing in the ES). Notably, hippocampus-lesioned participants were unable to consciously detect the contingency, although they showed an anticipatory skin conductance response; amygdala-lesioned participants were able to verbally report the contingency but did not show the skin conductance response; and participants with lesions in both structures showed no verbal or experiential learning at all. The Bechara et al. (1995) study therefore provides direct neurological evidence for the existence and functional as well as anatomical independence of two fundamentally different information processing systems, one entailing consciousness and the use of symbolic language and the other operating at a non-conscious, experiential level.

MOTIVE-GOAL DISSOCIATIONS IN EXPERIMENTS AND EVERYDAY LIFE

At this point, let's return to the problem precipitating the aforegoing theoretical analysis: Why have, as Klinger (1966) stated, so many experimental studies failed to find any direct and straightforward effects of implicit motives and behavior? Why have researchers sometimes obtained paradoxical effects where a motive had effects on behavior that were diametrically opposed to those hypothesized (cf. Lazarus, 1961)? I believe that the two-systems model of information processing presented above provides an answer to these questions if it is used to carefully dissect the mode of incentive presentation in a typical laboratory experiment.

Consider the case of an experimenter assigning an achievement goal to a participant with the words: "Next, you will work on an arithmetic task. Try to give your best and solve as many arithmetic problems in five minutes as possible" and trusting that this instruction will serve to engage the participant's implicit achievement motive in the subsequent task. The participant's verbal-symbolic system (VSS) readily processes this instruction and understands that the experimenter is placing value on high performance at this task. However, this information is not registering with the participant's experiential system (ES) and therefore not arousing her or his implicit achievement motive, because it is not presented in a format that the ES can process. Rather, the participant's ES is responding to experiential aspects of the situation, such as the experimenter's facial expression, tone of voice or behavior or other participants' behavior. This does not necessarily preclude that the participant's achievement motive (or another motive) may become aroused by situational cues in some other way, but these cues are most likely not under the experimenter's deliberate control. In fact, since the achievement motive also has a strong autonomy component which involves resistance to influence and conformity pressures (deCharms, Morrison, Reitman & McClelland, 1955; McClelland et al., 1953), uncontrolled experiential features of the testing situation, such as an experimenter's nonverbal "pushiness", can actually make participants with a strong achievement motive less willing to collaborate on an achievement-related task than participants low in achievement motivation. This line of reasoning may provide an explanation for the suppressor effects found by Spangler (1992), but further research is needed to clarify their nature and origin.

On the other hand, the experimenter's non-verbal behavior may also happen to be genuinely motive-arousing in some way. Interestingly, this notion is supported by some findings of a study that Klinger (1967) reports. In this study, an actor played either an achievement-oriented, an affiliative, or a neutral experimenter. Participants in a sound condition were in the same room with the experimenter and were exposed to his verbal instructions and behavior, while participants in a no-sound condition observed the experimenter in another room on a television monitor but could not hear his instructions. Afterwards, all participants were administered a TAT. Participants in the sound condition wrote TAT stories highly saturated with achievement imagery when the experimenter had acted in an achievement-oriented manner, but not if he had remained neutral or shown affiliative characteristics. Surprisingly, participants in the no-sound condition produced exactly the same differences in achievement imagery in response to the three different behavioral styles after just watching, but not hearing, the experimenter. This pattern of findings demonstrates that it may not actually be the content of an experimenter's instructions but other, non-verbal features of her or his behavior that arouse a person's implicit motives.

While this general analysis of experimental studies on implicit motives may, from the vantage point of the present information processing account, help explain why in the past researchers have sometimes obtained reasonable and predicted findings with motive measures (even though they may not have been aware of the situational factors that truly aroused participants' motives) and sometimes no or even paradoxical results (*because* they were unaware of these factors), it also highlights a central problem arising from the different operating characteristics of the ES and the VSS. As I have pointed out before, the ES responds to experienced features and stimuli of the present situation, whereas the VSS can receive, transmit, and deal with information that symbolically codes future (or past, or far-away) situations that cannot presently be experienced and processed by the ES. Since the goals that researchers assign to their participants in experimental studies, and even more so the goals people adopt from or negotiate with others in their everyday lives, typically precede the actual situation in which the goals are pursued and realized, the ES and the VSS do not process the same kind of information in parallel at the moment of goal choice or adoption. Rather, the VSS is now dealing with the future in the form of a potential goal that the individual can choose, adopt, or become committed to while the ES continues to process stimuli and incentives in the present situation. As a consequence, a person's goal choice or level of commitment to an assigned goal may not be influenced at all by the motivational contents inherent in the pursuit of goal but depend on experiential features of the goal-choice/adoption situation which, of course, can be completely dissimilar from the goal-enactment situation.

This account of goal-related information processing in experimental studies and real-life situations ties in with research demonstrating that individuals may use the output of their ES, namely, moods, feelings and affect, as input for their VSS and thus as information upon which they base their judgments and decisions, even though the ES's output may not be triggered by anything related to the decision at all (cf. Schwarz, 1990; Schwarz & Bohner, 1996). According to Schwarz, individuals often use a "How do I feel about it?" heuristic when asked to make a particular judgment or decision. The effects of this heuristic are nicely illustrated by a study by Saavedra and Earley (1991). They found that individuals exposed to a funny Woody Allen movie were more than twice as likely to continue pursuing an assigned goal than to change to a new goal, whereas individuals exposed to a documentary about torture were more than three times as likely to switch to a new goal than to stick to the assigned goal. Needless to say, the goals involved in this study (evaluations of the work of fictitious employees) were not in any way related to the mood-inducing content of the film clips shown. Thus, consistent with Schwarz's feelings-as-information model, the positive or negative emotions that the ES emits in response to experiential features of the goal-choice situation can influence the individual's goal choice, although not in a way that has anything to do with the goal itself.

This conclusion is also supported by findings regarding the role of implicit motives in goal choice and goal commitment. With the exception of a study by Emmons and McAdams (1991), who reported motive-goal correlations in the 0.30 to 0.40 range, survey studies of people's personal goals and strivings have consistently failed to produce significant or substantial correlations between individuals' sense of commitment to a goal or the motivational content of a goal and their implicit motives (Brunstein et al., 1998; Brunstein, Lautenschlager, Nawroth, Pöhlmann & Schultheiss, 1995; King, 1995). For instance, King (1995) found that the motivational content of her participants' goals and their TAT stories correlated only 0.18, –0.07, and 0.17 for the domains of achievement, affiliation, and power. Similarly, Brunstein et al. (1998) reported that students' implicit agency motive (i.e. need for power + need for achievement) correlated at –0.06 with their commitment to agentic goals (i.e. goals related to mastery and social influence) and their implicit communion motive (i.e. need for affiliation + need for intimacy) correlated at –0.09 with their commitment to communal goals (i.e. goals related to interpersonal closeness and friendly relationships). Consistent with the findings of these field studies, more highly controlled laboratory studies on the role of implicit motives in goal-choice situations also fail to show any influence of motives on participants' decisions (e.g. Brunstein & Hoyer, in press; Locke & Latham, 1990, p. 214).

However, while these studies document that, by and large, individuals' personal goals are not well-aligned with their implicit motives, Brunstein et al. (1998) found that progress on motive-congruent goals translated into enhanced emotional satisfaction, whereas progress on motive-incongruent goals did not provide individuals with an increased sense of satisfaction and contentment. Thus, although motives may not contribute to individuals' commitment to a goal, they determine how much pleasure they can draw from its enactment, which involves the consummation of motive-specific incentives. Viewed from a different angle, these results suggest that by pursuing motive-incongruent goals, a person is more likely to expose his or her ES to situations that do not contain motive-relevant incentives, and by allocating time to the pursuit of such goals to reduce his or her exposure to situations containing motivationally stimulating or rewarding stimuli. This notion is supported by Brunstein et al.'s (1998) finding that high levels of commitment to motive-incongruent goals led to slow progress on motive-congruent goals, which in turn was associated with increased feelings of dissatisfaction.

Taken together, these findings indicate that whether a person chooses or becomes committed to, for instance, an achievement goal does not depend on that person's implicit achievement motive, but whether a person can become happy with the chosen goal does. Thus, the VSS's capability to represent and deal with verbally coded future actions and end-states that are not accessible for the ES seems to put individuals at risk for choosing and pursuing goals that are not backed up by their implicit motives. The above analysis would suggest that even in those instances in which a chosen or adopted goal does correspond to a person's implicit motives, the choice may only indicate that the incentives present in the goal-choice situation for some reason happened to arouse the same motive that the goal is tailored to, but not necessarily that the person's ES is responding to the content of the verbally presented goal itself. But is there a way to make the ES process goal-related information that has been fed in symbolic form to the VSS and thus to ensure that a person's implicit motives are responding to the goal? In other words: Is it possible to pull the verbally coded future into the experiential present and make a person see, hear and feel what it would be like to pursue a goal, be it in a lab experiment or in real life?

THE GOAL IMAGERY TECHNIQUE IN RESEARCH ON IMPLICIT MOTIVES

I propose that goal imagery, defined as the perception-like mental representation of the pursuit and attainment of a goal (Schultheiss & Brunstein, 1999), can serve this function and be put to fruitful use in experimental research on implicit motives. Research on mental imagery has provided ample evidence that imagining an object, event or even a complex situation can be equivalent to actually perceiving it, both in terms of the information processing systems involved in and the emotional responses triggered by it. For instance, visual and auditory imagery activate the same brain areas that are involved in processing incoming visual and auditory information, which can sometimes even lead to direct competition between imagery and perception for processing resources (Farah, 1985, 1988; Farah, Peronnet, Gonon & Giard, 1988; Kosslyn, 1994; Kosslyn et al., 1993; Zatorre & Halpern, 1993). Moreover, studies using neuroimaging techniques, psychophysiological measures, self-reported mood or facial expressions as indicators of the emotional impact of mental imagery demonstrate that imagining an affectively charged situation can be just as emotion-arousing as actually experiencing it (Qualls, 1982/1983; Richardson, 1984; Schwartz, Weinberger & Singer, 1981; Shin et al., 1997; Sirota &

Schwartz, 1982). For example, Sirota and Schwartz (1982) found that individuals responded with increased corrugator activity (involved in furrowing the brow) to imagining a sad scene and with increases zygomatic activity (involved in smiling) to imagining an uplifting scene, and activity in these same muscles also accompanies the perception of negatively and positively valenced stimuli (cf. Caccioppo, Petty, Losch & Kim, 1986). Further evidence for the efficacy of imagery to elicit strong emotional responses comes from studies with clinical populations. Individuals suffering from generalized anxiety disorder show a preponderance of verbal-symbolic and a lack of imaginal thought, presumably because they try to avoid anxiety-inducing mental images (Borkovec & Inz, 1990). Snake phobics deteriorate in their ability to extract information from an imagined object once they are instructed to combine the object in their mind's eye with a snake or a snake-like piece of rope (Suler & Katkin, 1988). But the emotional power of mental imagery can also be used fruitfully in clinical settings, as, for instance, in the desensitization and treatment of patients suffering from a variety of anxiety disorders (e.g. Drobes & Lang, 1995). All in all, these findings suggest that mental imagery of an object or situation is equivalent to the direct perception of that object or situation in its ability to induce experiential processing and arouse motivational-emotional impulses.

Based on these lines of evidence, it seems plausible that vividly imagining the pursuit and realization of a potential goal should have the capacity to elicit a positive affective response and thus to motivate an individual to pursue a goal (cf. Paivio, 1985), provided that the goal fits, and resonates with, her or his implicit motive dispositions. A lack of fit, on the other hand, should become apparent by an absence of such emotional-motivational states in response to goal imagery or, in the case of goals that are directly opposed to a particular motive (e.g. an assertive power goal assigned to a person high in intimacy motivation), even by feelings of aversion. While the emotions triggered by goal imagery can have a direct, motivating effect on behavior, thus priming the individual for the pursuit of the goal, the individual can also use them to make an informed decision about whether or not to adopt and pursue a particular goal, because now her or his affective response to the goal actually reflects the goal's fit with her or his implicit motives. Without the translation of the verbal representation of a goal into imagery, however, the person's implicit motives cannot be aroused by the incentives associated with the goal, and her or his decision and motivation to pursue the goal should therefore not be influenced by the goal's match or mismatch with her or his motives.

I have tested these hypotheses in a series of four studies in which I used goal imagery as an experimental technique to engage participants' implicit motives in the adoption and enactment of an assigned goal by letting them explore the goal under the guidance of carefully constructed, tape-recorded imagery scripts. All goal imagery exercises were introduced by a short relaxation exercise in the course of which participants were asked to close their eyes and focus on their inner feelings and images. In the subsequently presented goal imagery scripts highly concrete and detail-rich language was used to describe the pursuit and attainment of the assigned goal, but participants' emotional or motivational response to various aspects of the goal were not specified. Rather, in each script the listener was prompted several times to pay close attention to his or her feelings and affective states after the description of a key sequence or element in the pursuit of the goal. The total length of the goal imagery exercises was typically around 10 min. Table 1 provides an example of a goal imagery script.

The effect of goal imagery on participants' motivation and behavior was assessed by a self-report measure of goal commitment (Study 1), task performance (Study 2), verbal and nonverbal behavior (Study 3) and hormonal changes (Study 4). In all studies, participants' motives were measured with a TAT-type measure at the beginning of a session and the goal imagery exercises (or control group procedures) were conducted after the experimenter had assigned participants the goal with precise and detailed verbal descriptions of the motivational incentives involved in its pursuit. Dependent measures were obtained subsequently.

Study 1: Implicit Power and Affiliation Motivation and Commitment to a Directive Counseling Goal

In an initial study, we (Schultheiss & Brunstein, 1999, Study 1) tested whether individuals' commitment to an assigned goal would reflect their implicit motives more closely after they had explored the assigned goal in their imagination than if they had only received the experimenter's description of the goal. The experiment was described to male and female participants ($N = 50$) as a comparative study of experts' and laymens' use of directive techniques in counseling a client. The experimenter explained that they were to meet another person (the "client") who was willing to discuss with them a problem that was currently troubling her or him. Participants were instructed to counsel their client in a directive manner, that is, to interrupt and advise the client whenever necessary, to keep her or him focused on the problem and to take an assertive lead in the conversation. The experimenter explained that prior research had proved this strategy to be useful in helping people cope with their problems effectively.

We expected this goal to provide an incentive for individuals high in the implicit needs for power and affiliation, because helping allows to both have impact on and to establish a positive, friendly relationship with someone. It should be less suitable for individuals high only in power or only in affiliation, though, because it required too much social moderation for the former and too indirect an opportunity to make friends for the latter. Finally, for individuals

Table 1. Sample Goal Imagery Script (used by Schultheiss, Campbell & McClelland, 1999).

The following goal imagery script was read by a native English speaker in a neutral tone of voice and tape-recorded. The speaker paused for 5 sec after each sentence and for 15 sec after each affect-focus question to give participants time to update their mental pictures and become aware of their emotional responses.

"Can you feel the weight of your body? Can you feel your hands and your feet? Can you feel that one arm is less relaxed than the other? Can you feel that one leg is more relaxed than the other? Can you close your eyes? Can you keep your eyes closed during the next few minutes? Can you imagine the distance between the top of your head and your chin? Can you imagine looking at someone who is standing far away from you? Can you feel the tension dissolve? Can you imagine the space inside your mouth? Can you feel a warm sensation somewhere in your body? Please keep your eyes closed and allow yourself to feel comfortably warm.

You are sitting on an uncushioned metal chair, the pencil is in your hand and the first test form is in front of you on the table. You can hear your competitor, who is sitting at the other desk, shuffling his feet. The air in the room is dry and carries the smell of old books and papers. You position the pencil on the number one on your test form. The experimenter says "Go!" and you start tracking the numbers as fast as you can. You can hear the other guy's pencil racing across his test form. He is fast – but you are faster. You can see that you are closing in on the highlighted last number. You are three numbers away, two numbers, one number – you reach the final number and cry "Stop." The other guy drops his pencil and exhales audibly. What do you feel right now?

You turn the page and position your pencil on the next test form. "Go", the experimenter says, and already you are tracking the numbers as fast as you can, your fingers tightly gripping the pencil. Again, you can see that you are approaching the highlighted final number. Suddenly your competitor cries "Stop" – and you have to stop and drop the pencil, still a few numbers away from the last number. What do you feel right now?

And off you go for a third time, racing through the numbers like a devil, determined to outspeed your competitor this time. And yes – now it's you who finishes first and cries stop. You hear the other guy grunting, but you are already eager for yet another test. And on and on you go, being the first to finish and keeping the other guy from finishing first more and more often. Finally, you have worked your way through all the tests. You realize that you scored first more often than the other guy and that you have won the competition. The other guy couldn't keep up with you in the end. What do you feel right now?

Now come back into this room slowly. Try to concentrate on your body. Take some deep breaths. And open your eyes."

low in both motivational dispositions, the incentives associated with the goal should not be motivationally arousing at all.

After the experimenter had assigned the directive-counseling goal to all participants, half of them (the experimental group) listened to a goal-imagery exercise that described the expected counseling session from the "therapist's" point of view, featuring a model scenario that contained all the elements of directive counseling that the experimenter had described before. Participants in the control group did not receive this treatment. Subsequently, all participants filled out a six-item goal commitment questionnaire that queried them about their affective involvement in the ascribed goal (e.g. "I am thrilled by the prospect of counseling my client in a directive manner"), the importance of the goal (e.g. "I find it important to counsel my client in a directive manner") and the effort they intended to invest in the goal (e.g. "I will try as hard as I can to counsel my client in a directive manner"). The experiment was then stopped and all participants were debriefed.

The results of this study were fully in line with our hypotheses. As Fig. 1 shows, participants in the experimental group who were high in power and affiliation motivation were strongly committed to the goal of counseling a client in a directive manner (it seems notable that they obtained an average score of 40.59 on a scale that ended at 42). Experimental-group participants who did not have this set of motivational dispositions, however, reported considerably less commitment to the assigned goal. In control-group participants, on the other hand, the power and the affiliation motive did not have any detectable conjoint influence on goal commitment. These findings suggest that participants' inclination to adopt an assigned goal reflected and was consistent with their implicit motives only after they had translated the goal into an experiential format through imagination. Without goal imagery, their decision to vigorously pursue the goal was unrelated to their motive dispositions, despite the experimenter's detailed verbal description of the motivational incentives inherent in the goal.

The results from the control group closely resemble those from many previous laboratory and survey studies on the influence of implicit motives on goal commitment. They thus reinforce the notion that feeding motivational incentives into the VSS without attempting to also make them accessible to the ES can readily lead to discrepancies between an individual's motivational needs and her or his goals. As the experimental-group findings demonstrate, however, this outcome is not inevitable and can be changed through an active effort to help the ES process the goal's incentives. But will the synchronizing effects of goal imagery on VSS and ES functioning also emerge for behavioral indicators beyond self-reported goal commitment? And is it really the motivational content of goal imagery that establishes between-systems alignment or is it simply the fact that a person relaxes or engages in imaginal activity, regardless of its content?

Study 2: Implicit Power Motivation and Performance in a Competitive Computer Game

To address these questions, we (Schultheiss & Brunstein, 1999, Study 2) conducted a second study in which we explored the effect of goal imagery on performance in a speed- and coordination based task. This time, we developed a task that contained only power-related and no affiliation incentives. Specifically, participants ($N = 52$) played a simple computer game ("Tetris") which allowed them to collect points on each game. Depending on the total

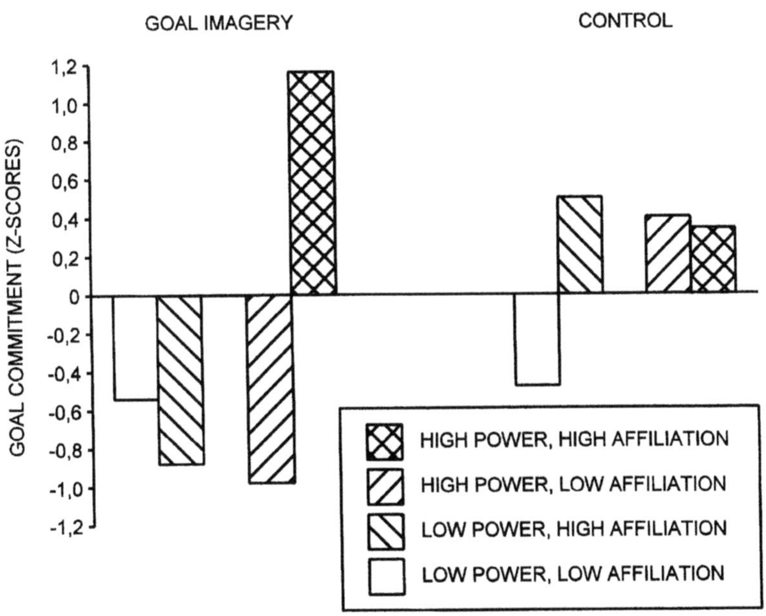

Fig. 1. Regression-estimated goal commitment as a function of experimental condition (goal imagery vs. control), power motive, and affiliation motive for values 1 SD above (high) or below (low) the means of the motive variables. From: Schultheiss, O. C. and Brunstein, J. C. (1999). Goal imagery: Bridging the gap between implicit motives and explicit goals. *Journal of Personality, 67,* 1–38. Copyright © 1999 by Blackwell Publishers. Reprinted with permission.

amount of points won in each game, they could enter their name in a highscore list presented at the end of each game. The goal assigned for this task was to surpass the current number one player on the highscore list (an entry at 52,087 points signed "Andreas Fischer") and thereby becoming the new number one player. The experimenter explained to participants that other indivduals had already played this game and thus created the highscore list they saw at the end of the first game. He went on to mention that he had been very impressed by the performance of the top-ranked player Andreas Fischer whose score had been truly outstanding and who, after becoming number one, had expressed his confidence that nobody would be able to beat him. He then suggested that the participant might try his luck and attempt to surpass Andreas Fischer.We expected that ascending in the highscore list and trying to beat the top-ranked player would provide an incentive for individuals with a strong implicit power motive because of their strong concern with social ranking and prestige (McClelland, 1987). This assumption is consistent with previous research documenting that power-motivated individuals often use performance goals as a means to gain recognition and fame (e.g. Veroff, Depner, Kulka & Douvan, 1980). Because this outlet of the need for power may be more characteristic of men than of women, however, only male participants were recruited for this study.

Participants in the goal imagery condition listened to a goal imagery script that described how, after some initial setbacks, they eventually managed to score high enough to enter their own name in the highscore list. Over the course of the next games, they were getting better and better until finally their performance surpasses that of the current number one and they eliminate his name from the highscore list by entering their own. In contrast, participants in the neutral imagery condition were presented a scenario in which they focused on the movements and properties of the game elements of Testris and their attempts to maneuver these elements across the screen. Neutral-imagery participants listened to the same relaxation exercise as goal-imagery participants before the imagery script.

After that, participants were allowed to play Tetris for a maximum of 30 min and the computer unobtrusively recorded their performance and highscore list entries on each game. As depicted in Fig. 2, the results obtained for the performance measure supported our general hypotheses. Using the highest score participants obtained in any of their games as a measure of their motivation to reach the top of the highscore list, we found that among goal-imagery participants, higher levels of implicit power motivation significantly predicted better performance and were also associated with a higher likelihood to become the new top-ranking player. In neutral-imagery participants, in contrast, the power motive was a negative but insignificant predictor of performance and top-rank attainment.[2] Notably, goal-imagery participants high in power motivation were also more likely than those low in power motivation or high- and low-power participants in the neutral-imagery group to "leave their mark" in the highscore list by signing their best game with their full or last name.

Complementing the finding from Study 1 that goal imagery makes individuals' commitment to a goal contingent on their motive dispositions, the results of this study thus demonstrate that translating a goal into an experiential representational format also generates the motivation in the ES that is necessary to pursue and realize an assigned goal, provided that it matches a person's implicit motives. Furthermore, this study yields evidence that it is not relaxation combined with imaginal activity per se that is "opening up" the ES for a verbal-symbolic goal but the actual content of individuals' imaginations. As the results in the neutral-imagery group show, relaxation plus mental imagery of motivationally irrelevant aspects of a goal fails to arouse a person's implicit motive and engage it in the enactment of the assigned goal.

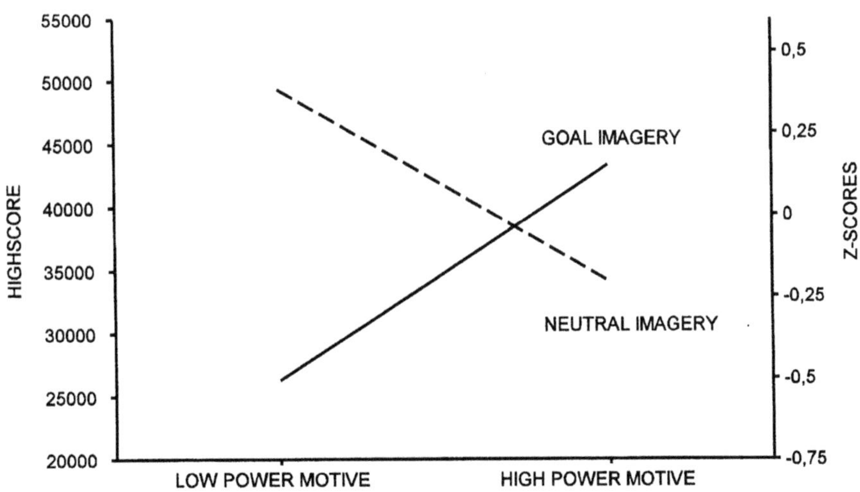

Fig. 2. Regression-estimated performance score on best game as a function of experimental condition (goal imagery vs. neutral imagery) and power motive for values 1 SD above (high) or below (low) the mean of the motive variable. From: Schultheiss, O. C. and Brunstein, J. C. (1999). Goal imagery: Bridging the gap between implicit motives and explicit goals. *Journal of Personality, 67*, 1–38. Copyright © 1999 by Blackwell Publishers. Reprinted with permission.

Study 3: Inhibited Power Motivation and Behavior in a Persuasive Communication Task

In a subsequent third study, we (Schultheiss & Brunstein, in press) explored the effect of goal imagery on the expression of implicit motives in complex social behavior. To do this, we used a persuasive communication task in which male and female participants ($N = 68$) were instructed to present their point of view on a controversial topic (i.e. ethical limits for experimentation with animals) to another person as convincingly as possible. Based on previous findings suggesting that power-motivated individuals may be especially adept at influencing others, provided that they can curb their more impulsive, antisocial impulses (e.g. McClelland & Boyatzis, 1982), we reasoned that this task would represent a strong incentive for individuals characterized by high levels both of implicit power motivation and activity inhibition, a TAT-derived measure of impulse control (cf. McClelland, 1979).

A goal-imagery condition, in which participants first listened to a relaxation exercise and then to a goal imagery script, was pitted against a relaxation condition, in which participants listened to the relaxation exercise only. The goal imagery script led participants to imagine how they presented convincing arguments in favor of their own point of view, while at the same time taking apart the opponent's position, and how the opponent becomes increasingly less confident of her or his own position. Afterwards, participants met their opponent (who was actually a confederate of the experimenter) in another room and started the discussion by presenting their own point of view for as long as they liked. Throughout this presentation, the "opponent" remained neutral, but attentive, and never commented participants' statements. After participants were finished, he stopped the experiment and debriefed them.

Participants' presentations were videotaped and later coded for a variety of verbal and nonverbal behaviors, such as number of arguments presented, balance of pro and con arguments, speech fluency, gesturing, eye contact, etc. Each videotaped speech was also judged by four observers on scales assessing the overall persuasiveness of participants' presentation. Once more, the results provided support for the validity of the information processing account of motive arousal and the goal imagery technique derived from it. As Fig. 3 shows, it was only among goal-imagery participants that implicit power motivation and activity inhibition combined in the expected manner to predict observers' assessments, with participants high in both variables being judged to have given the most persuasive presentation of all participants. In contrast, we did not obtain similar or substantial effects of personality variables on judged persuasiveness for participants in the relaxation group.

We were also able to identify behaviors that mediated the effect of participants' personality dispositions on judged persuasiveness in the goal-imagery group. Specifically, individuals with an inhibited power motive were judged to be highly persuasive because they spoke more fluently, were more likely to raise their eyebrows and gestured more than most other participants. These findings are in line with past research identifying these behaviors as effective peripheral indicators of the importance and persuasiveness of a message (e.g. Mehrabian & Williams, 1969; Miller, Maruyama, Beaber & Valone, 1976). Notably, we did not find any substantial effects of participants' implicit motives on the *verbal content* (e.g. the number or extremity of arguments presented) of their presentations. Although such an influence might

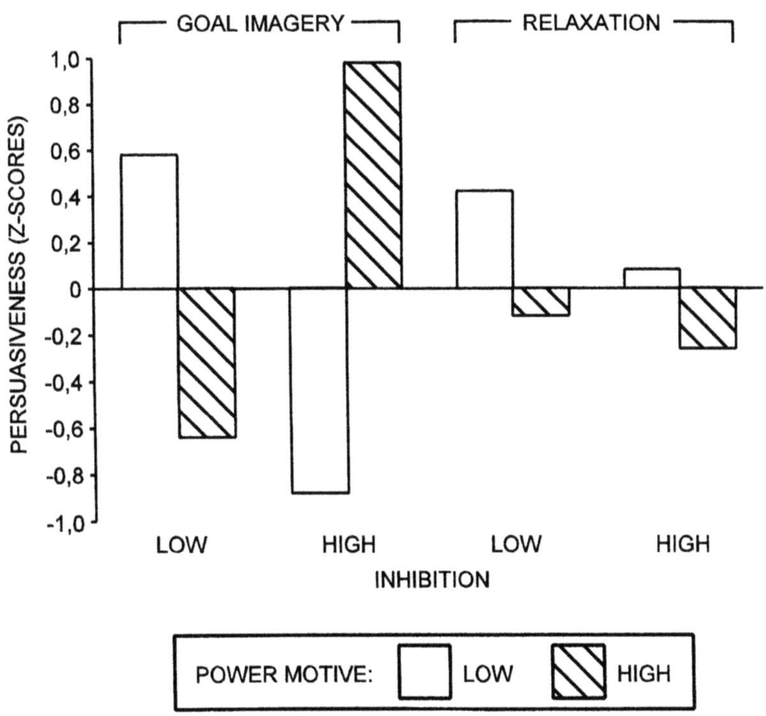

Fig. 3. Regression-estimated persuasiveness ratings as a function of experimental condition (goal imagery vs. relaxation), power motive, and activity inhibition for values 1 SD above (high) or below (low) the means of the personality variables. From: Schultheiss, O. C. and Brunstein, J. C. (in press). Inhibited power motivation and persuasive communication: A lens model analysis. *Journal of Personality.*

still be detected using more fine-grained measures of message content, this finding is fully compatible with and provides additional evidence for the notion that implicit motives operate at a nonverbal, experiential-expressive level.

Thus, the results of this study not only corroborate the general finding of the previous two studies that assigned goals can engage individuals' implicit motives only once they have been translated into an experiential format through goal imagery, but also demonstrate that the goal imagery technique can be used successfully to study the effects of implicit motives on complex and subtle social behavior in the laboratory. Since the predicted results of motives on dependent measures have never been obtained in the various control conditions of studies 1 through 3, I decided at that point to employ the goal imagery technique as a basic tool to get at individuals' implicit motives in my subsequent research.

Study 4: Personalized Power Motivation and Testosterone Changes in Response to Imagined Success in a Competition

The primary aim of this study was to test the hypothesis that the steroid hormone testosterone may represent a substrate of power motivation reward. More specifically, we (Schultheiss, Campbell & McClelland, 1999) predicted that individuals with an egoistical-assertive power motive (called personalized power or p Power) should show a testosterone increase in response to winning a competition against an opponent, whereas no such increase should be observable in winners lacking this type of power motivation or losers in general. The results of this study supported these assumptions, but more pertinent to the issues discussed in this chapter, they also provided evidence that goal imagery can have a direct effect on hormones.

Before participants (42 male students) competed against each other on a paper-and-pencil speed task in a one-on-one contest situation, they were first assigned the goal to beat their opponent in the contest and then listened to a goal imagery exercise which described the contest from the winner's perspective (cf. Table 1). Testosterone levels were assayed from saliva samples collected at the beginning of the session and immediately after the goal imagery exercise was over, but before the actual contest started. Regression analyses revealed that while among individuals showing signs of socialized power motivation (s Power), which is thought to act as a check on personalized power concerns, p Power was not associated significantly with testosterone changes from before to after the goal imagery exercise, higher levels of p Power strongly predicted increases in testosterone in no-s Power participants (see Fig. 4).

For lack of a non-imagery control group in this study, I cannot rule out that these changes in hormone levels may have been caused fully or in part by the experimenter's instructions before the goal imagery excercise. However, the persistent failure of verbal goal assignments to arouse implicit motives in control-group participants in the previous studies makes this an unlikely conclusion and strongly suggests that it was the goal imagery exercise and not the preceding instructions by the experimenter that instigated the observed motive-hormone relationships. To the extent that the results of this study can be interpreted as an extension of the previous findings, then, they make a compelling case for the efficacy of goal imagery to engage ES processing of a goal, because they demonstrate that goal imagery can affect the endocrine system, which is a major output of the ES, but not of the VSS.

SUMMARY AND CONCLUSION

Taken together, the results of these four studies consistently demonstrate that it is only after verbally assigned goals have been converted to an imagistic-experiential representational format that they can interact with implicit motives

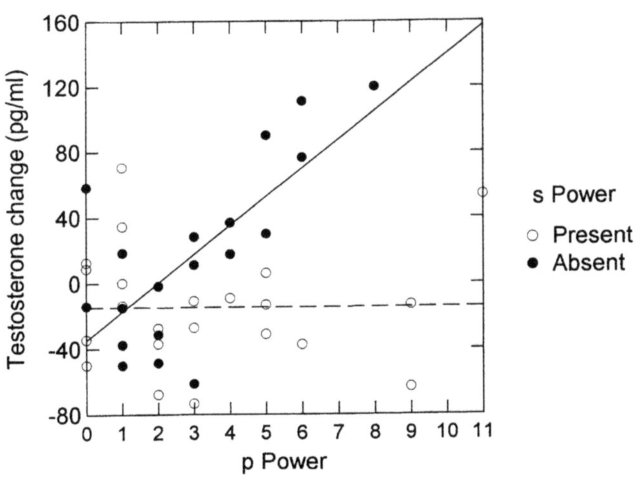

Fig. 4. Residualized changes in salivary testosterone (post-imagery minus baseline) as a function of s Power (present vs. absent) and p Power. From: Schultheiss, O. C., Campbell, K. L. and McClelland, D. C. (1999). Implicit power motivation moderates men's testosterone responsesto imagined and real dominance success. *Hormones and Behavior, 36*(3), 234–241. Copyright © 1999 by Academic Press. Adapted with permission.

to shape a person's motivation, performance and psychophysiological responses. Without goal imagery, and even despite clear-cut and detailed verbal descriptions of the motivational incentives associated with them, goals do not per se arouse an individual's implicit motives. At a more general level, these findings also support the distinction between a verbal-symbolic and an experientially driven information processing system. At a minimum, they suggest that under circumstances in which the verbal-symbolic system (VSS) deals with information pertaining to future states and actions, VSS and experiential system (ES) functioning are prone to become dissociated, because the ES continues to process features of the immediate environment and present situation, and that a realignment between the two systems requires an active effort to translate the content of one system into the format of the other. Finally, the results of these studies may help dissipate some of the concerns that Klinger, Lazarus and others have raised about the validity of implicit motive measures and better understand why researchers in the past may often have failed to obtain predicted motive-behavior relationships in experimental studies. I believe that it is one of the strengths of the present account that null effects and substantial and meaningful effects of motives on a variety of measures can be obtained side by side within one and the same study, which shows that presenting motivational incentives in the right format can make all the difference for success or failure in experimental research on implicit motives. I therefore suggest that the goal imagery technique described here may represent a valuable tool that researchers can use to study implicit motives en detail even in laboratory experiments which typically rely strongly on verbal instructions and experimenter-assigned behavioral goals.

CODA: BETWEEN-SYSTEMS INDEPENDENCE AND COMMUNICATION

In closing, I would like to return to the independence between the VSS and the ES once more. Throughout this chapter, I have emphasized that these systems differ in the kinds of information they process and the degree to which their inputs, operations, and outputs are reflected in a person's consciousness. Yet guided goal imagery, which after all relies on verbal language for instructing a person about what to imagine, has the power to bring the VSS in contact with the ES. Does this contradict the notion that the ES does not deal in verbal symbols or that the ES and the VSS are independent by virtue of their design and their origins?

I believe that this is not the case. As Paivio's (1986) research on verbal and nonverbal information processing shows, experiential stimuli always have an advantage over words when it comes to evaluating the valence or emotional meaning (and many other attributes) of a stimulus. Although this effect may be less pronounced for concrete words (like the ones that were used to construct the goal imagery scenarios in the studies described above) than for abstract words, it is robust and never completely abolished. According to Paivio, it is due to the fact that the processing of words for emotional meaning involves an active translation of a word into an imagistic format and thus requires additional time – time that is not needed for the processing of experiential information. Thus, to the extent that verbal language is highly concrete, it may help build a bridge from the VSS to the ES, but it still requires an extra effort to cross that bridge. I suspect that such active bridge-building efforts are more the exception than the rule in everyday life and depend on training and an awareness of its value. In order to efficiently coordinate our activities with others, we usually prefer highly condensed symbolic shortcuts to represent and communicate our goals and intentions and leave it to professional writers of fiction to delight us with the art of using concrete and epic language to evoke mental images and emotional experiences. Likewise, we also comparatively rarely make an effort to build bridges from the ES to the VSS and attend and carefully name the sensations, impulses, and emotions generated by the ES. According to the position presented in this chapter, the VSS has not developed to fulfill this function in the first place, neither phylogenetically nor ontogenetically. It therefore may require an active educational effort to train children in accurate "reading" of the ES and thus to make them emotionally and motivationally literate (cf. Buck, 1983).

In adulthood, people may differ intra- and inter-individually from each other in their ability to build such bridges due to differences in their socialization, their neurobiological setup, but also because of situational factors (see Bucci, 1995, for a measure of inter- and intraindividual variations in cross-modal connections). It is an intriguing but unexplored possibility that the better "bridge-builders" may also show a higher degree of correspondence between their implicit motives and their personal goals or explicit needs, or that goals that are represented in a person's mind as images and experiential scenarios are more likely to be congruent to the person's implicit needs than those that are coded in a primarily verbal format. The same idea, if applied to the TAT as the quintessential measure of implicit motives,[3] could mean that the motive scores of individuals who write very concrete and "visceral" TAT stories may be more valid indicators of their underlying needs than of those who write comparatively abstract and "brainy" stories. However, these ideas remain to be tested empirically.

All in all, I am firmly convinced that the implicit motive construct has suffered undue neglect in recent times, and that a better understanding of the nature and conditions of implicit motivational processes can open up new and fruitful avenues for research in motivational psychology. I hope that the information processing account presented here contributes to this goal and may help resolve some crucial issues and persistent problems in the study of implicit motives.

NOTES

1. Like the present theoretical account, Bargh and Ferguson's (2000; see also Bargh and Chartrand, 1999) model of controlled and automatic processes in goal-directed behavior emphasizes the fact that behavior can be triggered by environmental stimuli without the intervention of conscious volitional acts. However, Bargh and Ferguson base their conclusion on a body of research which typically involved activating individuals' verbally represented self-concepts and goals by external cues (usually words) and studying their effects on behavior. Thus, this research essentially demonstrates that the verbal-symbolic system can be triggered automatically and nonconsciously and that not all of its operations occur in a controlled fashion, a point that I do not debate. In contrast to their position, though, I contend that implicit motives are fundamentally distinct from verbally represented goals or self-schemata because they are represented nonverbally and usually do not show up in individuals' views of themselves or their goals. I should also point out that the conscious/nonconscious-distinction may not be the most critical one for differentiating implicit motives from other personality constructs. The more basic issue is, in my view, the independence between (or lack of fit of) an evolutionarily new system, which specializes on coordinating the individual's behavior with others' behavior through the use of symbolic language, and a more ancient system, which guides the organism's behavior based on experiential information processing.

2. In this study, as well as in Study 3, there is actually some evidence that without goal imagery, the power motive tends to be a *negative* predictor of power behavior, partly because individuals *low* in power motivation actually show more power behavior than those high in power motivation in their group or those low in power motivation in the goal imagery group. Although these trends never became significant in any single study, they come up consistently enough across studies (see also Spangler, 1992, for related results for the achievement motive) to require some explanation. I suggest that very low levels of a motive, especially when obtained with TAT pictures that have a considerable pull for this motive, reflect not just an indifference towards the motive's incentive, but may actually indicate a considerable level of fear or avoidance of the incentive (for related arguments, see Atkinson, 1957; Fenz & Epstein, 1962; Scott, 1956). In the case of the power motive, such a fear of having impact may be the result of early punishment for assertive behavior (cf. McClelland & Pilon, 1983) and, perhaps as a consequence of such punishment, be associated with increased obedience and conformity. This might explain why low-power individuals in this and other studies seemed to be relatively eager to follow the experimenter's instructions when they had not imagined the pursuit and attainment of the power incentive associated with the

assigned goal, but seemed to shrink away from executing those instructions after realizing, by means of the goal imagery exercise, that the goal was to have impact on others. Clearly, however, these issues merit further research.

3. Although the TAT procedure relies on individuals' verbal reports of their fantasies, I would like to point out that this does not necessarily contradict the main hypothesis presented here, namely, that implicit motives operate at the experiential, not at the verbal-symbolic level. The position taken in this chapter, namely that the VSS, but not the ES, is activated by and processes verbal symbols, does not rule out that spoken language as an instance of the behavioral *output* of information processing can be influenced both by the VSS and by the ES. However, whereas language should be primarily VSS-driven in response to verbal stimuli, particularly if aimed at the content of the VSS such as a person's self-schemata, goals, and other forms of declarative knowledge, and characterized by a self-reflective, declarative quality, it should be primarily ES-driven in response to nonverbal stimuli, particularly if they are in some way emotionally or motivationally arousing, and express the behavioral impulses elicited by the impinging stimuli. TAT stories clearly belong to this second category, and the way language is used in telling a TAT story has little to do with how it is used when a person is describing her or his personality, aspirations and motivations. Moreover, while in VSS-driven language the semantic content and self-relatedness of a message (i.e. self-reported preferences, attitudes, goals, etc.) are the important features and not necessarily the frequency with which the message is conveyed, it is precisely the frequency with which a particular concern shows up in language, typically in the absence of any reference to the self, that characterizes ES-driven language and which is assumed to be an index of the strength and thus arousability of an underlying motive disposition. Most researchers therefore assume that counting motive images in a person's TAT stories is equivalent to measuring the frequency of the person's motivational impulses in response to a particular situation (e.g. Atkinson & Birch, 1970; see also Cramer, 1999). This point of view has been summarized by Heckhausen (1968): "[. . .] we regard the apperception of a TAT picture situation –and the weaving of a story or plot in response – as operant behavior in a kind of miniature life situation." (p. 110).

ACKNOWLEDGMENTS

I would like to thank Kent Berridge, Joachim Brunstein, Martin Maehr, Bill McKeachie, Paul Pintrich, and Wendy Treynor for their helpful comments and suggestions on an earlier draft of this mansucript. The studies reported in this chapter were conducted while the author was supported by a doctoral stipend from the Studienstiftung des deutschen Volkes and by postdoctoral grants from the Deutsche Forschungsgemeinschaft (SCHU 1210/1–1, 1–2, 1–3).

REFERENCES

Atkinson, J. W. (1957). Motivational determinants of risk-taking behavior. *Psychological Review*, *64*, 359–372.

Atkinson, J. W. (1981). Studying personality in the context of an advanced motivational psychology. *American Psychologist, 36*, 117–128.

Atkinson, J. W., & Birch, D. (1970). *The dynamics of action*. New York: Wiley.

Atkinson, J. W., & McClelland, D. C. (1948). The effects of different intensities of the hunger drive on thematic apperception. *Journal of Experimental Psychology, 28*, 643–658.

Bechara, A., Tranel, D., Damasio, H., Adolphs, R., Rockland, C., & Damasio, A. R. (1995). Double dissociation of conditioning and declarative knowledge relative to the amygdala and hippocampus in humans. *Science, 269*, 1115–1118.

Bem, D. J. (1972). Self-perception theory. In: L. Berkowitz (Ed.), *Advances in Experimental Social Psychology* (Vol. 6, pp. 1–62). New York: Academic Press.

Berridge, K. C. (2001). Reward learning: Reinforcement, incentives and expectations. In: D. L. Medin (Ed.), *The Psychology of Learning and Motivation* (Vol. 40, pp. 223–278). New York, NY: Academic Press.

Biernat, M. (1989). Motives and values to achieve: Different constructs with different effects. *Journal of Personality, 57*, 69–95.

Borkovec, T. D., & Inz, J. (1990). The nature of worry in generalized anxiety disorder: A predominance of thought activity. *Behaviour Research and Therapy, 28*, 153–158.

Brewin, C. R. (1989). Cognitive change processes in psychotherapy. *Psychological Review, 96*, 379–394.

Brewin, C. R., Dalgleish, T., & Joseph, S. (1996). A dual representation theory of posttraumatic stress disorder. *Psychological Review, 103*, 670–686.

Brunstein, J. C., & Hoyer, S. (in press). Implizites und explizites Leistungsstreben: Motivmasse, Leistungsstandards und Verhaltenskriterien [Implicit and explicit achievement striving: Motive measures, performance standards, and behavioral criteria]. *Zeitschrift für Pädagogische Psychologie*.

Brunstein, J. C., Lautenschlager, U., Nawroth, B., Pöhlmann, K., & Schultheiss, O. (1995). Persönliche Anliegen, soziale Motive und emotionales Wohlbefinden [Personal goals, social motives, and emotional well-being]. *Zeitschrift für Differentielle und Diagnostische Psychologie, 16*, 1–10.

Brunstein, J. C., Schultheiss, O. C., & Grässmann, R. (1998). Personal goals and emotional well-being: The moderating role of motive dispositions. *Journal of Personality and Social Psychology, 75*, 494–508.

Bucci, W. (1995). The power of the narrative: A multiple code account. In: J. W. Pennebaker (Ed.), *Emotion, Disclosure, and Health* (pp. 93–122). Washington, D.C.: APA.

Buck, R. (1983). Emotional development and emotional education. In: R. Plutchik & H. Kellerman (Eds), *Emotion: Theory, Research, and Experience* (Vol. 2, pp. 259–292). New York: Academic Press.

Cooley, C. H. (1964). *Human nature and the social order*. New York: Schocken Books.

Corr, P. J., Pickering, A. D., & Gray, J. A. (1995). Personality and reinforcement in associative and instrumental learning. *Personality and Individual Differences, 19*, 47–71.

Corr, P. J., Pickering, A. D., & Gray, J. A. (1997). Personality, punishment, and procedural learning: a test of J. A. Gray's anxiety theory. *Journal of Personality and Social Psychology, 73*, 337–344.

Cramer, P. (1999). Future directions for the Thematic Apperception Test. *Journal of Personality Assessment, 72*, 74–92.

Deacon, T. W. (1997). *The symbolic species: The co-evolution of language and the brain*. New York, NY: Norton.

deCharms, R., Morrison, H. W., Reitman, W., & McClelland, D. C. (1955). Behavioral correlates of directly and indirectly measured achievement motivation. In: D. C. McClelland (Ed.), *Studies in Motivation* (pp. 414–423). New York: Appleton-Century-Crofts.

Dimberg, U., Thunberg, M., & Elmehed, K. (2000). Unconscious facial reactions to emotional facial expressions. *Psychological Science, 11*, 86–89.

Drobes, D. J., & Lang, P. J. (1995). Bioinformational theory and behavior therapy. In: W. O. Donohue & L. Krasner (Eds), *Theories of Behavior Therapy: Exploring Behavior Change* (pp. 229–257). Washington, D.C.: American Psychological Association.

Emmons, R. A., & McAdams, D. P. (1991). Personal strivings and motive dispositions: Exploring the links. *Personality and Social Psychology Bulletin, 17*, 648–654.

Entwisle, D. R. (1972). To dispel fantasies about fantasy-based measures of achievement motivation. *Psychological Bulletin, 77*, 377–391.

Epstein, S. (1994). Integration of the cognitive and the psychodynamic unconscious. *American Psychologist, 49*, 709–724.

Farah, M. J. (1985). Psychophysical evidence for a shared representational medium for mental images and percepts. *Journal of Experimental Psychology General, 114*, 91–103.

Farah, M. J. (1988). Is visual imagery really visual? Overlooked evidence from neuropsychology. *Psychological Review, 95*, 307–317.

Farah, M. J., Peronnet, F., Gonon, M. A., & Giard, M. H. (1988). Electrophysiological evidence for a shared representational medium for visual images and visual percepts. *Journal of Experimental Psychology: General, 117*, 248–257.

Fenz, W. D., & Epstein, S. (1962). Measurement of approach-avoidance conflict along a stimulus dimension by a Thematic Apperception Test. *Journal of Personality, 30*, 613–632.

Fineman, S. (1977). The achievement motive construct and its measurement: Where are we now? *British Journal of Psychology, 68*, 1–22.

Funder, D. C., Block, J. H., & Block, J. (1983). Delay of gratification: Some longitudinal personality correlates. *Journal of Personality and Social Psychology, 44*, 1198–1213.

Gupta, S., & Shukla, A. P. (1989). Verbal operant conditioning as a function of extraversion and reinforcement. *British Journal of Psychology, 80*, 39–44.

Heckhausen, H. (1968). Achievement motive research: current problems and some contributions toward a general theory of motivation. In: W. J. Arnold (Ed.), *Nebraska Symposium on Motivation* (Vol. 16, pp. 103–174). Lincoln: University of Nebraska Press.

Hunt, E., & Agnoli, F. (1991). The Whorfian hypothesis: A cognitive psychology perspective. *Psychological Review, 98*, 377–389.

Jacobs, W. J., & Nadel, L. (1985). Stress-induced recovery of fears and phobias. *Psychological Review, 92*, 512–531.

Jaynes, J. (1986). Consciousness and the voices of the mind. *Canadian Psychology, 27*, 128–148.

Jaynes, J. (1990). *The origin of consciousness in the breakdown of the bicameral mind* (2nd ed.). Boston, MA: Houghton Mifflin.

Kagan, J. (1994). *Galen's prophecy.* New York: Westview Press.

Kihlstrom, J. F. (1999). The psychological unconscious. In: L. A. Pervin & O. P. John (Eds), *Handbook of Personality: Theory and Research* (2nd ed., pp. 424–442). New York: Guilford.

King, L. A. (1995). Wishes, motives, goals, and personal memories: Relations of measures of human motivation. *Journal of Personality, 63*, 985–1007.

Klinger, E. (1966). Fantasy need achievement as a motivational construct. *Psychological Bulletin, 66*, 291–308.

Klinger, E. (1967). Modeling effects on achievement imagery. *Journal of Personality and Social Psychology, 7*, 49–62.

Koestner, R., Weinberger, J., & McClelland, D. C. (1991). Task-intrinsic and social-extrinsic sources of arousal for motives assessed in fantasy and self-report. *Journal of Personality, 59*, 57–82.

Kosslyn, S. M. (1994). *Image and brain: The resolution of the imagery debate*. Cambridge MA: MIT Press.

Kosslyn, S. M., Alpert, N. M., Thompson, W. L., Maljkovic, V., Weise, S. B., Chabris, C. F., Hamilton, S. E., Rauch, S. L., & Buonnano, F. S. (1993). Visual mental imagery activates topographically organized visual cortex: PET investigations. *Journal of Cognitive Neuroscience, 5*, 263–287.

Kuhl, J. (1978). Situations-, reaktions- und personbezogene Konsistenz des Leistungsmotivs bei der Messung mittels des Heckhausen-TAT [Situation-, response-, and person-based consistency of the Heckhausen measure of achievement motivation]. *Archiv für Psychologie, 130*, 37–52.

Lazarus, R. S. (1961). A substitutive-defensive conception of apperceptive fantasy. In: J. Kagan & G. S. Lesser (Eds), *Contemporary Issues in Thematic Apperceptive Methods* (pp. 51–71). Springfield IL: Charles C. Thomas.

LeDoux, J. (1996). *The emotional brain*. New York: Simon & Schuster.

LeDoux, J. E. (1987). Emotion. In: F. Plum (Ed.), *Handbook of Physiology. Section 1: The Nervous System* (pp. 419–459). Bethesda MD: American Physiological Society.

Lieberman, D. A., Sunnucks, W. L., & Kirk, J. D. (1998). Reinforcement without awareness: I. Voice level. *Quarterly Journal of Experimental Psychology B, 51*, 301–316.

Locke, E. A., & Latham, G. P. (1990). *A theory of goal setting & task performance*. Englewood Cliffs NJ: Prentice Hall.

Lundy, A. (1985). The reliability of the Thematic Apperception Test. *Journal of Personality Assessment, 49*, 141–145.

MacLean, P. D. (1987). On the evolution of the three mentalities of the brain. In: G. G. Neumann (Ed.), *Origins of human aggression: Dynamics and Etiology* (pp. 29–41). New York: Human Sciences Press.

Mandelbaum, D. G. (1963). *Selected writings of Edward Sapir in language, culture, and personality*. Berkeley CA: University of California Press.

Mazur, J. E. (1998). *Learning and behavior* (4th ed.). Upper Saddle River, NJ: Prentice Hall.

McClelland, D. C. (1958). The importance of early learning in the formation of motives. In: J. W. Atkinson (Ed.), *Motives in Fantasy, Action, and Society: A Method of Assessment and Study* (pp. 437–452). Princeton, NJ: Van Nostrand.

McClelland, D. C. (1979). Inhibited power motivation and high blood pressure in men. *Journal of Abnormal Psychology, 88*, 182–190.

McClelland, D. C. (1980). Motive dispositions. The merits of operant and respondent measures. In: L. Wheeler (Ed.), *Review of Personality and Social Psychology* (Vol. 1, pp. 10–41). Beverly Hills, CA: Sage.

McClelland, D. C. (1987). *Human motivation*. New York: Cambridge University Press.

McClelland, D. C. (1989). Motivational factors in health and disease. *American Psychologist, 44*, 675–683.

McClelland, D. C. (1995). Achievement motivation in relation to achievement-related recall, performance, and urine flow, a marker associated with release of vasopressin. *Motivation and Emotion, 19*, 59–76.

McClelland, D. C., Atkinson, J. W., Clark, R. A., & Lowell, E. L. (1953). *The achievement motive.* New York: Appleton-Century-Crofts.

McClelland, D. C., & Boyatzis, R. E. (1982). Leadership motive pattern and long-term success in management. *Journal of Applied Psychology, 67*, 737–743.

McClelland, D. C., Koestner, R., & Weinberger, J. (1989). How do self-attributed and implicit motives differ? *Psychological Review, 96*, 690–702.

McClelland, D. C., & Pilon, D. A. (1983). Sources of adult motives in patterns of parent behavior in early childhood. *Journal of Personality and Social Psychology, 44*, 564–574.

Mead, G. H. (1968). The genesis of the self and social control. In: C. Gordon & K. J. Gergen (Eds), *The Self in Social Interaction* (pp. 51–59). New York: Wiley.

Mehrabian, A., & Williams, M. (1969). Nonverbal concomitants of perceived and intended persuasiveness. *Journal of Personality and Social Psychology, 13*, 37–58.

Milgram, S. (1963). Behavioral study of obedience. *Journal of Abnormal and Social Psychology, 67*, 371–378.

Miller, G. A., Galanter, E., & Pribram, K. H. (1960). *Plans and the structure of behavior.* New York: Holt, Rinehart and Winston.

Miller, N., Maruyama, G., Beaber, R. J., & Valone, K. (1976). Speed of speech and persuasion. *Journal of Personality and Social Psychology, 34*, 615–624.

Mischel, W. (1996). From good intentions to willpower. In: P. M. Gollwitzer & J. A. Bargh (Eds), *The Psychology of Action: Linking Cognition and Motivation to Behavior* (pp. 197–218). New York: Guilford.

Mischel, W., Shoda, Y., & Peake, P. K. (1988). The nature of adolescent competencies predicted by preschool delay of gratification. *Journal of Personality and Social Psychology, 54*, 687–696.

Mischel, W., Shoda, Y., & Rodriguez, M. L. (1989). Delay of gratification in children. *Science, 244*, 933–938.

Murphy, S. T., & Zajonc, R. B. (1993). Affect, cognition, and awareness: affective priming with optimal and suboptimal stimulus exposures. *Journal of Personality and Social Psychology, 64*, 723–739.

Nisbett, R. E., & Wilson, T. D. (1977). Telling more than we can know: Verbal reports on mental processes. *Psychological Review, 84*, 231–259.

Öhman, A., & Soares, J. J. F. (1994). "Unconscious anxiety": Phobic responses to masked stimuli. *Journal of Abnormal Psychology, 103*, 231–240.

Öhman, A., & Soares, J. J. F. (1998). Emotional conditioning to masked stimuli: Expectancies for aversive outcomes following nonrecognized fear-relevant stimuli. *Journal of Experimental Psychology: General, 127*, 69–82.

Paivio, A. (1985). Cognitive and motivational functions of imagery in human performance. *Canadian Journal of Applied Sport Science, 10*, 22–28.

Paivio, A. (1986). *Mental representations. A dual coding approach.* New York: Oxford University Press.

Paivio, A. (1991). Dual coding theory: Retrospect and current status. *Canadian Journal of Psychology, 45*, 255–287.

Panksepp, J. (1998). *Affective neuroscience: The foundations of human and animal emotions.* New York, NY: Oxford University Press.

Qualls, P. J. (1982). The physiological measurement of imagery: An overview. *Imagination, Cognition and Personality, 2*, 89–101.

Reber, A. S. (1989). Implicit learning and tacit knowledge. *Journal of Experimental Psychology: General, 118*, 219–235.

Richardson, A. (1984). Strengthening the theoretical links between imaged stimuli and physiological responses. *Journal of Mental Imagery, 8*, 113–126.

Saavedra, R., & Earley, P. C. (1991). Choice of task and goal under conditions of general and specific affective inducement. *Motivation and Emotion, 15*, 45–65.

Schachter, S., & Singer, J. E. (1962). Cognitive, social, and physiological determinants of emotional state. *Psychological Review, 69*, 379–399.

Schultheiss, O. C., & Brunstein, J. C. (1999). Goal imagery: Bridging the gap between implicit motives and explicit goals. *Journal of Personality, 67*, 1–38.

Schultheiss, O. C., & Brunstein, J. C. (2001). Assessing implicit motives with a research version of the TAT: Picture profiles, gender differences, and relations to other personality measures. *Journal of Personality Assessment, 77*, 71–86.

Schultheiss, O. C., & Brunstein, J. C. (in press). Inhibited power motivation and persuasive communication: A lens model analysis. *Journal of Personality.*

Schultheiss, O. C., Campbell, K. L., & McClelland, D. C. (1999). Implicit power motivation moderates men's testosterone responses to imagined and real dominance success. *Hormones and Behavior, 36*, 234–241.

Schultheiss, O. C., & Rohde, W. (in press). Implicit power motivation predicts men's testosterone changes and implicit learning in a contest situation. *Hormones and Behavior.*

Schwartz, G. E., Weinberger, D. A., & Singer, J. A. (1981). Cardiovascular differentiation of happiness, sadness, anger, and fear following imagery and exercise. *Psychosomatic Medicine, 43*, 343–364.

Schwarz, N. (1990). Feelings as information: Informational and motivational functions of affective states. In: E. T. Higgins & R. M. Sorrentino (Eds), *Handbook of Motivation and Cognition: Foundations of Social Behavior* (Vol. 2, pp. 527–561). New York: Guilford.

Schwarz, N., & Bohner, G. (1996). Feelings and their motivational implications: Moods and the action sequence. In: P. M. Gollwitzer & J. A. Bargh (Eds), *The Psychology of Action: Linking Cognition and Motivation to Behavior* (pp. 119–145). New York, NY: Guilford.

Scott, W. A. (1956). The avoidance of threatening material in imaginative behavior. *Journal of Abnormal and Social Psychology, 52*, 338–346.

Serrano, J. M., Iglesias, J., & Loeches, A. (1992). Visual discrimination and recognition of facial expressions of anger, fear, and surprise in 4- to 6-month-old infants. *Developmental Psychobiology, 25*, 411–425.

Shin, L. M., Kosslyn, S. M., McNally, R. J., Alpert, N. M., Thompson, W. L., Rauch, S. L., Macklin, M. L., & Pitman, R. K. (1997). Visual imagery and perception in posttraumatic stress disorder. A positron emission tomographic investigation. *Archives of General Psychiatry, 54*, 233–241.

Sirota, A., & Schwartz, G. E. (1982). Facial muscle patterning and lateralization during elation and depression imagery. *Journal of Abnormal Psychology, 91*, 25–34.

Spangler, W. D. (1992). Validity of questionnaire and TAT measures of need for achievement: Two meta-analyses. *Psychological Bulletin, 112*, 140–154.

Springer, S. P., & Deutsch, G. (1998). *Left brain, right brain. Perspectives from cognitive neuroscience* (5th ed.). New York, NY: W. H. Freeman and Company.

Suler, J. R., & Katkin, E. S. (1988). Mental imagery of fear-related stimuli. *Journal of Mental Imagery, 12*, 115–123.

Veroff, J., Depner, C., Kulka, R., & Douvan, E. (1980). Comparison of American motives: 1957 versus 1976. *Journal of Personality and Social Psychology, 39*, 1249–1262.

Vygotsky, L. (1986). *Thought and language* (Alex Kozulin, Trans.). Cambridge, MA: MIT Press.

Weinberger, J., & McClelland, D. C. (1990). Cognitive versus traditional motivational models: Irreconcilable or complementary? In: E. T. Higgins & R. M. Sorrentino (Eds), Handbook of Motivation and Cognition: Foundations of Social Behavior (Vol. 2, pp. 562–597). New York: Guilford Press.

Whorf, B. L. (1971). *Language, thought, and reality. Selected writings*. Cambridge Mass.: MIT Press.

Wilson, T. D. (1985). Strangers to ourselves: The origins and accuracy of beliefs about one's own mental states. In: J. H. Harvey & G. Weary (Eds), *Attribution: Basic Issues and Applications* (pp. 9–35). Orlando, FL: Academic Press.

Winkielman, P., Berridge, K. C., & Wilbarger, J. (2001). Doing without feeling: Unconscious affect influences human consumption. Manuscript submitted for publication.

Winter, D. G. (1996). *Personality: Analysis and interpretation of lives*. New York: McGraw-Hill.

Winter, D. G., & Stewart, A. J. (1977). Power motive reliability as a function of retest instructions. *Journal of Consulting and Clinical Psychology, 45*, 436–440.

Zajonc, R. B. (1980). Feeling and thinking. Preferences need no inferences. *American Psychologist, 35*, 151–175.

Zatorre, R. J., & Halpern, A. R. (1993). Effect of unilateral temporal-lobe excision on perception and imagery of songs. *Neuropsychologia, 31*, 221–232.

Zivin, G. (Ed.). (1979). *The development of self-regulation through private speech*. New York: Wiley.

2. DYNAMIC MEASURES FOR STUDYING INTEREST AND LEARNING

Mary Ainley and Suzanne Hidi

Interest in the role of motivation in academic achievement has never been stronger. A wide range of constructs has been identified and the contributions they make to student achievement are being carefully researched. The general proposition advanced in this paper is that one way to expand our understanding of the character of specific motivational constructs, such as interest or achievement goals and their significance for academic achievement, is to develop methodologies and measures that access the dynamics of students' reactions. This need has been noted by a number of writers (see Alexander, 1997; Hickey, 1997; Jarvela & Niemivirta, 1999; Jetton & Alexander, 2001; Pintrich, 2000) and is being addressed in different ways by many of the papers in this volume. A common theme has been the need for research to focus more attention on "students' subjective experience while they are engaged in the learning activity" (Hickey, 1997, p. 182). The methods we are exploring direct attention to the microlevel of students' subjective experience monitoring and recording what students are doing as they proceed through a learning task. These methods complement what can be measured through the more common questionnaire and interview methods.

The approach we have adopted offers a number of advantages for research into the motivation of student achievement. It offers an insight into changes in motivation that might occur as students make choices and navigate their way through a learning task. An extensive set of behavioral indicators can be

New Directions in Measures and Methods, Volume 12, pages 43–76.

ISBN: 0-7623-0819-2

monitored with little interference to the ongoing learning task. For example, emotions and their intensity can be recorded at a number of points in one learning task, and so assist identification of how motivational variables interact. At the same time this approach preserves the real-time sequence of choices, decisions and reactions allowing interpretation of the sequential contingencies among important variables within the learning process.

The alternative methods we are exploring offer new insights into three critical issues that continue to be of concern for understanding the motivation of student achievement. The first issue concerns the relationship between person and situation (or, trait and state perspectives), the second deals with the question of identifying the specific processes through which interest influences learning and achievement, and the third focuses on the relationships between specific motivational constructs. Before describing in detail the methods we are developing in our research on interest, we will consider what our approach might contribute to understanding the relationship between motivation and academic achievement. Our analysis will concentrate on interest research but the approach has much to offer investigations of other motivational concepts.

INTEREST AND ACHIEVEMENT MOTIVATION

Current conceptualizations of interest owe a lot to the writings of Dewey (1913) who emphasized the interactive relation between the individual and environment that is expressed in what we refer to as 'interest'. Interest cannot be defined without reference to both person and object. It refers to the relation that exists between person and object when in Dewey's words "self and world are engaged with each other in a developing situation" (p. 126). This way of defining the substance of the term interest is the one adopted by most interest researchers (e.g. Bergin, 1999; Hidi, 1990, Hidi & Baird, 1986; Hidi & Harackiewicz, 2000; Krapp, Hidi & Renninger, 1992). At the same time interest researchers have made an important distinction between individual and situational interest (Hidi & Baird, 1988; Krapp et al., 1992). Individual interest, sometimes referred to as personal interest, has been described as an individual's relatively enduring predisposition to attend to certain objects, stimuli and events, and to engage in certain activities (e.g. Ainley, 1998; Krapp et al., 1992; Renninger, 2000; Schiefele, 1998). On the other hand, situational interest refers to interest that has been triggered by exposure to specific objects or experiences and refers to the heightened attention or concentration that is directed to the object or experience (Hidi & Berndorff, 1998).

From the perspective of understanding the experience of interest, both individual and situational factors are associated with a psychological state that involves focused attention and increased interaction with the object that can involve both cognitive and affective processing (e.g. Krapp et al., 1992, Rheinberg, 1998). It is the experience of the psychological state of interest that is at the heart of the approach we are developing. An important way of addressing educational questions concerning the role of interest in learning is to understand this experience of interest. It has been argued that interest is an important mental resource for learning (Hidi, 1990) and there is no doubt that both individual and situational interest influence learning (e.g. Hidi & Berndorff, 1998; Renninger, 2000; Schiefele, 1996). However, the specific ways in which this knowledge can be used to improve student learning depend on understanding the form and extent of interdependence between individual and situational factors in activation of the psychological state of interest. Questions concerning the relationship between situational interest and individual interests have special significance in this regard. For example, in order to trigger interest in a new science topic, a teacher includes personal examples. Is this likely to influence young adolescent students to engage more with the topic and develop longer-term interest in learning about science?

In our research we have focused on this issue and explored the processes that are implicated when students are first presented with the topic of a learning task. Investigating how both individual and situational factors contribute to the psychological state of interest promises to provide further understanding of how interest influences the learning process. Our methodology has been designed to document students' experience of a specific learning episode and to examine the dynamics of that experience as a sequence in real time. This involves tracking students' experience across the course of a specific learning activity.

Particular patterns of motivation triggered on initial presentation of a learning task are not necessarily maintained as students proceed through the task (Hidi & Baird, 1986; Mitchell, 1993). For example, some students may have their interest triggered by a topic when a text is first presented, but as they get further into the text their interest dissipates. Other students reading the same text may have a similar level of interest triggered by the topic and their interest in the text may be maintained or even intensified over time. The same kind of fluctuation may be found in other areas of research on student motivation. A student who has a strong mastery goal orientation may start a task with the intention of learning as much as possible about the topic. However, as the student proceeds through the task his/her mastery goal may dissolve into an intention to simply finish the task as quickly as possible. The ebb and flow of motivation as a student spends time with a specific task may be just as important for understanding the relationship between motivation and academic achievement as is the students' initial motivation.

Our research touches on all three of the general research issues for achievement motivation referred to earlier: the relationship between personal and situational perspectives, identification of processes mediating learning, and, relationships between motivational constructs.

INDIVIDUAL AND SITUATION IN MOTIVATIONAL RESEARCH

An approach that records student responses in real-time provides the opportunity to inspect dynamic features of students' reactions to specific learning tasks. It provides a new perspective from which to consider the relation between what the person brings to the learning task and what is generated by the task itself. In our research this issue has been addressed through investigation of the relationship between individual and situational interest. Before discussing our findings we review some of the current positions on this question.

Within motivational research constructs are often discussed in terms of their status as either trait or state and this continues to be a point of contention. Significantly, the issue is often framed in the form of an either/or question. Murphy and Alexander (2000) in their extensive review of motivation terminology refer to this issue as one of "variability – the degree to which identified constructs represent motivation traits or states" (p. 37), and later they summarize the issue described by them as a paradox.

> On the one hand, if students' goal orientations are truly orientations (i.e. motivational traits), then it is unclear what effect any manipulation of the instructional context should have on them. On the other hand, if sociocontextual factors have the power to transform students' perspectives on academic tasks, then it seems unlikely that the researchers are dealing with a motivational trait (p. 42).

One way of conceptualizing the relation between trait and state, individual and situation, is to see them in terms of levels of specificity. This is the argument advanced by Pintrich (2000) responding to Murphy and Alexander's (2000) critique of motivational concepts used in the study of student achievement. Pintrich stated that goals are not traits in the sense of fixed dispositions. Rather they are cognitive representations of what individuals would like to achieve and may show both intra-individual stability and contextual sensitivity. Drawing on the work of key goal theorists (e.g. Bandura, 1997; Ford, 1992; Locke & Latham, 1990), he suggested three levels of analysis for the achievement goal construct. At the general level are the reasons 'why' an individual is motivated that apply to broad areas of life. At the task-specific level it is appropriate to talk of target goals that express standards or criteria for evaluating performance. In between the general, global goals and the specific task goals, are achievement goals that are orientations toward achievement tasks. They represent an "integrated and organized pattern of beliefs about both the general reasons and purposes for achievement, and the standards for judging performance". The issue of trait and state is then addressed in terms of accessibility of goal schema and the ease with which they can be activated in specific situations. "Strong contexts can overwhelm chronically accessible traits, but in the absence of strong cues in the environment, then traits may influence behavior more" (Pintrich, 2000, p. 102). Wentzel's (2000) model of multiple goals in achievement situations makes a similar distinction between levels of complexity. At the most general level goals express "fundamental orientations toward the self and the social environment". Knowledge of the complementarity and hierarchical ordering between social and academic goals as well as the goal structure of classroom contexts are essential for understanding the interdependence of individual and situation in achievement behavior.

Despite important differences in specific constructs, both goal and interest perspectives within motivational research point to an essential interdependence between individual and situation. The active psychological state draws on both person and context and the problem is to determine how they interact in different types of achievement settings. As indicated above, the challenge is then to be able to identify within particular achievement domains the critical form(s) of interdependence between person and situation.

Predisposition and Psychological State in Interest Research

Interest researchers have consistently made a conceptual distinction between individual interest and situational interest (Hidi, 1990; Hidi & Baird, 1986, 1988; Krapp et al., 1992; Renninger, Hoffmann & Krapp, 1998). In the introduction to their widely cited volume documenting resurgence in research on the role of interest in learning and development, Krapp et al. (1992) defined three aspects of interest. The character of these aspects of interest in terms of their trait or state-like characteristics and the relationships between them form the theoretical background for our research.

> Three major points of view are reflected in interest research: (1) interest as a characteristic of the person; (2) interest as a characteristic of the learning environment; and (3) interest as a psychological state. Both individual interest, in the sense of relatively stable preferences, and interestingness can bring about experiences and psychological states in an

> individual that are generally referred to as interest. Typical characteristics of this state might include increased attention, greater concentration, pleasant feelings of applied effort, and increased willingness to learn, *although the extent to which these characteristics are generated by interest remains an open question* (our italics). Given that the theoretical interpretation and/or operationalization of the interest concept varies from author to author largely as a function of research questions, we suggest for now that the states of interest brought about by external stimuli be separated in theory and terminology from those generated by individual interest. *Although the state of interest, in the sense of an actualized individual interest, seems closely related to the experiential state of situational interest, it has not been demonstrated that the psychological processes and the effects of the two states are identical, or even comparable* (pp. 9–10, our italics).

The above paragraph acknowledges firstly a difference between interest as a general characteristic of the person, continuing over time and the situational interest triggered by specific properties of the situation. The question is whether the psychological state of interest experienced as the result of situational factors, is the same "or even comparable" to the psychological state that is the outcome of individual factors. For many of the specific learning tasks that are the concern of educators, it is likely that both individual and situational factors make joint and separate contributions to the learning outcomes. Although the definitions of individual and situational interest cited above have been widely used in subsequent research (e.g. Mitchell, 1993; Schiefele, 1996; Shraw, Bruning & Svoboda, 1995), it is clear that the relation between them in terms of the state that is activated, or triggered is not well researched or understood. In a later volume Renninger et al. (1998) proposed

> Both individual and situational interest can be analysed with respect to the underlying dispositional characteristics of the person, the structural characteristics of the learning environment, or with respect to an ongoing situation-specific process, where interest is experienced as a specific affective-cognitive (psychological) state (p. 12).

This more recent statement of the relation between the three aspects of interest acknowledges the potential complexity of the experience and the difficulty of casting it as either trait or state. Whereas the distinction between trait and state continues to be discussed in the motivational literature, the terms 'predisposition' and 'psychological state' are used in interest research to distinguish what the individual brings to the situation and what is aroused in a specific situation. It is central to interest theory that the psychological state is always the outcome of a person/environment interaction. What is common to both individual and situational interest is the individual's reactivity to some specific object. It may be that the object or some environmental factor triggers interest because of its novel or puzzling features. It may be that the object has some universal human significance. It may be that the object triggers interest in individuals who have a specific background that means they are primed to react to that object – the individual difference perspective. However, the relationship between interest triggered by individual factors and interest triggered by situational factors has not been clearly established. A critical agenda in interest research is to understand the nature of the psychological state of interest, and to determine whether the state triggered by individual factors is indeed the same, or in some way different to that triggered by situational factors.

It is our contention that part of the difficulty has been the lack of appropriate techniques for accessing the psychological state that ensues when interest is triggered. In our studies we are using computer-based techniques that record students' responses to specific learning tasks in their real time sequence. In one study dealing with students' reactions to sets of texts (see Ainley, Hidi & Berndorff, submitted) measures of individual interest allowed us to determine the contribution of individual interest to students' immediate reaction to each text title. Students were told they would be required to read a number of text passages. They were presented with the text titles and were asked: "How interesting do you expect this topic to be?" Responses were made on the screen using a five point Likert-type scale. A variety of analyses have been conducted using these measures to determine the contribution of individual interest to variations in intra-individual responses across the set of text titles as well as to inter-individual differences in the overall level of interest triggered by the text titles. Our findings have shown considerable variation in the levels of topic interest triggered by our four expository text-titles. Some of the wide variation between the responses to the text-titles could be attributed to individual interest factors. Individual interest in specific domains (e.g. science, personal health) accounted for some of the intra-individual variability in topic interest. More general individual interest variables were significantly related to inter-individual variations in topic interest. These effects although significant were generally small and suggest that topic interest is likely to be the outcome of both individual and situational factors, most probably operating in combination. Further investigation is needed to identify how both individual and situational interest factors operate for different students and different topics and the approach we are developing offers a means of addressing these questions.

Vollmeyer and Rheinberg (2000) have used a similar methodological approach in their investigation of the relationship between what they referred to as 'current' motivation, motivational state during the learning task, and specific learning process variables. They also employed computerized recording of student responses within a simulated biology-lab task. In one phase of the task students explored the system and then in a second phase had to apply the knowledge they had gained about the system. Measures of students' current motivation were taken before the task commenced and then at the end of every learning trial their motivational state was recorded.

The importance of this area of research lies in the theoretical and conceptual clarity that would result, and also the contribution it would make to our understanding of the development of individual interests. Development of measures that can reflect the dynamic of students' experience as they engage with a learning task will allow further identification of relationships between individual and situational factors. When this is combined with more macro-level or longitudinal perspectives it will contribute to understanding how generating situational interest can promote the development of longer term individual interests (see Hidi & Anderson, 1992; Hidi & Harackiewicz, 2000). At the practical level this may provide some insight into the perennial question of how to motivate the academically unmotivated.

IDENTIFICATION OF MEDIATING PROCESSES

At the heart of the vigorous research on academic motivation are questions about the relationship between motivation and academic achievement, between motivation and learning outcomes (see Murphy & Alexander, 2000; Schunk, 2000). In a number of reviews of research on interest and broader motivational dimensions, Schiefele and colleagues (Schiefele, 1996; Schiefele, Krapp & Winteler, 1992; Schiefele & Rheinberg, 1997) reported that for both general achievement and achievement in short-term learning tasks approximately 10% of the variance is associated with differences in motivational factors. Along with other researchers, Schiefele has pointed out that we know little of how this effect operates (see Schiefele, 1996; Vollmeyer & Rheinberg, 2000). With respect to interest, this means the path from the arousal of interest to specific learning outcomes needs to be more fully documented. Part of the difficulty for identification of the mediating processes has to do with methodological limitations. As pointed out by Schiefele and Rheinberg (1997), most studies that have attempted to identify how specific motivational dimensions influence learning have been cross-sectional and so the causal sequence has been difficult to determine. Longitudinal designs have been advocated as one way to address this problem (Schiefele & Rheinberg, 1997; Murphy & Alexander, 2000). An alternative, also advocated by Schiefele and Rheinberg, involves development of research designs that focus on what is happening in specific achievement situations. This is essentially the perspective behind the development of the On-line Motivation Questionnaire (OMQ, Boekaerts, 1997; Crombach, Boekaerts & Voeten, 1995). The OMQ was administered before and after specific learning tasks and students' current motivational state could then be related to different learning outcomes. An affect measure reported by Vermeer, Boekaerts and Seegers (1995) involved students reporting at fixed time intervals how they were feeling as a task proceeded, thereby measuring what was happening as students solved their math problems.

Looking specifically at interest research, questionnaires and self-rating scales have been widely used to measure interest. In terms of understanding the processes that contribute to learning outcomes, the timing of the administration of questionnaires and rating scales is critical for interpretation of their meaning. For example, when students are presented with a short description of a problem and asked to make a rating of interest, the measure is a forward projection, an expectancy measure. It represents the participants' estimation of how they expect that they will react to the learning task. On the other hand, when a rating of interest is made after the event, the participant is required to reflect back in time, to remember what they felt as they were performing the task. If the task involved reading text, students have already finished reading and their knowledge of the outcome cannot be ignored as a potential influence on their recollections of reactions at earlier points during the task. Thus, measurement of important indicators of mediating processes require a methodology sensitive to changes in students' reactions as they occur during the course of the learning task.

Availability of interactive, multimedia software, and data recording with modern computer networks and servers means that a wide range of reactions can be targeted. Exploring this direction for the development of research on students' motivation and achievement is in its infancy. Increasingly more software will be available to the motivation researcher and that software will have greater potential to be edited and modified to address sets of related research questions.

We have conducted some initial investigations of processes mediating the relationship between interest and learning (Ainley et al., 1999, submitted). Our results suggest that personal characteristics of gender, individual interests, general interest in learning, and prior knowledge of text content not only contributed to topic interest, the expectation of how interesting the text would be, but these variables also affected what happened in the course of text processing. After statistically controlling for the effects of the general personal factors, the effects of topic interest on learning were determined and we found that topic interest influenced students' affective responses. Affect influenced the degree that students persisted with each text, and persistence was related to scores on the test at the end of each text. Further studies using the same methodology are needed to confirm these patterns.

RELATIONSHIPS BETWEEN MOTIVATIONAL CONSTRUCTS

Renewed interest in the motivation of academic achievement over the last two decades has seen an increasing array of terms. Murphy and Alexander (2000) reviewed a large number of these concepts commenting that

> It is difficult to deal with one motivational construct without invoking the name of another . . . . It almost seems that the deeper we have delved into understanding the role of interest in academic development, the more often we have needed to speak about learners' *goals*, their *intrinsic* or *extrinsic motivations*, and their sense of *competence* (Murphy & Alexander, 2000, p. 40).

In the same vein, Renninger et al. (1998) when describing common bases for research on individual interest referred to interest as a motivational belief "Here, an interest is interpreted as a domain-specific 'personal goal' that has gained dominance in somebody's goal structure . . ." (p. 460). Clearly there is considerable need for clarification of the forms of relationship between these motivation concepts. Developing research strategies that focus on the processes operating in specific learning situations provides another form of validation of these concepts and the distinctions and interconnections between them. In his response to Murphy and Alexander's exploration of motivation terminology, Pintrich (2000) suggested that distinctions between motivational concepts should be based on "important and real differences in the terms, theories, and supporting empirical data" (p. 95). It is our contention that research strategies making use of the potential of interactive software to monitor and record large sets of reactions within a specific learning situation can provide a data base for testing these distinctions and interconnections. Earlier we have argued that this strategy allows the researcher to distinguish the separate and joint contributions of individual and situational factors. It also allows assessment of the dynamics of the interface between motivational constructs. Factor analytic studies, both exploratory and confirmatory test the structure of the relationships between motivational constructs within questionnaires and rating scales. Monitoring students' reactions as they progress through a learning experience provides the opportunity to test the predictive relations between motivational concepts. For example, in the pilot version of software that we have developed to monitor student responses to an instructional unit in physics we have included questions to assess students' general goal orientation (mastery, performance-approach, performance-avoidance, and work avoidant). The topic of the learning task concerned understanding what is happening when waves from two sources meet. This was described to students in terms of explaining the pattern of the radiating lines they could see in a photograph of a bee flapping its wings on the surface of a pond of water. Following this, the student's initial reaction was recorded by asking them to make a rating of how interesting they expected the learning task to be. From these responses the predictive relationship between students' academic goal orientation and their topic interest could be identified. In our pilot study using the *Waves* software with Introductory Psychology students' mastery goal orientation scores were significant predictors of topic interest scores.

In short, the development of techniques that monitor the dynamic properties of student reactivity to instructional tasks offers a new window into understanding the mediating processes that connect person and situation in achievement and learning.

THE DYNAMIC WITHIN A LEARNING EPISODE

In this section we will describe our basic research strategy and some of our initial findings. Monitoring the dynamics of student motivation within a learning episode requires development of techniques that allow us to observe what students are actually feeling, deciding, and doing as they engage with and disengage from the specific activity. We have employed computer-based techniques to record in their real time sequence behavioral reactions that may provide indicators of student involvement or disengagement. For example, with a task that consisted of reading sections of text we monitored the dynamics of students' subjective experience by recording a number of indicators as they progressed through the task. Students reported how they were feeling, choices between alternative paths within the learning activity, choices about whether to continue or quit, and their responses to items testing recall of text content. Development and subsequent refinement of these techniques will make a substantial contribution to knowledge and understanding of the ways students engage with and learn from academic activities.

The methods we are developing utilize the potential of computer-based data collection techniques to monitor students' reactions in a way that complements what is available with pencil-and-paper questionnaires. Of major significance is the potential of these technologies to allow researchers to automatically monitor and record extensive sets of indicators of students' reactions in their real time sequence across the full duration of a specific learning task. This critical feature offers possibilities for identifying the particular ways in which motivational variables interact and contribute to student achievement.

Computerized task presentation in educational research is not new and it has the advantage of providing sufficient flexibility to record responses that reflect students' interests and/or their learning goals. For example, in a recent study, McDaniel, Waddill, Finstad and Bourg (2000) combined both paper text materials and computer responses in their investigation of the way attention is deployed in association with text based interest. Students read from sets of paper-based texts previously determined to be of either high or low interest. While reading the texts students were required to simultaneously respond to a secondary stimulus administered by computer. When the distractor stimulus occurred, students had to press a key on the computer. Computer recorded reaction times to the distractor stimuli provided a measure of students' deployment of attention to the primary text material. In this way the researchers were able to identify the attention load associated with high and low interest texts.

Our research program is based on computerizing both the presentation of the learning tasks and the recording of responses. For example, we have examined interest as it relates to students' involvement with short texts. Students first recorded their impressions to a set of text titles and then chose which text they would work with first. A number of investigators have argued that student choice influences motivation (e.g. Schraw, Flowerday & Reisetter, 1998). In observational studies of intrinsic motivation, choice has been used in the form of time taken to re-engage with a task (e.g. see Deci, Koestner & Ryan, 1999). In our design the order in which texts were chosen was examined to determine how it related to interest in specific topics (topic interest). Interest was found to be a significant factor influencing order of choice though it was not the only factor (Ainley et al., submitted). When four topics were presented following the normal left to right reading orientation, there was a tendency for the order in which texts were chosen to match their order of presentation across the screen. After statistically controlling for this effect, the order of text choice was associated with levels of topic interest. In another study three text topics were presented in an irregular configuration. The first text chosen showed significantly higher topic interest than did the other two texts (Andrews, Hoey & Ainley, 2001).

In short, our studies use a task format that externalizes critical process dimensions and the real-time sequence of events is preserved. Monitoring the order of responses is especially important for analyses in this research because it allows researchers to identify sequences among variables in ways that are not possible with more conventional techniques.

TWO INTERACTIVE PROGRAMS

Between the Lines

The first of our research programs has focused on individual and situational interest and their effects on students' responses to short texts and used our interactive software called *Between the Lines* (*BTL*,[1] 1997; see Ainley et al., 1999, submitted; Ainley, Hillman & Hidi, in press). This software is described and the findings of our initial studies summarized. We also illustrate how this approach is being used to investigate two of the key issues referred to earlier: person and situation as they contribute to the psychological state of interest triggered in a specific learning task, and, processes that mediate the effects of interest on learning.

The software was designed to monitor students' interaction with the texts and this was achieved by recording students' responses to a series of structured decisions. Students could navigate through the software by answering a question on the screen, following a specific prompt, or by using a 'NEXT' button. The basic task sequence in the first versions of this software commenced with students recording their initial reactions to a set of topics in the form of text titles ("how interesting do you expect this topic to be?") Students then chose which of the texts they wished to read first. Each text consisted of three sections and when a specific text was chosen the first part appeared on the screen for the student to read. The length of time spent with this part of the text was under each individual student's control and from there they navigated their own path through the four texts.

The choices presented to students were designed to monitor individual reactions to the texts (e.g. to read what is on the screen or to move immediately to another text, how long to continue with the same text). At critical points, emotion probes consisting of a panel of face icons were used to record how students were feeling (e.g. surprised, bored, sad, interested). The intensity of the emotion chosen was also indicated using a Likert-type rating. Emotion probes were structured to allow students to choose more than one emotion if they so desired. When students chose to quit from a text or when they had accessed all three parts of that text, a set of multiple choice items assessed their recall of text content. The record of each student's responses was automatically logged and available for compilation with other students' logfiles and subsequent data analysis.

A record of the number of sections of text chosen and the amount of time spent with each section provided a detailed profile of student interaction with each text. In the initial studies an index of persistence was constructed that included both the number of parts of each text accessed and a time criterion. The time criterion identified students who after seeing a text on the screen chose to move on without spending sufficient time to actually read any substantial part of it. Pilot work with a group of senior secondary students indicated if students spent less than 35 seconds with a 250–300 word passage of text, they were unlikely to have read the full passage.

Mediating Processes

Using multivariate, multilevel modeling procedures (see Rowe, 2000) we tested a two-level hierarchical model of interest processing. This was basically a model separating what the individual brings to the task in the way of personal predisposition, (more specifically, individual interest), and what happens in the specific situation. For each of the four texts we modeled the contributions of topic interest, affect and persistence as predictors of learning outcomes and in each case found a significant path connecting topic interest and learning. The significant coefficients suggested that the level of interest recorded when the topic was first encountered contributed significantly to the emotion reported at the end of their time with the first part of the text. For each text, the emotion reported was significantly related to students' persistence. Students who reported that they expected to find a text interesting were more likely to report feeling interested, to choose to continue with the text, and to read more (to persist). On the other hand, students who reported less initial interest in a text-title were more likely to report feeling bored, and when given choice about continuing were more likely to quit. Persistence with each text was significantly related to the score on a short test at the end of each text (Ainley et al., submitted). One of the advantages of our methodology is that we have indicators of student disengagement with the task. When students activated a button to move them on to the next screen, the time they had spent with that section of text was recorded. Students were able to choose NOT to continue with a text. Knowing this we were able to determine that the relationship between persistence and learning was largely a function of the difference between those who disengaged quickly and those who continued to read.

In short, our modeling of the sequence of responses to the reading tasks suggested that affect and persistence were important variables mediating between the level of interest triggered by the text-title and the learning represented in the test score at the end of each text.

Individual and Situation

It was also important in this research to identify what influence the relatively stable personal interests that students bring with them might have on what happened in specific tasks. Therefore, the software was designed in such a way that students could be asked about their individual interests prior to their participation in the reading tasks. On the screen students were able record individual interests to prompts consisting of open-ended questions as well as to prompts in the form of Likert-type ratings. Our analyses of the relationships between responses to individual interest domains and topic interest ratings for the four texts indicated that individual interest made a significant contribution to intra-individual differences in topic interest as well as to inter-individual differences in the overall levels of topic interest that were triggered. Individual interest in the domain of personal health was significantly related to within person variation in topic interest to the four text-titles. Students who gave stronger ratings on the measure of individual interest in the personal health domain were more likely to report higher topic interest in the text title of 'Body Image' than they were to the other three titles. There was also significant between person variation in the students' level of topic interest averaged across the four texts that was associated with individual interest. Our measures of individual interest included a number of levels of generality. For example, we had measures that referred to very specific individual interest domains and others that related to broader individual interest concepts. Intra-individual differences in topic interest, responses within a set of text topics, were more likely to be related to specific individual domains while differences in the overall level of topic interest were likely to be related to the more general individual interest measures. These findings suggest that the question of generality (or specificity) within measures of individual interest is an important consideration for understanding how interaction between person and situation triggers interest. This needs further investigation.

An important advantage of computer-based data collection techniques for the study of motivation and achievement is that software can be written in forms that can be edited and adapted to test the range of hypotheses that are generated by these findings.

Waves

A second research program is investigating the processing of a unit of learning in physics. An instructional unit designed for web-based delivery (*Waves*)[2] has been developed. The same key features have been incorporated as in the *BTL* program. Students are required to make choices about their path through the learning task and their sequence of choices can be used to describe patterns of involvement with the learning task. Again, all responses have been monitored and recorded providing data for investigation of relationships between motivation and learning. Analyses are currently being conducted.

The instructional package, *Waves* deals with the physics of what happens when waves from two sources meet. To pose the problem a photograph is presented which shows a bee on the surface of a pond. The wave pattern produced as the bee flaps its wings shows a series of lines radiating out from the bee. Students are informed that the material they will encounter will give them an understanding of why this pattern is different to the increasing circles observed when a stone is dropped in the pond and how understanding this phenomenon is useful.

The learning package invites students to choose from two styles of learning, one more static the other more interactive. The more static path through the material presents a structured sequence of information much like a normal textbook with descriptions of the important concepts, images and explanations. The information and images address the key issue in terms of a cork in a pool of water being affected by waves from up to two sources. Although presented in a web-style, these pages are described to the student as being static ('like a textbook on the screen'). The range of choice available to the students is limited to how long they spend with each section of instruction (each individual screen), and whether they move forward to a new screen or look back to a previous screen.

The second path presents the same structured sequence of information but with an interactive component. The interactive component consists of a simulation that allows the student to actively explore what happens to the cork in relation to changes made to different elements of the situation, for example, its position, wave length, and, separation of the sources of the waves. Students are able to independently manipulate the important elements of the problem and to observe the effects of their actions as they work through the descriptions of basic concepts and explanations. As with the more static version, they are able to spend as much time as they would like with each screen and then choose to move forward or to go back to a previous screen.

We were interested to observe what students would do when given freedom to make choices about their form of instruction and so a further option open to students was the possibility of switching between forms of instruction at any time. Our first studies with *Waves* (Pearce, Ainley & Rodrigues,[3] work in progress) have incorporated a number of preliminary measures to record student motivational orientations, background experience in physics and a rating of how interesting they expected this topic to be. Within the learning unit itself we included an emotion and goal probe to record how students were reacting to the task. A set of emotions terms were presented to record how students were feeling and a number of goal statements monitored students' specific goals as they worked through the task. Each student encountered the probe twice. Pre- and post-tests on student understanding of the physics concepts were included and at the end of the session students completed ratings reporting on the specific strategies they had used to learn the content. All of the responses students made from the time they logged on to *Waves* were recorded on a server and then used to analyze patterns of responsiveness to the structure of the learning environment and how this related both to learning outcomes and to student variables.

SOME OUTPUTS

Monitoring Feeling with Emotion Probes

Contemporary research on motivation in learning acknowledges the importance of considering affect along with cognition. Whether the referent is interest, goals, or self-efficacy, affect is considered to be an important component of academic motivation (see Pekrun, 1992, 2000). In order to monitor what students feel as they progress through specific learning activities we have developed a number of emotion probes. The specific structure of each of the probes we have used reflects the age of the students as well as aspects of the specific issue being investigated. The basic theory of emotion informing the selection of emotions for these measures has been Izard's differential emotions theory (Izard, 1972, 1977), and his work on the measurement of emotion in children and adults (see Izard, 1972; Izard, Dougherty, Bloxom & Kotsch, 1974; Manstead, 1993).

The first of our emotion probes was used in a study of children's social problem solving (Ainley, Bretherton & Sanson, 1994). The changing emotions of fifth and sixth graders were monitored as they participated in a social problem-solving task. The software (*In the Picture*,[4] 1994) was designed to present a scenario that developed into a potential conflict situation and children were required to report what they would do to handle that situation. The potential conflict situation was presented through a series of graphics on the computer screen and as the scenario developed, a number of features in its design encouraged students to become involved and be the central character in the story. After each new graphic had been on the screen for a few seconds, a panel of emotion icons (faces) appeared on one side of the screen and the students had to click the mouse on an icon to indicate how they felt. The story involved a schoolyard event where the student received an award. The scene moved from the schoolyard where students were playing with their friends, through the Monday morning ritual of a school assembly where the Principal as part of her address to the school presented pupil awards. The Principal announced the 'Pupil of the Week Award' and the trophy showed the name of the student operating the computer. After receiving the award the student was surrounded by others wanting to see the award. The award ended up on the ground broken. All of this occurred across a series of graphics with minimal explanation, but at each point the student reported how they felt using the face icons. When plotted, the responses of a group of 164 fifth and sixth graders (approximately equal numbers of boys and girls) clearly showed a changing sequence of emotions as the scenario developed (see Ainley et al., 1994). Figure 1 illustrates this pattern and presents the percentage of respondents reporting each emotion for the seven graphics in this scenario sequence.

The smiling, happy face that was reported almost unanimously by students in response to playing in the schoolyard (Scene 1) was replaced by angry and sad faces in response to the award lying broken on the ground (Scene 7). Of interest also were the changes in the pattern of emotions chosen between Scenes 5 and 6. When called up to receive their award (Scene 5) most of the students chose the happy face, some chose embarrassed and a few chose scared and surprised. But when the other students were shown crowding around to see the award, scared and neutral were more common. The changing sequence of emotions chosen in response to the changing storyline suggest that this panel of eight face icons provided a simple and quick method of monitoring changes in affect. In addition, when a face icon was clicked a 'barometer' appeared in place of the face panel. The chosen face icon and a four point rating panel were used to record intensity of the emotion. The emotion probe could be responded to quickly and then children continued with minimal disruption to the main task.

The *BTL* software was designed to be suitable for use with secondary students and the set of face icons was extended to cover a broader range of basic emotions. Consistent with Izard's differential emotions theory (Izard, 1977), one icon was chosen to represent each of the basic emotions posited by that theory (happy, sad, scared, interested, surprised, embarrassed, angry, bored, disgusted, and sorry) with an additional face described as neutral. As with the *In the Picture* software, students had to click on a face to indicate how they were feeling whenever the panel of faces appeared. Selecting a face activated a screen that asked for a rating of emotion intensity. With the *BTL* format students were able to choose more than one emotion if they so desired, in order to describe how they were feeling.

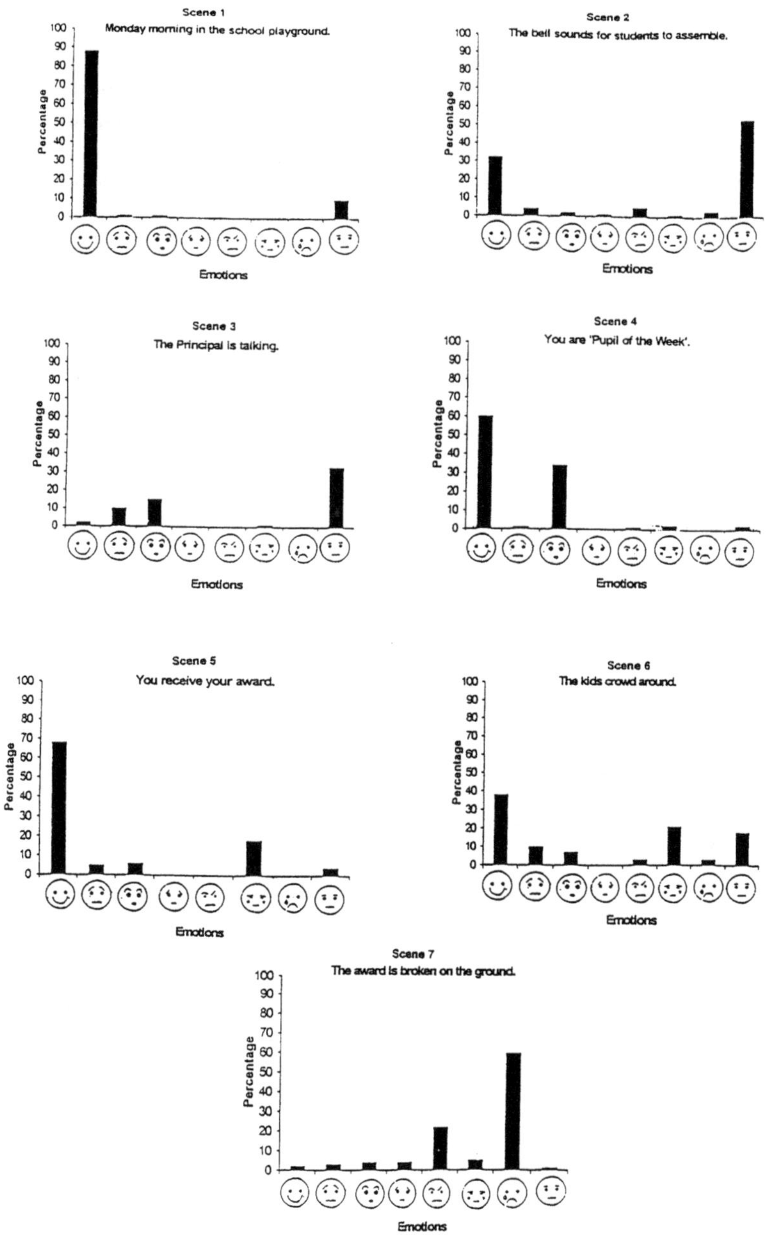

Fig. 1. School Assembly Scenario: The Emotions Students Reported.

Reliability and Validity

An important methodological issue that concerns all of the reaction data recorded through these techniques is the reliability and validity of these measures. First we will consider the issue of reliability, that is, reliability of measurement. With conventional questionnaire measures the two most common forms of reliability reported are *internal consistency* and what is becoming increasingly uncommon, *test-retest* reliability. The on-line recording of student responses as they proceed through a learning task requires some re-thinking of this issue. The responses that are of interest are students' immediate responses, choices, decisions, reactions. By definition many of these are transitory and it is important that immediate responses are recorded. As soon as the response is made the student moves on. Test-retest and internal consistency are not the measurement issues. With transitory responses reliability of measurement is more concerned with whether the recording is actually calibrated accurately. This is handled by checking that when a student clicks on the 'bored' icon that the correct code is recorded in the logfile of responses. However, what is more critical in this context is the question of validity. When a student clicks on the 'bored' icon, is it valid to interpret what they are feeling at that point in the learning task as boredom?

One form of validity relevant to an evaluation of these techniques is *discriminant* validity, the degree to which the measure yields different responses in substantively different situations. Two 'practice' trials at the beginning of the *BTL* provide a test of whether students are discriminating between situations in the way they use the face icons. In these trials students were asked to imagine two situations. Izard (1972) reported studies confirming the validity of using hypothetical situations with his pencil-and-paper versions of the Differential Emotions Scale. Following this model we included two 'practice' items. The first practice item asked students to imagine they were about to take a mathematics test. The emotion panel was presented and responses recorded. The second item asked students to respond imagining that they had just heard about winning a two week holiday of their choice. Clearly if students were responding to the content of these hypothetical situations they would report different emotions and so provide some indication of the discriminant validity of the measure. The proportion of students reporting specific emotions for these two situations is presented in Fig. 2. Only the first emotion chosen by any student was included but as can be seen there was good discrimination in students' responses for the two imagined situations. For the mathematics test the most commonly reported emotions were neutral, scared and interested. For the holiday scenario the most frequently reported were happy and surprised.

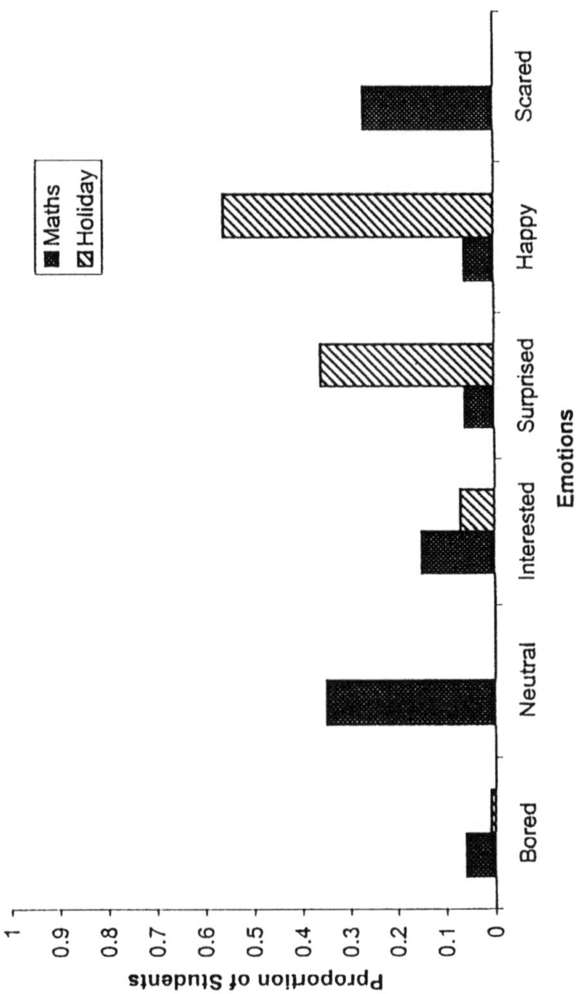

Fig. 2. Emotions Reported for the Mathematics Test and Holiday Situations.

Another relevant form of validity assessment is *predictive* validity (sometimes referred to as *concurrent* validity). This concerns the degree to which scores match predictions from a theoretical model of the relationships between variables. The emotions that students experienced while reading a text (*BTL*) or learning about something in the physical world (*Waves*) may not be as dramatic as those experiences represented in the practice trials, or in the social scenario depicted for the social problem-solving software (*In the Picture*). However, as affective responses are important components of motivation, we would expect differences in reported emotions in the *BTL* studies to be associated with differences in variables that are theoretically connected, for example, topic interest. How interesting a student expects a text to be when presented with a text-title should theoretically be positively related to the emotions they report after reading some part of the text. Of course, reading the text will contribute to the emotion reported. If the content of the text matches expectation, the emotion will be consistent; if the text does not meet expectations, emotions are likely to change. However, because the titles were constructed to fit the texts, the overall relationship between topic interest and emotion at the end of part one of each text would be expected to be positive. Ainley et al. (1999, submitted) found significant differences in the levels of topic interest associated with reporting feeling 'interested', 'neutral' and 'bored' at the end of the first part of the text. Students who reported higher topic interest when presented with the text title were more likely to report feeling 'interested' at the end of the first part of the text. Students with lower topic interest were more likely to report feeling 'bored'. When the emotion and its associated intensity ratings were combined into an index from 5 = 'very interested' through 0 = 'neutral' to –5 = 'very bored', there were significant positive correlations between how interesting students expected all four texts to be (topic interest), and their emotion responses. These correlations ranged from 0.44 ($p < 0.001$) for a text about popular science fiction videos and movies to 0.26 ($p < 0.001$) for a text about a physical science topic.

The *Waves* program incorporated probes designed to record the sequence of both emotions and goals as students progressed through the task. The probes appeared twice for each respondent. We describe some of the data from the goal items to comment on the predictive validity of these measures. Table 1 shows the means and standard deviations for the four goal statements represented in the probes indicating that the overall level of each was slightly lower for the second probe than for the first. In two cases the second probe level was significantly lower than it was for the first probe. For the probes to be a valid measure of what students are trying to achieve, overall, we would expect that there would be a significant positive relationship between like goals across

Table 1. *Waves*: Predictive Validity of Emotions and Goals Probes 1 and 2 (5 point Likert-type rating scales).

	Probe			
	First	Second		
Goal Probes	*M (SD)*	*M (SD)*	p^a	*r*
Mastery	3.35 (1.27)	2.96 (1.46)	*	0.58***
Performance – Approach	3.45 (1.40)	2.84 (1.27)	***	0.68***
Performance – Avoidance	3.08 (1.49)	2.80 (1.39)		0.44**
Work Avoidant	3.67 (1.21)	3.63 (1.13)		0.42**

* $p < 0.05$, ** $p < 0.01$, *** $p < 0.001$.
[a] Significance of difference between first and second probe means.

the two occasions. Table 1 confirms that there were strong positive correlations between the matching pairs of goal responses. The lowest correlation was between the 'work avoidant' goal pair ("Right now my aim is to finish as quickly as I can.") and the highest between the 'performance-approach' goal pair. The probe item in this latter case consisted of the statement "Learn enough to do well on the question at the end".

The probes in the *Waves* software were designed to capture the dynamics of students' task related goals as they might change and develop across the course of a learning task. As can be seen from the responses summarized in Table 1, there were some changes in the overall level of specific goals. Although correlations between matching goal items on the two probes were strong, there were individual changes in the degree to which specific goal statements were endorsed.

The range of measures that can be incorporated into this type of software allows us to identify important relationships between different motivational concepts. Commentaries on recent findings in the goal orientation literature have drawn attention to the variety of ways that mastery and performance goals might co-exist and interact having different effects on learning outcomes (e.g. Barron & Harackiewicz, 1999; Hidi & Harackiewicz, 2000; Harackiewicz, Barron, Tauer, Carter & Elliot, 2000). In addition, there is currently a wide concern for identifying the potential overlaps and the important distinctions between specific motivational concepts (see Murphy & Alexander, 2000;

Pintrich, 2000). Alongside these questions the role of affect in the relationship between motivation and learning is being addressed. For example, Pekrun (2000) has addressed this by distinguishing activating and deactivating achievement emotions. Monitoring a range of motivational and affective variables within one learning task can further these important research objectives. Our emotion and goal probes included a range of emotion terms. Exploratory factor analysis showed two groupings of these emotion terms. The first included high factor loadings for confused, surprised, challenged, and frustrated. The second grouping consisted of high positive loadings for the emotion terms interested and pleased, along with a high negative loading for bored. Factor scores for these two emotion groups were then used as the criterion variables in separate regression analyses with the goal orientation and topic interest scores as the set of predictor variables. Performance-avoidance goal orientation and topic interest scores were significant predictors for each of these two emotion groups. The direction of the relationships distinguished the two sets of emotions. Performance-avoidance goal orientation was a positive predictor and topic interest a negative predictor for the first group of emotions (confused, surprised, challenged, and frustrated). The reverse was true for the second group of emotions where topic interest was the significant positive predictor and performance-avoidance goal orientation a significant negative predictor. These findings are preliminary and will require replication. They do however suggest that the methodology we are using allows us to address a number of key research questions.

An Individual Path

An essential part of the design of our research measures has been the recording of student paths within the learning activity, that is, the order students chose to read a set of texts, when trying to learn about the physics of waves. Each measurement recorded provides an index of one aspect of the dynamic of student interaction with their learning. Some examples from our pilot study with *Waves* are described to illustrate the types of information we are accessing. The instructional package offered two separate types of instruction screen that we broadly characterized as 'static' and 'interactive'. Students could choose one of these and then stay with that type throughout the learning task or, they could switch between types. Figure 3 shows some examples of paths recorded in our pilot program and each path is displayed as a timeline. The horizontal axis shows time in seconds. The instruction screens are represented on the vertical axis. Each segment on the vertical axis represents one instruction screen. The segments above the mid-line represent the 'static' screens, those

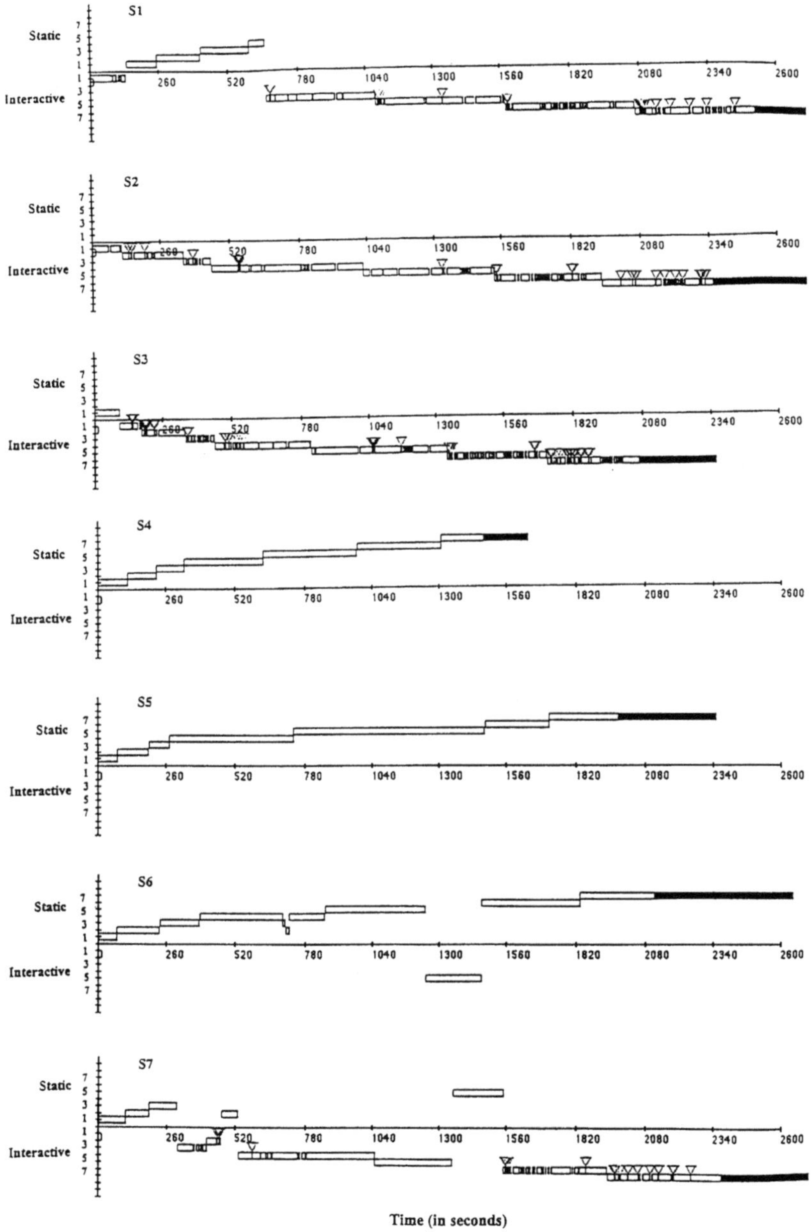

Fig. 3. *Waves*: Timelines of Screen Choice and Activity for Seven Individual Students.

below the mid-line the 'interactive' screens. For the 'static' screens time spent with the screen is shown as an empty block. For the 'interactive' screens each marker and each shaded portion within the block represents a specific action – the cork being moved, the wavelength changed, or the distance between the wave sources being moved. For all of the profiles the solid block at the end of screen seven shows the time taken to complete the post-test. For purposes of this display all of the paths have been cut-off at 2600 seconds (approximately 43 minutes).

The timelines in Fig. 3 show the paths taken by seven students (S1 to S7) with the solid block at the end of each timeline indicating the length of time spent on the post-test questions. The first three timelines at the top of the figure (S1 to S3) depict responses of students who predominantly worked with the 'interactive' screens. Their paths were different in important ways and suggest differences in how they engaged with the learning activity. The student represented by timeline S1 first chose the 'interactive' screens, tried a couple of the interactive features and then shifted to the 'static' screens. After working with four of these 'static' screens they returned to the 'interactive' screens. At the end of the 43 minutes shown in the graphs they were working on the post-test questions. Timeline S2 shows the path of a student who chose the 'interactive' version and stayed with that throughout. After 43 minutes they were well into the post-test. Of note from this display is the fact that their use of the interactive components intensified as they progressed through the task. The record for activity on screen six shows more intensive use of the interactive elements than was the case for all of the other screens. The student shown by timeline S3 first chose a 'static' screen but quickly switched to the first 'interactive' screen and then stayed with the 'interactive' version for the rest of the learning activity.

Timelines S4 to S6 all chose to work with the 'static' screens. They all spent approximately 5 minutes with the first three instruction screens. Differences can be seen in their interaction with screens four and five. The length of time spent with these screen varied. Student 6 (S6) made checks back to two of the earlier screens while working with instructional screen four and also sampled the interactive version but did not activate any of the interactive features. The final timeline (S7) shows that the student switched between the 'static' and 'interactive' screens a number of times and only towards the end of the task, especially screen six, did they make much use of the interactive components.

The plotting of these individual paths through the learning task makes it clear that there were many different ways that students engaged with the task. When linked with other aspects of each student's profile, for example, initial goal orientation, topic interest and post-test score, these paths can provide information about the dynamics of student involvement with particular aspects of instruction.

COURSES, CLASSES AND SPECIFIC TASKS

Our dynamic measures described above are one of a number of new approaches that are being used to investigate students' academic motivation. An important feature of our strategy is to monitor what is happening as the student engages with a specific learning task. This can be contrasted with other approaches that have concentrated on documenting students' experiences with larger behavioral units such as a set of lessons in one subject (e.g. Turner & Meyer, 2000), or blocks of time such as two weeks of a course (e.g. Wilde, Krapp, Schreyer & Lewalter, 1998).

When setting the context for describing her model of domain learning Alexander (1997) distinguished three levels of analysis that typify the units of learning and cognitive development in educational theories – macrolevel, midlevel, and microlevel. Analogous levels can be distinguished within the new techniques of motivational research. At the macrolevel are the techniques and measures addressing longitudinal or developmental questions and so involve the compilation of measures and assessments over extended periods of time. The term midlevel is used by Alexander to refer to domain learning, to theories of learning "more specific than the lifespan theories of human development, but generally more integrated than those that concentrate on change in individuals' understanding of particular concepts" (1997, p. 216). At the other end of the spectrum, the microlevel, are techniques and measures addressing questions concerning a specific learning episode. Our approach focusing as it does on a single learning episode addresses the dynamic of motivation at the microlevel and so is concerned with the compilation of records of students' responses to a specific learning activity and across a relatively short period of time. Some examples of approaches, mostly midlevel and microlevel approaches are described to highlight differences between these levels of analysis.

The Midlevel Perspective: Courses and Classes

The general strategy involved when motivational dimensions have been measured over time has been a repeated measures design. The same questionnaire or measurement is repeated at defined intervals.

Turner and Meyer (2000) used a questionnaire based on the experience sampling method (see Csikszentmihalyi & Larson, 1984) in an investigation of the relationship between patterns of teacher discourse and the quality of student experience in fifth and sixth grade classrooms. Students' subjective experience was the dependent variable in the study. A complete series of mathematics lessons were observed and after each class a small group of students, selected to represent a range of ability levels, were asked to complete a pencil and paper version of the Experience Sampling Questionnaire. The questionnaire consisted of ratings for 12 semantic differential items (e.g. happy – sad, proud – ashamed, excited – bored, etc.). In addition, students reported on how challenging the lesson was for them and how well they thought their skills met the challenges. The ratio of challenges to skills was used to characterize the quality of students' subjective experience for each classroom in terms of Csikszentmihalyi's 'flow' construct – flow, anxiety, boredom and apathy. Ratings of subjective experience were judgements about the whole class time made at the end of each class ("think about the maths class that just ended . . .", Turner & Meyer, 2000, p. 40). The questions being addressed in this kind of research concern student experience over extended intervals of time. Responses from the Experience Sampling Questionnaire were aggregated within classrooms and then used to determine differences in the typical character of students' affect associated with each type of classroom.

With post secondary vocational education students Wilde et al. (1998) used an electronic signalling device similar to that used by Csikszentmihalyi and Larson (1984) to measure the students' subjective experience in their natural learning environments (school and work). For a two week period students received five or six signals a day at random intervals, five days a week over two weeks. The specific rating scales included students' perception of the situation they were in at the time they received the signal, and included affect, activation level and motivation to learn. Responses were aggregated across signal points to assess whether the learning experience was related to gender and context.

In both of these studies (Turner & Meyer, 2000; Wilde et al., 1998), working with very different aged students, researchers collected a series of measures and addressed questions that concerned the overall or aggregated responses across the time interval concerned. A complementary perspective is to focus on change (or stability) across the time interval over which the measures were taken. For example, Prenzel, Kramer and Drechsel (1998) developed a 'Types of Motivated Learning' questionnaire based on theories of self-determination (Deci & Ryan, 1985) and interest (Prenzel, 1992). This was used with apprentices to compare motivation across their two learning settings, school and work. Questionnaires were administered to the apprentices at two-monthly intervals. At each testing the apprentices were asked for responses that referred generally to their last two months of training. A second administration was answered for the day prior to the interview. Prenzel et al. (1998) were able to map levels and changes in motivation across the two year period. Patterns of motivation were also plotted for individual apprentices within the group allowing some appreciation of the variability of individual apprentices across time as well as aggregated levels for the group.

The Microlevel Perspective: Specific Tasks

A number of investigations have monitored students' motivation as they engage with a specific task and some of these will be described to show the general strategies being employed. Boekaerts' On-line Motivation Questionnaire (OMQ, Boekaerts, 1997; Crombach et al., 1995) was designed to measure task-specific motivation. This scale requires students to complete a series of ratings measuring appraisals, attributions, affects and learning intentions. Two versions are administered, one prior to the task and one immediately following the task. Task specific appraisals, emotions and learning intentions are measured before the student commences the learning task. Emotions, invested effort, an estimate of achievement and attributions are measured after the learning task (see Seegers & Boekaerts, 1993). The sets of dimensions included in the two versions of the OMQ reflect differences in relevant dimensions of student experience prior to and after completing a learning task and so record some of the dynamic of the learning experience. The same questionnaire (OMQ) has been used in a diary format measuring task-specific motivation immediately before and after doing homework (see Boekaerts, 1997). In all of these studies it has been argued that the advantage of task-specific measures lies in the "dynamic indication of how student characteristics interact with learning tasks and learning environments" (Boekaerts, 1997, p. 177).

In a related study, Vermeer et al. (1995) used a Confidence and Doubt Questionnaire (CDQ) to measure five affective processes during mathematical problem solving. A series of five face icons ranging from very sad to very happy were printed to one side of the working space for the mathematical problems. Students were asked to mark a face to indicate the degree of doubt or confidence they were experiencing at designated points as they worked on the problems (viz. after having read the problem, every 40 seconds while working on the problem, and after having found an answer). However, when the results were reported, only the mean rating across the repeated measures was used.

Important questions concerning student motivation and experiences in learning situations can be addressed from the perspective of the general or typical pattern. In addition, it is also important to frame these research strategies in a way that is sensitive to the dynamics of the learner's experience as it might change and develop within classes and across time. These are complementary rather than alternative approaches. Aggregation of findings from research employing a variety of these techniques could ensure a robust knowledge base for classroom applications as well as providing insight into some of the continuing questions that confront motivation researchers.

Computerized data collection could be seen by some to be problematic for generating understanding of real students undertaking real learning tasks in real classrooms. While it is true that there may be some artificiality about the learning tasks, the rapid penetration of computer technology into classrooms in western industrialized societies makes this increasingly an authentic learning setting. Learning through the internet and the invention of e.books gives stronger ecological validity to our studies using text passages on computer screens. Any one specific learning task carries with it a number of situational and contextual properties that inevitably constrain interpretation of the specific findings. For example, data collected from tertiary students undertaking research participation for course credits requires certain caveats to be placed on generalization of findings to other learning settings. Even students in an elementary school classroom who participate in research on motivation and learning may approach the task administered by the visiting researcher in ways that are significantly different from 'normal' classroom learning activities.

Situational and contextual features of our data collection limit the range of learning tasks and learning settings to which the findings can be generalized. Therefore, understanding the complex relationships between student motivation and learning requires the pooling of empirical findings from a variety of complementary research methods and designs. It is our contention that further development of the types of research designs we have begun to employ in our research on interest will make a significant contribution to that understanding. Further development of its potential will provide a useful lens on what is happening as students variously engage and disengage themselves from learning experiences within the framework of schooling.

NOTES

1. Between the Lines (*BTL*) is a multimedia software package developed in the Psychology Department, University of Melbourne by Dr. M. Ainley and D. Tran in collaboration with Dr. S. Hidi at the Ontario Institute for Studies in Education of the University of Toronto.

2. The physics learning package was developed by J. M. Pearce. Software designed and developed by J. M. Pearce and S. Ainley in collaboration with Dr M. Ainley.

3. Australian Research Council Grant "Understanding the role that interactivity plays in promoting learning in science through Web-based materials."

4. *In the Picture* is a developmental software package developed in the Psychology Department, University of Melbourne, by Dr. M. Ainley, Dr. D. Bretherton and Dr. A Sanson in conjuction with software developer Leanne Renfree.

REFERENCES

Ainley, M. D. (1998). Interest in learning and the disposition of curiosity in secondary students: Investigating process and context. In: L. Hoffmann, A. Krapp, K. Renninger & J. Baumert (Eds), *Interest and Learning: Proceedings of the Seeon Conference on Interest and Gender* (pp. 257–266). Kiel, Germany: IPN.

Ainley, M., Bretherton, D., & Sanson, A. (1994). In the Picture: Accessing children's thoughts and feelings in interpersonal conflict situations. Paper presented at the P.P.O.W. and International Conflict Resolution Centre Conference, Melbourne, August.

Ainley, M., Hidi, S., & Berndorff, D. (1999). Situational and individual interest in cognitive and affective aspects of learning. Presentation at the American Educational Research Association Meetings, Montreal, April.

Ainley, M., Hidi, S., & Berndorff, D. (submitted). Interest, learning and the psychological processes that mediate their relationship.

Ainley, M. D., Hillman, K., & Hidi, S. (in press). Gender and interest processes in response to literary texts: Situational and individual interest. *Learning and Instruction.*

Alexander, P. A. (1997). Mapping the multidimensional nature of domain learning: The interplay of cognitive, motivational and strategic forces. In: M. L. Maehr & P. R. Pintrich (Eds), *Advances in Motivation and Achievement* (Vol. 10, pp. 213–250). Greenwich, CT: JAI Press.

Andrews, M., Hoey, L., & Ainley, M. (2001). Motivation and student achievement: topic interest and the assessment of reading competence. Paper for presentation at the Australasian Human Development Association Conference, Brisbane, July.

Bandura, A. (1997). *Self-efficacy: The exercise of control.* New York: Freeman.

Barron, K. E., & Harackiewicz, J. M. (2001). Achievement goals and optimal motivation: Should we promote mastery, performance, or both types of goals? *Journal of Personality and Social Psychology, 80*, 706–722.

Bergin, D. A. (1999). Influences on classroom interest. *Educational Psychologist, 34*, 87–98.

Boekaerts, M. (1997). Self-regulated learning: A new concept embraced by researchers, policy makers, educators, teachers, and students. *Learning and Instruction, 7*, 161–186.

Crombach, M. J., Boekaerts, M., & Voeten, M. J. M. (1995). On-line measurement of appraisals of students faced with curricular tasks. Presentation at the 6th European Conference for Research on Learning and Instruction, August, Nijmegen.

Csikszentmihalyi, M., & Larson, R. (1984). Validity and reliability of the experience-sampling method. *Journal of Nervous and Mental Disease, 175*, 526–536.

Deci, E., Koestner, R., & Ryan, R. (1999). A meta-analytic review of experiments examining the effects of extrinsic rewards on intrinsic motivation. *Psychological Bulletin, 125*, 627–668.

Deci, E., & Ryan, R. (1985). *Intrinsic motivation and self-determination in human behavior.* New York: Plenum.

Dewey, J. (1913). *Interest and effort in eduction.* Boston: Riverside Press.

Ford, M. (1992). *Motivating humans: Goals, emotions and personal agency beliefs.* Newbury Park: Sage Publications.

Harackiewicz, J. M., Barron, K. E., Tauer, J. M., Carter, S. M., & Elliot, A. J. (2000). Short-term and long-term consequences of achievement goals in college: predicting continued interest and performance over time. *Journal of Educational Psychology, 92*, 316–330.

Hickey, D. (1997). Motivation and contemporary socio-constructivist instructional perspectives. *Educational Psychologist, 32*, 175–193.

Hidi, S. (1990). Interest and its contribution as a mental resource for learning. *Review of Educational Research, 60*, 549–571.

Hidi, S. (2000). An interest researcher's perspective on the effects of extrinsic and intrinsic factors on motivation. In: C. Sansone & J. M. Harackiewicz (Eds), *Intrinsic and Extrinsic Motivation: The Search for Optimum Motivation and Performance* (pp. 309–339). New York: Academic Press.

Hidi, S., & Anderson, V. (1992). Situational interest and its impact on reading and expository writing. In: K. A. Renninger, S. Hidi & A. Krapp (Eds), *The Role of Interest in Learning and Development* (pp. 215–238). Hillsdale, NJ: Lawrence Erlbaum Associates.

Hidi, S., & Baird, W. (1986). Interestingess – A neglected variable in discourse processing. *Cognitive Science, 10*, 179–194.

Hidi, S., & Baird, W. (1988). Strategies for increasing text-based interest and students' recall of expository texts. *Reading Research Quarterly, 23*, 465–483.

Hidi, S., & Berndorff, D. (1998). Situational interest and learning. In: L. Hoffmann, A. Krapp & K. A. Renninger (Eds), *Interest and Learning: Proceedings of the Seeon Conference on Interest and Gender* (pp. 74–90). Kiel, Germany: IPN.

Hidi, S., & Harackiewicz, J. M. (2000). Motivating the academically unmotivated: A critical issue for the 21st century. *Review of Educational Research. 70*, 151–179.

Izard, C. E. (1972). Anxiety: A variable combination of interacting fundamental emotions. In: C. D. Spielberger (Ed.), *Anxiety: Current Trends in Theory and Research.* New York: Academic Press.

Izard, C. E. (1977). *Human Emotions.* New York: Plenum Press.

Izard, C. E., Dougherty, F. E., Bloxom, B. M., & Kotsch, W. E. (1974). The differential emotions scale: A method of measuring the subjective experience of discrete emotions. Unpublished manuscript. Vanderbilt University, Nashville, Tennessee.

Jarvela, S., & Niemivirta, M. (1999). The changes in learning theory and the topicality of the recent research on motivation. *Research Dialogue in Learning and Instruction, 1*, 57–65.

Jetton, T. L., & Alexander, P. A. (2001). The assessment of interest: Past explorations and future challenges for research and practice. *Educational Psychology Review, 13*, 303–318.

Krapp, A., Hidi, S., & Renninger, A. (1992). Interest, learning and development. In: K. A. Renninger, S. Hidi & A. Krapp (Eds), *The Role of Interest in Learning and Development* (pp. 3–25). Hillsdale, NJ: Lawrence Erlbaum Associates.

Locke, E., & Latham, G. (1990). *A theory of goal setting and task performance.* Englewood Cliffs, NJ: Prentice-Hall.

Manstead, A. S. R. (1993). Children's representation of emotions. In: C. Pratt & A. F. Garton (Eds), *Systems of Representation in Children: Development and Use* (pp. 185–210). New York: John Wiley & Sons Ltd.

McDaniel, M. A., Waddill, P. J., Finstad, K., & Bourg, T. (2000). The effects of text-based interest on attention and recall. *Journal of Educational Psychology, 92*, 492–502.

Mitchell, M. (1993). Situational interest: Its multifaceted structure in the secondary school mathematics classroom. *Journal of Educational Psychology, 85*, 424–436.

Murphy, P. K., & Alexander, P. A. (2000). A motivated exploration of motivation terminology. *Contemporary Educational Psychology, 25*, 3–53.

Pekrun, R. (1992). The impact of emotions on learning and achievement: Towards a theory of cognitive/motivational mediators. *Applied Psychology, 41*, 359–376.

Pekrun, R. (2000). A social-cognitive, control-value theory of achievement emotions. In: J. Heckhausen (Ed.), *Motivational Psychology of Human Development*. Oxford, U.K.: Elsevier.

Pintrich, P. R. (2000). An achievement goal theory perspective on issues in motivation terminology, theory and research. *Contemporary Educational Psychology, 25*, 92–104.

Prenzel, M. (1992). The selective persistence of interest. In: K. A. Renninger, S. Hidi & A. Krapp (Eds), *The Role of Interest in Learning and Development* (pp. 71–98). Hillsdale, NJ: Lawrence Erlbaum Associates.

Prenzel, M., Kramer, K., & Drechsel, B. (1998). Changes in motivation and interest in vocational education: Halfway through the study. In: L. Hoffmann, A. Krapp, & K. A. Renninger (Eds), *Interest and Learning: Proceedings of the Seeon Conference on Interest and Gender* (pp. 430–440). Kiel, Germany: IPN.

Renninger, K. A. (2000). How might the development of individual interest contribute to the conceptualization of intrinsic motivation. In: C. Sansone & J. M. Harackiewicz (Eds), *Intrinsic and Extrinsic Motivation: The Search for Optimal Motivation and Performance*. NY: Academic Press.

Renninger, K. A., Hoffmann, L., & Krapp, A. (1998). Interest and gender: Issues of development and learning. In: L. Hoffmann, A. Krapp & K. A. Renninger (Eds), *Interest and Learning: Proceedings of the Seeon Conference on Interest and Gender* (pp. 9–21). Kiel, Germany: IPN.

Rheinberg, F. (1998). Theory of interest and research on motivation to learn. In: L. Hoffmann, A. Krapp & K. A. Renninger (Eds), *Interest and Learning: Proceedings of the Seeon Conference on Interest and Gender* (pp. 126–145). Kiel, Germany: IPN.

Rowe, K. J. (2000). Simultaneous estimation of interdependent effects among multilevel composite variables in psychological research: An annotated example of the application of multilevel structural equation modeling. In: N. Duan & S. Reise (Eds), *Multilevel Modeling: Methodological Advances, Issues and Applications*. Hillsdale, NJ: Lawrence Erlbaum & Associates.

Schiefele, U. (1996). Topic interest, text representation, and quality of experience. *Contemporary Educational Psychology, 21*, 3–18.

Schiefele, U. (1998). Individual interest and learning, what we know and what we don't know. In: L. Hoffman, A. Krapp, K. Renninger & J. Baumert (Eds), *Interest and Learning: Proceedings of the Seeon Conference on Interest and Gender* (pp. 91–104). Kiel, Germany: IPN.

Schiefele, U., Krapp, A., & Winteler, A. (1992). Interest as a predictor of academic achievement: A meta-analysis of research. In: K. A. Renninger, S. Hidi & A. Krapp (Eds), *The Role of Interest in Learning and Development* (pp. 183–212). Hillsdale, NJ: Lawrence Erlbaum Associates.

Schiefele, U., & Rheinberg, F. (1997). Motivation and knowledge acquisition: Searching for mediating processes. In: P. R. Pintrich & M. L. Maehr (Eds), *Advances in Motivation and Achievement* (pp. 251–301). Greenwich, CT: JAI press.

Schraw, G., Bruning, R., & Svoboda, C. (1995). Sources of situational interest. *Journal of Reading Behavior, 27*, 1–17.

Schraw, G., Flowerday, T., & Reisetter, M. F. (1998). The role of choice in reader engagement. *Journal of Educational Psychology, 90*(4), 705–714.

Schunk, D. H. (2000). Coming to terms with motivation constructs. *Contemporary Educational Psychology, 25*, 116–119.

Seegers, G., & Boekarts, M. (1993). Task motivation and mathematics achievement in actual task situations. *Learning and Instruction, 3*, 133–150.

Turner, J. C., & Meyer, D. K. (2000). The relationship between teachers' instructional discourse and students' quality of experience in mathematics classes. Presentation at the annual meetings of the American Educational Research Association, April, New Orleans.

Vermeer, H., Boekaerts, M., & Seegers, G. (1995). Affective processes during mathematical problem solving. Presentation at the 6th European Conference for Research on Learning and Instruction, August, Nijmegen.

Vollmeyer, R., & Rheinberg, F. (2000). Does motivation affect performance via persistence? *Learning and Instruction, 10*, 293–309.

Wentzel, K. (2000). What is it that I am trying to achieve? Classroom coals from a content perspective. *Contemporary Educational Psychology, 25*, 105–115.

Wilde, K-P, Krapp, A., Schreyer, I., & Lewalter, D. (1998). The development of interest and motivational orientations: Gender differences in vocational education. In: L. Hoffman, A. Krapp, K. Renninger & J. Baumert (Eds), *Interest and Learning: Proceedings of the Seeon Conference on Interest and Gender* (pp. 441–454). Kiel, Germany: IPN.

3. THE ON-LINE MOTIVATION QUESTIONNAIRE: A SELF-REPORT INSTRUMENT TO ASSESS STUDENTS' CONTEXT SENSITIVITY

Monique Boekaerts

IS THERE A NEED FOR A SITUATION-SPECIFIC MOTIVATION INSTRUMENT?

Motivation researchers have always emphasized rigorous scientific design and methods. This approach has produced a large body of research findings that have found their way into the scientific journals. However, empirically supported knowledge does not naturally translate into classroom practice. There are many reasons for the occurrence of this bottleneck. One of the main reasons is that teachers and motivation researchers differ in their perceptions of what happens in the live classroom. A second, closely-related reason is that there is no common language to talk about these perceptions and about research findings. Indeed, the training that teachers have enjoyed is diverse and only a small percentage of the teachers are acquainted with motivation theories. Even fewer were trained to use and interpret psychological research methods to collect and evaluate information about teacher practice. Another bottleneck is that theory and research in motivation have not been integrated well into theories of learning and instruction. This implies that teachers, but also

New Directions in Measures and Methods, Volume 12, pages 77–120.

ISBN: 0-7623-0819-2

researchers who investigate good teaching practice, tend to consider findings from motivation research alien to classroom practice.

In the past, motivation researchers have tried to ensure functional relevance of the constructs studied by setting up research in the laboratory and subsequently field-testing their constructs by administering their motivation questionnaires to large groups of students. It is important to note, however, that before the 1990s, most motivation questionnaires were administered to students at one point in time, requesting them to give an indication of their commitment to school work. Typically, items of motivation questionnaires provided students with a set of short statements that described global experiences. Their task was to indicate on successive five-point-scales how much they agreed with these statements. For example: "I feel my heart beating fast when I take an exam".

Since it was shown that student motivation and cognitive strategy use differ by subject area (Pintrich & de Groot, 1990) the study of motivation as a personality trait has been largely abandoned. From then onwards, motivation questionnaires were designed to measure *domain-specific* commitment pathways. By the end of the 20th century, a general consensus exists that regularities in student behavior, defined in terms of stable motivational characteristics, should not be confused with their tendency to react favorably or unfavorably in relation to a domain of study.

At the time that I started my research on motivation, most motivation researchers were interested in describing student motivation in terms of stable domain-specific traits. Examples are: goal orientation in relation to math (Dweck, 1986; Nicholls, 1984; Pintrich & De Groot, 1990), intrinsic and extrinsic motivation patterns in the math classroom (Deci & Ryan, 1985), math anxiety (Martinot et al., 1988). Other motivation researchers studied the effect that different instructional contexts had on student motivation, as a group (e.g. Ames & Archer, 1988; Boggiano et al., 1989; Deci & Ryan, 1985; Meece, 1991). These authors showed that specific environmental conditions promote learning and motivation for most students (e.g. autonomy supportive teaching and the availability of peer support). Other conditions hinder learning because they affect students' motivational beliefs in a negative way (e.g. teacher time pressure, emphasis on evaluation procedures, and instruction and support that is not adapted to the needs and values of the students).

I entered this research from a particular perspective, viewing student behavior in the classroom as being directed by two main priorities. The first student priority is related to what teachers and parents consider a student's major job, that is, pursuing learning and achievement goals set by the teacher or the curriculum. The second student priority is to keep wellbeing within reasonable bounds, by pursuing personal goals, including socio-emotional goals that may or may not be compatible with the learning and achievement goals set by the teacher. This dual pathway was presented in my model of the adaptive learning process (e.g. Boekaerts, 1992, 1996). The theory of the adaptive learning process comprises all processes that mediate between students' general commitment toward learning and achievement, on the one hand, and their emotional state, learning intention, and enactment of that intention in a concrete learning situation, on the other. I wanted to construct an instrument that could register how students' implicit knowledge of learning situations and their domain-specific commitment affect their motivation in concrete learning situations. I intended to go beyond the description and assessment of favorable and unfavorable domain-specific motivational beliefs, because I wanted to challenge the assumption that favorable domain-specific motivational beliefs have a guaranteed positive effect on learning intention and that unfavorable motivational beliefs always affect learning intention negatively. Observations of student behavior in actual learning situations and stimulated recall of past learning experiences had convinced me that students' appraisal of the learning task and its context should be seen as mediators. More specifically, I argued that appraisals mediate between domain-specific motivational beliefs and the students' emotional state and their intended and actual effort investment.

The reason why it is necessary to postulate such mediators is that domain-specific motivational beliefs activated from memory do not take account of the current learning situation. Hence, students need to appraise (perceive and interpret) a learning opportunity in situ in order to take full account of the specific environmental conditions, including the exact content of the task, the local context, and rivaling goals at that very moment. For example, a student who dislikes reading comprehension tasks may nevertheless show commitment when he is invited to read and analyze a text on a topic he is interested in, and vice versa (cf. Ainley, 2001; Renninger, 2001). In a similar vein, a student who likes solving mathematics problems may not always be willing to invest a lot of effort. For example, he may invest little effort, when he realizes that he has to team up with poor students who need a lot of time to comprehend his solution steps. Also, rivaling goals at the time of solving a problem, including socio-emotional goals, may distract learners from the task at hand, as is reflected in low effort expenditure (see also, Boekaerts, 2001a, b). In short, I defended the view that, even though the chances are good that optimistic domain-specific motivational beliefs will have a positive impact on goal intention, perception of local learning conditions may counteract these beliefs.

My major point was (Boekaerts, 1985, 1992, 1996) and still is (Boekaerts, 1999, 2001a, b) that students' activated domain-specific motivational beliefs and the domain-specific commitment pathways based on these beliefs provide a *context* within which they appraise the current learning situation. In other words, I did not contest that activation of domain-specific motivational beliefs give meaning and value to learning activities that are part of a domain. Indeed, I agreed with my colleagues that the motivational beliefs of students, who have acknowledged that a new academic subject (e.g. physics) has its own inherent structure, rules and standards, differ from those of students who have not differentiated yet between the new domain and other subject areas. My main objective was to go beyond the description of domain-specific motivational beliefs and the way these beliefs are related to cognitive strategy use and achievement within a domain. What intrigued me most was how students assign meaning to functionally similar learning situations presented at different points in time, or embedded in different learning contexts. Do they create a unique mental representation of each learning event, taking account of specific cues in the learning environment? Or, do they make use of implicit heuristics to set goals for all situations within a domain? If their behavior is domain-specific their learning intention should be quite consistent across situations that belong to the same domain. On the other hand, if students are sensitive to specific aspects of the task and its context, their behavior will be context-specific, reflected in moment-by-moment changes in their appraisal of the learning situation. The theory of the adaptive learning process predicts that appraisals of a learning situation will explain more variance in learning intention, emotional state, and reported effort than domain-specific measures (superiority of situation-specific measures) mainly because appraisals incorporate students' perception of local conditions.

THEORY BUILDING AND DEVELOPMENT OF THE ON-LINE MOTIVATION QUESTIONNAIRE (OMQ)

Our initial attempt to construct an instrument to register situation-specific motivational beliefs (appraisals) and emotions were guided by Stress and Coping theory (Lazarus & Folkman, 1984) and Emotion theory (Frijda, 1986; Leventhal, 1980). We also used common sense and student reports about their cognitions and feelings while working on various curricular tasks and exams. It was proposed that, in addition to learning conditions that are perceived by most students as favorable or unfavorable for learning, there are certain cues in an actual learning situation that students may appraise as threatening or challenging. We noticed that the perception of cues that are related to excitement and challenge, as well as feelings of autonomy, competence or social relatedness lead to optimistic appraisals of a learning situation. In contrast, cues that are related to threat, loss, harm, boredom or damage lead to pessimistic appraisals. Based on Frijda's (1986) extensive research in mainstream psychology, it was assumed that pessimistic appraisals turn a learning situation into an "annoyer" (problematic situation that may cause damage, loss or harm) whereas optimistic appraisals turn it into a "satisfier" (nonproblematic situation, associated with positive cognitions and emotions). It is noteworthy that the same or similar environmental cues, may be viewed as dissimilar by different students and by the same students on a different occasion. It is also important that teachers are aware that their students may appraise the same learning activity differently and that they may attribute a similar learning outcome to different causes. Knowledge about a student's appraisal and attribution process will help teachers to create learning environments that are considered to be "powerful for learning" by the students themselves.

The on-line motivation questionnaire that was developed together with my colleagues over the last 15 years is an experience sampling method. This self-report instrument makes it possible to determine whether learning situations are basically appraised as "a satisfier" or "an annoyer" by a particular student or a group of students. More specifically, this self-report instrument was developed to measure students' cognitions and emotions about various curricular tasks while the learning process is unfolding. The questionnaire registers "student by situation transactions" (Boekaerts, 1985, 1987, 1992, 1996a, b, 1999; Boekaerts & Otten, 1992, 1994; Boekaerts, Crombach & Voeten, 1998; Crombach, Voeten & Boekaerts, 1994; Crombach, Voeten, Boekaerts & Seegers, in press; Seegers & Boekaerts, 1993, 1996; Vermeer, Boekaerts & Seegers, 2000). The questionnaire consists of two parts. The first part is completed after the learning task has been introduced and before the student starts with the actual task. Students are asked to glance at the task to form an impression of its content and then give an indication of their appraisal processes and the emotions that are elicited by the task. They are also asked to report on their intention to invest effort in the task. The second leg of the questionnaire is completed as soon as the task is finished or is discontinued. At that point, students report on their emotional state and effort expenditure. They also assess their result and attribute it to one or more causes.

Appraisals, Learning Intention and Emotional State at Task On-Set

The model of adaptive learning that guided the construction of this instrument (e.g. Boekaerts, 1992, 1995, 1996) specifies that the mental representation that students make of a familiar learning task differs from the mental representations they make of unfamiliar learning tasks. When a learning task is unfamiliar, students have no way of knowing whether or not they are competent to do the task or how difficult it will be. They also cannot predict their success ratio and they may have no idea as to whether or not they will value the task (personal relevance and task attraction). At best, they can make an intelligent guess about these issues. For this reason, it is essential that the tasks or learning activities used to measure student appraisals are familiar to the students. This will allow them to make a mental representation of the task and the context within which the task has to be performed and give an indication of the emotions they experience and the commitment they feel (learning intention).

The model of adaptive learning specifies that appraisals mediate between domain-specific motivational beliefs and various outcome variables, measured at task onset, including learning intention and emotional state. Many theoretical connections can be drawn between domain-specific motivational beliefs (e.g. math goal orientation, interest in math, math anxiety, concept of math ability, pleasure in math) and specific aspects of the appraisal process. These connections will not be the same for different students because they have been established during a student's unique learning history. For example, two students who experience math anxiety may differ in the links they have established between this particular domain-specific belief and their appraisal of actual math problems. The first student may focus on cues that inform him that he cannot master the task or cannot complete it without help (negative link between math anxiety and subjective competence). The second student may focus on his feelings of displeasure, finding the task boring and irrelevant (negative link between math anxiety and task attraction and perceived relevance). It is assumed that the strength of the associations that have been established in the past between specific task appraisals and one or more domain-specific motivational beliefs determines students' context sensitivity, i.e. which cues in the learning environment they pay attention to.

Consequently, the mental representations that students will form of a specific math task in situ will differ as a function of their context sensitivity. It was hypothesized that students' appraisal of a concrete learning task or exam will affect their commitment to the task (learning intention) as well as their emotional state. More specifically, it was argued that students who report dominantly optimistic appraisals at task onset indicate that they intend to invest effort as well as positive emotional state. By contrast, dominantly pessimistic appraisals lead to a low learning intention and negative emotional state. In other words, students will form a learning intention and report a positive emotional state, when they attach value to the learning task, either because they consider the task to be attractive (fun to do, or interesting) or because they view the task as relevant/important to them as a person. Students will also express commitment and report positive emotional state when they are confident that the learning task is "manageable", meaning that they think that they have the ability to do it, that it is not too difficult, and that they expect success. On the other hand, students will not be inclined to invest effort in a learning task and report negative emotional state when they find the task of little value and/or express low confidence that it will work out.

Emotional State, Reported Effort, Result Assessment and Attribution at Task Completion

The model of adaptive learning also specifies that students' mental representation of a task may undergo some changes during task performance, mainly because students interact with the task and its context. As such, it is interesting to study the relation between emotional state at task onset and task completion and the relation between students' learning intention and their reported effort at task completion. Differences between these variables are an indication that the students' perception of the task have changed while the learning episode was unfolding. It is also informative to examine how students' attributions affect their emotional state and reported effort at task completion.

Attribution processes can be seen as causal beliefs mediating between students' perception of the outcome of the task and: (1) their emotional state upon completion; and (2) the amount of effort (personal resources) they admit they invested in the task. Weiner (1986) argued that neither success nor failure as such will affect future representations of a task, but the causal attributions that students make about these outcomes. He assumed that students use domain-specific motivational beliefs about the why's of their successes and failures to make a mental representation about the outcome of the completed or discontinued task. Weiner proposed three dimensions to categorize students' attributions, namely locus, stability, and control. We argued that students attribute their successes or failures in a specific domain basically to either stable or variable (controllable/non-controllable, internal/external) causes, but may nevertheless, report different attributions in relation to specific learning outcomes within that domain. In accordance with our argument about context sensitivity of the appraisals, the model of adaptive learning assumes that attributions, registered in relation to a specific outcome, will reflect the students' causal beliefs about value and competence. Furthermore, it is theorized (Boekaerts, in preparation) that students' reported effort and emotional state upon task completion is influenced by their result assessment and their attribution of this outcome. More concretely, it is hypothesized that students who assess their learning outcome as successful (e.g. "I did OK", "I guess I passed the exam", or "I got a satisfactory outcome") report more effort when they attribute perceived success to value-related aspects of the task rather than to competence-related aspects. In a similar vein, students who assess their learning outcome as a failure will report less effort when they attribute this outcome to competence-related aspects of the task rather than to value-related aspects.

CONSTRUCTING THE OMQ

In this chapter, I will describe the construction and validation of the OMQ and summarize the results of several psychometric analyses. The on-line motivation questionnaire went through several revisions that were based on an extensive research program conducted at Leiden University. The development started in 1983 and consisted of four successive stages. We started with the development of the first part of the OMQ (administered at task onset) followed by the development of the second part of the OMQ (administered at task completion). We set up several field studies to examine the psychometric properties of the two parts and conducted longitudinal research to test the mediating role of the appraisals and the attributions. During the developmental stages, central issues were the definition and operationalization of learning intention and the various appraisals and emotions that are related to learning intention, the construction of item pools to measure these three central constructs of the OMQ, and the choice of response categories. A set of pilot studies was set up to determine the utility, validity and reliability of the preliminary version of the first part of the OMQ which will henceforward be called "the appraisal part" of the OMQ. In the meantime, the OMQ was extended to include a second part that had to be administered upon task completion to measure the students' emotions, their result assessment and corresponding attribution process, and their reported effort. This second leg of the OMQ will be referred to as "the attribution part" of the OMQ. Next, a wide variety of field studies were set up in primary education (age range from 10 to 12), secondary education (age range 12 to 16), and vocational school (age range 16 to 20) to determine the structure of the successive versions of the OMQ and to validate the instrument.

In this chapter, I will focus on the psychometric properties of the final version of the OMQ, namely the OMQ91, which has been translated into several languages. Where appropriate, I will refer to earlier versions of the questionnaire. To date, authorized versions of the OMQ exist in English,

German, Spanish and Dutch. A version developed for younger children (age 8 to 12) is also available.

The aim of the first few pilot studies was to formulate the definition of the various hypothetical constructs and to formulate items that could register students' appraisals for various curricular tasks, their learning intention and emotional state at task onset. We examined whether students were able to answer the OMQ within a reasonable time period, whether or not they grasped the meaning of the various questions and perceived the instrument as valuable. Cooperation was started with various primary and secondary education schools. There were successive formats of the on-line motivation questionnaire. The first version (OMQ-84) consisted of eight dimensional judgments of the perception of curricular activities, including task attraction, self-efficacy, success expectation, task difficulty, perceived relevance, peer success expectation, perceived teacher relevance, and familiarity. These appraisals were registered before the students started on the task. In addition, learning intention was measured with one item (Boekaerts, 1985). The first version of the questionnaire was discussed with students and teachers A later version of the questionnaire already consisted of the two parts (e.g. OMQ-85).

The appraisal part of the OMQ now included 7 appraisals: self efficacy (2 items), task attraction (2), perceived personal relevance (1), perceived difficulty (1), success expectation (1), learning intention (2), and 6 items measuring emotional state. The attribution part consisted of the same items registering emotional state and three extra items tapping emotions related to task completion (e.g. I feel relieved), 2 items on reported effort, 1 on result assessment and 4 on attribution. Panels of experts, including several teachers and researchers, evaluated the new version of the OMQ. Item analyses and explorative principal component analyses helped us to gain insight into the utility and applicability of the questionnaire (see Boekaerts, 1987; Crombach, in press; Crombach, Voeten & Boekaerts, 1994; Seegers & Boekaerts, 1993, 1996). On the basis of these insights, items were reformulated, answering categories were adapted and various scales were extended. The final version of the OMQ is based on our emerging theory about various aspects of the affective learning process. This includes insights about: (1) aspects of the appraisal process that are essential to form a commitment toward curricular tasks; (2) aspects of students' learning intention that are most salient to measure their situation-specific commitment; (3) the number and type of emotions that should be registered to provide an indication of dominantly positive or negative emotional state; (4) aspects of students' reported effort that are most informative about the quality of the effort they invested in the task; and (5) how best to assess students' attribution of the perceived outcome of the task, taking into account situation-specific aspects as well as the more situation-neutral aspects (domain attributions). These theoretical insights resulted in the OMQ-91. The structure of the final version of the OMQ can be seen in Fig. 1.

The appraisal part of the OMQ includes 23 items that measure three aspects of task motivation, viz. Appraisals, emotions and learning intention. Appraisals are registered in 13 items that together measure three aspects of task judgment. These aspects are: personal relevance of the curricular task (e.g. How useful do you consider this task), subjective competence (e.g. How good are you at doing this type of task?), and task attraction (e.g. How much do you like this type of task?). Six items refer to emotional state (e.g. How do you feel now? Nervous . . . not nervous; happy . . . not happy). Four items measure learning intention (e.g. How much effort are you going to invest in the task).

The attribution part of the OMQ consists of 23 items of which 7 measure the emotion students felt after doing the task. Three items measure invested effort (e.g. "How hard did you work on this task?"), 2 items register result assessment (e.g. "How well did you do on this task?") and 8 items measure the attribution process. Students are requested to select either the questions that relate to successful or unsuccessful task completion (e.g. "I completed this task (un)successfully, because I am (not) competent to do this type of task). The complete questionnaire can be found in the appendix.

PSYCHOMETRIC QUALITIES OF THE OMQ

The psychometric qualities of the OMQ91 were examined in several studies. All the scale scores, except Emotional State1 and Emotional State2 have a normal distribution. The emotion scales display a skewed distribution to the left. Students indicated that, on the whole, they do not experience intense negative emotions in relation to curricular tasks, except under exam conditions. Since there were, at the time the research started, no gold standards available to register students' situation-specific motivation, content and construct validity of the scales used in the OMQ were important issues to consider when testing the validity of the OMQ. Basically, two strategies were used to test the validity of the OMQ, viz., logical analysis and internal structure analysis. In addition, reliability was tested, using two indices, namely test-retest reliability and internal consistency estimates. We also did a number of multi-sample analyses to test the fit of the proposed appraisal model. I will review the main findings of these validation studies, referring briefly to studies that have already been published. The results of the studies that have not yet appeared in print will be presented in more detail. Table 1 summarizes the characteristics of the studies that I will refer to in this chapter.

	Dimensions	N of items	Type of items	Name of scale	N of items	Measurement Categories
Part: 1 Appraisal Model	Emotions	6		Emotional State 1	6	Symmetric four-print scales measuring intensity of emotions
to be completed at task onset	Appraisals	13	perceived difficulty (3) success expectation (2) self-efficacy (3)	Subjective Competence	8	four-point likert scales measuring degree of competence, relevance, task attraction etc. (very much------⇒not at al)
			task attraction	Task attraction	3	
			perceived relevance	Perceived relevance	2	
	Learning intentions	4		Learning intentions	4	
Part: 2 Attribution model	Emotions	6		Emotional state 2	10	intensity of emotions
	Result assessment	3		Result assessment	2	four-point scale measuring degree of success-failure
to be completed upon task completion	Reported effort	2		Reported effort	3	four-point scale measuring degree of invested effort
	Attributions	8	Effort (1) Attraction (1) Mood (1) Luck (1)	Value-related Attributions ⇑	3 /4	four-point scales measuring agreement with statement
			Difficulty (1) Ability (1) Familiarity (1) Strategy (1)	⇓ Competence Related Attributions	4 /5	(very much------⇒not at al)

Fig. 1. Descriptions of OMQ91; its two legs, dimensions, number of items, and scales.

Table 1. Characteristics of the Studies on Which the Validation is Based.

	Characteristics of the sample	Tasks	Instruments used	Results	Source
Study 1 (1991)	$N = 221$ primary school age: 11–12 9 schools Boys: 108 Girls: 113	• **domain**: math • 2 tasks • tasks randomly selected from national math test (PPNO'88) • **interval**: 2 weeks	• OMQ91 • Goal orientation • Non-verbal IQ • Self-concept-M • Attribution-M	• Appraisals mediate effect of domain-specific motivational beliefs on learning intention, emotional state and task performance • Evidence for a value-directed and outcome-directed pathway • Indicators of competence (IQ) do not influence students' appraisals • Model fit at t1 and t2, $N = 221/221$; $\chi^2 = 79{,}92/108{,}28$; df = 58/58; GFI = 93/0.91; AGFI-0.88/0.84; RMS-0.06/0.07 • identical appraisal model fits for boys and girls $\chi^2 = 127.87$; df 69; GFI-0.91; AGI = 89; RMS-0.06	• Seegers and Boekaerts (1993) • Seegers and Boekaerts (1996) • Boekaerts (1999)
Study 2 (1994)	$N = 361$ primary school age: 11–12 14 schools Boys: 183 Girls: 178	• **domain**: math • 2 tasks (see Study 1) • conditions differ: students are told that task is part of exam or just exercise (random order) • **interval**: 2 weeks	Idem Study 1	• Task condition does not affect task performance • Appraisals differ: subjective competence is higher, personal relevance is lower, and learning intention is higher when students assume that performance on the task is consequential in nature (exam)	• Seegers (1994)

Table 1. Continued.

Study 3 (1995)	$N = 276$ primary school age: 11–12 12 schools Boys: 129 Girls: 147	• **domain**: math • 2 tasks (a) computational problems (b) application problems • **interval**: 2 weeks	Idem Study 1 • Confidence-and doubt questionnaire ($N = 160$)	• Students' appraisals and learning intentions on computational problems are higher than those on the application problems • Gender differences in motivational beliefs were found at the domain specific level: goal-orientation-M, self-concepts-M. At the situation-specific level gender differences were evident with respect to application problems only: Boys higher on subjective competence, they listed more unconventional solution strategies. Boys scored lower on persistence after failure than girls. Girls attributed a poor result more often to lack of capacity and difficulty level than boys did	• Vermeer (1997) • Vermeer, Boekaerts and Seegers (2000) • Boekaerts (1994) • Boekaerts, Seegers and Vermeer (1995)
Study 4 (1996)	$N = 415$ primary school age: 11–12 17 schools Boys: 205 Girls: 210	• **domain**: math • 2 tasks • tasks were randomly selected from national math test • **interval**: 2 weeks	Idem Study 1	• Students have similar appraisals when they are confronted with similar assignments 2 weeks later, provided they have assessed their performance positively • Negative result assessment decreases subjective competence on the subsequent task	• Seegers (1996)

Table 1. Continued.

	Characteristics of the sample	Tasks	Instruments used	Results	Source
Study 5 (1993)	$N = 327$ secondary school age: 12–14 10 school Boys: 159 Girls: 168	• **domains**: math, history, Dutch, French • 2 tasks per domain • each task is composed of regular curriculum assignments • **interval**: 3 months	• OMQ91 • SAS-M (Martinot) • ACTION CONTROL (Kuhl)	• Appraisal model proposed by Seegers and Boekaerts (1993) [see Study 1] was confirmed for secondary school students • Model fit at t1 and t2 math $N = 327/323$; $\chi^2 = 65.15/70.76$; df = 31/31; GFI-0.97/0.96; AGFI-0.93/0.92; RMS-0.05/0.05 • Indicators of objective competence (GPA) do not influence students' appraisals of the curricular tasks • ego orientation directly affects emotional state	• Boekaerts (1999) • Boekaerts and Otten (1994)
Study 6 (1988)	$N = 113$ secondary school age: 12–13 4 schools Boys: 56 Girls: 57	• **domains**: math, history, Dutch • 2 tasks per domain: regular exams administered under exam condition • **Interval**: 2 months	• State anxiety (Spielberger) • OMQ87	• When asked to generate attributions and text analyses spontaneously, students attribute math outcomes dominantly to external factors (task difficulty) and to a lesser extent to ability and effort. History outcomes are dominantly attributed to effort and to a lesser extent to task difficulty, followed closely by ability attributions. • Very few students attribute their successes or failures spontaneously to luck	• Boekaerts (in preparation)

Table 1. Continued.

Study 7 (1992)	$N = 506$ secondary school age: 12–13 6 schools Boys: 259 Girls: 245	• **domains**: math, history, Dutch • **tasks**: national exams in math, history and Dutch • **interval**: 3 weeks	• OMQ91 • SAS-H (Boekaerts and Otten) • SAS-M (Martinot et al.,) • AMS (Gjesme)	• Students are poor at assessing their result when they completed an exam. More than 1/3 incorrectly judged successful math performance as a fail. More than 2/3 of the students who failed the text analysis exam incorrectly judged their performance as a pass. • Students spontaneous attribute perceived success on a history exam dominantly to effort. • Perceived success on a math and text analysis exam is spontaneously attributed to effort, ability or task difficulty. • Luck is hardly used in spontaneous attributions • Spontaneous causal ascriptions of exam results are school-subject dependent rather than exam-specific.	• Otten (1997) • Boekaerts, Otten and Voeten (1997) • Boekaerts (in press)

Table 1. Continued.

	Characteristics of the sample	Tasks	Instruments used	Results	Source
Study 8 (1989)	$N = 108$ secondary school age: 12–13 3 schools Boys: 52 Girls: 56	• **domains**: math, history, Dutch • 2 tasks per domain: • curricular assignments selected by a team of teachers • **Interval**: 3 weeks	• OMQ88	• Students' causal attributions of math homework split up factor-analytically into (1) competence-related and (2) value – related attributions • Luck attribution clustered with affect-related attributions	• Otten (1997)
Study 9 (1992)	$N = 262$ secondary school age: 12–14 8 schools Boys: 134 Girls: 128	• **domains**: math, history • **tasks**: two teacher made curricular assignments per domain • **interval**: 3 months between domain sessions	• OMQ90 • SAS-M • SAS-H • AMS • GPA-M/H	• The mediating role of self-efficacy between domain specific traits and other appraisals (cf. Eccles et al., 1985) was only partially confirmed. Self-efficacy only mediated the effect of fear of failure, math anxiety and report mark on success expectation and task attraction. • The appraisal model was found to be stable over time, subject-area and gender.	• Crombach, Voeten, Boekaerts and Seeger (in press) • Crombach (in press)

Table 1. Continued.

Study 10 (1995)	$N=718$ secondary school age: 13–16 8 schools Boys: 338 Girls: 380	• **domain**: math • **tasks**: regular homework assignments • diary was kept during 3 two week periods, separated by 3 months	idem Study 7 • action control (Kuhl) • social support (Boekaerts) • learning style (Vermunt)	• Appraisal model proposed by Seegers and Boekaerts (1993) [see Study 1 and 5] was confirmed for homework assignments for secondary school students • Model fit at t1 and t2 for math: $N=349/263/244$, $\chi^2=53.15/48.90/78.25$; df = 32/31/30, GFI = 0.97/0.97/0.95; AGFI = 0.94/0.93/0.89, RMS = 0.04/0.04/0.06 • Fear of failure as a trait directly affects emotional state and is not mediated by the appraisals. • The causual attributions of math homework split up factor-analytically into (1) competence-related and (2) value – related attributions • Luck attribution clustered with competence-related attributions	• Boekaerts (1999) • Boekaerts (2001) • Boekaerts (in preparation)

Logical Analysis of the Questionnaire

What is the utility of the OMQ? Are the items of the questionnaire perceived as relevant by the students themselves and do the various items measure what they intend to register? In order to answer these important questions, we observed students in the process of completing the OMQ and discussed their answers afterwards to make sure that they grasped the meaning of the subtle differences between some of the items. This procedure revealed that almost all students understood the questions and knew what was expected of them. We observed that almost all children were able to complete the questionnaire without experiencing difficulty. However, it was noted that the younger age groups of primary education (below the age of 11) needed help. In those classes, the teacher or the research assistant had to read the questions out aloud to the children, not only because hearing the questions facilitated understanding and allowed students to ask informative questions (e.g. explanation of a difficult word), but also because working individually took too much time. It was decided that the OMQ91 could not be used for children below the age of 11. A special version was developed for the younger age groups (cf. Boekaerts, in preparation). The average time that students needed to complete the OMQ91 was 15 minutes for the appraisal part and 10 minutes for the attribution part. After some practice, most secondary school students could complete the first leg in less than 10 minutes and the second leg in less than seven minutes. Nevertheless, researchers were asked to make sure that the task, sandwiched in between the first and second leg of the OMQ was never longer than 20 minutes on average. This precaution ensures that the completion of the OMQ in connection with the selected curricular activity could be performed within one lesson period. If, for some reason, it was not possible to reduce the task to 20 minutes, researchers had to make arrangements with the school to extend the lesson period. This foresight is necessary to guarantee that students do not view the OMQ as a speed test. Although the OMQ has been used with different types of tasks (worksheets, papers, homework assignments, exams, group assignments, etc.,) it works best with tasks that students are familiar with (reading comprehension tasks in the native or foreign language, math tasks, study texts). In primary school, middle school and vocational school we recommend that the task should have a clear structure so that students can represent its action path mentally, without the need for extra instruction or explanation.

In most of our studies, students understood the system of the questionnaire immediately (after one trial run). However, it was necessary to have two and even three trial runs for the attribution questions in vocational school. Indeed, students tended to answer the attribution questions blindly. They did not understand that they had to complete the first set of questions if they assessed the outcome of the task as "perceived success" and the second set on the event of "perceived failure". After the developmental stage, the format of the questionnaire was changed slightly to remind students of this arrangement. We wanted to ensure that the various sub-scales discriminate well between the appraisals, learning intention, reported effort and attributions of students, who belong to different subgroups (boys and girls, indigenous vs. immigrant children, low ability vs. high ability students). For this reason, we identified outliers on some of the items in the respective subgroups. These students were asked to rephrase the relevant questions afterwards and to elaborate on their own answers. In all cases, students seemed to have grasped the meaning of the questions as intended. Exceptions were students who had recently immigrated and still had language problems. These students were eliminated from the analyses. Crombach (in preparation) also examined answering tendencies in various groups of students and concluded that there was no indication that such tendencies existed.

Internal Structure of the OMQ

Internal structure analysis was used as a second strategy for assessing construct validity. As all the constructs of the OMQ are subjective constructs, the emerging factor structure gives us an indication of importance of the various aspects of situated motivation registered by the OMQ, as indicated by the students themselves. At the onset, there were five clear cut theoretical scales, namely emotional state 1 and 2, learning intention, reported effort, and result assessment. With respect to the appraisals and the attributions, the theoretical model still needed to be tested. In the next few paragraphs, I will describe some studies in which we validated the hypothesized scales of the OMQ, focusing explicitly on the appraisal and attribution part of the OMQ.

The Appraisal Part of the OMQ

Seegers and Boekaerts (1993) first examined whether students' appraisals of a specific task are distinct from their expressed learning intention vis-à-vis that task as was assumed in the model of the adaptive learning process. A confirmatory factor analysis was applied to all the items of the OMQ that measured student cognitions (13 appraisals and four learning intention items). The items that registered emotional state were analyzed separately. The results confirmed the theoretical structure: a model with four latent variables explained the data pattern adequately. The first three factors grouped the appraisals. The first factor tapped the students' judgment about their subjective competence, the second factor related to task attraction, the third factor measured perceived personal relevance. The fourth factor described the students' learning intention. In various studies, we tested whether the hypothesized structure of the appraisals fitted the actual data. The psychometric qualities of the resulting scales were also inspected. Table 1 summarizes the characteristics of these studies.

Seegers and Boekaerts (1993) were the first to examine the appraisal model. They used confirmatory factor analysis to examine the structure of the 13 appraisal items. Confirmatory factor analysis by means of linear structural equation modeling (Jöreskog & Sörbom, 1993) is an appropriate method because we had access to a model of the underlying factors of the appraisals. Three factors were found with an Eigenvalue greater than 1. The variance accounted for by the three unrotated factors was 63%. The correlation between factor 1 (subjective competence) and factor 2 (task attraction) was moderate (0.29) which necessitated oblique rotation. However, oblique rotation yielded the same three-factor structure as varimax rotation.

In Table 2, the two and three factor structure found in different studies conducted in primary education is described. The fit measures are also reported. Examination of the scree plots informed us that a three- factor solution is the most appropriate internal structure in all the reported studies. This means that a three-factor solution can be forced. Using the Kaiser criterion, a two-factor solution is preferable in some studies and a three-factor solution in other studies. Where there is a two-factor structure task attraction and personal relevance (the two aspects of task value) load on the second factor. However, inspection of the various fit measures warrants the conclusion that the hypothesized three-factor model best fits the actual data sets. Indeed, the Chi-square of the three-factor model is significantly lower than that of the two-factor model in each study. Also, Akaiki's information criterion and the average absolute standardized residual are lower in the three-factor model than in the two-factor model. A better fit of the three-factor model is also suggested by the Normed (NFI) and the Non-normed fit indices (NNFI) and the comparative fit index (CFI). The values for the three-factor models lie closer to 1 than those of the two-factor models. The percentage of the variance explained by the three-factor solution in the various studies ranges between 59% and 70%. The correlations between the appraisals and the two outcome measures are to be found in Table 3 (primary education: studies 1–4) and Table 4 (secondary education: studies 5 and 10).

A close look at the correlations between the three appraisals in connection with the math tasks shown in Table 3 reveals that in the primary school samples there is no association, or only a modest one, between perceived relevance and

Table 2. Fit measures of Confirmatory Factor Analyses for the 2 and 3 Factor Model Found in Primary Education.

	χ^2 (df)	AIC	NFI	NNFI	CFI	Av. Res.
Study 1	121.40 (62) $p<0.001$	−2.60	0.86	0.91	0.93	0.048
task 1	187.21 (64) $p<0.001$	59.21	0.79	0.82	0.85	0.069
3-factor model						
2-factor model						
task 2	107.44 (62) $p<0.001$	−16.56	0.91	0.95	0.96	0.052
3-factor model	251.37 (64) $p<0.001$	123.37	0.78	0.78	0.82	0.093
2-factor model						
Study 2	157.64 (62) $p<0.001$	33.64	0.94	0.95	0.96	0.036
exam condition	292.36 (64) $p<0.001$	164.36	0.88	0.88	0.90	0.054
3-factor model						
2-factor model						
exercise condition	243.45 (62) $p<0.001$	119.45	0.90	0.90	0.92	0.052
3-factor model	337.15 (64) $p<0.001$	209.15	0.86	0.86	0.88	0.065
2-factor model						
Study 3	106.34 (62) $p<0.001$	−17.66	0.91	0.95	0.96	0.036
computational	178.27 (64) $p<0.001$	50.27	0.85	0.88	0.90	0.056
problems						
3-factor model						
2-factor model						
application	122.67 (62) $p<0.001$	−1.33	0.85	0.90	0.92	0.051
problems	154.26 (64) $p<0.001$	26.26	0.82	0.86	0.88	0.057
3-factor model						
2-factor model						
Study 4	206.29 (62) $p<0.001$	82.29	0.92	0.92	0.94	0.043
task 1	315.61 (64) $p<0.001$	187.61	0.87	0.87	0.89	0.056
3-factor model						
2-factor model						
task 2	247.13 (62) $p<0.001$	123.13	0.91	0.91	0.93	0.053
3-factor model	449.20 (64) $p<0.001$	321.20	0.84	0.83	0.86	0.076
2-factor model						

Note: AIC = Akaike's information criterion, NFI = Normed fit index, NNFI, Non-normed fit index, CFI = comparitive fit index, Av. res = Average absolute standardized residual.

subjective competence (0.01 to 0.19). A modest to moderate correlation is found between perceived relevance and task attraction (0.21 to 0.51), and a moderate to high correlation between subjective competence and task attraction (0.36 to 0.66). Scanning the upper half of Table 4 informs us that a similar pattern of correlations is found in relation to the math homework condition in

Table 3. Pearson Product-Moment Correlations for Studies 1–4 (Primary Education). On the Diagonal Test-Retest Measures are Reported.

	sc	*ta*		*pr*		*li*		em_1	
Subjective Competence	*0.82*	**0.36**	**0.39**	–0.10	–0.11	0.02	0.15	**0.52**	**0.51**
	0.80	**0.56**	**0.48**	0.11	0.01	0.14	0.10	**0.59**	**0.52**
	0.60	**0.53**	**0.66**	0.19	0.17	**0.35**	**0.36**	**0.50**	**0.54**
	0.78	**0.51**	**0.44**	0.07	–0.02	0.26	0.14	**0.53**	**0.47**
Task Attraction		*0.63*		0.24	**0.38**	**0.40**	**0.47**	**0.51**	**0.57**
		0.59		**0.38**	0.28	**0.37**	**0.36**	**0.52**	**0.46**
		0.60		**0.42**	**0.42**	**0.46**	**0.62**	**0.52**	**0.63**
		0.74		**0.42**	**0.51**	**0.51**	**0.56**	**0.48**	**0.41**
Perceived Relevance				*0.65*		**0.55**	**0.59**	–0.12	–0.06
				0.60		**0.70**	**0.67**	0.01	–0.01
				0.49		**0.46**	**0.55**	0.19	0.21
				0.71		**0.67**	**0.72**	0.08	0.03
Learning Intention						*0.67*		–0.03	0.13
						0.71		0.07	0.10
						0.63		0.26	**0.37**
						0.73		0.22	**0.37**
Emotional $State_1$								*0.57*	
								0.86	
								0.53	
								0.58	

Top line refers to the two measurement points in Study 1, followed by Studies 2,3 and 4
Correlation above 0.30 are printed in bold.

the secondary education sample (study 10). Low to modest correlations are reported between perceived relevance and subjective competence (0.11 to 0.31), moderate correlations between perceived relevance and task attraction (0.44 to 0.58), and moderate correlations between subjective competence and task attraction (0.49 to 0.53). This pattern of correlations is also evident in the secondary school sample for various curricular assignments (lower part of Table 4). More specifically, the correlations between perceived relevance and subjective competence range between (–0.06 to 0.01), and between (0.49 to 0.58) for perceived relevance and task attraction. However, the size of the association between subjective competence and task attraction is slightly lower (0.19 to 0.28), but still significant, in this sample compared with the other two samples.

Table 4. Pearson Product-Moment Correlations for Study 10 (Secondary Education; Homework for Math at 3 Points in Time) Above the Diagonal and Study 5 (Math, History, Dutch and French) Below the Diagonal.

	Sc	Ta	Pr	Li	Em_1
Subjective Competence	–	**0.49** **0.55** **0.53**	0.11 0.14 **0.31**	0.02 0.20 0.07	**0.35** **0.35** **0.37**
Task Attraction	0.27 0.21 0.19 0.28	–	**0.51** **0.58** **0.44**	**0.47** **0.57** **0.46**	**0.31** 0.28 0.26
Perceived Relevance	–0.06 0.05 –0.00 0.01	**0.49** **0.58** **0.58** **0.58**	–	**0.53** **0.65** **0.66**	0.18 0.22 **0.33**
Learning Intention	**0.32** 0.28 **0.39** **0.40**	**0.48** **0.52** **0.46** **0.54**	**0.53** **0.58** **0.58** **0.60**	–	0.08 0.27 0.19
Emotional $State_1$	0.19 0.17 0.15 0.17	**0.52** **0.63** **0.57** **0.60**	0.25 **0.40** **0.30** **0.46**	**0.35** **0.40** **0.30** **0.36**	–

Correlations above 0.30 are printed in bold.

Inspection of the patterns of correlations between the appraisals and the two outcome variables reveals that learning intention is positively associated with perceived relevance (0.46 to 0.72) and with task attraction (0.36 to 0.62) in all the samples. The association between learning intention and subjective competence is below 0.40 in all the studies. It is lowest in the homework study (0.02 to 0.20) and highest in study 5 (0.28 to 0.40). Examination of the patterns of correlations between the appraisals and emotional state1, informs us that task attraction has a positive association with emotional state1 (0.26 to 0.63). It is noteworthy that subjective competence has a moderately positive association with emotional state in the primary school samples (0.47 to 0.59) and the homework condition in the secondary school sample (0.35 to 0.37). The association is only modest in the classroom assignment condition (0.15 to 0.19). By contrast, the association between emotional state and perceived relevance is moderate in the classroom assignment condition (0.25 to 0.46), modest to moderate in the homework condition (0.18–0.33). and low to modest (–0.12 to 0.21) in the primary school sample.

The Attribution Scale Part of the OMQ

Development of the attribution part of the OMQ progressed in parallel to the development of the appraisal model. First, a logical analysis of the attribution items was undertaken to examine construct validity. Since it was hypothesized that students' attributions mediate between, on the one hand, their assessment of the outcome of a curricular task, and on the other, their emotional state and reported effort, we wanted to make sure that the attributions were outcome generated. In order to gain insight into the attribution that students spontaneously generate, the OMQ was extended with an open question. The open question was phrased as follows: Judy thinks she has failed her exam. When I asked her how that happened, she said "I was ill yesterday, so I did not have time to prepare for the exam". I also asked John and he said that he had been very lucky. Why did you perform well/or not so well on this exam? Mention one cause.

Examination of the answers that students generated in this study (study 6), revealed that the outcome of both mathematics and text analysis exams were predominantly attributed to task difficulty (e.g. because I think math (text analysis) exams are too difficult (easy) for me to do). Ability and effort attributions also occurred frequently in relation to math and text analysis exams. By contrast, the outcome of history exams was predominantly ascribed to effort (internal, unstable cause). The second most frequently generated attribution was task difficulty and ability. Students hardly ever volunteered "luck" as an explanation of either a successful or unsuccessful exam performance, despite the fact that this attribution was primed in the example. There were two types of attributions that students frequently generated spontaneously. The first category was related to mood (because I did not feel in the mood to do the exam), the second to perceived attractiveness of the tasks (because, I liked the exam questions). There were still a number of alternative explanations that we put into the category "other". A limited number of students was asked to indicate the emotions that were associated with the attributions they had formulated. This yielded a number of attribution dependent emotions: feeling (dis)satisfied, feeling good/bad, disappointed, irritated, or surprised.

We repeated the procedure described above with a larger group of students (Study 7) and examined whether the pattern of spontaneously generated attributions revealed in Study 6 could be found again. We also examined students' result assessment in relation to their attributions. We were surprised that a number of secondary school students were not able to assess the result of an exam correctly. More than one third of the students, who objectively passed their math exam, assessed it as a fail, while more than two thirds of the students who failed the history exam, assessed their exam as a pass. Examination of the spontaneously generated attributions revealed that students ascribe perceived success on history exams mostly to effort (unstable, internal attribution). Success on math exams and text analysis exams was ascribed to ability, task difficulty, or effort. The picture was less clear in relation to failure attribution. Similarly to what was found in Study 6, luck was infrequently used as a spontaneous explanation for one's exam result. This finding is in line with other research.

Based on insights gained in these studies, it was decided to extend the attribution scale of the OMQ. The original four attributions measured in the OMQ87 (ability, luck, task difficulty and effort) were supplemented with attributions that students typically use when ascribing the outcome of curricular assignments or exams (i.e. mood, task attraction, familiarity of the task, access to specific strategies). As can be seen in Fig. 1, the OMQ91 consists of eight items tapping the attribution process. In Studies 1–4 (primary education), Study 8 (secondary education) and Study 10 (homework in secondary education) the structure of the attribution scale was further examined. Inspection of the means and standard deviations on the various attribution measures revealed that primary school students, who assess their performance as "successful", attribute this outcome predominantly to effort (variable, internal attribution) and to a lesser degree to ability (stable, internal). Students, who assess their performance as "less successful" mostly attribute this perceived outcome to task difficulty (variable, external) and somewhat less to ability (stable, internal). They infrequently ascribe failure to lack of effort (variable, internal) or bad luck (variable, external).

Boekaerts, Otten and Voeten (1997) investigated whether the causal attributions used by secondary school students to ascribe exam outcomes can be explained as a function of their perceived outcome (success or failure) of the exams in the different subject areas (most restricted model = *model a*). Alternative models were formulated as well. As can be seen in Table 5, the fit of the null model was compared to four alternative models. *Model b* took also account of the observed frequencies in the three attributional categories (ability, task difficulty and effort). In *model c*, the perception of exam conditions was taken into account. In *model d*, the school subject in which the exam is taken was added and, finally, *model e* incorporated both school subject and exam conditions. In order to determine which model fitted the data best, a set of

Table 5. Fit Names for the Four Relevant Models

Models	χ^2	df	F	S
SER				
model a	334.70	48	6.97	
SER, A				
model b	260.29	46	5.66	0.19
SER, RA				
model c	183.97	44	4.18	0.26
SER, SA				
model d	139.75	42	3.33	0.41
SER, EA				
model e	254.01	40	6.35	–0.12

Note: S = school subject; E = Exam; R = Result Assessment; A = Attribution; RA = Interaction between result assessment and attribution, etc.

hierarchically nested log-linear models was fitted to the data using the SPSSX-program HILOGLINEAR. Inspection of the Chi square and goodness-of-fit indices for the relevant models showed that *model d* fits the data best. This means that students' exam attribution is largely outcome and school subject dependent. The particular exam that provides the context of the attribution process seems to be less relevant (*model e*). Hence it seems that in the first form of secondary education, students have construed specific views about exam outcomes in various school subjects and use this knowledge to infer causality when assessing exam results in different school subjects.

Otten (1997) factor-analyzed the attributions that students reported when assessing their outcome on curricular tasks in a classroom context (study 8). She found that secondary school students mostly used two patterns of ascription when asked to give an indication of their causal beliefs about success and failure. Two factors emerged with an Eigenvalue greater than 1 and the scree plot also indicated a drop after the second factor. As can be viewed from Table 6, items that are traditionally referred to as "variable, external and internal causes" grouped on the first factor (mood, task attraction, effort and luck). Items that are considered to be non-controllable causal beliefs (ability and task difficulty) clustered on the second factor. It is noteworthy that luck clustered with mood, task attraction, and effort in this sample. Otten concluded that of the three dimensions that Weiner (1986) proposed, only the stability dimension emerged. I would, however, prefer to re-label the first factors she found as "affect-related attributions" and the second factor as "competence-

Table 6. Factor Structure for Attributions of Math and History Tasks at t_1 and t_2 (Study 8)

	Math				History			
	t_1		t_2		t_1		t_2	
Item	Factor 1	Factor 2	Factor 1	Factor 2	Factor 1	Factor 2	Factor 1	Factor 2
Mood	0.87	–	0.75	–	0.75	–	0.83	–
Attraction	0.81	–	0.62	–	0.62	–	0.79	–
Effort	0.79	–	0.86	–	0.86	–	0.80	–
Luck	0.52	–	0.46	–	0.46	–	-	–
Difficulty	–	0.88	–	0.89	–	0.87	–	0.51
Ability	–	0.83	–	0.87	–	0.82	–	0.54
Cronbach's Alpha	0.74	0.69	0.66	0.78	–	0.67	0.65	0.61

related attributions. Re-labeling the factors may help us to understand why "luck" is clustered with the affect-related items in this sample. This patterning suggests that these students consider "luck" in class as part of the affective learning process (hot cognition). Inspection of the Table suggests that the two-factor structure is consistent across subject-matter areas and across curricular tasks. The internal consistency of the various scales is satisfactory, with Cronbach's alphas ranging from.78 to 0.61 (see Table 6, bottom line).

In Study 10 the internal structure of the extended attribution scale was investigated, separately for students who assessed their homework performance as "successful" and "unsuccessful". As can be seen in Table 7, two factors emerged for both the math and the history tasks. The structure of these two factors is similar to the factor structure that was displayed in Table 6. Again, task attraction, mood and effort grouped on one factor, which was labeled "affect-related attribution" (hot cognition). Items that loaded on the second factor bear on the students' causal beliefs about their competence (cold cognition), reflected in attributions to ability, difficulty, familiarity, and strategy use). Note, that luck now clusters with the "cold cognition" items, which suggests that these students view luck in relation to homework tasks (mathematics and history) as part of the task completion process rather than as part of the motivation process. It is interesting, in this respect, that luck clustered modestly, or moderately, with strategy use. This pattern was evident for both school subjects at the three data collection points. The internal consistency of the two factors is satisfactory when students attribute to success.

Table 7. Factor Structure for Attributions of Math Homework at t_1 and t_2, Separately for Students who Reported a Successful and Unsuccessful Outcome (Study 10).

	Attribution of success				Attribution after failure			
Item	t_1 $N = 336$		t_2 $N = 250$		t_1 $N = 48$		t_2 $N = 31$	
	F1	F2	F1	F2	F1	F2	F1	F2
Mood	–	0.82	–	0.87	–	0.91	0.79	–
Attraction	–	0.81	–	0.83	–	0.89	0.74	–
Effort	–	0.68	–	0.61	–	0.58	0.74	–
Difficulty	0.79	–	0.81	–	0.80	–	–	–
Familiarity	0.66	–	0.73	–	0.77	–	–	0.84
Ability	0.81	–	0.78	–	0.61	–	–	–
Strategy	0.75	–	0.71	–	0.60	–	–	0.78
Luck	0.34	–	0.35	–	–	–	–	0.75
Variance Explained	36.42	18.90	37.41	18.90	31.25	20.65	27.10	21.90
Eigenvalue	2.9	1.5	3.0	1.5	2.5	1.6	2.1	1.7
Cronbach's Alpha	0.72	0.70	0.72	0.71	0.73	0.61	0.68	0.55

Cronbach's alpha ranges from 0.72 to 0.70. The structure of the attribution scale after failure still needs some further study, since the group of students who attributed their result to failure was quite small in the homework condition.

Pearson product-moment correlations were computed for the group of students who assessed the outcome of the two mathematics homework tasks as "a pass" at each of the data collection points (see Table 8). As can be learned from the data displayed in the table, the Pearson product-moment correlations between the two attribution scales are modest to moderate. A close look at the Pearson product-moment correlations of the other scales of the attribution part of the OMQ reveals that in the primary school sample (lower part of Table 8) there is no association, or only a modest one, between reported effort, on the one hand, and emotional state (–0.09 to 0.17) and result assessment (–0.03 to 0.17) on the other. The association between emotional state and result assessment is moderate to high (0.48 to 0.58). Inspection of the upper part of Table 5 shows that a similar pattern of correlations is found between emotional state upon task completion and result assessment in the homework condition

Table 8. Pearson Product-Moment Correlations for Studies 1–4 (Below the Diagonal) and Study 10 (Above the Diagonal).
Test-Retest Values are Printed on the Diagonal (Italics).

	Emotional $State_2$		Reported Effort		Result Assessment	CO Attribution	AO Attribution
Emotional	*0.49*		0.26		0.45	0.13	0.12
$State_2$	*0.48*		**0.33**		0.46	0.12	0.12
	0.66		**0.33**		0.51	0.24	0.11
	0.56						
Reported	–0.04	–0.09	*0.77*		**0.34**	0.03	**0.34**
Effort	–0.07	0.02	*0.53*		**0.45**	0.10	0.19
	0.15	0.17	*0.42*		0.21	0.05	0.05
	0.00	–0.03	*0.63*				
Result	**0.54**	**0.48**	–0.04	0.08	*0.34*	**0.38**	0.25
Assessment	**0.51**	**0.58**	–0.03	0.02	*0.47*	0.26	0.07
	0.51	**0.58**	0.12	0.09	*0.44*	**0.32**	–0.04
	0.51	**0.53**	0.06	0.06	*0.45*		
CO							0.29
Attribution							**0.31**
							0.13
AO							
Attribution							

Correlations above 0.30 are printed in bold.

(Study 8). In contrast to the pattern of correlations found in the primary school sample, modest to moderate correlations are found between reported effort, and emotional state (–0.26 to 0.33) and between result assessment and reported effort (0.21 to 0.44).

Reliability of the OMQ

Test-retest reliability should be tested by comparing students' scores on the questionnaire at two measurement points, separated by a relatively short period. There is however a problem here. Normally, a high intercorrelation between two measurement points is taken as evidence that the questionnaire reliably measures the construct. However, very high correlations also suggest low context sensitivity, unless the two situations are identical or very similar indeed. Moderate to high correlations indicate that the OMQ taps situation-specific motivational belief. As can be seen in Table 1, students who participated in the four first studies (primary school samples), were asked to complete the OMQ at least twice in relation to highly similar math tasks. The period in between these test sessions was never more than 14 days. Test-retest measures were calculated and are printed in Table 3 (appraisal part of the model) and in Table 8 (attribution part of the model). Test-retest scores were quite high for perceived subjective competence (0.82 and 0.60) and moderately high to high for learning intention (0.73 and 0.63), task attraction (0.74 and 0.59), personal relevance (0.71 and 0.49), emotional state1 (0.68–0.53), reported effort (0.77 and 0.42) and emotional state2 (0.66–0.48). The reported values are in accordance with the assumption of context-sensitivity of the constructs. On the basis of a content analysis of the tandem tasks in each of the studies, one would expect that the test-retest estimates would be highest in Studies 1 and 4. In these studies, both sessions had been organized on the basis of a random split between the math tasks of a national math test. This expectation was confirmed in the data for the three appraisals, learning intention and reported effort. Modest to moderate test-retest values were evident in all the studies for emotional state1 and 2 and result assessment. This finding is in line with the idea that a particularly emotional state, and also the result assessment are heavily influenced by situation-specific cues generated in the actual situation. Our students told us that task conditions influence emotional state (e.g. anxiety or irritation) and result assessment (e.g. some students judged their performance as less (more) successful, if other students completed the task much faster (much slower) than they did themselves). The test-retest values for both the competence-related attributions and the value-related attributions can also be measured reliably in this group. Test-retest estimates for the affect related attributions ranged between 0.69 and 0.75 and for the competence related attributions between 0.59 and 0.74, which is satisfactory for a situation-specific measure.

Table 9 displays the internal consistency estimates for all constructs, except the attribution scales which are shown in Tables 7 and 8. As can be seen, internal consistency (Cronbach's alpha) of the various scales is satisfactory. Cronbach's alpha for all scales, except result assessment, was higher than 0.70. However, only two of the 17 result assessment scales yielded insufficient values. These values were obtained in the same study at both data collection points.

Convergent Validity

In most of the studies conducted in secondary education, students had to complete the OMQ as well as a set of instruments that measured domain-

Table 9. Internal Consistencies for the Different Studies.

	Study 1		Study 2		Study 3		Study 4		Study 5		Study 9 Math				Study 10 History		
	t_1	t_2	t_1	t_2	t_1	t_2	t_1	t_2	t_1	t_2	t_1	t_2	t_1	t_2	t_1	t_2	t_3
Subjective Competence	0.88	0.89	0.90	0.90	0.85	0.91	0.88	0.89	0.70	0.74	0.70	0.74	0.87	0.83	0.91	0.89	0.90
Task Attraction	0.78	0.84	0.80	0.78	0.77	0.82	0.81	0.84	0.85	0.89	0.85	0.89	0.88	0.88	0.87	0.90	0.87
Perceived Relevance	0.73	0.86	0.75	0.68	0.69	0.77	0.70	0.81	0.70	0.73	0.73	0.70	0.71	0.82	0.81	0.77	0.81
Learning Intention	0.74	0.80	0.72	0.69	0.66	0.71	0.71	0.75	0.75	0.76	0.75	0.76	0.73	0.74	0.85	0.77	0.82
Emotional $State_1$	0.71	0.71	0.78	0.78	0.69	0.76	0.70	0.73	0.78	0.86	0.78	0.82	0.84	0.82	0.88	0.83	0.88
Emotional $State_2$	0.77	0.73	0.80	0.83	0.85	0.81	0.77	0.84	0.78	0.82	0.78	0.81	0.83	0.79	0.83	0.88	0.91
Reported Effort	0.81	0.80	0.77	0.74	0.74	0.75	0.74	0.82	0.72	0.72	0.72	0.72	0.73	0.83	0.85	0.81	0.81
Result Assessment	0.44[1]	0.54[1]	0.64	0.61	0.72	0.78	0.68	0.64	0.70	0.70	0.68	0.71	0.65	0.70	0.80	0.83	0.80

Note: [1] Only two values are below 0.60

specific motivational beliefs. In Study 10, the scores on the School subject Attitude Scale (SAS) were compared with those of the corresponding appraisals. The SAS-Mathematics (Martinot et al., 1988) as well as its twin instrument, the SAS-History (Boekaerts & Otten, 1992) consist of four subscales, namely domain-specific pleasure, domain-specific relevance, domain-specific anxiety and perceived difficulty, and domain-specific interest and effort. In other words, this instrument has the same object of measurement as the appraisals of the OMQ, albeit at the domain-specific level. Study 10 has a longitudinal design, in which the OMQ was completed several times in relation to homework sessions in history and mathematics. The SAS-M and the SAS-H were also completed at each measurement point. The correlation between the respective measures of math and history competence (i.e. appraisal subjective competence of the OMQ and the Anxiety and perceived difficulty of the SAS-M/H) were high, ranging between 0.67 and 0.73. The correlations between the pleasure scales of the SAS and task attraction of the OMQ are also high, ranging between 0.57 and 0.61. The associations between the perceived relevance scale of the OMQ and the relevance scale of the SAS M/H are moderately high, ranging between 0.39 and 0.41.

Predictive Validity

The power of the situation-specific measures, registered by the OMQ relative to domains-specific measures was demonstrated in Study 10. As can be seen in Table 10, reported effort after completing math homework was predicted with a four predictor model, namely: (1) intelligence; (2) learning style; (3) action control; and (4) motivational beliefs. Motivational beliefs were measured at three different levels, namely the general level (with Gjesme's Need Achievement Scale; AMS), the domain-specific level (with Martinot's SAS-M and Boekaerts & Otten's SAS-H) and at the situation-specific level (with OMQ91). Table 10 shows that when the appraisals were added to the first three predictors more variance in reported effort can be explained than adding either the domain-specific or the general measures of motivational beliefs. At the first measurement point, 32.6% of the variance in reported effort can be explained when the appraisals are included in the predictor set, compared to 26.5% when the domain-specific measures were included. At the second and third measurement point, including the appraisals in the regression equation results in, respectively 61.5% variance explained (compared to 39%) and 51.3% explained (compared to 31.5%). The picture is similar for history tasks. For more information about these results, see Boekaerts (in preparation).

Table 10. Summary of Multiple Regression Analyses with Reported Effort on Mathematics and History Homework as the Criterion Variable and a 4-Predictors Set as the Independent Variables.

Predictor set		Mathematics						History					
		t_1 $N = 272$		t_2 $N = 154$		t_3 $N = 192$		t_1 $N = 243$		t_2 $N = 140$		t_3 $N = 182$	
		R^2	β	R^2	β	R^2	β	R^2	β	R^2	β	R^2	β
Intelligence (Evers and Lucassen)		1.1%	–0.03	5.1%	–0.07	2.5%	–0.07	0.4%	–0.2	0.2%	–0.13	0.4%	–0.4
Learning style (Vermunt)		12.7%		21.9%		9.7%		6.6%		17.9%		9.2%	
Surface			0.16		0.10		0.03		0.13		0.06		0.10
Concrete			0.03		0.08		0.00		0.13		0.06		0.05
Deep			0.04		0.08		–0.07		–0.11		0.05		0.05
Action control	I	16.3%	0.08	28.9%	0.16	19.4%	0.19	10.0%	0.13	26.2%	0.08	18.2%	0.21
(Boekaerts and Otten)	P		0.09		0.02		0.04		0.01		0.18		0.09
	D		–0.02		–0.11		–0.18		–0.14		–0.05		–0.16
General motivation (Gjesme)	AchM	17.6%		31.4%		21.4%		12.3%		28.4%		18.7%	
	FOF												
Domain Specific (SAS-M/H)		26.5%		39.0%		31.5%		35.8%		23.8%			
Appraisals	ATTR	32.6%	0.22	61.5%	0.13	51.3%	0.21	28.0%	0.20	56.8%	0.28	39.1%	0.23
	COMP		–0.13		0.05		–0.19		–0.01		0.12		–0.15
	PR		0.30		0.51		0.52		0.29		0.31		0.35
Total Model with appraisals	R	0.571		0.784		0.716		0.529		0.754		0.625	
	R^2	32.6%		61.5%		51.3		28.0%		56.8%		39.1%	
	Adj R^2	30.1%		58.9%		48.6		24.9%		53.5%		35.5%	

Testing the Tenability of the Appraisal Model

The Mediating Role of the Appraisals

The model of adaptive learning assumes that appraisals are superior to domain-specific measures in explaining the variance in learning intention, emotional state and reported effort. In other words, students' appraisals of the here-and-now-situation are considered to be the connecting link between stored domain-specific motivational beliefs and their willingness to invest effort in situ as well as their reported emotional state. The proposed appraisal model (see theory building section) was tested in various studies. The appraisal model explained a substantial percentage of the variance in emotional state, learning intention, and reported effort in each of the studies. In Table 1, fit measures for the appraisal model at time 1 and time 2 are given, for Studies 1, 5 and 10 respectively (see also Boekaerts, 1999). We therefore concluded on the basis of these findings that the proposed model fits the data well. Moreover, evidence was found for a value-directed and an outcome-directed pathway in students' appraisals.

In Studies 1, 5 and 10 we tested the mediation hypothesis for two affective outcome variables, namely learning intention and emotional state. In accordance with our basic assumptions, we first tested a model where no direct links from the exogenous variables were allowed on the outcome variables (restricted model). This model was compared with a less restricted model in which direct links between domain specific variables and outcome variables were allowed. In Study 1, the less restricted model did not improve the fit of the restricted model. All the variance in learning intention and emotional state was mediated by the appraisals. This implies that primary school students' intention to invest effort in curricular assignments depends largely on the way they appraise these tasks in situ. Interestingly, in the 7th (Study 5) and 9th grade sample (Study 10) the fit of the unrestricted model slightly improved the fit of the restricted model. Inspection of the parameter estimates revealed that the appraisals fully mediated the effect of domain-specific motivational beliefs on learning intention in both samples. However, one direct link had to be allowed to emotional state in each study. Ego-orientation (measured by the "hiding mistakes sub scale") triggered negative emotional state in the 7th grade sample and fear of failure had the same effect in the 9th grade sample (homework condition). Accordingly, it was concluded that the effect of avoidance ego orientation and fear of failure is not mediated by the appraisals. These motivational beliefs have a direct detrimental effect on emotional state in middle school students (see Boekaerts, 2001 for discussion of this effect). The effect of other unfavorable motivational beliefs, for example having a negative self concept of mathematics, are mediated by the appraisals. More concretely, students report negative emotional state in relation to curricular assignments in the classroom (Study 5) and homework (Study 10) if they have a low self concept of mathematics, reflected in low subjective competence, and if they also express low liking in relation to a concrete math assignment. In Study 9, Crombach et al., also found that fear of failure and math anxiety directly affected emotional state (task anxiety) but not intended effort. The results from these four studies support the conclusion that the appraisals fully mediate the effect of domain-specific motivational beliefs on learning intention. This conclusion does not hold for the effect of domain-specific motivational beliefs on emotional state. The appraisals mediate this effect only partially.

Gender Differences

Significant gender differences were found in mean scores on a number of domain-specific and situation-specific variables (cf. Crombach et al., in press; Seegers & Boekaerts, 1996; Vermeer et al., 2000). For example, Vermeer et al., reported that boys differ significantly from girls on subjective competence. Boys score generally higher on emotional state before and after doing a math task. They report feeling more at ease and being more enthusiastic before and after the task. Boys also score significantly higher on result assessment. Interestingly, boys use more unconventional solution strategies. Girls score higher than boys on persistence after failure and they attribute a poor result more often to lack of capacity and difficulty level than boys do (competence-related attribution). Other studies also yielded significant differences between boys and girls with respect to average scores on a number of variables (for review, see Wigfield et al., 1998). In some studies, significant differences between boys and girls were found on task attraction (boys higher than girls), personal relevance (girls higher than boys), intended effort (girls higher than boys), and reported effort (girls higher than boys).

Seegers and Boekaerts (1996) predicted and found that identical models are adequate to explain the underlying relationships between the variables in the data for both boys and girls (see Table 1). Boekaerts & Otten (1992) compared a restricted appraisal model (an identical structure is assumed for the two groups) with a less restricted model in which different parameter-values for boys and girls were allowed. As can be seen in Table 11 (top part), the unrestricted model (model b) did not improve the fit of the restricted model (model a) in relation to any domain, meaning that identical appraisal models can be accepted for the two groups in mathematics, history, text analysis, and French.

Table 11. Summary of Fit Measures for the Appraisal Model for Boys and Girls in Different Domains. Top Half Displays Fit Measures for Study 5. Bottom Half Displays Fit Measures for Four Models in which Increasing Restrictions are Added (Study 9).

Domain	χ^2	df	GFI	RMS		Study 5
Mathematics	265.33	205	0.915	0.070		
	239.46	176	0.921	0.066		
History	291.41	205	0.930	0.058		
	270.61	176	0.919	0.066		
Dutch	280.37	205	0.910	0.069		
	247.77	176	0.918	0.064		
French	333.03	205	0.917	0.067		
	305.07	176	0.922	0.061		
Math	**χ^2**	**df**	**NNFI**	**RMSEA**	**BIC**	**Study 9**
Model a	55.77	42	0.96	0.051	–178.10	
Model b	80.24	63	0.96	0.045	–270.57	
Model c	87.36	72	0.97	0.041	–313.56	
Model d	106.76	87	0.97	0.042	–377.69	
Model d (t_2)	162.21	87	0.91	0.081	–324.85	

Note:
Study 5: math: Boys 167, girls 170; history: boys: 175, girls 205; Dutch: boys 170, girls 172; French: boys 180, girls 200.
Study 9: first data wave: boys 134, girls 128. Second data wave (t2): boys 139, girls 131

Crombach et al. (in press) fitted four versions of the appraisal model to the data of Study 9 (see Table 1) in order to test for interaction effects with gender. They started with the least restricted model (*model a*) which assumes identical structures for the two groups. In the successive models (b–d) more restrictions were added to the null model. *Model b* tests whether all regression coefficients and residuals are the same. *Model c* examines whether all co-variances of the dependent variables are the same. Finally, *model d*, which is the most restrictive model, tests whether the variances and co-variances of the exogenous variables are the same for boys and girls. By adding the mean differences between boys and girls to the final model, these authors explored whether gender differences could still be found in the endogenous variables (appraisals, learning intention, and emotional state) after controlling for the independent variables in the path equations.

Inspection of the fit measures in Table 11 (bottom part) informs us that *model d* fits the data best. Accordingly, Crombach et al., concluded that mean gender differences can be explained from the exogenous variables, particularly math anxiety (sub-scale of the SAS-M) and fear of failure (sub-scale of Gjesme's AMS). In other words, there is no need to include gender in the appraisal model, since identical appraisal models are adequate to explain the underlying relationships between the variables in both data sets.

Crombach et al., also examined whether *model d* is adequate for the history data as well. They found that the math model fits the history data quite well at both data collection points. Hence, it can be concluded that the appraisal model is stable across school-subjects and time, as well as gender.

CONCLUSIONS

As stated in the introduction, we wanted to gain insight into students' commitment about various learning tasks and used the model of adaptive learning to construct a self-report instrument. It was argued, that the best way to register students' cognitions and affects in situ, is to present them with familiar learning activities and ask them to report on their cognitions and affects while the learning episode is unfolding. The studies reported here support the conclusion that the OMQ is an experience-sampling method that can reliably capture students' cognitions and feelings in relation to specific learning tasks, without disturbing their task focus. As such, the OMQ can open new ways of studying motivation in the classroom. The instrument may play a significant role in gaining information about the various reasons why students are not willing to invest effort in class. In addition, the OMQ can provide valuable information on the effect that different cognitions and feelings have on task engagement and wellbeing in the classroom. Up to now, researchers on task engagement and school satisfaction (class wellbeing) have followed different avenues of inquiry. By using the OMQ, motivational researchers can increase their knowledge of the mediating effect of appraisals on these two important, intertwined aspects of the learning process.

REFERENCES

Ainley, M., & Hillman, K. (in press). Gender and Interest processes in response to English texts: situational and individual interest. *Learning and Instruction*, (special issue).

Ames, C., & Archer, J. (1988). Achievement goals in the classroom: Student learning strategies and motivation processes. *Journal of Educational Psychology*, *80*, 409–414.

Boekaerts, M. (1985). Some new developments in the study of motivational processes in a classroom context. In: G. d'Ydewalle (Ed.), *Cognition, Information Processing, and Motivation*. Amsterdam: North Holland.

Boekaerts, M. (1987a). Situation specific judgments of a learning task versus overall measures of motivational orientation. In: E. De Corte, H. Lodewijks, R. Parmentier, & P. Span (Eds), *Learning and Instruction* (pp. 169–179). Oxford/Leuven: Pergamon Press/Leuven University Press.

Boekaerts, M. (1987b). Die Effekte von state- und trait-motivationaler Orientierung auf das Lernergebnis. *Zeitschrift für Pädagogische Psychologie*, *1*(1), 29–43.

Boekaerts, M. (1992). The adaptable learning process: Initiating and maintaining behavioural change. *Journal of Applied Psychology: An International Review*, *41*(4), 377–397.

Boekaerts, M. (1995). The interface between intelligence and personality as determinants of classroom learning. In: D. H. Saklofske & M. Zeidner (Eds), *Handbook of Personality and Intelligence* (pp. 161–183). New York: Plenum Press.

Boekaerts, M. (1996). Personality and the psychology of learning. *European Journal of Personality*, *10*, 377–404.

Boekaerts, M. (1997). Capacity, inclination, and sensitivity for mathematics. *Anxiety, Stress, and Coping*, *10*, 5–33.

Boekaerts, M. (1999). Motivated learning: studying student *situation transactional units. In: M. Boekaerts & P. Nenniger (Eds), *Advances in Motivation from the European Viewpoint* [Special issue]. *European Journal of Psychology of Education*, *14*(1).

Boekaerts, M. (2001a). Motivation, Learning, and Instruction. In: N. J. Smelser & P. B. Baltes (Eds), *The International Encyclopedia of the Social and Behavioral Sciences*. Elsevier Sciences Ltd., Oxford.

Boekaerts, M. (2001b). Context sensitivity: activated motivational beliefs, current concerns and emotional arousal. In: S. Volet & S. Järvelä (Eds), *Motivation in Learning Contexts: Theoretical Advances and Methodological Implications* (pp. 17–31). New York: Pergamon Press.

Boekaerts, M., & Niemivirta, M. (2000). Self-regulated learning: Finding a balance between learning goals and ego-protective goals. In: M. Boekaerts, P. R. Pintrich & M. Zeidner (Eds), *Handbook of Self Regulation* (pp. 417–450). San Diego, C.A.: Academic Press.

Boekaerts, M., & Otten, R. (1992). *Motivatie en Inzet. (Motivation and Effort). Leiden University: Unpublished manuscript.*

Boekaerts, M., & Otten, R. (1994). Motivatie en Schoolsucces (Motivation and School Achievement). Leiden University: Unpublished manuscript.

Boekaerts, M., Crombach, M. J., & Voeten, H. J. M. (1998). Task attraction as a determinant of intended effort on curricular tasks. *Scientifica Paedagogica Experimentalis*, *2*, 493–512.

Boekaerts, M., Otten, R., & Voeten, R. (1997). *Exam Performance: Are Students' Causal Ascriptions School subject-specific?* Unpublished manuscript.

Boggiano, A. K., Main, D. S., Flink, C., Barrett, M., Silvern, L., & Katz, P. A. (1989). A model of achievement in children: The role of controlling strategies in helplessness and affect. In: R. Schwarzer, H. M. van der Ploeg & C. D. Spielberger (Eds), *Advances in Test Anxiety Research* (pp. 13–26). Amsterdam: Swets & Zeitlinger.

Crombach, M. J. (in press). Appraisal processen van brugklasleerlingen ten aanzien van schoolse taken (7th graders appraisals of curricular tasks). Academic dissertation. Leiden University.

Crombach, M. J., Voeten, M. J. M., & Boekaerts, M. (1994). A model for explaining individual differences between students in intended effort on curricular tasks. *Tijdschrift voor Onderwijsresearch, 19*, 301–317.

Crombach, M. J., Voeten, M. J. M., Boekaerts, M., & Seegers, G. Development of a model to explain students' willingness to engage in actual curricular task situations (submitted for publication).

Deci, E. L., & Ryan, R. M. (1985). *Intrinsic motivation and self-determination in human behavior.* New York: Plenum.

Dweck, C. S. (1986). Motivational processes affecting learning. *American Psychologist, 41*, 1040–1048.

Eccles, J., Adler, T. F., Futterman, R., Goff, S. B., Kaczala, C. M., Meece, J. L., & Midgley, C. (1985). Self perceptions, task perceptions, socializing influences, and the decision to enroll in mathematics. In: S. F. Chipman, L. R. Brush & D. M. Wilson (Eds), *Women and mathematics: Balancing the Equation* (pp. 95–121), Hillsdale, NJ: Lawrence Erlbaum.

Frijda, N. H. (1986). *The emotions.* Cambridge (Great Britain): Cambridge University Press.

Jöreskog, K. G., & Sörbom, D. (1993). *Lisrel 8: Structural Equation Modeling with the SIMPLIS command language.* Chicago, Il: Scientific Software International.

Leventhal, H. (1980). Toward a comprehensive theory of emotion. In: L. Berkowitz (Ed.), *Advances in Experimental Social Psychology* (Vol. 13, pp. 140–228). New York: Academic Press.

Martinot, M. J., Kuhlemeier, H. B., & Feenstra, H. J. M. (1988). Het meten van affectieve doelen: De validering en normering van de belevingsschool voor wiskunde. (Psychometric Qualities of the Attitude Scale for Mathematics). *Tijdschrift voor Onderwijsresearch, 13*(2), 65–76.

Meece, J. (1991). The classroom context and students' motivational goals. In: M. Maehr & P. Pintrich (Eds), *Advances in Motivation and Achievement* (Vol. 7, pp. 261–285). Greenwich, CT: JAI Press.

Nicholls, J. (1984). Achievement motivation: Conceptions of ability, subjective experience, task choice, and performance. *Psychological Review, 91*, 328–348.

Otten, R. (1997). *School Subject Motivation.* Unpublished manuscript.

Pintrich, P. R., & De Groot, E. V. (1990). Motivational and self-regulated learning components of classroom academic performance. *Journal of Educational Psychology, 82*, 33–40.

Renninger, A. (2002). Individual interest as context in expositionary text and mathematical word problems. *Learning and Instruction* [Special issue].

Seegers, G., & Boekaerts, M. (1993). Task motivation and mathematics achievement in actual task situations. *Learning and Instruction, 3*, 133–150.

Seegers, G., & Boekaerts, M. (1996). Gender-related differences in self-referenced cognitions in relation to mathematics. *Journal for Research in Mathematics Education, 27*, 215–240.

Vermeer, H. J. (1997). *Sixth-grade students' mathematical problem-solving behavior.* Leiden University: Academic Dissertation.

Vermeer, H. J., Boekaerts, M., & Seegers, G. (2000). Motivational and gender differences: sixth-grade students' methematical problem-solving behavior. *Journal of Educational Psychology, 92*, 308–315.

Weiner, B. (1986). *An attributional theory of motivation and emotion.* New York: Springer.

Wigfield, A., Eccles, J. S., & Rodrigues, D. (1998). The Development of Children's Motivation in School contexts. Review of Research in Education, 23, Washington; AERA.

Pre-task Questionnaire

Name: .... Grade: .... Subject: ....

Date of birth: .... O boy O girl

We will ask a number of questions about how you view the task you are about to start.
Read every question and fill in the circle that suits you best.
There are no correct or incorrect answers.
Fill in one circle per question. Work quickly.

1. Are you in the mood to start the task?

   O not at all in the mood
   O not much in the mood
   O in the mood
   O very much in the mood

2. How good do you think you are at this type of task?

   O not at all good
   O not so good
   O good
   O very good

3. How useful do you consider this task?

   O not at all useful
   O not so useful
   O useful
   O very useful

4. How easy is this task for you?

   O not at all easy
   O not so easy
   O easy
   O very easy

5. How well do you expect to do on this task?

   O not at all well
   O not so well
   O well
   O very well

6. How enthusiastic are you about this task?

   O not at all enthusiastic
   O not so enthusiastic
   O enthusiastic
   O very enthusiastic

7. How often can you succeed at this kind of task?

   O hardly ever
   O now and then
   O regularly
   O nearly always

8. How much attention do you plan to devote to this task?

   O not much attention
   O some attention
   O much attention
   O very much attention

9. How important do you find it to do well on this task?

   O not at all important
   O not so important
   O important
   O very important

10. How difficult do you find this task?

    O not at all difficult
    O not so difficult
    O difficult
    O very difficult

11. How pleasant do you find this task?
    O not at all pleasant
    O not so pleasant
    O pleasant
    O very pleasant

12. How much effort do you have to put into this task in order to get a passing grade?
    O I don't have to do my best at all
    O I have to make a bit of an effort
    O I have to try hard
    O I have to try as hard as I can

13. My goal on this task is . . .
    O to just get a pass
    O to make sure I pass
    O to make sure I perform well
    O to make sure I perform very well

14. What sort of grade do you expect to get for this task?
    O below passing level
    O around passing level
    O above passing level
    O considerably above passing level

15. How much effort are you going to put into this task?
    O very little
    O some
    O much
    O my very best

16. How good are you at this task in comparison to your classmates?
    O far below average
    O just below average
    O just above average
    O far above average

17. If you could take as much time as you want, how long would you spend on this task?
    O I'd just begin and decide later how long to keep working
    O I'd work until I think I've *just* made a passing grade
    O I'd work until I've done a reasonably good job
    O I'd work until I feel truly satisfied with myself

18. How do you feel right now, just before starting the task?

a. not at ease	O	O	O	O	at ease
b. not nervous	O	O	O	O	nervous
c. not fine	O	O	O	O	fine
d. not worried	O	O	O	O	worried
e. not confident	O	O	O	O	confident
f. not annoyed	O	O	O	O	annoyed

19. What is the time now?

    Note the time here please ....

Good luck with the task!

Post-task Questionnaire

Name: .... Grade: .... Subject ....

Now that you have finished the task, we have some more questions for you.
Choose the answer that suits you best. There are no correct or incorrect answers.
Fill in one circle per question.

As you answer the questions, keep in mind the task you have just finished.

0. What is the time now: ....

1. How do you feel just after finishing the task?

a. not relieved	O	O	O	O	relieved
b. not at ease	O	O	O	O	at ease
c. not nervous	O	O	O	O	nervous
d. not satisfied	O	O	O	O	satisfied
e. not fed up	O	O	O	O	fed up
f. not fine	O	O	O	O	fine
g. not worried	O	O	O	O	worried
h. not confident	O	O	O	O	confident
i. not annoyed	O	O	O	O	annoyed
j. not concerned	O	O	O	O	concerned

2. How carefully did you do the task? I paid

   O not much attention
   O some attention
   O much attention
   O very much attention

3. How difficult did you find this task?

   O not at all difficult
   O not so difficult
   O difficult
   O very difficult

4. How long did you continue working on the task?

   O I started, but I dind't continue very long
   O I worked until I thought I would just pass
   O I worked until I thought I'd done a reasonably good job
   O I worked until I was really satisfied with myself

5. What sort of grade do you expect to get for this task?

   O below passing level
   O around passing level
   O above passing level
   O far above passing level

6. How much effort did you put into this task?

   O very little
   O some
   O much
   O my very best

7. How well did you do this task?

   O not at all well
   O not so well
   O well
   O very well

8. How useful do you consider this kind of task?

   O not at all useful
   O not so useful
   O useful
   O very useful

Answer either question 9 or question 10
Answer question 9 if you did well on the task
Answer question 10 if you did not do well on the task

Questions 9 and 10 list reasons for succeeding or failing on a task.
For every reason, indicate to what extent this reason explains your performance on this task.

An example:
Suppose you think that you performed the task well because the task was really very simple. In question 9e you would then choose the answer: 'strongly agree'
(the first circle)

9. I did well on this task . . .

	Strongly agree	Agree	Disagree	Strongly disagree
a. because I am good at this type of task	O	O	O	O
b. because I was in the mood to do the task	O	O	O	O
c. because I was lucky	O	O	O	O
d. because I did my best	O	O	O	O
e. because I found it an easy task	O	O	O	O
f. because I thought it was a pleasant task	O	O	O	O
g. because I knew how to handle the task	O	O	O	O
h. because I already knew a lot about the subject of this task	O	O	O	O

10. I did not do well on this task . . .

	Strongly agree	Agree	Disagree	Strongly disagree
a. because I am not good at this type of task	O	O	O	O
b. because I don't like doing this type of task	O	O	O	O
c. because I had bad luck	O	O	O	O
d. because I didn't do my best	O	O	O	O
e. because I found it a difficult task	O	O	O	O
f. because I thought it was an unpleasant task	O	O	O	O
g. because I didn't know how to handle the task	O	O	O	O
h. because I hardly knew anything about the subject of the task	O	O	O	O

4. METHODOLOGICAL ISSUES AND ADVANCES IN RESEARCHING TACTICS, STRATEGIES, AND SELF-REGULATED LEARNING

Philip H. Winne, Dianne Jamieson-Noel and Krista R. Muis

Scientific inquiry into self-regulated learning (SRL) inherently couples theory to methodologies for examining and revising empirical claims that emerge from theory. We do not take up debates about whether theory or methodology does more work in moving the other forward but we observe that chapters in this volume and other chapters (e.g. Winne & Perry, 2000) and books (e.g. Schraw & Impara, 2000) indicate keen interest in scrutinizing methodological issues concerning research on SRL.

We begin by presenting a model of SRL to make explicit the sort of phenomena being researched and its main components, such as metacognition, motivation, and strategic action. Next, we review the state-of-the-art in measuring SRL. Because self-report methods dominate, we give detailed attention to issues that bear on gathering, analyzing, and interpreting these kinds of data in a third section. Finally, we survey an assortment of proposals that need more methodological attention in advancing theory and research on SRL. We also introduce methodological issues that arise because tactics, strategies, and other aspects of SRL are events that most research represents as aptitudes. Where appropriate, we contrast views of SRL generated by

New Directions in Measures and Methods, Volume 12, pages 121–155.

ISBN: 0-7623-0819-2

minimizing its event-related qualities with views of SRL as dynamic event that spans actions over time.

SELF-REGULATED LEARNING

We highlight three features of the construct of SRL. First, SRL theory describes forms of cognition. Thus, self-regulating events and features of those events are not available for direct inspection by researchers; they must be inferred in relation to researchers' operational definitions. A plausible hypothesis, which we accept, is that SRL shares significant commonalities with other forms of cognition. For example, SRL fundamentally depends on the contents of long-term memory and on cognitive operations, such as searching, that the learner performs on that content.

Second, SRL is an expression of agency even when learning appears to be regulated automatically, without deliberation. Underlying this claim are two assumptions: (a) automated regulatory actions (other than physiological reflexes) were, at a prior time, deliberately designed; and, (b) under appropriate conditions, an automated regulatory action can be inspected and modified. Characterizing SRL as agentic entails the learner has a cognitive representation of goals. Thinking about approaching a goal and acting to approach a goal are expressions of motivation. Like other theorists (Carver & Scheier, 1998), we hold that goals are not isolated from one another but exist in a complex, probably hierarchical relationship. That is, some goals have priority over others.

Third, SRL can be analyzed into two principally different activities, metacognitive monitoring and metacognitive control. Metacognitive monitoring is the cognitive operation by which a learner examines the degree to which features of the current state of (a) a task and (b) work done on it correspond to standards that constitute goals. Metacognitive control is the cognitive mechanism that accounts for what learners do in relation to perceptions they generate by monitoring.

One way to link monitoring to control uses an If-Then representation, also called a condition-action rule. IF the current conditions (features) of a task have particular values or qualities, THEN (and only then) is a particular action carried out. We consider the packet of an IF-THEN rule as a *tactic*. For example, IF a word in a chapter is in bold format, THEN highlight the word and immediately adjacent text that defines or describes it. Tactics can be arrayed to create larger patterns or designs for approaching distal goals or goals with multiple parts. Applying a tactic generates up-to-the-minute feedback. An array of tactics is a *strategy*. A strategy extends the If-Then representation of a tactic to form a network in which the fundamental unit is an IF-THEN-ELSE rule. Strategies are structurally more complex than tactics, that is, they have a larger grain size (Howard-Rose & Winne, 1993). Also, compared to a tactic, a strategy has potential to yield more information in the form of feedback (Winne, 2001).

Winne and Hadwin's (1998) Model of SRL

Winne and Hadwin (1998; see Fig. 1) proposed a model of SRL for a generic task called studying. Studying is inspecting information under a general goal to learn some or all of it. The model represents SRL as having three necessary phases and an optional fourth phase. Cognitive operations applied in each phase construct products of information. The topic(s) of these products is what distinguishes one phase from another. The box labeled Products in Fig. 1 identifies the four main kinds of topics we distinguished: definition of the task, goals and plans, tactics, and adaptations.

In our model, information the learner generates or that is available in the environment can play four roles: as a condition (If), a product, an evaluation about features of a product (feedback), or a standard. The arrows in Fig. 1 are paths along which newly generated or received information flows to update prior conditions, products, evaluations, and standards. The two cognitive operations powering SRL, metacognitive monitoring and metacognitive control, are centrally positioned in Fig. 1 to reflect their centrality in SRL.

Phase 1: Defining the Task

Cognitive activities in Phase 1 account for how the learner develops a perception of the task at hand and perceptions of updates to the task that are created by working on it. These definitions of the task are multifaceted and, because they are constructed partly using information stored in long-term memory, they are inherently idiosyncratic to a degree (Butler & Winne, 1995; Winne, 1997). In Fig. 1, *task conditions* refer to information in the environment that the learner attends to, such as a teacher's or task's time limit or a heading in a text. At the outset, then, SRL is mediated by what a learner registers about the environment. *Cognitive conditions* refer to information the leaner retrieves from long-term memory, for example: knowledge in the domain(s) of the task (e.g. Tennyson's writings, oxidation-reduction reactions), memories about self related to this kind of task (e.g. expectations about efficacy, interest), and memories about tactics and strategies previously used with similar tasks.

For logical reasons, Hadwin and Winne conjecture that learners often create two products in Phase 1. One is a "default" perception about the task as it would be if addressed using a "standard" routine or habitual approach. The

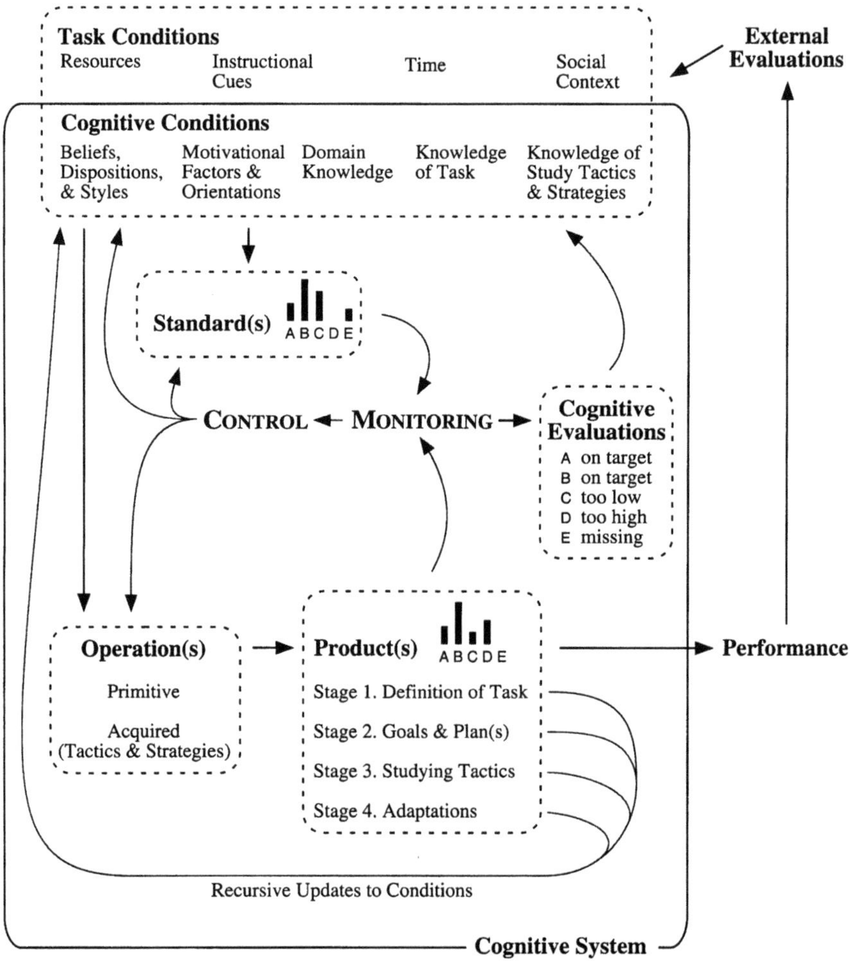

Fig. 1. Winne and Hadwin's Model of SRL.

Source: From "Studying as self-regulated learning," by P. H. Winne and A. F. Hadwin (1998). In: D. J. Hacker, J. Dunlosky & A. C. Graesser (Eds), *Metacognition in Educational Theory and Practice*. Hillsdale, NJ: Erlbaum. Copyright 1998 by Lawrence Erlbaum Associates. Printed with permission.

second product is an estimate about what will happen if a non-standard approach is taken. This second option is logically necessary because, even if there is no alternative tactic other than the standard routine, the learner can exercise agency in Phase 3 by not applying that tactic (see Winne, 1997), in effect, quitting the task.

Phase 2: Setting Goals and Developing a Plan to Reach Them

In Phase 2, having constructed a definition of the task in Phase 1, the learner sets goals to achieve by engaging with the task. Tasks can have multiple goals, for example, when there is a mixture of performance and learning orientations. Also, learners' goals can differ from those intended by a teacher or curriculum developer, for example, when learners set self-handicapping goals to avoid exposure to information that indicates low ability (Covington, 1992).

Once goals are framed, memory may automatically retrieve tactics or a strategy coupled to them (McKoon & Ratcliff, 1992). Plans created this way are a sign of expertise. Alternatively, the learner may construct a plan by retrieving tactics and then forecasting how well the products they would create match standards in an incremental way. The information generated by metacognitively monitoring these unfolding thought experiments can guide further search for tactics in long-term memory or provide the basis for modifying a prior strategy. Or, it might invite the leaner to return to Phase 1 to re-inspect the task and perhaps redefine it. Any of these actions reflects the exercise of metacognitive control.

Phase 3: Enacting Tactics

When tactics and strategies from Phase 2 are applied, the learner makes a transition into Phase 3 where work to approach the goals begins. Using terminology from the literature on problem solving, the givens of the task – task conditions, cognitive conditions, their articulation in the learner's definition of the task, tactics and strategies – provide raw materials for generating a solution to the task. Better solutions match, as closely as possible, standards that define the goal(s). We agree with other theorists (Pintrich, Marx & Boyle, 1993; Winne, 1995, 1997, 2001; Winne & Marx, 1989) that this complex bundle of informational raw material fuses "cold" with "hot" information. "Cold" propositions describe "facts" of the task, such as what a tactic (or strategy) is and does. "Hot" propositions – for example, efficacy expectations, outcome expectations, incentives associated with the completing (or failing to complete) the task, and attributions – are motivational beliefs that give rise or link to affect. While cold and hot propositions can be separated for analysis, the amalgam as a whole is processed when tactics are enacted.

The products that tactics create are cognitive. These may be but are not necessarily expressed as behavior that a researcher can observe. When a learner metacognitively monitors cognitive products – that is, when thought is self-observed – internal feedback is generated (Butler & Winne, 1995). External feedback may also be generated as the learner interacts with the material environment, for example, when a learner's contribution to a shared activity invites peers' evaluative feedback or when unexpected results are returned from a search on the internet.

Phase 4: Adapting Metacognition

Phase 4 of the model is optional. If engaged, this is where a learner makes major adaptations to controllable elements of SRL (versus following an alternate path toward goals already set out within a strategy). We borrow Rumelhart and Norman's (1978) framework to describe three forms of adaptations: (a) accreting (or deleting) conditions that determine when a tactic is appropriate, or adding or deleting tactics in a strategy; (b) tuning either or both of the conditional knowledge that triggers tactics or operations that carry out actions, or improving how tactics articulate in strategies; (c) restructuring cognitive conditions, tactics and strategies in a major way to create markedly different definitions, goals, or plans for tasks (Winne, 1997).

Although Fig. 1 may imply that SRL unfolds sequentially from Phase 1 to 2 and so on, this is unlikely. SRL is recursive. Information generated in a given phase can feed into that same phase or almost any other phase because memory can automatically trigger conditional knowledge (McKoon & Ratcliff, 1992). We consider SRL to be weakly sequenced. After a first description of a task is constructed in Phase 1, information subsequently generated in continuing that phase or by work in another phase may jump phases or feed back into the same phase.

Issues for Research on SRL

The events portrayed by Winne and Hadwin's (1998) model of SRL have a common structure. Conditions, cognitive as well as external, provide raw materials (information) on which cognitive operations work. Operations construct informational products, and products are further operated on when their properties are evaluated by monitoring them relative to standards the learner holds for the task being performed. These conditions, operations, products, evaluations, standards can be modeled as a COPES script (Winne, 1997, 2001), a modest elaboration of Miller, Galanter, and Pribram's (1960) seminal TOTE (test-operate-test-exit) unit. COPES scripts interact with one another over time and, most likely, in a hierarchical or cascading manner (Carver & Scheier's, 1998; see Fig. 2). They are "event units" in SRL.

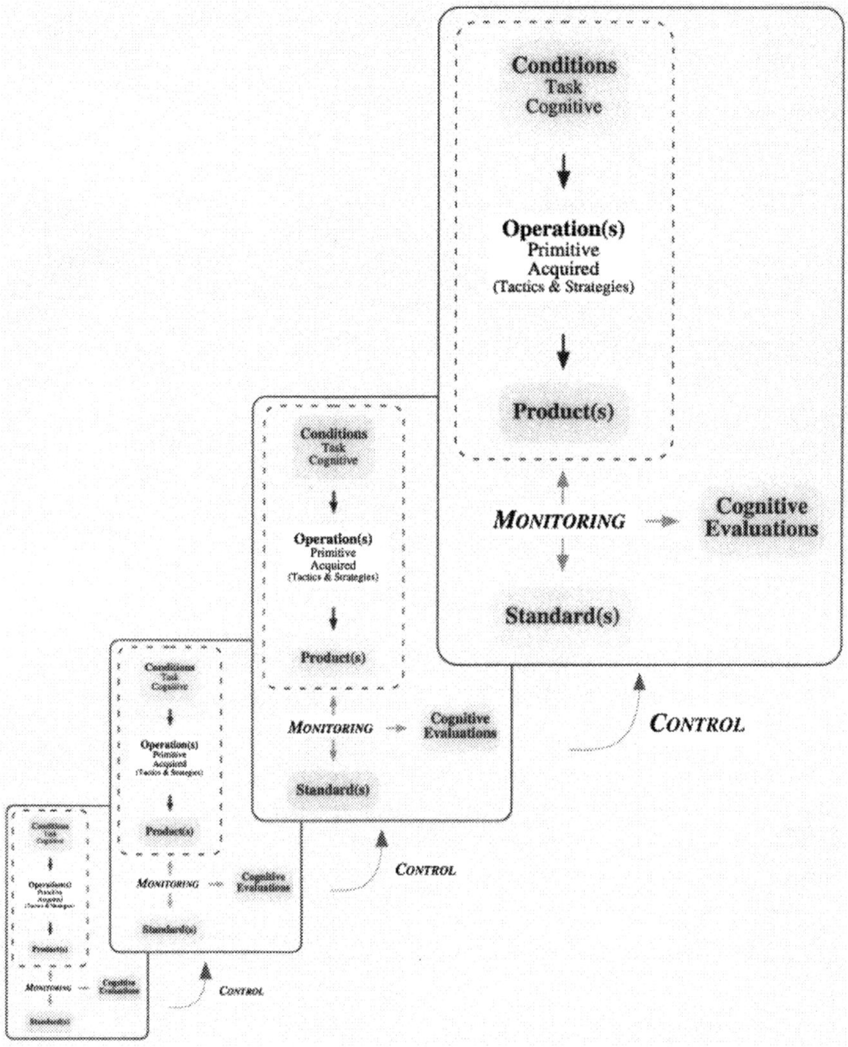

Fig. 2. Cascade of SRL.

Viewed from this perspective, SRL has a dual character, as aptitude and as event. "An aptitude describes a relatively enduring attribute of a person that predicts future behavior . . . An event is like a snapshot that freezes activity in motion, a transient state embedded in a larger, longer series of states unfolding over time" (Winne & Perry, 2000, p. 534). Two views of SRL as event and as aptitude are not antithetical.

> Although our everyday sense of time is one of a unbroken flow, measured time is not continuous. At fundamental physical levels and at levels that characterize SRL, time "happens" in discrete chunks. As a temporal entity, an event therefore has a beginning and end, for example, an endpoint in an oscillating crystal or a decision to try a different tactic when studying doesn't seem to be progressing well enough that is made following deliberation. The event prior to the current one is like a brief-lived aptitude that may predict the next event. (Winne & Perry, 2000, p. 534)

COPES scripts and SRL's dualistic character as an aptitude-event set the stage for us to address several issues relating to research on SRL and the tactics and strategies that comprise SRL. To foreshadow our developments, these are: What data can represent SRL as aptitude and as event? What properties do different kinds of data have and how do these relate to decisions about gathering and analyzing data? What are the relative strengths and weaknesses of different kinds of data and how are these best balanced in relation to topics that researchers investigate?

A SUMMARY OF ISSUES IN MEASURING TACTICS, STRATEGIES, AND SRL

We recap four of five key areas of concern about measuring SRL that Winne and Perry (2000) addressed: targets of measurement, metrics, sampling, and technical issues. These issues pertain mostly to how previous research has measured SRL as an aptitude.

Targets for Measurement

Measurements of complex phenomena such as SRL intrinsically arise from models of those phenomena. Winne and Perry (2000) marked these elements as "targets" for measurement. Models for tactics specify two key targets, IFS and Thens. Models for strategies specify three targets, IFS, THENS, and ELSES. Using COPES scripts as a representation of SRL specifies five targets for measurement: conditions, operations, products, evaluations, and standards. To the extent an interpretation of a measurement excludes reference to one or more targets of the model from which it arises, it is incomplete relative to the model that data are supposed to represent and, consequently, invalid in kind or degree.

We concur with Winne and Perry's (2000) observation that, at present, no measure of SRL simultaneously and fully represents all targets of its model. Thus, evidence for the validity of constructs is under-represented in measurements currently used in research. Under-representation is probably unavoidable and, correspondingly, care should be taken to avoid inappropriately generalizing to targets not part of a measurement.

Pintrich, Wolters, and Baxter (2000) offer another view of targets for measuring SRL that reflects a multi-facet characterization of judgments involved in SRL. Their first category relates to judgments a learner makes about his or her knowledge of cognitive processes and how they may be regulated. For example, what does a learner know about the cognitive operation of rehearsing, about tasks in which rehearsing is appropriate, about his or her skill in rehearsing, or about forms of rehearsal? (See also Alexander, Schallert & Hare, 1991.) A second collection of metacognitive judgments result when learners monitor information about a particular task. Ease of learning (EOL) judgments are created during Winne and Hadwin's (1998) first phase, constructing a definition of the task. Here, learners are theorized to search memory for knowledge of similar tasks and of the task's domain, then monitor the new task's difficulty (conversely, the ease of learning) in relation to information returned by these searches. Judgments of learning (JOL) are formed during Winne and Hadwin's phase three, engagement. As the learner applies tactics and strategies to approach learning goals, attributes of engagement are monitored (see Winne, 2001). Theoretically, positive JOLs would be proportional to perceptions about some attributes of a task or work on it, such as the effort applied or about the brevity of time to complete the task. Negative JOLs may be founded on a learner's recognition that standards are not met, or that they are vague or lacking (as in ill-structured problems). Negative JOLs are theorized to be occasions where learners might adapt tactics for learning, perhaps in a self-regulated way. After engaging with and completing the task, a third kind of judgment can arise that represents the learner's confidence that products are correct, sufficient, or satisfactory relative to a set of standards (e.g. Schraw & Dennison, 1994).

Our review of literature accords with Pintrich et al.'s (2000) that contemporary studies focus on one or rarely two of these judgments. We observe that no study represented each kind of judgment that is theoretically characteristic of full-fledged SRL. Again, this raises concerns about under-representation of targets in measurements currently used in research and possible inaccuracies in interpretations about SRL.

Metrics

The second issue Winne and Perry (2000) raised was that of metrics. For our purposes, the concept of metric refers to units used to represent a phenomenon and rules for working with measures expressed in those units.

Units

Defining units of measurement poses challenges. It involves categorizing unique instances as being sufficiently similar so they can be considered equivalent or mutually substitutable with respect to the category. Simultaneously, it requires justifiably disregarding features of each instance that constitute its uniqueness. In the case of a self-report questionnaire, two concerns arise about categorization: (a) whether a set of self-report items forms a unidimensional and internally consistent subscale (category), and (b) whether semantically identical points on a scale for responding (e.g. typical of me) represent the same quantity for each item responded to within the subscale. For self-report items using a researcher's response format, an armamentarium of quantitative techniques, such as factor analysis and analyses of internal consistency, are available to help researchers investigate and justify the equivalence of items in relation to a latent construct.

In the context of verbal accounts collected according to a protocol for eliciting think-aloud reports, retrospective descriptions, or remarks made by participants in a solo interview or a focus group, concerns about categorization arise as researchers: (a) sort individual propositions into representative and salient themes, reserving those that don't "fit" as a list of "singletons;" and, (b) judge the extent to which individual propositions that have been categorized within a theme contribute equivalent meaning to the category. Techniques that have been applied to address these issues include member checking, having multiple researchers search for emergent themes, and progressively refining categories as one collects information from successive samples (e.g. see van Meter, Yokoi & Pressley, 1994; Wyatt, Pressley, El-Dinary, Stein, Evans & Brown, 1993).

Winne and Perry (see also Howard-Rose & Winne, 1993) observed that the "grain size" or the dimensions of a unit is another metrical concern. In relation to Winne and Hadwin's model of SRL, a tactic is commonly a finer grained event in SRL than a strategy. A tactic involves just one schema that defines conditional knowledge, cataloged in an IF, and one set of actions appearing in the THEN. A strategy adds at least a simple ELSE to a tactic and possibly a different kind of judgment about how a profile of IFS must match standards in relation to choosing between the THEN and ELSE. It is in this sense that we view a strategy as a larger topic of deliberation, a longer event, a more complex activity, all of which can contribute to the strategy yielding more feedback than a tactic.

Based on our survey of recent research, we found little methodological work has been done to probe and clarify issues about units of SRL. To our knowledge, only one study (Howard-Rose & Winne, 1993) investigated how units of different grain sizes and data represented as different response formats might have differential relations to other variables. We found no formal studies of scaling. Surprisingly, we found no research that investigated how units of one self-report inventory correspond to units of others', that is, a multitrait-multimethod study. Nor could we locate research that investigated the correspondence between learners' possibly differing meanings conveyed by self-report gathered using verbal report methods relative to quantitative facets revealed by self-report questionnaire items.

We observed two other methodological issues that arise when researchers collect learners' self-generated descriptions about SRL, as in think alouds, categorize them into themes, and then illustrate categories with selected examples drawn from the categories in reporting the research. While these studies are usually clear that the method used is constant comparison of propositions within the corpus (see Pressley, 2000 for a basic description), this declaration does not equate to a replicable method for sorting propositions into categories. Categories or themes are generated by a researcher or research team rather than by an explicit, relatively objective protocol that exists independently from the researcher(s). No studies in our sample provided anything by way of an operational definition of this process beyond describing it using paraphrases of "constant comparison" or "identifying themes that emerged from the data." Thus, in these studies, unitization is confounded with researcher(s). No studies in our sample explicitly compared two or more independent researchers (i.e. not members of a pre-existing team) or independent research teams in terms of their convergence in generating categories the same corpus of learners' self-generated descriptions. Instead, agreement among members of a pre-established research team is used, usually achieved after a discussion among the members about which nothing specifically is documented other than reaching agreement. Individuals likely form a team because they share theoretical or pre-theoretical views. In this light, concern is warranted about the dependability of categories or themes generated in a single study, and about bias in assigning propositions in the full corpus of data to categories.

Second, it is almost universal that researchers offer examples drawn from propositions in a category to clarify the meaning of that category. We found no occasions where researchers supplemented these reports with two essential kinds of information: (a) In what way or to what degree is the example representative of the population of propositions found in the category? To borrow language from quantitative orientations, what is the spread of the web of meaning attributed to propositions the researcher placed within a category and where, within this spread, is the example located and offered as a median or modal representation of the category? (b) What makes the example representative, that is, what principle(s) is the basis for deciding that any randomly chosen proposition with the category is not as representative as the one chosen to reflect the category? We are concerned here that selection of examples may be an instance of the fallacy *post hoc, ergo prompter hoc*.

In the context of all these issues about units, work on synthesizing findings across studies is open to various concerns about the extent to which variance among findings arises due to variance attributable to method rather than genuine variance in latent variables that reflect tactics, strategies, and SRL. The validity of inferences based on aggregations across samples, tasks, and studies is blurred in proportion to this confound.

Rules for Working with Units

Once units are defined, rules for manipulating units are applied. In the case of self-report questionnaire items, it has been universally assumed that responses learners make using dichotomous (e.g. yes-no) and Likert scales (e.g. typical of me) are interval measurements. Under this assumption, each response is the same grain size and data on unique items can be added to form subscale scores that represent a quality (e.g. frequency, importance, typicality, or utility) of that category of tactics, strategies, or some other facet of SRL.

Although rarely explicit, we judge that researchers performing qualitative analyses of verbal reports have relied on approximately these same assumptions. There are two indicators for our inference. First, in research that uses these methods, we observe very little evidence that propositions categorized into a theme are accorded differential influence or other ordinal (rank) demarcations – all members of a category or theme are treated as equivalent if not equal. Second, the attribution of ordinality, if not additivity, is implicit when researchers characterize particular themes as "more common," "less useful," or "about as effective" in relation to others.

Research on SRL is not unique in adopting these assumptions. Nonetheless, we believe the field would profit if future research delved into metrical matters of units and rules for working with them. At the least, such research might justify current practices.

Sampling

"Every measurement is a sample of behavior" (Winne & Perry, 2000, p. 558). This fact invites concerns about (a) how the population of behavior is defined and (b) the extent to which a sample in hand reflects characteristics of the population it is supposed to represent. One manifestation of sampling (or situatedness) is the context relative to which data about SRL are gathered: Learners are instructed to report about SRL in relation to various contexts: a particular assignment or task, "this course," or "when you study." These context-setting instructions are important because all current models of tactics, strategies, and SRL assign a critical role to context in the form of conditional knowledge (IFs) that learners use to judge the appropriateness of tactics and strategies. Measurements that generalize over differentiated contexts, like the average or the theme that exactly represents no one person in a group, are troublesome in light of several studies (Hadwin, Winne, Stockley, Nesbit & Woszczyna, 2001; Wolters & Pintrich, 1998) that found differences in self-reports about SRL and its components as a function of variation in task or cognitive context factors that Winne and Hadwin's (1998) model indicates to affect SRL from the outset.

Another concern for sampling arises when learners self-report about SRL, regardless of response format. This is that learners must search memory for information on which to base judgments about a tactic or strategy such as it frequency of use, typicality (generalization over tasks and context), or effectiveness. There is considerable research (e.g. Tourangeau, Rips & Rasinski, 2000) documenting that people's self-reports in response to questions about such topics are often generated by heuristics rather than by thorough searches of memory and accurate quantitative summarization of the products of those searchers. We address this issue in more detail in a subsequent section on Detailed Consideration of Self Reports.

Technical Issues

We highlight two main technical issues of measurement (a) reliability or dependability and (b) how meaning is constructed in relation to nomological networks. Reliability concerns the dependability of a measurement or trustworthiness of an account. In research using self-report inventories with researcher-provided response formats, reliability is almost universally reported as a coefficient of internal consistency, usually alpha. Indeed, as we noted earlier, a definitional criterion for positing a category, be it subscale or theme, is that it have adequate internal consistency. We also point out that a crucially important feature of measurements about SRL is stability, the degree to which behavior changes or does not change over time. With respect to SRL, stability has a particular focus because SRL entails changing tactics and reforming strategies in adaptive ways. Thus, tactics and strategies themselves will be unstable when learners self-regulate. As a result, direct measures of tactics and strategies should show instability when learners self regulate learning. In light of this account, how could self-report data correlate with achievement? We conjecture that such correlations reflect the effects of using tactics. Using tactics without adaptation is the most minimal form of self regulation: IF conditions are such-and-such, THEN apply a tactical operation. The challenge to the experimenter is to distinguish: (a) deliberate adaptation that *is* SRL from (b) random changes in learners' use of tactics that are the bane of reliability or dependability.

No study in our survey distinguished these two kinds of change over time. None investigated stability other than taking at face value learners' descriptions that, "I usually do it that way." None examined variation over time, such as multiple episodes of learning, that might provide data with which to distinguish self-regulated experimentation a learner carries out (Winne, 1997) in the service of adaptation that Winne and Hadwin's (1998) model describes.

More challenging than a simplistic concern about the "degree" of change is the need to characterize features *of* change in SRL, that is, representations of (a) the adaptive patterns among use of tactics that constitute strategies as well as (b) adaptations to individual tactics (e.g. liberalizing conditional knowledge) and strategies (e.g. re-ordering the sequence of tactics). We return to this in a later section on Traces as Representations of Events in SRL and ways to use tools from graph theory to characterize SRL as an event.

Researchers have used several response-generating methodologies – self-report inventories with various response formats, think aloud, and so forth – and have aggregated raw data to propose a variety of factors, latent variables, scales, or dimensions of SRL. In this context, two natural questions arise beyond ones we previously considered about categorization: To what extent are various facets of SRL alike or different? And, what influence(s) do response formats, situational factors, other methodological features (e.g. instructions defining context for responding), and the temporally unfolding nature of SRL within a complex task have on facets? Both matters are reflected in Campbell and Fiske's (1959) seminal proposal to investigate similar data using multitrait-multimethod techniques. We found no multitrait-multimethod investigations about SRL other than Howard-Rose and Winne's (1993). Consequently, it is not yet known: (a) how similar representations of SRL are across instruments; or (b) the degree to which representations vary as a result of features of instrumentation and other methodological factors such as response format, contexts for responding that are introduced by directions learners are given, the domain in which SRL is considered (Schraw, 2000), and so forth.

FURTHER ISSUES ABOUT MEASURING SRL

We have already reviewed a collection of issues about measuring SRL. In this section, we refocus our perspective to examine: (a) methods for collecting data about these cognitive events; and (b) the logic underlying inferences about the occurrences of these cognitive events and their properties.

Detailed Consideration of Self-Reports

Self-report inventories such as the Metacognitive Awareness Inventory (MAI; Schraw & Dennison, 1994), Motivated Strategies for Learning Questionnaire (MSLQ; Pintrich, Smith, Garcia & McKeachie, 1991), and the Learning and Study Strategies Inventory (LASSI; Weinstein, Schulte & Palmer, 1987) are widely used in research and on university campuses as diagnostic inventories. Each instrument derives from a model of metacognition and SRL, and all have undergone relatively intense scrutiny to insure psychometric quality in the classic sense. Moreover, dozens of studies provide material for developing a nomological network of the constructs these inventories reflect. Despite these plusses (for reviews see Pintrich et al., 2000; Winne & Perry, 2000) and the earned respect these instruments merit on those grounds, we believe there are substantial issues to face when considering how these and other less extensively validated self-report inventories are used in research to map and explain SRL.

Winne and Perry (2000) noted that most measurements, including self-report inventories, are interventions designed "to cause the learner to recall or to generate a particular kind of response" (p. 532). Three universal components of self-report inventories – instructions that establish context, response scale, and items – typically are assumed *a priori* to influence or cause respondents to answer in particular ways.

Although "one might expect that survey researchers [including developers of self-report inventories] would long ago have developed detailed models of the mental steps people go through in answering survey questions, models that spell out the implications these steps have for survey accuracy . . . study of the components of the survey response process is in its infancy, having begun in earnest only in the 1980s" (Torangeau, Rips & Rasinski, 2000, p. 2). To our knowledge, there is no work of this kind specifically in the context of self-report methods used to examine SRL. In this section, we bring forward matters we believe are important in interpreting research already done and in framing future investigations. We use the COPES model to frame our discussion and occasionally refer to representative items from the MSLQ (Pintrich et al., 1991). This survey instructs learners to "answer the questions about how you study in this class as accurately as possible" using a 7-point scale anchored by "not at all true of me" (recorded as a 1) and "very true of me" (recorded as a 7). Items include simple propositions (e.g. "I make good use of my study time for this course") and IF-THEN relations (e.g. "When reading for this course, I make up questions to help focus my reading").

Conditions

There are at least two and often three task conditions that might affect responses to items on self-report inventories. One is the context relative to which learners are to consider a feature of cognitive engagement. (In passing, we note that some self-report inventories provide no context relative to which learners should respond to items.) The context posed in the MSLQ is a particular course. Courses, however, almost surely are not unidimensional. For example, in his 3rd-year course on instructional psychology, Winne assigns various tasks including: preparing for in-class discussions, studying for exams, reading chapters in a required textbook, developing segments of lesson plans justified by findings from research, and generating questions to share with peers in small group tutorials. These activities take place under a variety of conditions: studying alone in the library or while riding a bus traveling a busy city street, working with a peer who has prepared for class or with one who has not, suffering from a cold or feeling fit, being distracted by an argument with a mate or elated by an unexpected good grade in another course. To the extent these various assignments and their variable contexts present learners with different conditions (IFs), as Winne intends and as much collateral research documents, they theoretically would trigger distinctive tactics arrayed in varying and sometimes dissimilar strategies. Some research documents these variations. Hadwin et al. (2001) found that, when learners respond to a single set of self-report items about tactics and SRL in relation to different assignments, responses to the same self-report item varied in level (frequency of use) as a function of context. As well, after correcting for attenuation, correlations among items varied as a function of context, indirect evidence that strategies and SRL also were differentiated by context. Pressley and Afflerbach (1995) documented a variety of circumstances to which sophisticated readers report attending in reading. The implication of such findings for interpreting self-report items is that, unless the researcher is clear about which context(s) respondents adopt when self-reporting about features of tactics, strategies, and SRL, there is ambiguity in what self-reports represent.

Another issue regarding responses to self-reports arises when items on an inventory or incidents in a think-aloud protocol are considered in temporal relation to one another rather than in isolation. The sequence of items on surveys can create contexts that have transitory effects on responses (Menon & Yorkston, 2000; Tourangeau et al., 2000). We account for this cognitive condition as a result of search through a network of associated information in long-term memory. Suppose the topic of either item no. 10 or of some information the respondent retrieves from memory in the course of answering item no. 10 is, for that learner, associated with the topic presented in item no. 11. If so, the learner's basis for searching memory to create a response to item no. 11 will be influenced by the residual content of working memory about item no. 10. Had item no. 10 been located as item no. 20 in the inventory, cognitive conditions influencing the response item no. 11 would differ and, correspondingly, the response to item no. 11 might differ.

It might be countered that, because researchers randomly distribute items in most self-report questionnaires, there is no concern about sequence. We are not so sanguine. If information that learners retrieve from memory in answering a first item has some relationship in the learner's view to the topic of a following item, even randomly distributed items can create context effects if they jointly reflect a correlation that characterizes a population. An example might be when a first item concerns use of a tactic and the following item invites a motivational interpretation about effort. Suppose learners in a particular population fuse memorial representations of tactics' "cold" IFS and THENS with "hot" motivational and affective content (Boekaerts, 1995; Pintrich et al., 1993; Winne, 2001) in particular ways – for example, as a body of research might demonstrate to be characteristic among undergraduates in studies of the affective states associated with cramming for final exams. Their memories about the first item about a particular tactic will likely bias search of memory for responses to the immediately following item about motivation. Such context effects are even more likely in think-aloud and interview protocols when researchers ask follow-up probes that the researcher intends to contribute to data for correlating factors in a population. Here, such probes purposefully ask for generalization, specialization, or elaboration contingent on a learner's first response, so search of memory is quite likely constrained. And, because the researcher is seeking a general principle, the nature of the context effect also will be general.

A similar concern about self-report items in inventories and probes in think aloud protocols arises when items pose a conditional relation in an IF-THEN form ("When reading for this course, I make up questions to help focus my reading."). While this item may appear straightforward, the constraint of "this course" is imprecise about conditions (IFS). In the selected example, is the context of "reading for this course" what one does in skimming assigned reading to develop a plan for studying? How one reads when assigned to lead a seminar discussion next class? A variable activity depending on how much time is available relative to the length of the text? Depending on which search path is followed in long-term memory, information returned about THENS of tactics, and THENS and ELSES of strategies can differ unpredictably because THENS and ELSES are inherently sensitive to conditions (Ifs) that identify the search path.

Relief from this concern might be obtained by asking respondents: (a) to describe what they interpret by the antecedent clause, (b) to select instances of these conditions in a task, and by the researcher (c) examining correlations or correspondences across repeated self-reports. To our knowledge, these tacks have not been taken in research. If conditions like these affect self-reports, several issues arise. First, levels of responses can be over- or under-represented. Second, when an unintended context effect applies to multiple self-report items or probes, correlations will inflate so that the ability to differentiate latent traits is undercut (e.g. communality in a principal components analysis is invalidly elevated) or an unnecessarily complex representation of traits will emerge (e.g. in oblique rotations of principal components or factors). Third, when reports are given about closely spaced activities or when learners are probed about the specificity or generality of specific activities, misrepresentation can emerge if researchers' don't "bundle" data in the same way as respondents do.

Search Operations

Researchers' questionnaire items or on-the-spot probes always are mediated because learners interpret those requests for information. Speed in responding is partly a reflection of automated perceptual and linguistic scripts that construct interpretations of those stimuli. Once a learner interprets conditions of the task and constructs a context for self-reporting about a tactic, strategy, or feature of SRL, the next two steps in self-reporting are: (a) carrying out a search of memory to locate information relevant to this context; and (b) developing a response on the basis of information retrieved. Our review of recent research that used self-report methods of any sort reflects scant attention to either of these distinct cognitive operations. We note three issues about search in this section. Issues relating to framing a response are taken up in the following section.

Along with the learners' construction of what the self-report task is, qualities of information stored in long-term memory about SRL co-determine how memory can be searched (Anderson, 1991). First, if tactics and strategies are stored as unitized and automated scripts, reporting about their features and even their use is likely compromised. Such automated skills operate without attention and their IF-THEN components do not exist in memory as separable elements: (e.g. see McKoon & Ratcliff, 1992). Under these circumstances, mental records of the frequency with which a tactic is used may substantially underestimate actual use. And, the ability to recognize conditions (IFS) under which specific actions (THENS) are enacted can be diluted.

Second, we interpret that strategies have a degree of stability in the sense that learners do not create a new strategy for each task if they perceive it to be a minor variant of other tasks they have experienced. Under our model, where strategies are structured as serially and conditionally ordered tactics, a tactic that is positioned in the middle or toward the end of a strategy may be difficult to locate in a search unless tactics prior to it in the strategy serve as salient cues (see Winne, 1997). Again, under-representation of such tactics would be predicted to characterize self-reports. It may be that the production deficiency, that is, situations where learners who know a tactic fail to use it, can be partially explained by this hypothesis.

Third, it is well known that so-called memory search is often more of a constructive process than a retrieval process (Bartlett, 1932). Asked to describe a script, learners sometimes opt to use a less cognitively demanding process of heuristic construction to develop a response rather than carry out a relatively exhaustive search of memory for it. Because construction creates rather than recapitulates information, the result may distort qualitative features of SRL or inaccurately characterize the frequency of a component of SRL. We suggest that all three effects lay grounds for plausible conjectures about why learners' self-reports of study tactics calibrate poorly to moderately with traces of tactics actually used while studying (Winne, Hadwin, Nesbit & Stockley, 2001; Winne & Jamieson-Noel, in press).

Evaluating Memorial Content and Responding

Self-reports about incidents of SRL that occur just once, which we term singleton events, or occasionally, which we term rare events, could be theoretically interesting. Singleton events may be indicators of phase four of Winne and Hadwin's (1998) model that reflect learners' attempts to adapt tactics and strategies that failed and that are subsequently rejected for some reason such as requiring too much effort or being too unpredictable. Rare events may be especially clear indicators of SRL because they may indicate the learner was particularly sensitive to conditions (IFS) of a task's state and engaged in more than usual deliberation to choose actions (THENS) that respond to those uncommon conditions.

Singleton events and rare events are not frequent topics of self-report inventories that use a scaled response format such as true/not true of me or typical/not typical of me. (At least, this is our interpretation of the semantics of not true or typical of me.) We also observed that qualitative analysts and researchers who used think aloud protocols seem to steer away from interpreting singleton and rare events exactly because they do not fit into themes that researchers construct as accounts about how learners enact SRL (e.g. see Pressley & Afflerbach, 1995).

There is evidence that learners underestimate frequency of occurrence in reporting about various phenomena. For example, the extent of underestimation for how often items appeared in a study list ranges from approximately 5 to 35% (Begg, Maxwell, Mitterer & Harris, 1986). Winne and Jamieson-Noel (2001) found that learners were not very accurate when, after studying, they reported the frequency of using study tactics. Median calibration (correlation) of the match between self-reported frequency of using specific tactics and traces we gathered of those same tactics was $r = 0.34$. Also, learners' varied unpredictably in the degree to which they overestimated and underestimated their use of study tactics. If calibration were viewed as a kind of interrater agreement, undergraduates would be deemed quite unreliable in reporting the frequency they use tactics.

How do learners create the basis for reporting about the frequency with which tactics are used and SRL is applied? Several models have been proposed. In one model, frequency of use is stored as an attribute of an event. In another model, frequency is estimated on the basis of other attributes of events, such as how familiar an event is judged to be or how variable the contexts (IFS) are in which Thens are carried out (Tourangeau et al., 2000). The latter model, supplemented by other influences, has current favor in the literature on how people respond to surveys where they estimate the frequency of events (Menon & Yorkston, 2000).

Menon and Yorkston (2000) reviewed research showing that when events occur irregularly, people are less accurate in reporting about the frequency of those events compared to events that occur at regular intervals. They illustrate with an example about two people who both drink about seven cans of soda a week. One person drinks one can each day of the week whereas the other consumes soda less regularly, two or three cans some days and none on other days. The regular soda drinker is more accurate at estimating consumption than the drinker with a shifting pattern of consumption. If this finding generalizes to self-reports about SRL, we hypothesize that more adaptive learners who have and act on relatively differentiated conditional knowledge (IFs, a cognitive condition in Winne & Hadwin's [1998] model) will provide less reliable accounts of SRL because the regularity of tasks they survey in memory as they form a response about SRL will vary. Self-report inventories that set a "large" context such as "this course" would hypothetically be susceptible to this effect. In think aloud methodologies, learners are commonly asked to comment on the typicality of a reported event or incidentally comment on this themselves. Their choice of context relative to which they frame this response could yield quite different information and, consequently, if they do not describe that context, we would counsel researchers to probe for it.

Learners who have considerable experience with the tasks about which they self report also are likely to have a larger store of memories about a greater variety of tactics, strategies, and qualities of SRL. Except for self-reports about a singleton and rare COPES script, whenever learners must aggregate over memories to report about qualities such as frequency, typicality, usefulness (utility), or difficulty, some form of mental arithmetic and judgment is involved. We first consider self-reports about frequency, then take up issues bearing on judgments concerning qualities of SRL.

Reporting the Frequency of Elements of SRL

All self-report inventories we examined and many follow-up probes in think-aloud protocols ask learners to estimate how frequently they use a tactic or a strategy in a task. When asked to self-report about the frequency of an event, survey respondents probably respond using the least cognitively taxing method. We concur with Tourangeau et al.'s (2000) synthesis of relevant research that learners probably do not store in memory a tally of the frequency with they engage in particular activities. That is, they don't answer questions about a tactic's use by simply retrieving a tally. An alternative is that learners search memory for all the episodes in which a tactic was used, within the parameters set by instructions to self-report (e.g. "this course") and an item (e.g. "when reading"), and create a tally of the number of episodes retrieved. A third alternative is that learners exercise judgment or apply heuristic estimating methods to estimate the frequency with which they have used a tactic, experienced a condition, or shaped studying strategies in relation to conditions.

The literature seems relatively consistent that "respondents rarely recall-and-count all the episodes of a frequent behavior (i.e. an episodic recall strategy). Instead, they rely on a heuristic and estimate the frequency from other, more available information" (Menon & Yorkston, 2000, p. 65). Using estimation strategies rather than a recall-and-count method for self-reporting is more likely when one or more of these conditions holds: (a) the event is more frequent, which would require a large number of events to be reviewed and counted; (b) the context in which the event might occur is broader (e.g. a course vs. a recent study session, which would require a correspondingly broad search of memory); and (c) the wording of a question or its response scale implies counting ("How many times do you . . .?") versus reporting rough categorizations ("On average, . . .?"). While researchers might prefer learners to tally episodes, heuristic estimation seems much more likely. Researchers need to be concerned about this to the degree that heuristic estimation methods are biased, erratic (unreliable), or both.

In circumstances where learners find it difficult to retrieve direct representations of events used in counting or as a basis for heuristic estimation, coincidental features about their cognitive attempt to respond may be used to answer questions rather than any information actually retrieved. One well known bias in this case is the availability heuristic (Tversky & Kahneman, 1974), the case where a learner substitutes a judgment about the degree to which information is retrievable for actual retrieval of information about an event. In a similar vein, a learner can use features of memory search per se, such as time to retrieve an item, as an estimate that correlates inversely with the frequency of an event.

Judging Elements of SRL

Judging a quality about a feature of SRL differs from reporting its frequency and such judgments are inherently more cognitively demanding in two ways. First, except for the case where a tactic or strategy or condition is a singleton (i.e. it occurred only once), the learner and the researcher alike need to consider the representativeness of the sample of the element upon which a judgment is made. Second, the method used to make a judgment on the basis of the sample demands cognitive resources and skill. If the sample of an event is unrepresentative, skill in judgment can not compensate. If the sample is representative, inaptitude or bias in rendering judgments can reduce the accuracy of self-reports.

We interpret that when learners judge the typicality of a feature of SRL they are rendering a judgment about the probability or likelihood this feature is characteristic of their studying, or the probability or likelihood they vary tactics depending on particular task or cognitive conditions. In other contexts (judging risks), Tourangeau et al. (2000) reported that people are likely to underestimate the likelihood of rare events, overestimate the likelihood of common events, and that "we seem to make finer discriminations among probabilities that are near 0 and 1 than among less extreme probabilities" (p. 161). People also appear, in some circumstances, to violate laws of probability. For instance, if asked to judge how typical a condition (IF) is separately from how typical a cognitive operation (THEN) is, the likelihood of a tactic (IF-THEN) constituted from this condition and this tactic should be equal to the product of these separate likelihoods. Although never studied in the setting of self-reports about SRL, in other contexts, this expectation is often violated. Compound events (tactics) are often judged more likely than indicated by their components.

Inferential Measurement and Comparison Groups

In most studies of SRL, measurements of SRL are "temporally and/or logically separated from ongoing strategic activity," a form of measurement that Kail and Bisanz (1982, p. 231) term inferential measurement. Consider this seemingly well-designed experiment as an example. Suppose a random half of a large sample of learners is assigned to a treatment group that receives training in each of several tactics for studying. They are not trained to use tactics strategically, however, because the experimenter intends to assess self-regulation. After training, each participant in this group demonstrates "mastery" in using each of the tactics. Subsequently, these learners study a text on DNA cloning and take a well-constructed and psychometrically sound achievement test. While the treatment group is learning about study tactics, the randomly constituted remaining half of learners participate in a placebo activity. They take approximately the same time as treatment group learners spent on training to read a text on the history of British Columbia, and then they take a test on this material. Next, placebo participants study the same text on DNA cloning and take the same achievement test as the treatment group. A statistical test detects a difference in achievement that favors the treatment group. The experimenter attributes this to treatment group learners' self-regulated use of the study tactics with which they had demonstrated proficiency after the training phase of the experiment.

In this fictional study, random assignment, experimental controls, the measure of mastery with respect to tactics trained in the treatment group, and achievement differences provide strong grounds for inferring that *tactics* learners mastered account for differences observed in achievement. No data were gathered, however, about any learner's self-regulated articulation of tactics during studying. Because achievement has many sources, one of which may be self regulation of study tactics, it is possible that self-regulation contributed to the observed difference in achievement. But in this fictional experiment, and in every other study we have examined, measures of achievement are temporally separated from when tactics are used and when tactics are articulated in a self-regulated way. SRL may be a sufficient but is not necessary precursor of achievement so an inference about self-regulated use of tactics is not warranted.

In this apparently well-designed mock study, there is also the potential for invalidity of a putative cause (Cook & Campbell, 1982) because there are other empirically grounded accounts for the observed difference in achievement. Here is one theoretically interesting possibility. Eisenberger (1992) surveyed a wide variety of research that supports the hypothesis that people who apply effort to tasks and then succeed at those tasks learn that effort per se, not necessarily a particular manifestation of effort – e.g. particular study tactics – is a key to success. In a study about study tactics, Rabinowitz, Freeman and Cohen (1993) found that a first experience in applying an effortful study tactic can, under certain conditions, be a poor predictor of learners' re-use of that tactic in a subsequent task (see also Winne, 1995). That condition is when effort called for in a first studying situation is less than the effort required in a second. In this light, our mock experimenter's inference that learners trained to use study tactics actually used them would be undercut if studying material on DNA cloning is more taxing than studying material that was the vehicle for learning study tactics. In most experimental contexts, this would be the case. Experimenters usually design training sessions so that learners can focus attention on mastering the tactics rather than coping with difficult material.

It might be countered that learning study tactics is equally as challenging as studying material on DNA cloning, in which case the preceding threat to a valid inference is reduced. But, there is another potential concern. Every model of SRL with which we are familiar is consistent with the claim that strategic SRL is quite effortful. In our mock experiment, we suggest that studying the material on DNA cloning in a self-regulated way is more effortful than studying about the history of British Columbia because of differences in familiarity. If so, according to Eisenberger's theory, learners in the placebo group would generalize low effort to the session when they studied the DNA cloning chapter, engaging in less intense self-regulated use of tactics. This allows the possibility that learners in the placebo group learn less than they otherwise might when they study the DNA cloning chapter because they apply less effort. If the placebo group's mean is depressed, it is not clear that mean achievement in the treatment group is elevated due to simple use of or even self-regulated use of trained study tactics. The experiment was supposed to determine that by contrasting the treatment group's mean to a mean representing "regular" effects of studying. But, if that contrasting mean is depressed, there's no way to know whether the treatment group's mean reflects "regular" studying or studying enhanced by SRL.

There is yet a further issue bearing on our mock experiment that is tacit in our first criticism: There is no direct evidence that learners in the treatment group actually used the study tactics while studying the chapter on DNA cloning. We turn to this in the next section.

Traces as Representations of Events in SRL

Ludwig Wittgenstein (1968) claimed, "An inner process stands in need of outward criteria." One form of outward criteria for activities constituting SRL is traces. Traces (Winne, 1982; see also Winne, 1992; Winne & Perry, 2000) are a form of (relatively) unobtrusive data that parallel what Webb, Campbell, Schwartz and Sechrest (1966) called a running record of deposit data. A trace is created, for example, when a learner highlights a clause in a text or chooses an option from a menu in software. Recorded simultaneously in the course of a learner's studying, traces can indicate occurrences of cognitive events and, in some instances, properties of cognitive events. If experimenters design traces that indicate significant cognitive events during learning and if each trace datum includes the time of its occurrence, the resulting stream of trace data is a timeline of indicators of significant features of the learner's cognitive engagement with a task.

Consider a trace, the information a learner highlights (or underlines) while studying a text. Highlighting particular text while leaving other text unmarked unambiguously indicates the learner discriminated some information relative to other information in the text. In addition, it is plausible that an instance of highlighting indicates the highlighted information was rehearsed as the learner chose a specific word at which to begin highlighting and, while drawing the highlighting tool across text, re-read and attended to its meaning to provide a basis for deciding where to stop highlighting. While syntactic cues, such as a comma or period, might be used to trigger stopping, highlighting often spans such marks. We posit that highlighting requires making semantic decisions about where information ceases to be relevant for highlighting.

A second example of a trace is choosing an option from a menu in software. Menu options allow software users to perform actions, for example, making previously selected information act as a hyperlink to another document or pasting information into another location. When learners select a particular menu option, this directly indicates a decision to perform that particular function. Depending on context, characterized by other traces, and what the chosen function is, plausible inferences might be drawn from such a trace. For example, having highlighted several sentences in a text and, choosing an option that provides the learner with a "tool" to create a "hot-linked" index term seems a strong indicator about the learner having a plan to return to that selected information later. Jamieson-Noel and Winne's (2001; Winne & Jamieson-Noel, in press) studies illustrate operational definitions of traces for several common cognitive activities in studying such as planning, comparing information, generating self-questions and analogies, and reviewing (see also Howard-Rose & Winne, 1993).

Using Trace Data to Describe SRL

As we previously described, when the IF-THEN structure of a tactic is elaborated by adding an option, the resulting IF-THEN-ELSE structure constitutes the simplest form of a strategy. Graphically, a tactic has a shape like a line, IF-THEN, like the path from A to B in Fig. 3. A strategy has a forked shape like a Y rotated 90° clockwise. One branch of the Y is the THEN and the other branch is the ELSE, as represented by C and D in Fig. 3. Complex strategies array multiple forks. Self-regulation is disregarding Yogi Berra's advice, "When you come to a fork in the road, take it." SRL requires at least deciding on-the-spot. Better yet, it involves planning that creates a "map" of studying tactics and conditions for following particular paths (THENS and ELSES) to achieve goals.

As we noted earlier, data characterizing some aspects of linear tactics and forked strategies often are gathered using self-report formats, and several well-established qualitative and quantitative techniques are available for examining these kinds of data. In most rating items, learners describe THENS. Less often, rating items record learner's assessment of a full IF-THEN tactic by describing particular conditions and specific cognitive actions taken in response to them. In some interview formats and think-aloud protocols, the full structure of IFS, THENS and ELSES can be represented as the learner perceives them. (We repeat, however, that learners' calibration may not be high.) These data can identify tactics but rarely have yielded information about properties such as the length of multiple concatenated tactics, the shape of complex forked structures representing self-regulated study strategies, or the degree to which alternative tactics and strategies are similarly structured. We view these kinds of properties of SRL as central to describing events of self-regulation.

Winne, Gupta and Nesbit (1995) tackled the problem of how such properties of SRL might be characterized quantitatively. Winne et al.'s methods begin with a stream of event data, such as traces gathered in a software environment that serves as both medium of instruction and tool for gathering trace data (e.g. see Hadwin & Winne, 2001; Winne, 1991). Winne and Nesbit (1995) extended this work and illustrated how it can describe both individuals' studying and a group's aggregate approach to studying. They devised their methods for trace data but their techniques apply to data gathered using interview and think aloud methodologies. (In the latter context, however, it would be essential to take steps to insure that events were not omitted from the learner's report due to lapses in attending to events' occurrences, misconstruing what constitutes an event to be reported, or loss of memory for an event due to cognitive load.)

Raw data for analyses of structure in learners' SRL are a series of time-sequenced codes that correspond to each traced event (see Fig. 3). This stream of codes is then transcribed into an adjacency matrix. The process is of transcribing serially arrayed codes to a transition matrix straightforward.

Data Stream: A B C A B C A B D D

trace	A	B	C	D	P(y|x)
A		///			.33
B			//	/	.33
C	//				.22
D				/	.11
					N=9

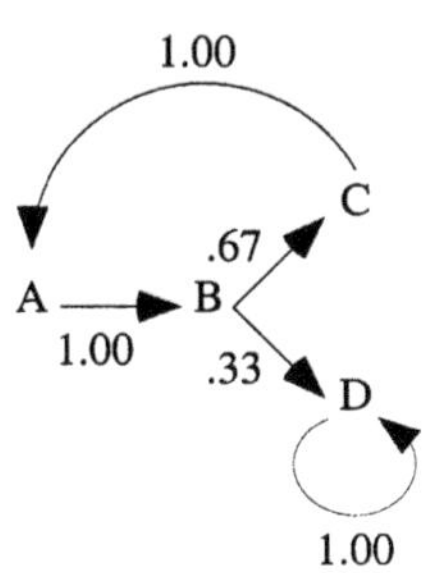

Fig. 3. A stream of trace data, its transition matrix, conditional probabilities of transitions from row traces to column traces, and a graphical representation of transitions that represents a simple strategy.

Create a square matrix that lists each unique trace as a row and transposes that list in the same order into columns. This matrix has the same form as a square correlation matrix of variables. The first trace in the data stream identifies the row of the adjacency matrix in which a tally will be made. The next (second) trace in the data stream identifies the column, and a tally is made in the cell at the intersection of that row (1st trace) and column (2nd trace). To enter the next tally for a transition, the second trace is now used to identify the row of the adjacency matrix in which a tally will be entered, and the third trace marks the column. A tally is placed in that cell. At step three, the third trace determines the row, the fourth trace specifies the column, and a tally is made. Tallying transitions between temporally adjacent traces continues until the final tally is made for the transition from the N-1st trace to the Nth trace.

Each cell in an adjacency matrix represents the number of transitions from each kind of trace (event) to every other trace that immediately followed it, including itself (to allow repetition). The conditional probability of a transition from a the trace in a row to a trace in a column is computed by dividing the sum of traces in a row by the total number of traces in the adjacency matrix. A graphic representation of the complete studying session can be developed from the matrix that shows linear, forked, and looping patterns, a picture of the strategy the learner used to study labeled by the probability of the learner followed each path in the strategy.

Beyond depicting what a learner's SRL looks like, various statistics can be calculated to describe properties of a learner's approaches to studying, and that compare tactics to one another or strategies to one another. First, counting tallies in a row and dividing by the total number of tallies in the matrix creates an index of a trace's relative use in the study sessions(s) represented in the adjacency matrix. These might be interpreted as a learner's preferences for particular tactics or, if assumed the learner has no preferences, a profile of how the learner perceived the task in terms of tactics judged appropriate to achieve goals. By using graphical representations (e.g. the diameter of a circle circumscribing each tactic), features of the learner's enacted plan can be visualized. This might be compared to self-report data to examine questions such as: Were any tactics actually used during studying omitted from self-reports? Does the learner's perceptions about the relative utility (frequency) of a tactic for the studying task correspond to actual use; that is, is the learner accurately calibrated about how studying actually was enacted? Does the learner's recollections about sequences and about decision making (at forks) match actual studying? Other statistics describe other properties of tactics, strategies and SRL.

Linearity (also called density; Winne & Nesbit, 1995) is a statistic computed by dividing the number of cells in the adjacency matrix that have at least one tally by the total number of cells in the adjacency matrix (number of rows × number of columns, or N^2). This index ranges from a minimum of $1/N^2$ to a maximum of 1. A linearity index of $1/N^2$ indicates that a particular tactic might be followed by any other tactic observed in the data stream, including the same tactic. In other words, having just enacted a particular tactic, it is completely unpredictable which tactic the learner will use next. As linearity approaches 1, a graphical representation of the tactics represented by traces in the data stream looks more and more like a straight line with no forks or loops.

Suppose a learner studies the same material twice (reviews) or studies two different chapters. In this case, two adjacency matrices can be constructed, each based on one of the two streams of trace data. Winne and Nesbit (1995) proposed a measure of similarity they called S*. It gauges how similar the pattern of studying is across two data streams. S* can be used to compare different learners or to gauge the consistency of studying patterns by comparing a single learner's studying at different times or in different contexts. Computing S* requires both adjacency matrices to have the same tactics listed in the same order down the rows (and across the columns). Tallies of each transition in each cell of the adjacency matrix are first converted to proportions relative to the total of all tallies in the matrix. Then, representing the first adjacency matrix as A and the second as B, and indexing each cell in a matrix by i, S* is calculated as the ratio

$$S^* = \frac{\sum_{i=1}^{N^2} \min(A_i \cdot B_i)}{\sum_{i=1}^{N^2} \max(A_i \cdot B_i)}.$$

In this calculation, min and max are operators: min returns the smaller of the two proportions found the ith cell of A and its twin cell in B; max does the opposite, returning the larger of the two proportions in twinned cells of the two adjacency matrices. If cells with tallies in matrix A never have twins with tallies in matrix B, S* is 0. This indicates that the pattern of studying represented in the first adjacency matrix has zero overlap with the pattern of studying represented in the second. When the proportions of transitions for pairs of tactics are identical in the two data streams, S* reaches its maximum value of 1.

An important issue to explore in research on SRL is whether tactics that seem superficially different, or that learners report as being different in their perception, play different roles in a strategy. For instance, we have observed that learners sometimes study like this: sometimes they highlight a clause in text, sometimes they draw a vertical line in the margin adjacent to some material in text, and sometimes they put a star in the margin. Do these traces represent different cognitive events? Some learners to whom we've put this question say these traces reflect different cognitive activities. If that is true, we would expect patterns of traces – strategies – to show differences, too. A graph theoretic statistic called structural equivalence (Winne et al., 1994) can be used to explore this issue.

Structural equivalence compares two traces in terms of the pattern of relations each traced event has to all other traces in the adjacency matrix. The logic underlying this measure is this: Suppose we suspect highlighting and starring are equivalent, even though a learner reports otherwise. If the learner is correct, transitions from any other trace "into" highlighting would not be expected to have an identical pattern to transitions from any other trace into starring. In other words, the conditions (IFS) that lead to highlighting should not be identical to the conditions that lead to starring. Correspondingly, transitions from highlighting "out" to other traces should not be the same as transitions out from starring. This would be a differentiation of ELSES. To the extent transitions into and out of these two superficially different traces are the same, however, we might entertain the hypothesis that highlighting and starring are not differentiated strategically because they have identical relations with the other traces that reflect cognitive activities in studying.

If we adopt terms that describe the "structure" or shape of a graph like that in Fig. 3, traces that are not strategically differentiated would be structurally equivalent, serving the same roles as one another in a larger pattern. Mathematically, structural equivalence is a measure of the distance that separates two traces in a graph. A distance of 0 indicates the traces play "the same" role in the graph when considered in relation to all other traces. Thus, the structural equivalence statistic, d_{ij}, has a value of 0 when trace i and trace j have identical patterns of relation to all other traces in the graph; it has a value of 1.0 when i and j have a maximally dissimilar pattern of relations to all other traces in the graph. Formally, for each pair of traces i and j, the structural distance between them is calculated relative to all other traces, k,

$$d_{ij} = \sqrt{\sum_{\substack{k=1 \\ k \neq i,j}}^{N} (x_{ik} - x_{jk})^2 + (x_{ki} - x_{kj})^2},$$

where i, j, and k are events in a graph, and x_{ij} is the entry in the ith row, jth column of the adjacency matrix.

The methods Winne et al. (1995) described offer promise to elaborate descriptions of SRL. We stress, however, that because they have not yet been used much, judgments are pending about how useful they will be and what shortcomings they may have. Moreover, because these quantitative measures generate new descriptions of SRL, it will be important to triangulate across methods to establish what these descriptions represent. We view these as challenges that merit approach rather than reasons not to explore the patterns of events that comprise SRL.

CONCLUSION

Research on SRL has made significant strides over the past decade. Models of the phenomenon have become appropriately more sophisticated and better coupled with a wider scope of research. Compared to the vigor of work on theorizing about and modeling SRL, however, relatively scant attention has been paid to methodological features that round out paradigm(s) for research. Pintrich et al.'s (2000) and Winne and Perry's (2000) reviews highlighted major issues regarding measurements of facets of SRL, particularly SRL as aptitude. We continued this line of review in this chapter. Our analyses emphasize issues that arise when SRL is considered as a complex whole, a whole that we illustrated by representing and contrasting SRL as a COPES script and as a series of traced events. Scripts and events can be treated as units per se and as components within larger structures. As well, scripts and events can be decomposed. All three perspectives present methodological challenges that we believe merit attention in future research.

An important and likely useful tension is beginning to arise relating self-reports as learners' interpretations about their SRL compared to traces or other forms of data that reflect what learners do as they enact SRL. We reviewed literature suggesting that methods by which learners create self-reports are themselves a topic worthy of study in research on SRL. Such studies into learners' interpretations of current and past episodes of SRL offer interesting methodological puzzles of their own, puzzles that we predict are central to understanding more clearly what theorists should and can infer from self-report data. Because learners' interpretations are central to all models of SRL, we believe that such research should investigate individual differences that bear importantly on how learners proceed through phases 1 (definition of task) and 2 (goal/standard setting and planning) of Winne and Hadwin's model of SRL.

Complementing deeper probes of what is represented by self-report data is a need to better understand what learners do as they enact SRL. We view this as important because researchers design and do research under models in which the terms refer to learners' behaviors, events and activities learners carry out. In contrast, the vast majority of data about behaviors are learners' interpretations about what they do when they engage with tasks. We believe that studies of the calibration or match between self-reports and traces are essential. Finding ways to offset the strengths of each kind of data against weaknesses of the other presents intriguing challenges.

We echo Winne and Perry's (2000) observation that there is very little research documenting SRL as a progression of events that evolves over time in response to feedback (Butler & Winne, 1995; Winne, 1997). The methodological challenges of such research are formidable but, if these challenges can be conquered, there likely will be large payoffs to understanding the workings of conditional knowledge and metacognitive control. Some purchase on these issues may be gained by experimenting with the graph theoretic techniques Winne et al. (1994) and Winne and Nesbit (1995) proposed. At least three challenges need to be met when data are viewed as a stream of evolving, recursive events. The first is how to identify segments within a sequence. The second is to consider what is theoretically important, if anything, in the interval between adjacent events in the sequence. The third is how to represent recursion and on-the-fly adaptation, situations where prior products of cognitive engagement serve as input to subsequent regulative cognitive action. All three matters are central to current models of SRL but they are not well represented in current research.

Another strong recommendation we make for enhancing work on SRL is that the field investigate how metrics relate to representations of SRL. Grain size issues and issues of categorization need more penetrating address. We urge that this not be a "horse race" to account for variance in achievement. Rather, we suggest carrying out studies that compare and triangulate data cast in differing metrics before trying to relate those measures to achievement.

Finally, we identify an issue that, as best we can tell, has not been researched and that we believe very much needs it. We observed frequent and sometimes fervent call for studies of SRL in "authentic" settings, whatever these may be. We believe these calls arise, in part, from convictions that studies occurring in less than or other than "authentic" settings intrinsically yield impoverished data or data that provide less sturdy grounds for crafting models and theories of any relevance. We certainly do not contest others' beliefs or our own model or mountains of data demonstrating that conditions do affect SRL. Indeed, variations in conditions, the IFs of tactics, occasion SRL. What we do contest, because we believe it has not yet been demonstrated, is that one kind of setting is a more productive one than another for researching SRL. We point out that whether setting matters and how it matters are empirical questions and we urge that such questions be tested rather than assumed. Doing comparative research like this will, we forecast, help the field to better understand the nature of methodological issues we identified. Hopefully, it also will lead toward resolutions of some of these issues.

ACKNOWLEDGMENTS

Support for this research was provided by grants to Philip H. Winne from the Social Sciences and Humanities Research Council of Canada (no. 410–98–0705) and from the Simon Fraser University-Social Sciences and Humanities Research Council of Canada Institutional Grant Fund.

REFERENCES

Alexander, P. A., Schallert, D. L., & Hare, V. C. (1991). Coming to terms: How researchers in learning and literacy talk about knowledge. *Review of Educational Research, 61*, 315–343.

Anderson, J. R. (1991). The adaptive nature of human categorization. *Psychological Review, 98*, 409–429.

Bartlett, F. C. (1932). *Remembering: A study in experimental and social psychology*. New York: Cambridge University Press.

Begg, I., Maxwell, D., Mitterer, J. O., & Harris, G. (1986). Estimates of frequency: Attribute or attribution. *Journal of Experimental Psychology: Learning, Memory, and Cognition, 12*, 496–508.

Boekaerts, M. (1995). Self-regulated learning: Bridging the gap between cognitive, motivation and self-management theories. *Educational Psychologist, 31*, 195–200.

Butler, D. L., & Winne, P. H. (1995). Feedback and self-regulated learning: A theoretical synthesis. *Review of Educational Research, 65*, 245–281.

Campbell, D. T., & Fiske, D. W. (1959). Convergent and discriminant validation by the multitrait-multimethod matrix. *Psychological Bulletin, 56*, 81–105.

Carver, C. S., & Scheier, M. F. (1998). *On the self-regulation of behavior*. New York: Cambridge University Press.

Cook, T. D., & Campbell, D. T. (1982). *Quasi-experimentation: Desing & analysis Issues for field settings*. Chicago: Rand-McNally.

Covington, M. V. (1992). *Making the grade: A self-worth perspective on motivation and school reform*. Cambridge, U.K.: Cambridge University Press.

Eisenberger, R. (1992). Learned industriousness. *Psychological Review, 99*, 248–267.

Hadwin, A. F., & Winne, P. H. (2001). CoNoteS: A software tool for promoting self-regulated learning in networked collaborative learning environments. [Special issue]. *Evaluation Research in Education, 7*, 313–334.

Hadwin, A. F., Winne, P. H., Stockley, D. B., Nesbit, J. C., & Woszczyna, C. (2001). Context moderates learners' self-reports about how they study. *Journal of Educational Psychology, 93*, 477–487.

Howard-Rose, D., & Winne, P. H. (1993). Measuring component and sets of cognitive processes in self-regulated learning. *Journal of Educational Psychology, 85*, 591–604.

Jamieson-Noel, D. L., & Winne, P. H. (2001). *Comparing self-reports about studying and traces of actual studying behavior as representations of how learners' perceive achievement and studying*. Manuscript submitted for publication.

Kail, R. B. Jr., & Bisanz, J. (1982). Cognitive strategies. In: C. R. Puff (Ed.), *Handbook of Research Methods in Human Memory and Cognition* (pp. 229–255). New York: Academic Press.

McKoon, G., & Ratcliff, R. (1992). Inference during reading. *Psychological Review, 99*, 440–466.

Menon, G., & Yorkston, E. A. (2000). The use of memory and contextual cues in the formation of behavioral frequency judgments. In: A. A. Stone, J. S. Turkkan, C. A. Bachrach, J. B. Jobe, H. S. Kurtzman & V. S. Cain (Eds), *The science of self-report: Implications for research and practice* (pp. 63–79). Mahwah, NJ: Lawrence Erlbaum Associates.

Miller, G. A., Galanter, E., & Pribram, K. H. (1960). *Plans and the structure of behavior.* New York: Holt, Rinehart & Winston.

Pintrich, P. R., Marx, R. W., & Boyle, R. A. (1993). Beyond cold conceptual change: The role of motivational beliefs and classroom contextual factors in the process of conceptual change. *Review of Educational Research, 63*, 167–199.

Pintrich, P. R., Smith, D. A. F., Garcia, T., & McKeachie, W. J. (1991). *A manual for the use of the Motivated Strategies for Learning Questionnaire (MSLQ)* (Technical Report No. 91-B-004). Ann Arbor, MI: University of Michigan, School of Education.

Pintrich, P. R., Wolters, C. A., & Baxter, G. P. (2000). Assessing metacognition and self-regulated learning. In: G. Schraw & J. C. Impara (Eds), *Issues in the Measurement of Metacognition* (pp. 43–97). Lincoln, NB: Buros Institute of Mental Measurements.

Pressley, M. (2000). Development of grounded theories of complex processing: Exhaustive within- and between-study analyses of think-aloud data. In: G. Schraw & J. C. Impara (Eds), *Issues in the Measurement of Metacognition* (pp. 261–296). Lincoln, NB: Buros Institute of Mental Measurements.

Pressley, M., & Afflerbach, P. (1995). *Verbal protocols of reading: The nature of constructively responsive reading*. Hillsdale, NJ: Erlbaum.

Rabinowitz, M., Freeman, K., & Cohen, S. (1993). Use and maintenance of strategies: The influence of accessibility to knowledge. *Journal of Educational Psychology, 84*, 211–218.

Rumelhart, D. E., & Norman, D. A. (1978). Accretion, tuning, and restructuring: Three modes of learning. In: J. W. Cotton & R. Klatzky (Eds), *Semantic factors in cognition* (pp. 37–53). Hillsdale, NJ: Lawrence Lawrence Erlbaum Associates.

Schraw, G. (2000). Assessing metacognition: Implications of the Buros symposium. In: G. Schraw & J. C. Impara (Eds), *Issues in the Measurement of Metacognition* (pp. 297–321). Lincoln, NB: Buros Institute of Mental Measurements.

Schraw, G., & Dennison, R. S. (1994). Assessing metacognitive awareness. *Contemporary Educational Psychology, 19*, 460–475.

Schraw, G, & Impara, J. C. (Eds) (2000). *Issues in the measurement of metacognition* (pp. 297–321). Lincoln, NB: Buros Institute of Mental Measurements.

Tourangeau, R., Rips, L. J., & Rasinski, K. (2000). *The psychology of survey response*. Cambridge: Cambridge University Press.

Tversky, A., & Kahneman, D. (1974). Judgment under uncertainty: Heuristics and biases. *Science, 185*, 1124–1131.

van Meter, P., Yokoi, L., & Pressley, M. (1994). College students' theory of note-taking derived from their perceptions of note taking. *Journal of Educational Psychology, 86*, 323–338.

Webb, E. J., Campbell, D. T., Schwartz, R. D., & Sechrest, L. (1966). *Unobtrusive measures: Nonreactive research in the social sciences*. Chicago: Rand McNally.

Weinstein, C. E., Schulte, A. & Palmer, D. (1987). LASSI: Learning and study strategies inventory. Clearwater, FL: H & H Publishing.

Winne, P. H. (1982). Minimizing the black box problem to enhance the validity of theories about instructional effects. *Instructional Science, 11*, 13–28.

Winne, P. H. (1992). State-of-the-art instructional computing systems that afford instruction and bootstrap research. In: M. Jones & P. H. Winne (Eds), *Adaptive Learning Environments: Foundations and Frontiers* (pp. 349–380). Berlin: Springer-Verlag.

Winne, P. H. (1995). Inherent details in self-regulated learning. *Educational Psychologist, 30*, 173–187.

Winne, P. H. (1997). Experimenting to bootstrap self-regulated learning. *Journal of Educational Psychology, 89*, 397–410.

Winne, P. H. (2001). Self-regulated learning viewed from models of information processing. In: B. J. Zimmerman & D. H. Schunk (Eds), *Self-regulated Learning and Academic Achievement: Theory, Research, and Practice* (pp. 153–189). New York: Longman.

Winne, P. H., Gupta, L., & Nesbit, J. C. (1994). Exploring individual differences in studying strategies using graph theoretic statistics. *Alberta Journal of Educational Research, 40*, 177–193.

Winne, P. H., & Hadwin, A. F. (1998). Studying as self-regulated learning. In: D. J. Hacker, J. Dunlosky & A. C. Graesser (Eds), *Metacognition in Educational Theory and Practice* (pp. 277–304). Hillsdale, NJ: Erlbaum.

Winne, P. H., Hadwin, A. F., Nesbit, J. C., & Stockley, D. B. (2001). *Calibrating traces and self-reports about study tactics and predicting achievement from each*. Manuscript submitted for publication.

Winne, P. H., & Jamieson-Noel, D. L. (in press). Exploring learners' calibration of self-reports about study tactics and achievement. *Contemporary Educational Psychology.*

Winne, P. H., & Marx, R. W. (1989). A cognitive processing analysis of motivation within classroom tasks. In: C. Ames & R. Ames (Eds), *Research on Motivation in Education* (Vol. 3, pp. 223–257). Orlando, FL: Academic Press.

Winne, P. H., & Nesbit, J. C. (1995, April). *Graph theoretic techniques for examining patterns and strategies in learners' studying: An application of LogMill*. American Educational Research Association, San Francisco.

Winne, P. H., & Perry, N. E. (2000). Measuring self-regulated learning. In: M. Boekaerts, P. Pintrich & M. Zeidner (Eds), *Handbook of Self-regulation* (pp. 531–566). Orlando, FL: Academic Press.

Wittgenstein, L. (1968). *Philosophical investigations*. New York: Macmillan.

Wolters, C. A., & Pintrich, P. R. (1998). Contextual differences in student motivation and self-regulated learning in mathematics, English, and social studies classrooms. *Instructional Science, 26*, 27–47.

Wyatt, D., Pressley, M., El-Dinary, P. B., Stein, S., Evans, P., & Brown, R. (1993). Comprehension strategies, worth and credibility monitoring, and evaluations: Cold and hot cognition when experts read professional articles that are important to them. *Learning and Individual Differences, 5*, 49–72.

5. IN THEIR OWN WORDS: STUDENTS AND TEACHERS TALK ABOUT LEARNING AND SCHOOLING

Elisabeth Vialpando De Groot

In the last volume in this series, Jere Brophy (1999) examined the development, present concerns, and potential future considerations of research on motivation in education. He noted the significant progress psychological research has made in understanding human motivation and the benefits of such work for education. However, Brophy also pointed out that the questions that drive research on motivation in psychology are often different than those asked by educators, thus potentially limiting the applicability of research findings to educational concerns. He argued that research on motivation in education needs to focus on educational questions and more work is needed that investigates whether and how motivation principles derived from non-school-based psychological research operate in educational contexts. Further, he suggested that addressing the often more application-oriented educational questions regarding motivation may require the adoption of alternative methods and perspectives than those traditionally used in psychological research.

Brophy's comments regarding the nature of the questions we ask and the methods we use have particular relevance for the topic of this chapter, the use of interviewing to enhance our understanding of motivation and self-regulated learning. To date, self-report questionnaires have been primary vehicles for inquiring into issues of motivation and learning in the classroom (Brophy,

New Directions in Measures and Methods, Volume 12, pages 157–206.

ISBN: 0-7623-0819-2

1999; Winne & Perry, 2000). Research relying on self-report data has yielded important results about two general issues. First, in terms of students, studies have found that adaptive motivational beliefs such as high self-efficacy, task value, interest, and mastery goals foster student commitment and engagement in learning including more use of cognitive and self-regulating strategies (e.g. Nolen, 1988; Pajares, 1996; Pintrich & De Groot, 1990; Pintrich & Schunk, 1996; Wigfield, Eccles & Pintrich, 1996; Wolters, Yu & Pintrich, 1996). Second, in terms of the role of context, research has shown that factors such as perceived teacher support and goals for learning emphasized in the classroom/school are linked to critical outcomes such as perceptions of competence, task value, feelings of school belonging, social and academic goals, and academic performance (e.g. De Groot, 1997: Goodenow, 1993; Midgley, Feldlaufer & Eccles, 1989; Roeser, Midgley & Urdan, 1996; Wentzel, 1994). However, self-report questionnaires do not allow for an in-depth exploration of how students and teachers come to construct their own understandings within classrooms and schools or how contextual factors affect the development of individuals' motivational beliefs. I suggest that interviewing might be a more appropriate method to use for gaining a better understanding of these two issues regarding individuals' experiences and the meaning of these experiences for them, and for exploring the complex interrelations between individuals and contexts.

Through participation with colleagues in several research studies over the last few years, I have had the privilege of interviewing well over 200 students and teachers in a variety of different school settings. In this chapter, I will share students' and teachers' perceptions of their experiences of learning and schooling obtained by using three different interview approaches. Of particular interest was the role of interpersonal relationships (e.g. teacher support and caring), as well as school/classroom policies/practices and organizational features (e.g. goal structure, school structure, principal leadership) that can facilitate or hinder motivation and self-regulated learning. This work is informed by social cognitive models of self-regulated learning (e.g. Pintrich & De Groot, 1990) and motivation (e.g. Ames, 1992a, b; Anderman & Maehr, 1994; Eccles, 1983; Eccles & Midgley, 1989; Maehr & Midgley, 1996), and work from a sociological perspective on school organization and structure, and social capital (e.g. Bryk, Lee & Holland, 1993; Bryk, Lee & Smith, 1990; Coleman, 1988; Lee, Bryk & Smith, 1993). While the purposes for conducting the individual research studies varied widely, concerns for understanding informants' experiences, what they considered important, and how they made connections between individual and contextual factors were common to all endeavors.

For this chapter, I have selected examples I believe illustrate the three different interview approaches and what can be learned from them. In each of the first three sections, brief descriptions of studies and interview strategies are provided, followed by samples of data generated. I conclude with comments regarding some of the advantages and challenges I found when utilizing each approach, as well as speculations about future directions in research on motivation and self-regulated learning in educational contexts where interviewing might be a valuable approach to inquiry.

STUDENTS TALK ABOUT THEIR EXPERIENCES OF SCHOOLING AND LEARNING IN UNSTRUCTURED INDIVIDUAL INTERVIEWS

Study 1: The Experience of Dropping out of High School (De Groot)

The purpose of this study was to gain a better understanding of dropping out of high school among White, middle-class, academically capable young people. Individual unstructured interviews were conducted with four adolescents, two males and two females. When interviewed, informants were attending an alternative high school program especially for former dropouts.

I began each interview by asking my informants to "Tell me about your experience of dropping out of high school." Adolescents were invited to tell their own stories in their own way rather than structuring the interviews based upon the extant literature. What was gained was not only an understanding of the reasons and influences involved in leaving school but also which experiences were most salient and why, and how these adolescents interpreted their experiences and connected these over time. A richer, more coherent picture of their schooling experiences emerged. Individual profiles were assembled from students' own descriptions of themselves and their experiences. Interview transcripts were also scrutinized for emerging patterns and themes.

As these students recounted salient experiences in their lives, their construction of "school" emerged. School appeared to be synonymous with the interpersonal interactions that occurred there. Indeed, one could say that these students saw school as a social-relational context, rather than an academic context. Interpersonal relationships are what gave school meaning and were of paramount importance. The quality of these relationships seemed to profoundly influence their perceptions of themselves, their academic engagement and performance, their beliefs about others, and their beliefs about the institution. The following are examples of what was learned:

Interactions With Teachers

Each student, when recounting their previous experiences in mainstream high schools, talked about teachers as having control over their academic success or failure. Although these students believed they had the ability to master the academic content, they attributed their failure to do so to lack of acceptance by teachers and lack of teacher care. If teachers didn't like someone, then they wouldn't give them the help they needed to understand the content, therefore impeding continued progress. They also believed that teacher acceptance dictated the actual grades they received in their classes. Therefore, academic outcomes had more to do with whether they could gain social acceptance from their teachers, something they came to believe they could not do, than their actual performance. Further, these students saw teacher acceptance linked to and reflective of the same rigid categorization "system" (status hierarchy) that defined relations between students. Therefore, academic outcomes had more to do with teachers' perceptions of them as a "certain type of person" rather than on their academic skills. This was noted again and again in their statements:

> . . . a lot of us I would say have been treated badly by teachers in regular high school because of the fact that we were different. A lot of the teachers in high school are there for the summertime vacations and they really don't care about the students and they don't . . . they're like my father. If they don't like somebody then they're not going to give them a good grade and they're not going to work with them, and make them feel wanted . . . it's that simple.

> She categorized me as someone who would be a loudmouth and you know somebody who smoked pot and smoked cigarettes. Which I did but that had nothing to do with gym class you know. She kept giving me E's.

> It's just that they don't help you and, you know, you have a question and they don't help.

> I liked being in high school. It's just that the teachers . . . you ask the teacher 'What's this mean?' and she goes, 'Go sit down. You're just trying to waste time.' They won't help. Probably over half of them, they didn't, they won't help you.

This belief that the type of person one is dictates one's academic success can be extremely debilitating. First, these students perceived themselves to have no control over their achievement because their progress depended on teacher helping and caring. Since they believed there was nothing they could do to get the teacher to like them, their persistence at classroom tasks declined, as did their sense of efficacy. Some began showing their frustration by failing to complete homework assignments, skipping class, talking back to the teacher, and engaging in minor disruptive behavior or daydreaming while in the classroom. Further, if one's academic progress was dictated by the relationship one had with the teacher, then one would focus on that relationship, rather than on the actual academic tasks and building the academic skills necessary to improve academic performance. This could lead to a cycle where the longer one stayed in school the further behind one would fall until actual academic failure would be the end result. This seemed to be the case for three of the four students.

Second, these students were trying to figure out who they were, struggling to develop their own identities. They were trying to find out how they were distinct from others, as well as how they were like others in their social milieu. Therefore, to be categorized as a certain type of person regardless of what they actually did or didn't do just added to their confusion. The feedback they received from teachers seemed to indicate that their distinctiveness lay in their less likable qualities. They appeared to form their ideas about themselves as students through these interactions with teachers, and then seemed to act in accordance with what they thought were teachers' expectations of them. This appeared to lead to increased self-doubt and lower self-esteem.

> (on the effect of others' expectations on self) "Ya, if it's positive, I'm positive. If it's negative, I'm negative. What the hell, everybody knows more than I do, right? So let them . . . or should I say, everyone knows more about me than I do so let's hear what they have to say and prove them right. Keep them happy.

Perceptions of the Institution

My four informants were unanimous in their denunciation of school as an unfair institution. They noted a severe discrepancy between stated school policies and actual practice. Although they believed some policies, especially those pertaining to entry and exiting school grounds, to be silly, they also believed that school rules and policies were necessary. What led to their beliefs about unfairness was what they perceived as inconsistent enforcement, especially concerning the discipline and attendance policies. As was noted previously, these adolescents believed that students received differential treatment depending on their status in the school hierarchy.

> Ya, okay, like my friend said, this guy Vaughn. If somebody walks down the hall all dressed up, nice clothes, dress pants on, dress shoes, and somebody walks down the hall dressed in jeans and a tee shirt and a leather jacket, the person with the leather jackets is gonna get stopped and asked for a pass, not the person dressed up and looks like a preppy. They don't bother them; they just let them walk right by. They do that all the time.
>
> Like last year, this guy got busted with heroin. They didn't call the cops and they only gave him five days suspension instead of 15 days suspension and calling the police like they would've with somebody who was a burnout or anything.

From these students' descriptions it seemed as if two separate "schools" existed within the confines of the same building. The "school" they experienced appeared to be more oriented toward control of student behavior and less focused on academics. Infractions of rules led to frequent detentions and suspension. Students reported they were given no opportunity for in-put or questioning of rules. Participation in school extra-curricular activities was neither expected nor encouraged (Students had to have a "C" or better in all of their classes in order to be eligible to participate in extra-curricular activities).

> I told you. It was like a jail over there. I felt like a dummy, literally. Doing what I was told and, you know, following the rules.

> I asked her if I could go to the bathroom and she says, 'cause I had to go, she says 'No you can't go to the bathroom'. I went to the principal. I says, 'When someone tells you you can't go to the bathroom that's (expletive), 'cause, you know, that's not right. And he just didn't do anything about it, he just sent me back to class.

This stood in sharp contrast to their descriptions of the other "school." From their vantage point, students attending this "school" appeared to be allowed greater freedom to move around the building at will, to question school policies and to pursue personal interests. Rules appeared to be more flexible and enforcement more corrective than punitive. Academics and participation in school activities were emphasized, recognized and rewarded. (Interestingly, differential treatment of students and enforcement of rules depending on status was noted in interviews with honors and general track students (Damico & Roth, 1993) and with high and lower achieving students in Study 3 in this chapter.)

One issue for these students was equity. They believed that all people should be treated the same when it came to rules, especially by the teachers and administrators in school. The differential treatment they believe they received brought about feelings of anger, frustration and powerlessness.

The second issue was captured by statements dealing with being "treated as an adult." These students believed they had few choices in this rule governed environment and were not respected by the adults. This was especially difficult because they were assuming adult roles and responsibilities outside the school setting.

> You should be treated more like an adult, given choices and responsibilities to your adult level. (*choices important?*) Uh huh. Knowing that you have them and knowing that you're able to use your own judgment, looking at the good and bad and making your own choice instead of having someone tell you what to do and having to do it.

> So they're probably gonna start putting bars on the windows over there or something, who knows . . .

These are only two examples of what was learned through interviews regarding dropping out. Students also talked extensively about their relationships with peers, their own attitudes and behaviors (e.g. not caring about school, "partying" that led to missing school), and out-of-school influences (e.g. family problems) that impacted in-school functioning.

This study was an exploratory investigation into dropping out among White, middle-class, academically capable adolescents. I included the study in this chapter because of what was learned through in-depth, unstructured interviews regarding the meaning of school for these students. Their whole experience of school seemed to be embedded in their social relations with others. For example, their experiences with teachers affected their control beliefs, self-perceptions, persistence at classroom tasks, attitudes toward school and their behavior. This suggests that academic motivation and cognition cannot be considered in isolation from these social dynamics. Additionally, although questionnaires have been used productively to examine the relations between individuals' perceptions of interpersonal relationships and their motivation and cognition, and even the importance of interpersonal relationships to them, they cannot get at the meaning people make of their experiences with others that can help us understand their behavior.

Study 2: Quantitative and Qualitative Approaches to the Study of Motivation and Self-regulated Learning Among Early Adolescents (Pintrich & De Groot)

The purposes of this study were: (1) to explore students' motivational beliefs and self-regulated learning; and (2) to examine intra-individual differences in beliefs and learning across different subject domains by integrating data obtained using the MSLQ (Motivated Strategies for Learning Questionnaire, see Pintrich & De Groot, 1990), a self-report instrument, with qualitative data gathered through interviews. Sixteen seventh grade students were interviewed individually using an unstructured, in-depth interview approach. Two experienced interviewers were used. Practice interviews were conducted and interviewers worked together for many hours developing their interviewing skills. Each interviewer began by asking the informant to "tell me how you go about learning things for school." The students set the pace and direction of each interview with the interviewer asking clarification questions and reflecting back what was heard, attempting to see through the students' eyes how they experienced the phenomena of school learning. The interview data provided an opportunity to "hear" students as they generated rich descriptions about their own learning processes. Some of the findings regarding the first purpose of the study are presented below.

An analysis of the qualitative data about students' experience of learning suggested that the three motivational (self-efficacy, intrinsic value, and test anxiety) and two cognitive (cognitive strategy use and self-regulation) components tapped in the MSLQ also emerged as students talked about their own learning. However, the relations between these five components were somewhat different because of differences in the meanings students attached to these cognitive and motivational constructs.

From students' statements, learning takes place over time and has four general components: memory, strategies for information acquisition and demonstration, comprehension monitoring, and specific goals for learning. Each is necessary for learning but the process cannot be defined by any single component.

> Learning is acquiring new skills and acquiring new knowledge, something that you haven't already known. I know (when I've learned something) when I can remember most everything from what people are talking about and I know when I can think about it and tell myself everything about what I am supposed to know. I know when I know it when I can say to somebody, for instance, give them a complete answer about everything that's included in the chapter.

Students, when asked to elaborate, made particular reference to the distinction between learning and memorization. This distinction seems to be an important assumption for students that can lead to differential use of strategies for information acquisition and different goals for their learning.

> See, if I memorize it for the test or the quiz then I forget it later . . . if you learn it, it's pretty close to remembering it years later and putting that, like applying it to something else. But if you just memorize it you might remember some of the things but that's it. Memorizing is more like to get the grades and stuff.

> If it makes sense to you like if you're learning a definition and you say whatever the word is and it's right but you still don't understand it, you still don't, you still wouldn't be able to use it in a sentence then you know you don't understand it. You memorized it but you don't understand it. You didn't learn it. Just because you memorize doesn't mean you understand. And learning is when you understand *and* memorize.

Memorization operated as a mechanism or facilitator in the service of the learning process, linked more strongly to a performance goal such as passing the test or getting the grade than a mastery goal such as understanding the subject matter. (Although this was true for the majority of the students interviewed, three students made no distinction between memorization and learning. Two students could not articulate how they learned).

The facilitator function of memorization was referred to again when students were probed about the information acquisition component. When asked what happens to information so that it could be used in the learning process, students said the following:

> When your brain gets more information about something, you remember it sometimes until just that unit is over, and then sometimes, if it's really interesting, for a long, long time. I

> remember it more if I have to do it over and over. It just sticks in my mind 'cause I might have to do it again in something.
>
> Learning you can't forget as easy as you can memorizing. Once you learn something it kind of sticks in the back of your head so if you want to go back to it like if you read a book and if you're thinking about it, you'll remember it.

Students' descriptions seemed to call forth the image of the mind as "Velcro" with certain information sticking, to be translated into understanding and learning, and other information not adhering. Students also described a variety of learning strategies they used that helped them retain and understand information such as paraphrasing, mnemonic strategies, self-testing and self-questioning, note taking, outlining, and asking others for help. Interestingly, these strategies were the same ones asked about in the quantitative data, providing some face validity to the questionnaire we developed, at least in terms of students' views of learning.

> I talk into a tape recorder, the question, and then like eat dinner or something and then come back to it and play the tape and answer the questions. And at the end of what I recorded I have all the answers. I just keep playing it . . . I can just ask myself questions and that's how I understand it.
>
> You have to take the time to sit down to understand what they're trying to say . . . if I can write it down into a sentence and see if I can figure the sentence out (then it's in there).
>
> I just like write it down and then like test myself. Sometimes my mom will give me a question and I'll write it (the answer) to see if I understand it.
>
> I usually try to think up like a story or something. Like I had to do a test today on South America and I kept forgetting Argentina so I thought of something like 'are Jenny and Tina home'? You know, you think of something weird like that and you go over and over it.

Most students seemed to be able to talk easily about what learning strategies they used. There was variability among students, however, with regard to the actual number of different strategies each had at their disposal to employ. It appeared that students who described themselves as better students had a greater number of strategies to choose from and used these with discretion. Those who described themselves as less effective students relied primarily on rehearsal strategies to retain and acquire information.

From their descriptions, most students were aware that the process of learning and understanding involved both activities that observers would be able to recognize as taking place and internal activities known only to the learner. Thinking about their own thinking (metacognition) seemed to be crucial in helping them make decisions about whether they were actually comprehending information.

> Sometimes you just have to sit there and try to brainstorm through what to do and stuff . . . I usually just concentrate on it and I don't talk much . . . the whole time I try to think of stuff and keep working on and on.

> Like when the teacher asks questions and you think to yourself if you remember the answer to that you know it's in there (in your head).

Descriptions of the learning process for the students were not confined to purely cognitive or metacognitive strategies, however. Motivation in terms of goals for learning was also a component. Having goals was mentioned again and again. In general, there seemed to be agreement that the goal of understanding the material (a mastery goal) was important and partially defined learning. However, students also thought getting good grades (a performance goal) played a role in learning as a kind of feedback or regulatory mechanism. For example, getting a good grade on a test in some cases was a way to validate whether the student really understood the material or not. Additionally, the knowledge that what they were studying was important to learn for future success or to meet future goals seemed to serve a self-regulatory function in terms of effort management. Here we see the close relationships between students' goals and their cognition, paralleling the strong correlations found in the quantitative data for intrinsic value, cognitive strategy use, and self-regulation (see Pintrich & De Groot, 1990).

> Some people don't care if they learn or not, so maybe they don't have a motive to learn. I do because I want to get good grades and if I get good grades I want to go to U. of M. That's my motive for learning. The more I learn then the more knowledgeable I'll be and I'll get better grades. And the better grades I get, I can get into a better college and I want to go to U. of M.

> I (try to) understand what we're learning, what we're talking about. I know I'm going to use it. I know I'm not going to get annoyed that I used to like English and it just doesn't help me now. I mean, I know I'm, whatever I'm going to have to do, I'm going to have to spell words right. I mean spell something right on a job application or something.

This, however, was not the entire story for these students. There were other factors that students said influenced their learning, but were not essential or necessary components for learning; they either helped or hindered the process. First was intrinsic interest in the material. If material was intrinsically interesting, the interest helped them control their attention and sustain their effort even if the material was difficult.

> I guess like when it's interesting you wanna sort of learn a little bit more . . . it's easier for me to learn if I'm interested in it usually. Well, it's like, if the subject's interesting it's something that I want to know about. Then if they start going into something that's part of it but it's not the same thing, it's, so it gets boring because I don't really want to learn about it. It's hard for me to, um, keep it in there (in her head) if I'm not interested in it.

> In Art, like I really like it and am interested in it so I just try to do better and whenever she shows me stuff I try to improve all my stuff.

> It's easier to learn if it's more interesting. It's easier learning it – starting it and studying it or memorizing it. Your mind is thinking about that subject.

When something was perceived as "boring", students had a much harder time regulating their own learning.

> Your mind wanders off and you have to study it more . . . your mind's not paying attention or you just don't pay attention.
>
> I usually just sort of sit there. Most of the time I try to listen but it's too boring. It just, well sometimes I try to listen and then I start doodling or something. You know, just look around the room.
>
> After a while you just get too bored and though you're reading over the words you're just not learning anything.

Of particular note, especially with regard to distinctions between what was learned through the questionnaire and interviews, the terms "interesting" and "boring" seemed to take on different meanings depending upon whether students defined themselves as being better or poorer students. For better students, interesting meant the subject presented a challenge or they themselves wanted to learn more about it and boring appeared to mean the material or subject was uninteresting or the task was too easily accomplished. In addition, these students were able to design strategies to regulate their attention or keep their cognition "on-task" as they coped with an easy/boring task.

> Well, I enjoy geography and Social Studies. I wanted to test my knowledge.
>
> Science, but it seems almost too easy. It starts getting boring . . . but if you're getting everything right and just getting a very good average, maybe once in awhile I'll lay my head down because I don't really need to hear it because I already know it.
>
> Well, I try to make it more interesting in some way or another. Thinking about what he said, you'd be replacing some of the vocabulary with it or something. It is something to do.

For poorer students, boring or the state of being bored seemed to mean that the material was too difficult to grasp or required too much time to understand.

> Yeah, um, I, well, it's Geography-World Culture and Geography. It's, I don't really do so good. I have a B- now, but I really have to work at it real hard, cause, it's really difficult for me . . . I guess cause she makes us read a lot of the information, I just think it is really boring.
>
> I look at my grades and my feelings. They were really bad, D's and E's. I noticed that when I studied, I might be studying for like 5 minutes and I'd get really bored. Then, I'd get upset and go watch TV, or talk, or something.

The second set of factors that played a role were those associated with the learning environment. Again, however, there appeared to be variability among students. Poorer or less effective students' learning seemed to be much more susceptible to or under the control of environmental influences such as the teacher's behavior, whether they liked the teacher, others' behavior in the classroom, and the nature of the classroom tasks.

> (how much you get out of class) Yeah, I think it depends, like a lot of it is if you like the teacher or not . . . 'cause in 4th grade, like, I had a teacher who me and her just didn't get along. And then it reflected in my grades and then, you know, like before I had done really good in reading 'cause that's one of my best subjects and that year it just dropped. So I think it has a lot to do with if you like the teacher or not. 'Cause like, I might be so mad at the teacher I won't even listen.
>
> . . . like maybe for a grade you'll blame her for it even though you got it (the grade), even though it was on you you'll blame her for marking it like that. Instead of you, you blame the teacher. A lot of times you feel like she's the one who marked it like that. She could have given you a break and everything or it was her fault she didn't teach it well enough.
>
> . . . like when she gives us something we don't even know. She'll just go 'do this page'. We say 'we don't know how to do it', and she'll say, 'I don't care, still do it. I'll do it and I'll do it all wrong too! If I get it wrong I get it wrong. She should have taught it. She was just trying to be mean and so she goes 'Do this page'. So everyone goes, 'well I'm not doing it'. Then, she'll, she it, I hate her!
>
> Cause you might be laughing about something and you'll totally miss what the teacher just said or you might be paying attention to someone else getting in trouble and you'll miss what you're supposed to be doing.
>
> I was just laughing 'cause this boy was trying to make everyone laugh. Everyone was laughing and she goes, "T. we don't need this. You go out in the hall." She acts like no one else talks and mess, act like I always talk. (That's how I miss stuff).
>
> Like in Science – dissection. Me and my partner like we did really good on that 'cause it's like kind of fun, it was something different, it just wasn't lectures and everything. It was something different to do . . . you could learn more, you could actually participate in it. I think it helps to learn when you participate in it. Like if it's just copying down notes that gets real boring sometimes.

Average students did seem to be sensitive to some task demands and try to adapt their learning accordingly. They also seemed to be somewhat more susceptible to outside influences in comparison to the better students.

> Well, I'll read the questions before I read the story. I mean, that one thing, you know, and then I'll find out what the question is and then I'll read it and then if I come across the thing that sounds like the answer then I'll write it down.
>
> I'd like the answers to be right there (in the book).
>
> Well, I only study for the tests.
>
> If there's not going to be a test, just whatever they say to do. Like if they say read and take notes, I'll do that. If it just says read it or it says learn something, I'll do that.
>
> Liking class has a lot to do with liking the teacher. I'll still study for it and stuff, you know, to get a good grade but it could be harder.
>
> Well it also depends on the teacher. If the teacher's nicer or boring or harder. If they just run off facts and don't give examples, you know, they're not really interesting. It's harder to learn.

Better students seemed to acknowledge that these were factors that could influence learning. To what extent, however, was under their control. They seemed to be much more successful at self-regulation. For example, because they were concerned with task demands, they were more likely to spend more time and effort on school tasks and persist in the face of difficulty than other students were.

> Mentally you have to work harder at being able to work at it. I have to, um, get myself to concentrate before 'cause otherwise I don't remember it and it becomes harder . . . I just try to get myself to focus in on what I'm doing and think about it as I'm reading. That's for everything because if I don't concentrate and I don't know a fair amount already and then I go to study for a test it takes a lot.
>
> You do extra work just to have it. You can also do them (extra credit) just for fun. That's what I usually do to keep my A+ average.
>
> If I don't understand it I'll spend a lot of my time on it.
>
> I read over my notes and I read over the material in the textbook and I make sure I know it. Sometimes I have my parents ask me questions about it. That's pretty much how I study . . . I'm pretty known for taking a lot of notes. The more I know the easier it is, like, in an essay question to answer the question . . . I keep going over everything and think about what the teacher said in class. Then I think about what it said in the textbook, and with all that combined . . . (You do that for every subject?) For every subject.

Taken together, findings from both qualitative and quantitative perspectives suggest that motivational beliefs and cognitive and self-regulatory strategies are linked in important ways to one another in the classroom context. In addition, the interview data suggest that students may have both intrinsic, mastery goals as well as performance goals. Specifically, these data suggest that performance goals can lead students to be more aware of their own strengths and weaknesses and facilitate self-regulation of learning.

What was especially interesting was that prior to any comparison between student responses to the questionnaire and the quantitative data with regard to individual and contextual factors and achievement, it was possible to hear differences in the interviews between better, average and less effective students from their reflections on how they experienced their own learning. These differences were evident in three ways: how they spoke about what learning strategies or resources they used to study, their skill in regulating their effort and persistence, and how factors in their learning environment affected their own learning processes. These differences were borne out in the quantitative data. Students who appeared to be better, average, and less effective learners in the qualitative data did differ in actual achievement in terms of grades (see Pintrich & De Groot, 1990). Thus, although only 16 students were interviewed, they can be seen as being representative of the different levels of students that we found in the quantitative data. Here is a case where interviews not only added depth and richness to the quantitative data but also provided insights into how students made connections between motivational and cognitive constructs important to their learning, and how contextual factors (e.g. teacher and peer behavior) not tapped by the questionnaire could influence their learning.

STUDENTS TALK ABOUT THEIR EXPERIENCES IN A MIDDLE LEVEL SCHOOL THAT HAD ALTERED ITS STRUCTURE IN A SERIES OF STRUCTURED INDIVIDUAL INTERVIEWS

Study 3: Perceptions of the School Environment and Adaptive Functioning Among Early Adolescents (De Groot, Fravil & Pintrich)

A four-year school/university collaborative study of the influence of the school environment on early adolescents was initiated because school staff was interested in monitoring student outcomes as school reform initiatives were implemented. In response to staff concerns over the results of a school-wide (grades 7–9) student survey and recommendations from the school improvement team, the school restructured its seventh and eighth grades. The seventh grade moved to a "team" or "house" concept. Two teams of approximately 150 students and five teachers remained together for the entire year. Students traveled with the same 30 students throughout the school day in their academic classes and gym. Students were tracked based upon math ability into two groups, yielding a total of four classes of high achievers, and six classes of average and lower ability including special education students per team. An advisory period was built into the school day. Teachers were allocated an extra planning period to meet in teacher teams.

The major goals of the reform were: to ease the transition into junior high school; to promote a sense of community and help build positive relationships and reduce conflicts between students and between students and staff; to promote students' investment in education; to increase students knowledge of and use of effective learning strategies to enable them to be more effective learners; and, to increase students' self-esteem. In addition to these general goals, the seventh grade structural change was accompanied by several changes in educational practice: (1) the adoption of a common philosophy among seventh grade teachers regarding what constituted appropriate educational experiences for early adolescents including an emphasis on collaborative learning, academic skill building, and the design of thematic units and projects to foster an understanding of the interconnectedness of disciplinary knowledge; (2) the adoption and uniform implementation of a common approach to discipline across seventh grade; (3) the designation of each teacher as an advisor for one group of students for the year which involved monitoring student attendance and academic progress, as well as serving as a resource for students to go to for help with academic and other problems; and, (4) the adoption of a seventh grade motto that stressed responsibility, reliability and mutual respect (the three R's) between teachers and students to encourage better teacher/student and student/student relations.

As the first group of seventh graders moved to the eighth grade, an alternate, loosely coupled configuration of the team concept was adopted. Whereas seventh grade was viewed as a transition into junior high school, eighth grade was seen as preparatory for high school. Even though students did not leave the school building for ninth grade, they did begin earning credits toward graduation. Changes in eighth grade were focused more on curriculum than creating a fundamentally different environment for students. Core academic teachers were divided into three teams and worked together on curriculum planning. However, teachers functioned more autonomously than did seventh grade teachers and there was no coordinated approach in dealing with students either academically or in terms of discipline. In addition, the students were no longer assigned to specific teams. Students traveled in groups of twelve to maximize their exposure to different peers and were detracked for all subjects except math. There was no advisory period built into the day.

Students in the first class to enter the restructured school were followed from seventh grade entry through the first semester of ninth grade. Four self-report questionnaires tapping the areas of interest to school and research staff were administered in English and Math classes over two days during the first semester and toward the end of the second semester of both seventh and eighth grade, and during the first semester of ninth grade. Data from classroom observations, informal discussions with teachers, and teachers' written reflections were collected. In addition, interviews were conducted with 38 students. In late October, each team of seventh grade teachers nominated 6 to 8 students who they believed fell into the following categories: (1) high achiever, positive relationships with peers; (2) high achiever, little or negative relationships with peers; (3) average achiever, positive relationships with peers; (4) average achiever, little or negative relationships with peers; (5) low achievers, positive relationships with peers; and (6) low achievers, little or negative relationships with peers. Random selection yielded 19 students per team. Students were interviewed individually in November, March and June of their seventh grade year, in November and June of eighth grade, and again during the Fall of their ninth grade year. For the purposes of this study, only seventh and eighth grade interview were used. Because of attrition, 35 students completed all interviews over the first two years.

Interview protocols were developed and tailored for administration during the seventh and eighth grade years. Questions were developed that reflected staff interests including students' understanding of and attitudes toward reform measures (e.g. teaming, advisory) and reform values (e.g. respect for self and others, responsible and reliable behaviors, effort and progress in schoolwork), as well as interests of the research team pertinent to the goals of the study. The initial interview protocol contained 25 predominantly open-ended questions regarding the seventh grade program, policies and classroom practices, teacher behavior, student self-perceptions and behavior, and perceptions of peers. In later versions, more questions about specific instructional practices, help seeking, peer relationships, student behavior, and school safety were added. Students also were asked at the end of 7th grade and during the first semester 8th grade what they thought were the benefits or detriments of the team concept. Initially, two experienced interviewers conducted all interviews. However, two additional interviewers with little experience were added during the second year. Each interview began with asking the student to "Tell me about the seventh grade (or eighth grade)", followed by "How is it different from 6th grade (or the beginning of the year)?" and "What did you expect the 7th grade (the 8th grade) to be like?." Other questions included:

How would you describe the program in 7th grade?
Describe your teachers.
What are the students like in your team?
How do students treat one another in your team?
How would you describe a "good" student? "bad" student? "average" student?
How would you describe yourself to others?
How have others described you?

Examples of questions added after the first interview:

How do you feel about the team program now?
Is there anything different about the team program now versus the beginning of the school year?
What do your parents think of the team program?
Do you think there are more discipline problems now versus the beginning of the year?
I'd like you to think of a time when you are working on your math problems and you're having some difficulty. Sometimes you might ask for help and other

times you might not. What are some reasons you might not ask for help? What are some reasons you would ask for help?
Do you think teachers really listen to you?
Do students compete against each other for grades in your classes?
What is the most important thing about school to you?

Because of the longitudinal nature of the study, it was possible to examine students' perceptions of the school environment and their own functioning over time. Results from the self-report questionnaire data suggested that students did change their perceptions of the school environment and of themselves over the two years. Overall, these changes were in a less favorable direction. In terms of the school environment, students in general viewed teachers as less supportive and caring and thought more stress was placed on relative ability and competition and less on task mastery, personal progress, and cooperation among students over time. Within this general trend, steeper declines in task focus and teacher support occurred during eighth grade than during seventh grade. Although the change in ability focus overall from the beginning of seventh grade to the end of eighth grade reflected an increase, the greatest significant increase came between the beginning and ending of eighth grade. While there are a number of possible explanations for such negative changes in perceptions of the school environment, student interviews provided not only corroboration for the quantitative data but also some additional insights into students' experiences over time.

At the beginning of seventh grade, students reported feeling they were adjusting to their new environment. They were still unsure about what to expect academically because most of the material covered to this point had been review. However, some stated they expected the work to get harder as the year progressed. Students in general expressed positive feelings about school, their teachers and peers. While few could describe the team program or its goals in any detail, some did recognize they traveled with the same group of students in their academic classes, that teachers worked together and talked with one another about students, that there was a uniform discipline policy and that the motto, the three "Rs" (respectful, responsible, reliable), was stressed.

> (the program) It's not trying to make you fail, it's just trying to help you succeed. In your grades and stuff. Like if you get a bad grade on a test, they ain't gonna make you fail. They let you take it over to get a better grade and succeed in grades.

> (about teams) I don't know. I just heard some of the teachers talking about how it, how they say it's supposed to help because they all get together and talk about the same problems that one person or student has and then they just talk about the whole thing.

> (about teachers) I like them all pretty good. Mr. S., he gives us a lot of work. But the other thing is he gives us plenty of time to do it. And I like all my teachers pretty good.

(about teachers) Mr. S., he's pretty funny. Mr. K., he's good, magic tricks and stuff. Mrs. S.'s a good math teacher. My fourth hour, I had to go to a study skills class because my grades went down a little bit too much. Then my fifth, Mr. B., he's a good teacher. Mrs. M., she's good. (what makes them good?) You get to work with them. They, like, you know, some teachers you just don't like and some teachers you just like because you get along so well. (these teachers?) They're kind. They don't yell at you or anything. Because some teachers, if you kinda go the other way and you say "white", they'll say "black" and they kinda get really mad.

(about peers in team) I like it. It's really neat. You get, like, comfortable. They're not, like, always putting you down and stuff. (behave well toward one another?) Ya.

(about peers in team) They're all good friends. Except a couple of them . . . . I mean, I knew, the first day I was kind of scared about going into a first, new class. But the second or third day, I mean I knew them just as well as I knew my other class (6th grade).

(about encouragement) Well, they're not really encouragements, they're just like, they're just telling you "come on, you'd better do your homework" stuff like that. "You gotta keep up", stuff like that. They really don't tell you much.

(about encouragements) I don't know, they're always saying I *can* do it. I just don't wanna do it. They say I rush through all my work and – they always try to help.

By seventh grade mid-year, all students were able to identify the team program and describe individual components such as the advisory period, the use of collaborative learning projects and students moving together as measures adopted to support students academically and socially in the junior high environment. Students also recognized that the teachers worked together on both curriculum and student advising. They talked of the discipline code, the three "Rs", and were able to list benefits of the program for themselves.

In general, students viewed the team program as supportive and most felt they were doing better in school because of the amount of support they received from teachers and peers. In terms of policies and instructional practices, students gave several reasons for the use of collaborative learning in the classroom and the discipline code. This may be due to the fact that teachers explicitly discussed reasons for both with students on a regular basis. In the interviews, many students commented on the importance of being able to work cooperatively in the classroom as preparation for their future work lives. Other students noted the help peers can provide in understanding concepts and completing difficult assignments. Indeed, it appeared that students wanted to be able to engage in more group work in all subject areas. As far as the discipline code was concerned, students saw it as fair and felt it was applied fairly to all students. However, they did state that some teachers were more likely to give detentions than others were.

Toward the end of seventh grade, student responses became more variable. When asked about differences between the beginning and ending of the school year, some students felt there were few differences. However, many felt things had changed:

> The teachers are, like, they try to get more out of you to get it right and stuff.

> It's a lot harder now than at the beginning of the year because they wanted to get you off to a good start. And the more harder the work gets, the more bad grades I get – because it teaches me more. I think I'm getting more out of it now.

> Teachers have gotten a lot stricter .... When we came from 6th grade, they just wanted to start us off on a slow process. But now we're getting to really, to a curriculum that's really more fast-paced. But we're used to it. It's getting harder but we're used to it.

> I think I'm learning more now because I'm understanding the teachers more and getting to know their policy and how they teach and stuff.

> I think we're learning a lot more now because we're trying to pack it in, finish the books before the semester. Like, I'll use Ms. P. as an example because she's one of my favorite teachers, but Mr. G.'s is my favorite class. Um, like she, we're learning like all of Asia, we've learned it like in the last three weeks. Like all of Asia! It's kinda hard on the students but as long as she explains it fairly well and we take it home and we read the chapters, like instead of reading in class we mostly read it at home, so we have more time to work in class.

Interestingly, many students felt they were learning more at the end of the year than earlier. However, it appeared that what some students meant was that *more material was being presented to them to learn*, not that they were actually mastering the content. In addition, many students felt teachers were more demanding. Although effort was still stressed, the emphasis seemed to have shifted from making progress to "getting it right". Differential treatment of high and lower achieving students was becoming more noticeable. High achieving students reported they received more opportunities for interactions with teachers, group work, and special projects. Some low achieving students felt they were not treated as well as high achieving students by teachers and some of their peers. At this time, all students recognized they were grouped by ability within the team. Further, students seemed to be slightly more negative towards school, but were looking forward to the eighth grade.

Students also commented extensively about the assignment notebooks, something they had only talked about in passing during the previous interview. To assist students in developing appropriate study strategies and monitoring their own progress and behavior, each student was given an assignment planner at the beginning of the year. As two students described it:

> We have to, like, write down what we did in that class and like on that date. We wrote like what we did and what we have to finish .... They're good. They helped me out. Like, I would look back like after 7th hour and see like what homework I have and like take what I had to do (home with me). I'd probably still be organized, but not as much as I am. (What do parents think?) They like them because they know what I'm doing.

> I like it a little, but it just bugs me a little because you forget it sometimes. But I like it because you look back and you go "Oh no, I forgot the questions" and you can do it again. If you left out your class and you look back and "Let's see if I got any homework" and you could take it home. Instead of thinking in your head "Let's see, did I forget anything?" and then you forget and you get an E on that thing.

Students were required to have the assignment notebooks signed by parents after every week. On Mondays, teachers checked to make sure parents had signed the books and students had filled the information in properly. As the quotes above suggest, some students, especially average achievers, believed the planners helped them to monitor and regulate their own behavior. However, high achievers had more negative reactions. They seemed to believe they were self-regulating already and did not need teachers to monitor their behavior.

In terms of the team program, all students listed a number of benefits. Average and lower achieving students were particularly complimentary, whereas most of the high achieving students felt they would not have needed the team structure to assist them in the transition because they were sufficiently mature, organized and academically capable to adapt well on their own. The majority of the students felt the team program was beneficial to incoming seventh graders and wanted to see it continued for this group. The program allowed students to adjust more easily to a bigger school with many more people and a number of different teachers. Many felt that having teachers who talked with one another about students made absences and difficulties easier to manage. However, only about 25% wanted the teams continued into eighth grade. The main reason for discontinuation was social – they wanted to meet more students. Starting at mid-year, students had begun expressing dissatisfaction with traveling with the same 30 students throughout the academic portion of the day and this trend continued to escalate as the year drew to a close. In addition, although students still saw the discipline policies as fair, some students stated that punishment for infractions was more severe for low achieving than high achieving students over time. They also said they thought students were getting in trouble more now than at the beginning of the year and teachers were giving more detentions overall. It appears, then, that the increased negativity toward school was due not only to end of year pressures and differential treatment of high and lower achieving students, but also to the change in discipline and the desire to connect with a greater number of peers.

During the first interviews in the eighth grade, students did not recognize that even a modified team structure existed (there were three teacher teams for the eighth grade). Although they thought the teachers were supposed to be working together, they saw no evidence that this was happening. More students saw the benefits of the team concept and the accompanying instructional practices now.

In particular, they missed how the teachers worked together in providing support for students and in coordinating instruction and homework demands. They spoke critically of the lack of a consistent discipline policy and the variability among teachers in terms of grading practices. They also said that teachers called attention to grades and treated those students who got good grades better than those who did not perform as well. They also felt a lack of closeness to teachers and reported they did not talk much to their teachers about school or other issues. Students were able to see how small measures such as the 7th grade motto (the three "Rs") made a difference in the school/classroom environment and in student motivation. On the whole, students were more critical of their teachers and the school in general. In general, the high-achieving students were the ones who continued to be the most motivated in their studies and positive about school.

Interestingly, many students thought the seventh grade had been "harder" in some ways than the eighth grade. Eighth grade was harder than seventh grade because teachers were more demanding in terms of homework assigned and the material was being presented at a faster rate primarily through lectures. However, students thought their seventh grade teachers had been tougher overall, and their grades had been lower (subsequent analysis of report card grades supported students' remarks). They also stated that teachers last year were more responsive to student questions and provided more solicited and non-solicited help. This year it is much more dependent on the teacher.

> Once you get into higher grades, teachers get harder. Lectures, notes and more homework. (more demanding?) Ya . . . . Lectures, notes and tests. That's all we do.
>
> This year your teachers don't really know what your other teachers are assigning. You might get a ton of homework from all your teachers. Last year they wouldn't really do that. It'd be like one teacher one night, next teacher the next night.
>
> Some of the teachers are really quick to give you detention. Like you do anything wrong, you get detention. Like if you forget to bring something to class or something, they'll give you detention or sentences and other teachers just don't care. (it doesn't really matter what you do?) No, it's just the type of teacher.
>
> (discipline practices) Like last year it was all the same thing. (this year different?) Ya. It depends on the teacher.
>
> (teachers listen to students) Ya, some of them do, some of them don't.
>
> (teachers listen to students) Some do. Some just don't want to.
>
> (teachers giving encouragements) Usually they give a lot of credit to those people who get good grades mostly, and the people that get bad grades, I don't think they respect them as much as the people with good grades.

As part of the changes from seventh grade, students now traveled in groups of 12 and were de-tracked for all classes except math. Although few students recognized that they now moved in groups of 12, they did recognize they were in mixed ability groups. Students liked this change, especially those who had been in the average/lower ability classes in seventh grade.

By the end of the eighth grade, many of the students were nostalgic about the seventh grade team program. They spoke about how they had been able to have more interaction with the teachers, had been given more help, and had done more group work in all of their classes. The eighth grade teachers were seen as more distant and less caring. Students rarely worked in groups in any classes besides science. Although they thought the teams were better for teacher/student relationships and instructional practices, few missed being with the same students for all of their academic classes. They liked getting to know a greater number of peers and having students of differing ability levels in their classes. This made classes more interesting and fair to all students. When asked about their expectations for ninth grade, most students believed it would be the same as eighth grade.

Although it is beyond the scope of this chapter to present all the data or to talk about the patterns that seemed to emerge over time in the interviews with these 35 students, it may be useful to draw attention to some of the changes students perceived in the school/classroom environment and in their attitudes and behaviors. First, students noted changes in specific instructional practices and teacher behaviors. There was a decline in opportunities for students to work together in groups, the amount of content covered increased while the amount of explanation and discussion of content decreased, instruction became more teacher-lead and less student-centered, and there was increased variability among teachers in terms of their grading practices. In addition, it appeared that the school/classroom goal structure did become more ability focused and less task focused, teacher support in terms of perceived helping, caring, and listening to students declined, and students reported an increase in differential treatment of students by teachers.

Second, as these changes in perceptions of the school environment occurred, students also reported changes in their own attitudes and behavior. Although the higher achieving students remained the most positive about school, students generally became more negative. They became more critical of their teachers, especially during eighth grade. Students seemed to become more focused on grades. When asked what frustrates them in school, responses moved from "Nothing" or feelings of frustration when they wanted to understand something but were having difficulties to frustration over not getting better grades. In addition, social comparison increased. When asked about whether students competed against each other for grades, the responses shifted from "No" accompanied by puzzled looks to answers such as, "They fight about who gets the best grades, who made the honor roll." Further, when asked about the definition of a good student, early answers reflected a concern with being nice to others, not misbehaving in class, trying hard, and getting their work done, whereas later responses focused on going to class, doing the work and getting good grades. Finally, peer relationships seemed to change. In early interviews, students reported that they liked their classmates, everyone got along well and everyone talked with everyone. Over time, although students still reported liking their classmates, responses were more variable and qualified. "Everyone" changed to "some people." Indeed, some students reported that peers were "mean" to one another, and there was an increase in conflicts among students. While these tendencies toward more negative changes in important indices of adolescent functioning are consistent with the literature on early adolescence (Eccles et al., 1993a, b), they are troubling nonetheless. From student interviews and questionnaires, it would appear that differences in the seventh grade and eighth grade environments might play a significant role, and teachers' concerns over providing a fundamentally different middle-level school environment for students had merit.

In this study, questionnaires and interviews were used to complement one another to yield a better picture of how students experienced the school environment, how they perceived themselves over time, and the relations between the two. While the questionnaires could provide data on some of the areas of concern to school personnel (e.g. use of learning strategies, motivational beliefs and strategies, feelings and perceptions about school and schoolwork), the interviews could provide additional information on some of these areas as well as home in on others (e.g. relationships between teachers and students, peer relationships, perceptions of reform measures) that were not tapped by the questionnaires. Although the interviews were structured and inquired only into specific areas, what was learned through these interviews was critical and could not have been obtained through our questionnaires alone. For example, students identified specific instructional practices, teacher behaviors, and policies that made a difference in their learning and motivation over time. It also was possible to hear differences between the experiences of high achieving and low achieving students, and how student-student relationships changed in general and for different students over time. While it may be possible to design questionnaires that would provide data similar to those obtained through structured interviews, I suggest it would be necessary to spend considerable time in the setting to become familiar enough with school/classroom practices and the areas of concern to educators to know what to include if the study was to be of practical value and also contribute to theory as we hoped this one would.

TEACHERS AND STUDENTS TALK ABOUT THE SCHOOL CONTEXT, TEACHING, AND LEARNING IN SEMI-STRUCTURED INDIVIDUAL, TEAM, AND FOCUS GROUP INTERVIEWS

Study 4: Social Capital and its Effects on the Academic Development of Adolescents at Risk for Educational Failure (Lee and Croninger)

Beginning in 1997, I had the opportunity to work with Valerie Lee and Robert Croninger, sociologists of education, on their research project. While both are known for their work using quantitative methods, qualitative methods were employed in this study. The purposes of the study, as articulated by Lee and Croninger, were to examine: (1) how social capital is generated and sustained in high schools; and (2) how social capital in schools promotes the academic and social development of students at-risk for educational failure. To address these study questions, six schools were explored in depth using multiple inquiry approaches and case studies were written for each school.

Teams of researchers (2–3 individuals per team) assumed responsibility for gathering data in each school. I will focus on one school, St. X. (pseudonym), a small Catholic high school, in which I functioned as Lead Researcher working in collaboration with Doug Ready and Bob Croninger in gathering and analyzing the data, and writing the case study. Primary data collection occurred during two one-week visitations, one in the fall and one in spring of a single school year. While data used to inform the case study of each school came from a variety of sources including written artifacts, responses to questionnaires, classroom observations, and fieldnotes, the interviews conducted with staff and students are the focus here.

Semi-structured focus group interviews were conducted with students and teachers. Numbers in these groups varied from three to ten. Interview guides with open-ended questions tapping specific areas of interest to researchers were used. Each began with an introductory script reviewing the nature of study and the approximate duration of the interview. A general question followed by more specific questions and probes were provided in each guide. However, these guides were to function more as a tool for interviewers to help focus the discussion than as a set of questions to be asked in a specific order. Interviewers were to follow the lead of their informants, working the areas of interest into the conversation as appropriate. Questions focused on five areas for student focus groups: beliefs about the school's mission, the school's social environment, the kinds of problems students have in school, the assistance provided to students to resolve problems, and students' perceptions of teachers. The first four areas were the same for teacher interviews, while the fifth area concerned teachers' perceptions of teacher-parent and school-community relations. In addition, some teachers and other members of the school staff were interviewed individually using semi-structured and unstructured approaches. Occasionally, staff members were interviewed more than once to help clarify perspectives and perceptions.

As in previous sections of this chapter, it is impossible to do more than touch upon some of what our informants shared with us about their perceptions of their school experiences. Because of its relation to the issue of the role of context, one of the two general issues that are the focus of this chapter, I will share what emerged as a central theme in our inquiry – the "sense of relationship" or "community" in this school. What follows is offered as a brief introduction to the kind of information gained primarily through focus group interviews.

Teachers Talk About School:

They just kinda, they become a whole person here. They develop a confidence and a broad perspective. They're better prepared for college and for the world because of the sense of relationship they had here.

We create an environment. The school as an institution has always worked hard to create that environment.

What I realized (after spending time in another school) was, because, I just hadn't spent much time in other schools, is how engaged our students and our faculty are. So engaged. The engagement, the interaction, the relationships . . . . here there's always a give and take, whether it be in the hall and in this school, constantly, you'll always see teachers in the hall talking to the kids and visa versa, always. About all kinds of things. There's this whole thing going on. It states that there really is a sense of place about this program.

I think we are a fairly traditional school in some ways and not only in the structure. We offer a stability. We're not going to expect one thing one day and then change another day.

My feeling is that when a student is admitted here it's almost a contract between the school and the student. Somebody is working with them. A teacher, a counselor . . . if things aren't looking too well.

. . . And one of the things I like to tell parents and students when they inquire about the school, I like to promote the family atmosphere that exists.

. . . to relate that to what sets us apart from other schools is the faculty here doesn't talk much about pension plans . . . . They talk about kids . . . it's networking among the faculty, not gossip . . . to help the kid. . . . You're here for the kids.

(why she stayed) . . . But, I really do enjoy every minute of it. You know, I don't want to leave. I wanted to stay here because of the support that I get from faculty and I love the

> kids. I don't want to leave to go any other place. What I found here is actually, pretty much a sharing, supported, kind, pleasant, at the same time pretty much strict, you know, atmosphere.
>
> You show them respect, they'll show you respect. They show you respect.
>
> One of the strengths which sets it apart from other schools is how very accepting our students are of one another.
>
> If a teacher cares about teaching, you care about kids.

As these quotes suggest, teachers believed "There's this whole thing going on" that sets this school apart from others. The majority of the adults in this school had made a commitment to a common vision, to creating an environment described in words such as: family atmosphere, sense of place, stability, support, strict, helping, accepting, caring, and relationships. Indeed, as one teacher in a large focus group articulated, many teachers who choose to remain here despite more lucrative prospects elsewhere do so because they feel a sense of mission or purpose. Another teacher followed up on his colleague's comment by saying, "Talk with those who have left for the public schools, for the higher salaries or what have you. Almost without exception, they'll say, 'Ya, salary's great; but I miss the community. I miss the kids.". The word "community" was used again and again and it took us a while to realize that what people were talking about was the school as "community", a feeling of belonging or sense of place not a geographic locale. This school had a clearly stated mission statement and goals that are published in the student handbook and the faculty handbook and that the staff worked hard to carry out. Further, a particular route had been chosen to accomplish their purpose and new faculty and students were socialized accordingly.

Teachers spoke about what they thought promoted the kind of environment they were trying to create. Teachers communicated high expectations for academic performance and appropriate behavior to students, but also actively helped students to meet these expectations. They held study groups, made themselves available for individual help before or after school, helped arrange peer tutoring, talked informally with students about problems, and adopted an attitude that they expected the best from their students at all times but tempered these expectations with understanding. Teachers stated that some of the most important things they try to convey to students are attitudes of tolerance and understanding, and that school was more than academics. They believed everything students did in school, including extra-curricular activities and the community service component (requirement for juniors and seniors), was important to their growth and development as individuals. To this end, they actively encouraged students participate in clubs and sports. Further, they modeled what they expected from students in their own behavior. Many teachers either sponsored clubs and activities themselves or attended after school events on a regular basis They spoke about the support and help they gave and received from other teachers and the administration, and the informal expectations regarding what it meant to be a teacher in this school.

In the teacher focus groups, we heard a remarkable degree of agreement about "how things worked" in this school. There appeared to be some very strong norms at work regarding how they wanted to be perceived and how they wanted to present their school to outsiders. This suggests one of the difficulties that may arise as a function of conducting focus group interviews in a small school (approximately 700 students and 63 full and part time teachers). Individuals may be reluctant to express divergent opinions in a highly public forum such as a focus group of their peers. After all, they will continue to live in this environment long after researchers have left. To explore this and other issues further, we made the decision to conduct more individual interviews with adults than we had planned. Some areas of disagreement did emerge. These seemed to revolve around structural and organizational concerns such as the way the school day was divided, communication within and across different units, and curriculum planning (e.g. the need for more cross-disciplinary coordination), not those that reflected fundamental differences in vision for the school. While these types of structural/organizational concerns sometimes create serious divisions within a school and animosity between staff members, that was not the case here. Staff members did disagree with one another, but they did so in a way that conveyed respect. Indeed, it appeared that differences of opinion were viewed by some as evidence that the school was healthy and functioning properly.

Students Talk About School:

In focus group interviews, students were very willing to express their opinions about the school in general and to share their personal experiences openly with peers. Indeed, one of the challenges was to manage the time so that all students who wanted to could give their perspective. Most students felt that the school helped prepare them academically, that there were supports available to them for academic and personal difficulties, that most teachers held high expectations for students, and that they received encouragement to do their best. They also spoke of the opportunities provided to become involved in activities that matched their interests and the recognition that there was a basic set of rules by which everyone abided, including teachers.

> I think its supportive because I've been through a lot home-wise and I've had teachers help me through things with my school, and plus like with problems I have at home. They've been there for me.
>
> I think this is a good school because I mean, like, this whole little thing is supposed to be about relationships, and at my old school people weren't very friendly to me. And this is the first place, the first school, where I've ever had any friends. And everybody here is really supportive and they really help to make it a good place. The teachers and the students and that's what I like best about it.
>
> Mainly, they offer programs; basketball, football, intramural games for kids, clubs. They have plenty of clubs.
>
> The teachers will let you know that this is how ethics works here. If you want to get by this is how you want to do it. Some do it in a nice way, some do it in a not so nice way. It just depends on the teacher.
>
> The school has high expectations for you and so everyone is going to do their best to reach those expectations.
>
> They push you, they push you really hard. They make you do better. They just drum it into your head until you get it. They work with you one on one if you ask for help. They'll make the opportunity available to you.
>
> It comes to a point with some of my lower grades that the teachers will tell my parents, 'She's not working up to her full potential.' They expect you to do what you can and they notice what it is that you can do and they'll push you to achieve that.

In contrast to what we heard from teachers, students seemed to believe there was considerable variability among teachers in terms of who could be relied upon for support and what form that support might take, equal treatment of students, and disciplinary practices.

> Participation makes you learn, participation is like huge in her class, is about 75%. She let's you have fun but controlled fun and once you get comfortable she'll throw stuff at you that you can take and she puts it in such a comfortable way that you adapt to it very quickly.
>
> Some teachers, like if you're behind in something, like if you've been having a rough time lately at home, a couple of teachers they'll cut you a little bit of slack like if you're falling behind in your work . . . . It's not necessarily the teachers that don't like make you do any work. It's the teachers that understand when you're having a problem and they give you a chance to, like, work on that. Not the teachers that are like, 'Ok, don't do anything.'
>
> I don't really feel close enough to any of my teachers to talk to them about stuff like that, like any personal stuff. I mean, like schoolwork, maybe, but other than that, no.
>
> Well, I would, see like, it would basically depend on the teacher because if you have a certain teacher that you trust who will help you. There are certain individuals in this school who say 'I won't go to this teacher because they might not help me with my work'.
>
> The teachers are probably a friend who I would go to for help with anything
>
> Like, I mean he just doesn't seem like a helpful person to me. I don't know, like when I ask questions in class he will just kind of give me like one answer, just like a one word

> answer and doesn't really explain to me and I'm just like, I don't really learn. He doesn't explain anything to me.
>
> I have a math teacher and he's also my baseball coach. And like in some instances I may have problems and when we're in the classroom or when I have a problem with work, he kind of relates both to the situation. It really does help me out because it kind of makes me feel like as if I don't have to carry the load myself.
>
> You can say anything to him and he'll give you, he'll try to see both sides. He'll listen.
>
> I think it's just because she's a teacher, like she just here to teach. So, she's not here to do anything else but teach. So, she just comes and teaches and if you got a problem – Well, what I was saying was like, I mean, yah, that is the job of a teacher, to teach. But, I mean, like some of these other teachers, they don't just teach. They teach and they can help you with a problem with any of your friends or whatever like that. But, she's just like the teacher that comes to teach, and she goes home.
>
> I mean, I don't even have Mr. A. I have Mr. D. for Western Civ but Mr. A. was tutoring me. (how did that happen?) I'm in his homeroom. We were just talking about it and he offered. So, he works with me on my Western Civ.
>
> Some teachers do communicate favoritism or dislike to students by what they say.
>
> If this teacher doesn't like you, you're pretty much gonna fail the year, 'cuz most of her grade is based on participation, you know, on your participation. Luckily, she likes me though.
>
> (On rules and enforcement) It varies by teachers. You gotta know your teachers that's probably the first rule.

As these quotes suggest, some teachers were seen as providing academic help to students by what they did instructionally in the classroom. At the extremes were those teachers who students would go to for anything and those who were perceived as unapproachable.

A similar range of responses was garnered when students spoke about differential treatment. When queried about what form this took, students gave several examples. What was mentioned most frequently was that teachers called on certain students in class either first or more often than others. Since participation was figured into students' grades in most classes, this could give some students an unfair advantage. Additionally, favored students were given more latitude in terms of their behavior. This was a particular issue since students were very sensitive to differences between teachers in terms of discipline.

There seemed to be general agreement that rules such as talking in class, mobility within the classroom, the necessity of hall passes, and bathroom access were under the discretion of the individual teacher and there was little consistency across the school in these areas. The comment about having to know the teacher applied here. What also began to emerge, however, was an impression that the consequences of violating some rules, including cheating, were much more discretionary than teachers had led us to believe. Students suggested that some teachers would assign students personal detention (detention to be served with the teacher in the individual classroom and not reported on students' disciplinary record) while others would assign detention (to be served in the detention hall and reported on disciplinary record) for the same offense. What was remarkable, however, was that students noticed variations in these areas among teachers, expressed their feelings about them, but didn't seem to focus on these as things that interfered with the overall sense of "community" most felt was present in this school.

The sense of community arose again when students spoke about their relationships with peers.

> Unity. Like everybody's so, it's like a whole big family here. If one person has a problem, everybody has a problem.
>
> Ok, I don't talk to some of these people everyday, but this is like my family, kind of. I might not get along with all of them, but we still, I just don't know how I would graduate without them or whatever.
>
> . . . they were about to fight each other and then everybody was like, no, just stop, and they grabbed them and held them back.
>
> (fighting) We had three (the entire year).
>
> (cliques at school?) Yes, definitely!
>
> It's not so much that it's in school because the school pushes you to meet other friends . . . It's more of a clique when you leave out of school, like 2:35, everybody's with their little group and everything. At school, they're all like together.
>
> (racism?) Like last year in the bathroom, there were a whole lot of swastikas in the bathroom, all of this stuff saying White Power and everything.
>
> Like if a blind person came to this school, you'd think everybody was the same. It's like, there's no racial problems in this school because there are so many different people and everybody has friends of each.
>
> It's not because people don't like other groups, its because they have that (interests and background) in common.

Most students believed that the school was like a family. They felt peers got along well with one another and that there were few students in the school who did not seem to fit in socially. Although there were comments that freshman year was particularly difficult because students had not learned the norms regarding appropriate behavior yet, only a few students continued to have problems being accepted. Students indicated that participation in clubs and sports as well as religion classes were where you met and got to know people, resulting in friendships that extended beyond the school day. In this school, like any other, groups or cliques did form. However, these were viewed as permeable and based on common interests more than a deliberate attempt to be exclusionary.

As in any "family", however, conflicts did occur. When asked if there was animosity between groups, responses were mixed. One student suggested that there was a group of racists in the school, however, another African-American student in the same focus group disagreed as did students in other focus groups. Indeed, most reported that conflicts were not a group phenomenon but occurred more often between individuals. Unlike teacher reports, however, students did indicate that small fights or what they termed "skirmishes" happened regularly among both males and females. These arguments seldom escalated into large fights mainly because students intervened with their peers to calm the situation.

Further, students helped one another academically. Indeed, they believed the help and support they received from peers was as important to their success as that provided by teachers. At the same time, the majority of students reported that intense competition for grades went on in this school.

> Well, for me mostly, like me and my friends, in school and out of school, we always comparing grades. Like some people out of school and even some people in school, they, like, some people seem kind of proud to be doing bad in school. But other people, I don't know why, we are always comparing saying, ah, I got better than you second quarter. You stupid. We just playing around and stuff and so we always like compete with each other and get our better grades than each other. But, we mostly support each other like that.
>
> (o.k. to be smart in this school?) Yah, I think that's good because if you live around, report cards come out, it's like a competition with just about downright everybody. Who's going to make the honor roll? Everybody's running to the board and saying, 'What's your GPA?' They're like, 3.6, they're like, ha, 3.714. I'm saying the numbers just roll right off their tongue and they'll see it one time and they'll, 4.372. And they just come right out with it and it's like everybody's trying to be better than their friend and their friend's got 3.7 and they're trying to get 3.8. (what if somebody doesn't do well?) You encourage them. Ya, that's what I like about this school. Because if you do something good, it's not just one person will congratulate you. The whole school will be behind you. They'll be like, 'Ya, you did good, good job, good job.' But if you did bad, they ain't gonna put you down or nothing. They'll just, everyone will be like, oh, you can do better, you will do better. I'll help you.

There was a great deal of comparison of grades and a heightened awareness of where students ranked relative to their peers. As one student said of another, "Everybody knows she sits on top."

Interestingly, the majority of students said that the competition and social comparison that went on did not have a negative impact in this environment. Rather, it provided them with an incentive to want to do better and it did not interfere with their relationships with one another. Indeed, even students who didn't do well felt supported by their peers, especially when they became discouraged. No one was going to put them down, only try to help. Given the current debate among motivation researchers coming from a goal theory perspective regarding the operation of mastery and performance goals (e.g. Midgley, Kaplan & Middleton, 2001), these student descriptions are particularly provocative.

It was evident that teachers and students had different perceptions of what went on in this school. However, there seemed to be general agreement among informants that a sense of "community", a feeling of belonging, was fostered in this school. Within this context of community, there appeared to be active participation and investment in school among the majority of faculty and students.

As one can see, the use of the semi-structured interview approach with focus groups and individual teachers allowed us access to students' and teachers' perceptions of this school, particularly the nature of the social relations between school members (teachers, administrators, students, and parents) and beliefs regarding the school's purpose and what was expected of individuals in this school. That the school as "community" emerged from interviews as key in understanding this school is very interesting. A subsequent examination of the some of the research on school as community revealed remarkable congruence between what Bryk and his colleagues (Bryk & Driscoll, 1988; Bryk et al., 1993) identified as three essential features of what they termed communal school organization and what we heard from our informants regarding their school. The three features are: (1) a shared set of values among school members and common beliefs about the school's purpose, member behavior, what students should learn, and who students are as people and the kind of people they can become; (2) shared activities that provide opportunities for social interaction among school members and connections to school traditions; and (3) a pattern of caring, respectful social relations (Bryk & Driscoll, 1988, p. 5). These researchers also indicated that this communal school organization is very often found in Catholic high schools. Thus, the fact that we found these communal organizational features here is consistent with other research on Catholic schools. However, what is more critical for this chapter is what we learned regarding the role of context, specifically the school as community, in student motivation and learning.

Studies relying primarily on self-report questionnaires have found that communal school organization, sense of community in schools/classrooms, and similar constructs (e.g. feelings of belonging) were positively related to outcomes such as teacher efficacy and enjoyment of work, staff morale, and student academic interest, effort, liking of school, task orientation, self-efficacy, acceptance of outgroups, concern for others, and academic achievement (Battistich, Solomon, Kim, Watson & Schaps, 1995; Bryk & Driscoll, 1988; Goodenow, 1993). Many of these attitudes, beliefs, and behaviors were noted in our interviews along with high educational aspirations and involvement in school activities. Thus, our investigation definitely supports these findings regarding the relations between context and attitudes, motivational beliefs and behaviors, and the positive consequences of having a sense of community for teachers and students, I suggest that what we learned through interviews, however, goes far beyond the finding of relations between variables. As students and teachers talked about their experiences, we were able to hear the importance and impact of a powerful school culture on social relations and individual functioning and development. The data from this study suggest that school culture plays an important role in students' academic and social development and needs to be considered when trying to understand motivation and learning in school.

Study 5: Teachers as Struggling Learners (Yochum & De Groot)

This study is different from others included in this chapter in several respects. First, the study grew out of our interest as teacher educators in developing a learning community at Cranston Elementary School (pseudonym), the university's professional development partner. Initially, the partnership centered on the development of a multiage primary program, a district-wide initiative. As part of the changes, teachers were experimenting with teaming and inclusion models and were involved in extensive curricular revisions including transitioning from traditional basal reading programs to more literature-based approaches. Since we had just been granted permission to conduct an on-site course for preservice teachers that integrated literacy methods, psychological foundations, and field experience, we saw an opportunity to expand the university-school relationship that had already been active for three years. We wanted to provide a venue for professional development, an opportunity for teachers, university faculty, and preservice teachers to engage in joint inquiry into issues of teaching and learning, and to connect research and practice. As a first step in developing the learning community we envisioned, we proposed a semester-long inquiry project. Nine teachers, seven early elementary and two upper elementary, volunteered to participate. They wanted the focus of the project to be exploring ways to support the learning efforts of the struggling readers in their classrooms.

Second, the study began as a short-term investigation into the experiences of teachers as they participated in the semester-long Literacy Inquiry Project. However, it grew into a three-year study of teachers as learners as they endeavored to make and sustain changes in beliefs and instructional practices at a time when major changes were occurring at the building, district, and state levels. Teachers agreed to be interviewed as part of the initial inquiry project. As this project progressed, we saw a gradual shift from a focus on struggling students to a broader focus on issues of practice taking place. In working with the interview tapes and transcripts, we noted that teachers seemed to be struggling right along with their students. They also seemed to be struggling in different ways. Thus, we thought it important to continue to follow these teachers and document their experiences over time.

Third, we viewed ourselves as co-learners as we worked in classrooms and participated in the Literacy Study Group, the lunch time discussion group that had been established and continued to function after the Literacy Inquiry Project ended. Therefore, we thought it appropriate to inquire into our own practice as we engaged in professional development activities. We included our reflections and fieldnotes as part of this study.

In the initial phase of the study, the nine teachers were interviewed one month into the Literacy Inquiry Project (February) and again toward the end of the school year. These interviews were conducted by a research assistant with an extensive background in in-depth interviewing techniques. A semi-structured interview approach with open-ended questions was used that explored teachers' perceptions of the project, the difficulties students were having, teachers' instructional practices, how they collaborated with others, and their perceptions of their own learning. Teachers were interviewed either individually or in their teams. Each interview lasted 1–1 1/2 hours and was tape-recorded for later transcription. Pseudonyms were given to participants and the school. The following are examples of questions used in the first two rounds of interviews:

Tell me why you chose students' literacy learning as the focus for this project.
Describe the specific difficulties that your students are having.
What has worked with these students? What hasn't worked?
Describe your own learning over the course of the project.

After this first set of interviews we chose to focus on a subset of five teachers because we felt they represented the diversity of perspectives that was present within the larger group of nine teachers. These five teachers were re-interviewed at the end of Year 2 and Year 3. Nina Yochum and I conducted the last two rounds of interviews. The last two interviews were less structured than the first two to allow the teachers to explore those areas that seemed most critical to them over time.

"When Children Struggle, You Also Struggle."

This comment was made by Carol as she talked about her experiences as she worked with struggling readers in her classroom. What became apparent through interviews was that teachers were struggling right along with their students. And, like their students, they were struggling in different ways. Three themes emerged from working with the interview data that seemed central to understanding the experiences of the teachers within the nested contexts of their work. The themes were: the culture of competence, letting go, and trust and support. Because I think it might be of particular interest to motivation researchers since it deals with the interrelations between individuals and context, I will focus on the competence theme.

The Culture of Competence

The issue of competence was related to teachers' views of student learning, their perceptions of themselves as teachers and learners, and their perceptions of the meaning of competence in this school. How the teachers described the problems their students were experiencing and how they approached these problems seemed to reflect their beliefs about the nature of student learning as well as their own learning. In addition, teachers' sense of efficacy appeared to be linked to their prior experiences, their on-going observations of student progress, and the daily issues of classroom and school practice. Further, changes over time in working conditions and in school and district priorities and emphases regarding the goals for learning and teaching played a role in competence perceptions. The descriptions of three teachers' experiences help illuminate these points.

Nancy and Barbara (20 + years teaching) who team taught a grades 1–3 class with inclusion in Year 1 and 2, focused on individual learners having difficulties. In the first year's interviews, they gave lengthy descriptions of their six target students and the specific skills each had developed, as well as the difficulties each was having regarding reading and writing. They assumed that everyone will encounter challenges; this was just a part of the learning process.

Nancy and Barbara seemed to view learning from a mastery perspective. Learning was an incremental, on-going process for both students and teachers. From their perspective, student progress required the active participation of both the teacher and the student and involved making complex decisions as learning unfolded over time. The instructional process was one of constant adaptation based upon information gleaned from interactions with individual students, as well as data from observations of student work. Nancy said, "... You have to use a lot of different strategies and from each strategy, some part of it works. And some part of it doesn't, but at least we are constantly trying different things." Barbara added, "We take guidance from the kids too in regards to what way to try with them. ... I just think that in talking with them that we make some changes, by the reactions we get from them or the ideas we get from them. I think we change all the time ...."

Nancy and Barbara acknowledged that they had not seen a great deal of growth in target students' learning over the January to May project period (Year 1). Indeed, one student had made little reading progress the entire year. While the teachers were very concerned about the one student in particular, overall, they were positive about student learning potential and confident in their own ability to help struggling learners. However, they also stated they had encountered students that they were not able to reach. Although this was reality, it was still very frustrating for them.

What seemed critical to these teachers was that they continued to build their own knowledge base, learn from their mistakes and model these behaviors for their students. They also believed that a year is a short period of time, too short for some students to make significant progress. Teachers need to have the latitude to give students that time, which is why the multi-age program was so valuable. What was important was to keep students motivated and to keep building their skills so that they can make continuous progress.

> Well, I like the fact that even if we didn't see a tremendous growth, we have shown these university students that this is what you have to expect when you do start teaching. That even though we have been at it 20 to 30 years, we don't have the answers and they need to see that they may not have all the answers within five or six years of actual teaching. They have got to see that each child is going to present some kind of a challenge and some you are not going to be able to meet the needs of. It bothers the daylights out of us ... There was one behavior problem, but that is fixed, and that is what makes it so frustrating is here you have got a child that's basically a good kid and we still can't reach that kid, and it's frustrating.

> See, I need to look at the QRI (Qualitative Reading Inventory) now and see where the specifics are. ... Four of those (target students) we will get back next year. I guess that's why I don't feel like a failure with it, ... because you know that you get them back again. This is not the end ...

> I used to think, you know, that if the kid wasn't reading by the time, you know, third grade level that maybe he was going to be a non-reader. I don't think that is true either. I'm not, you know, when they have struggled so long sometimes you lose the motivation, you know, and then I think you lose the child. But if we can keep the child, to love this book and feel stimulated by those books then I wouldn't give up hope for those kids. I just think that, you

> know, as long as that desire is still there and that love, you know, there is still a chance that you can get that child to read. . . . I won't give up on those kids. M. loves books and he is starting to perceive that he may be able to read and once a child believes in themselves then maybe I'll be able to, I think there is still every possibility of that child being a reader.

During the interview at the end of Year 2, Nancy and Barbara engaged in an exchange that seems to capture their beliefs about themselves as teachers and learners:

> Barbara: Don't you think three years we have been struggling learners?
> Nancy: I just feel like I am kind of getting to where we feel kind of comfortable.
> Barbara: Yeah, I don't feel I'm good yet, well, no, that's not true. I feel I'm good, but I feel like I have a long way to go, that I could be better. Let me put it this way. You know, I feel we are good. I really do.
> Nancy: Yeah, I do too.
> Barbara: But I still feel that we have a lot of areas yet that we could still make improvements on, so I think that we struggle. I don't feel like I am struggling as much with reading, but that doesn't mean I've got it all together. We still have some other areas, especially this writing area, that we are not happy with, you know, and so for next year that would have been probably our focal point. We are feeling a little better about our reading, let's keep on doing what we are doing there but now look to some focus here on this writing and see where we go. So in some ways I think a teacher always ought to be a struggling learner. I think that is important. If we know, then we are not, you know, we won't make the progress that we should make as a professional I think.

Carol, who had been teaching for three years at the start of the study, was also in a grades 1–3 multi-age, team-teaching situation. She was the teacher who said "When children struggle, you also struggle", the quote that introduced this section. When describing the difficulties her students were having, Carol said: "The students that I chose (target students) were second graders and they just weren't near where they should be in fluency or comprehension or, basically the children that I chose had very, very limited abilities so I was concerned about all aspects of literacy." She made no distinctions between students in her description and talked about general difficulties all target students were having. At the end of Year 1, Carol said she had seen some definite student progress and that was rewarding. She was especially pleased that after spending eight weeks on one book, the students felt "a level of competence because they could actually read a book from cover to cover and they really liked that and it gave them, it made them feel good, so I think it bolstered their self-esteem". Further, the students were using words in their writing that they had learned in reading. However, she qualified her statements each time by saying that students still weren't where they should be.

> They, it just hasn't made a connection yet, so specifically, I just have to say that they are just all around struggling and trying to come up with a way to help themselves and they are not using what they should be able to use to help themselves.
>
> They came a long way, but they still have a long way to go.
>
> (future interventions?) Give them more time. We have two groups of three students, we have six, obviously six students total, so that is almost one-on-one help and just to continue that because they have made gains and I hate to see them slide back. None of them still are what you would call grade level reading . . .

In Year 1 and Year 2, Carol appeared to be very focused on performance for herself as well as her students. She believed it was the teacher's responsibility to "fix" the learning problems of her students and her competence as a teacher was related to her perceptions of her ability to do so. She felt she should have The Answers and she should have them right now so that she could bring all of her students to grade level. While she felt that she had learned "a lot" and had made changes that had positively influenced student learning, since her students still were not reading at grade level neither she nor her students quite measured up yet.

> But I guess I have a low frustration with the reading process I guess. (In terms of?) Of after knowing what is wrong, what to do about it. (How to help?) Yeah. I don't know if it is something that comes with more experience. I don't know, or whether I should know it all. I feel like I should know it all now because I am doing these kids a disservice, you know.
>
> Well, I hate to say this, because it goes against really my philosophy, but I used to be, for lack of a better word, very un-skill oriented. You know, totally out there with whole language . . . but I have had to find myself, and I don't really like it, but kind of swinging over a little bit to the skill way of thinking. . . . I just figured, you know, they would just know or it would become battered in or whatever, and I have had to back up on that as well. Obviously they are not going to just 'get it'.
>
> . . . whether you can be developmentally appropriate and also reach the outcomes that those kids have to meet at third grade in ___ (the district). So I take reading, study, you know, on what a teacher can do to facilitate the learning process, developmentally as well as moving these kids along to these specific benchmarks. I worry about it every single day. You know, I wake up thinking about it, I go to bed thinking about it. And I don't know what the answer is.
>
> I feel pressure for all the kids to work the same, for all the kids to progress the same way . . .

Carol was questioning everything to do with teaching reading, including her own ability to be effective with emergent readers. Her struggles were evident in her interviews which included statements such as: "I am still perplexed", I am at a loss", ". . . but, see, then I get that information and then I don't know what to do with it". Interestingly, this lack of confidence in her abilities was confined to reading.

> I don't feel like, see, I am very confident and qualified in the math and science areas. . . . But in the teaching of reading, I don't feel the confidence as a teacher that I feel I should. So that is a pressure I feel. That I don't have enough tricks in my bag so to speak to help them just where they need it.

Year 2 was a particularly difficult year for Carol. A new principal was assigned to Cranston School. Whereas the former principal was an advocate for the multi-age, continuous-progress model and had an authoritative leadership style, the new principal was more authoritarian and was putting significant pressure on teachers to raise state assessment test scores in reading. The emphasis at the district and school levels was no longer on mastery and continuous progress in student learning, but on student performance on test day. Test scores had dropped from one year to the next at Cranston. There was considerable tension in the building and some blaming of lower elementary teachers and the multi-age curriculum for the decline. These factors served to heighten Carol's anxiety and her concerns about her competence as a reading teacher.

To this point, I have focused on Years 1 and 2 in terms of the competence theme. Now I will discuss briefly what happened with these three teachers in Year 3. Nancy was reassigned to teach a fifth/sixth grade combination after having taught at the early elementary level for over twenty years. She believed she had been given this assignment as a punishment because she had questioned the principal's policies. She was very frustrated with her performance as a teacher and questioned her ability to meet the needs of this age group. She said, "I was doing well just to keep up in the subject matter, let alone any modern methods at this point. And that disturbed me". Nancy said she had felt very competent as a teacher in lower elementary, but not in her new assignment: "And I really felt, how did I feel here? Ill-prepared I guess". Besides subject matter concerns, she said she had not been prepared for the discipline problems she encountered. She said she had to spend most of the first semester socializing appropriate student behaviors (i.e. respecting self and others, working collaboratively) so that teaching and learning could take place. While she believed that most of the students had made progress over the year (especially in reading), the price she had paid for that progress was too high. Nancy decided to retire at the end of the year.

Barbara was made the "floating" special educator for the building for the first part of the year and then became a permanent team member in the grades 1–3 inclusion classroom. She was now working with Carol and Margo, the teacher who had been Carol's teammate for Year 1 and 2. The three teachers decided they wanted to be interviewed as a team.

All three agreed that this had been "a very rough year". They believed that what was happening in the district and under the current principal was in conflict not only with the kinds of changes they had been encouraged to make with the initial switch to multi-age, but with the changes they had been making in practices and beliefs as a function of their own professional development. They felt increasingly devalued as professionals, had little autonomy as curricular decision makers, and believed that the main criterion for judging teacher competence was student performance on the standardized test. As one put it, "I have felt like I am just trying to keep my head above water this year . . . I am pleased because I survived the year and so, and that was my goal, okay". Other comments included:

> They value you or they don't. They do this or they don't. So, they jump on so many bandwagons you don't know whether you are coming or going . . . it is hard.

> . . . I for some reason bit the multi-age hook, line, and sinker. I thought, but this was, and they were making such a pull for it and sometimes it is so disheartening to see that (pulling away from multi-age and focusing on curriculum driven by the state-wide test).

> Yeah, but, you know . . . but there is some really good things that came out of that (the switch to multi-age) for me as a professional. Whether or not the district maintains what it is that they believe about multi-age, I have made some personal growth, okay, and I have some things that are my belief system. I, you know, I found that some place in all of that digging around . . . even though they will jump on multi-age or they won't, it was still worth that trip in order for me to get to the way I am now.

> Well, because it has come down to, now they are going to be looking and saying, okay Teacher A's kids did this well on the ___ (state-wide test) but Teacher B's kids didn't so what did A do that B didn't and that – I mean **to compare teachers**!

> (dilemmas?) Well, the curriculum being driven by the ___(state-wide test). And less choice coming down for us as professionals to choose the way, you know, it is just back to, you know, 'This is what you teach', and it is set in stone and you don't have a lot of flexibility.

Despite the tensions, teachers said they had become a "well-oiled machine" in terms of how they worked together to help students learn. However, in order to do what they believed was in the best interests of the students, they found they had to engage in subterfuge, a form of "cheating":

> And we believe that we make decisions on the basis of the children, and we believe that is our Number One reason for what it is that we are doing and so we close the door. We share those things that are what we know is expected of us by individuals, so those are the things that we share and the other things we just keep quiet and do it on our own. And you know who you can talk to and you know who you can't. It's like being politically correct.

> It's analyzing anything we do. That is, analyzing what we put out in the hall . . . . So the things we brag about are the things you know will be acceptable by everyone.

They felt they were continuously engaged in a "balancing act"; trying to maintain what they thought important while having to turn in weekly lesson plans that were scrutinized by the principal for the extent to which what they were teaching reflected an emphasis on what would be tested on the state-wide assessment.

At the individual level, Barbara was angry about what happened to her and Nancy. However, she appeared to concentrate on her current teaching situation rather than dwell on the past, and had retained her mastery focus. She referred to herself as "a continual learner" and said that she felt very challenged by the students she has had this year.

> Well, this is the strangest group I have ever had in my life. Well, this is a group of high functioning first graders who, the light bulbs turn on all the time. So, what a wonderful experience. I have never had a group that has been that receptive and picking up as quickly as it did. . . . It is a very rewarding situation. I just love it, you know, and that is why I have them for reading and Margo gets them for math, okay, because you couldn't stand a whole day of these kids (laughs), or of the other ones that I have left because they are struggling in everything. We just have a group who really struggle, so we flip-flop those.

When asked whether she has changed how she approaches instruction with struggling readers, Barbara's answer was clear: "NO". While the response seemed inconsistent with her "continual learner" self-appraisal, this was not the case. She firmly believed "because of the kids that change daily I think you need to change daily", words almost identical to those she had used in her interview two years ago. She felt she needed to be constantly refining, experimenting and trying to get better at her craft. She seemed to approach teaching and learning with the attitude that the more you know, the more you know you don't know, and the more you want to know. Perhaps it is this perspective that has allowed her to remain confident in her ability to be effective with emergent readers and as a teacher in general at a time when teacher competence was being questioned.

Carol was still questioning her competence in teaching Reading and her ability to be effective with struggling readers.

> I struggle every day and I question myself a lot about, just, am I doing what is right for these kids. I don't know, I think, you know I can hear them reading, I will listen to them and, you know, some of the insights they have are wonderful and they get so depressed after their ____ (state-wide) test results come, or the MAC or the QRI comes back. So then I think well, back off, Carol, you know, obviously you are not doing what, I am missing the boat here somewhere, and I struggle and I have now for five years. Reading is what I struggle with the most. . . . I just really don't still feel like I have a good handle on it.

Although the quote appears to reflect the same problems she had been having for years, there appeared to be subtle but important differences in how she now was viewing and analyzing her teaching and learning, and student learning. She seemed to be recognizing individual differences in students, pointing out both strengths and weaknesses, and making more fine-grained distinctions in terms of what she and individual students were doing. Rather than the "can'ts" that characterized her descriptions in the past, she was making statements such as: "I now know how to use that"; "I can see"; "But when they get to the comprehension they can't answer it, I think this expository is a lot more difficult than the narrative"; "I have made changes in the kinds of questions I ask".

Carol stated she had learned a great deal through her Masters in Reading program, participation with colleagues in the Literacy Study Group, Reading Recovery training and working with her team-mates that had helped her to make "tremendous changes" in her beliefs and values. While she had used the terms "developmental" and "process" when she spoke about learning in the past, these words appeared to take on added significance. Although she was still looking for Answers so she can do what is "right for these kids", she seemed to be trying to fit pieces together rather than feeling "like I should know it all now" as she stated in Year 1. While she was still feeling frustrated, she also appeared to be more accepting of herself and her students as learners who struggle as they try to understand and make progress. Ironically, these changes were coming at a time when performance not progress was being stressed. Although she was very disheartened by the developments within the school, she appeared more confident and less vulnerable to environmental pressures:

> That has changed my (values and beliefs), and it won't matter whether they (district moves away from emphasis on multi-age and developmentally appropriate practices), I've got that insight now. . . . I just remember all the teachers saying:'I'm not going to do that! You're not going to catch me doing that'. But, you know, sometimes I almost feel like I am going to end up being one of those teachers. If it goes against my value system, of what I have, and then I think, oh my goodness, these are the people that I thought, 'What is your problem?' And now I am going, 'Excuse me, I'm not going there because, you see, I really truly believe THIS!'

While I only drew upon what was shared with us by three of the five teachers, I believe this was sufficient to illustrate what was learned regarding the issue of competence. Through the interviews we were able to hear differences among teachers as they talked about student learning and themselves as teachers and learners. It also was possible to link what teachers said they believed with how they described what they did as learners and teachers. For example, two teachers with a mastery perspective focused on building knowledge and skills, learning from mistakes, trying different strategies and adapting strategies to individual learner needs, These teachers also felt confident that they could help struggling readers and were positive about student learning potential. Because of the longitudinal nature of the study, it was possible to see changes in competence perceptions, the contextual factors (e.g. principal leadership, goals for learning emphasized in the district/school, relations between teachers) that appeared to be related to teacher efficacy, and the change in what it meant to be considered a successful teacher or student in this school.

This study focused on the experiences of teachers as they tried to make changes in beliefs and practices, and to sustain these changes during a time when major changes also were happening at the school, district and state levels. I only presented a portion of one of the three themes that emerged from interviews here. Classroom observations and fieldnotes also were used to gain a better understanding of informants' perspectives. What was clear to us as we followed these teachers over time was that understanding the teacher as learner requires attending to the contexts that can serve to nurture or constrain growth and development. While considering the environment is old news, what is sometimes overlooked is that environments are not static entities. As I have stated previously in this chapter, I think interviewing is an especially useful tool for inquiring into the complex interrelations between individuals and contexts.

ADVANTAGES AND CHALLENGES OF INTERVIEW APPROACHES AND FUTURE DIRECTIONS

In this chapter I provided examples of different study designs and interview approaches as well as samples of the data generated by different studies. I attempted to select studies that were sufficiently different from one another to invite comparisons. I tried to make explicit how interviewing could provide information and address questions regarding student and teacher motivation and learning, and the role of context that self-report questionnaires can not. Briefly, I would like to comment on what I believe to be some of the advantages and challenges of using the interview approaches introduced above. This is not intended to be a comprehensive examination of the various approaches, merely some practical considerations I found that I think would be useful to point out for those interested in using interviewing in their work. Several excellent resources are available that explore the different approaches and their utilization in depth (e.g. LeCompte & Schensul, 1999; Schensul, Schensul & LeCompte, 1999; Schensul, LeCompte, Nastasi & Borgatti, 1999; Seidman, 1998; Weiss, 1994.).

In the first section, individual in-depth, unstructured interviews were conducted to explore students' experiences of dropping out and their perceptions of how they learned things for school. In both studies, I was interested in how students made meaning of their experiences and seeing phenomena through their eyes as much as possible. The unstructured format allowed students to tell their own stories in their own way, yielding rich descriptions of themselves and their experiences that, in my opinion, could not be obtained in any other way. The second study had both interview and self-report questionnaire components. The two components were treated as separate entities and only later combined to yield what was presented here. The interview component was designed to explore students' perceptions of their own learning and what they considered important, not to find support for the constructs tapped in the questionnaire or to gain answers to specific questions.

Conducting these interviews was no easy task and required a significant investment in terms of time and effort. It was critical that informants had enough time to talk until they believed they were finished. This was especially challenging since we were interviewing students during the school day and considerable negotiation with school staff ahead of time was necessary. In addition, utilizing this approach effectively requires that interviewers develop considerable skills in in-depth interviewing techniques so they can facilitate rather than direct, and seek to uncover informants' perspectives not assume shared understandings. Since two of us were conducting the interviews for the second study, we worked together for several hours practicing our skills and learning from one another before entering the field. If more than one interviewer is used to gather data for any study regardless of the interview approach taken, I believe it is critical that adequate time is allocated for training and practice.

In contrast to the studies in the first section, the third study used a structured interview approach. A series of five individual interviews were conducted over two years. Interview protocols with primarily open-ended questions were developed and tailored for administration during the seventh and eighth grade years. Questions reflected staff interests as well as those of the research team concerning students' perceptions of the school environment and their own functioning.

There were several advantages to the use of a structured interview. We found that it was possible to gather student perspectives on a variety of different areas of interest in a relatively short period of time, while the open-ended nature of the questions still allowed students the opportunity to shape their responses in any way they saw fit. In addition, although this approach still required interviewers to possess some interviewing skills, these could be developed in less time as part of the training in the use of the interview instrument. Since training took less time, it was possible to add interviewers at a later date. Further, we found that having an interview protocol was very helpful when it came to data analysis, especially since students were interviewed five times over two years. Preliminary analyses could be done in a relatively short period of time and the findings reported to our collaborators in the school who needed them to make school improvement decisions.

While there were advantages to this approach to inquiry, challenges also were identified. Perhaps the most significant was in the development of the instrument itself. Because of the number of areas of inquiry that were significantly different from one another, we found it very difficult to craft a protocol where the questions built upon one another so that there would be a flow to the actual interview. This was my first attempt at protocol design and it showed. Transcripts from the practice interviews read like disjointed verbal questionnaires and students' responses reflected the abrupt shifts in thinking that were needed to respond to questions as they were asked. Although adjustments were made and useful information was gained from the interviews, this experience clearly demonstrates the need to devote significant time and attention to instrument development.

A second area merits mention. By its very nature, the structured format is limiting. We designed the interview portion of the study to supplement the quantitative piece. While this format served our research needs, we were very aware that we were making choices to explore some areas and not others as we initially designed the protocol. However, some significant issues emerged during the first years' round of interviews that we had not considered previously. As a function of what we learned, we altered our protocol for the next rounds to allow us to explore these areas. Because of the longitudinal nature of the study, we were able to do so. However, it made us very aware of what could be missed when using this interview approach.

In the fourth study, focus groups of students and teachers were interviewed using a semi-structured interview format. Interview guides with open-ended questions were developed. Interviewers were to use the guides as tools for themselves, not as interview instruments to be followed precisely during interviews. This approach was chosen for this study to insure a degree of comparability across sites and yet allow for sensitivity to each school's uniqueness (Miles & Huberman, 1994). As the name implies, this approach combines some of the advantages of both the unstructured and structured formats discussed above and also shares some of the drawbacks.

Since the number of multiple-case research studies is increasing, I think our experiences are worth sharing. Of particular concern for this study was the use of multiple researchers in multiple sites. While the interview protocols used were consistent across sites, researchers were not. A different team assumed responsibility for each school. In addition, not all researchers who were part of a team in a given school were from the same institution. While these may seem like small matters, we found they could present significant challenges. It was very difficult to conduct any kind of extensive training for all interviewers before entering the field. This approach to interviewing requires a good deal of skill on the part of the interviewer, especially when conducting focus group interviews. Interviewers need to be able to attend to many individuals at the same time as well as providing some direction to the discussion. Pairing an experienced interviewer with a less experienced one when conducting focus groups, as we did as much as possible for this study, can be very helpful. However, providing training and practice beforehand is always the preferable option.

The second concern involves choosing to conduct focus groups rather than individual interviews. Since we were interested in gathering as much information as possible in a short period of time about individuals' perceptions of their school and how individuals interacted with one another, the focus group was a good choice. However, we also became aware of some limitations of group interviews. First, the larger the group, the more difficult it was to gather multiple perspectives on the range of areas that we thought important to investigate. Second, in our small school, we became concerned that teachers in particular were reluctant to offer divergent opinions regarding the school in a group setting. While we had the opportunity to enhance our understanding of individuals' perspectives by conducting individual interviews, I think these are important considerations.

The third area involves the management and analysis of the interview data. Researchers conducted many interviews at each of the six sites during their two week-long visitations. The shear amount of data was overwhelming and managing these data was a persistent challenge, particularly keeping track of the transcription and verification of transcripts necessary so that data analysis can proceed. Further, and perhaps most importantly, data analysis was a challenge. Each team of researchers produced their own case summary. Because the summaries after the initial visitations were so different from one another, the decision was made to provide an outline for all groups to follow. While this practice facilitates cross-case analysis to permit speedier reporting of findings, in my opinion a great deal of the richness of the data that utilization of the semi-structured interview approach can provide could be lost.

Semi-structured interviews were also used in the fifth study. Teachers were interviewed either individually or in their teaching teams. Semi-structured interviews were utilized for the first two rounds because this was to be a short-term investigation of teachers' perceptions of their experiences as they participated in the Literacy Inquiry Project. The decision to follow these teachers for another two years was not made until after these interviews were conducted. We were able to obtain the services of an interviewer with extensive experience in in-depth interviewing. However, she was not a permanent part of the research team and had not spent much time in the school. Therefore, we felt we had to craft interview protocols with open-ended questions for each round of interviews because we wanted to inquire into specific areas but also wanted the flexibility to explore other areas as they arose during the course of the interview. Because of interviewer expertise, we felt we could use this approach successfully. In addition, we had our fieldnotes and classroom observations to supplement the interview data.

Although semi-structured interviews were used for the remaining two rounds, no interview protocols were developed. Since we were conducting these interviews ourselves, we constructed a short interview guide for each round to remind us of issues that had been raised in previous interviews or in informal conversations during the school year we felt needed clarification. However, our primary purpose in these interviews was to give our informants the opportunity to explore areas they thought were important. Because we had been working in classrooms with these teachers for a long period of time, we thought this approach was appropriate and consistent with our research goals. Through these series of semi-structured interviews we were able to hear how teachers described themselves as teachers and learners over time, how they changed (or didn't change) their ways of thinking about instruction and learning, and the ways in which the context changed and the influence of these changes on teacher growth and development. Further, the interview and classroom observation data worked together to provide us with a better understanding of how teacher beliefs were reflected in their choices of instructional strategies.

To this point I have dealt with practical matters regarding the use of the different interviewing approaches. While this is important, I do not want the message of this chapter to be lost. What I hoped to convey in these pages was the power and utility of interviewing as an approach to inquiry into issues related to motivation and learning in educational contexts.

Looking toward the future, I suggest that interviewing will continue to be a very valuable method to use for gaining a better understanding of complex educational phenomena. As we focus more attention on understanding the individual in context, an important direction for future research (Pintrich, 2000), interviewing will become particularly important. Further, as we move beyond basic research to conducting interventions in classrooms and schools, it seems critical that we investigate individuals' experiences in depth to determine the effectiveness of interventions. As I have tried to point out throughout this chapter, interviewing can be especially effective for inquiring into individuals' perceptions of classrooms/schools and their own functioning that can give us insight into how different contexts or contextual features of classrooms and schools affect student and teacher motivation, learning, and development.

REFERENCES

Ames, C. (1992a). Achievement goals and the classroom motivational climate. In: D. Schunk & J. Meece (Eds), *Student Perceptions in the Classroom: Causes and Consequences* (pp. 327–348). Hillsdale, NJ: Erlbaum.

Ames, C. (1992b). Classrooms: Goals, structures, and student motivation. *Journal of Educational Psychology, 84*, 261–271.

Anderman, E., & Maehr, M. L. (1994). Motivation and schooling in the middle grades. *Review of Educational Research, 64*, 287–309.

Battistich, V., Solomon, D., Kim, D., Watson, M., & Schaps, E. (1995). Schools as communities, poverty levels of student populations, and students' attitudes, motives, and performance: A multilevel analysis. *American Education Research Journal, 32*(3), 627–658.

Brophy, J. (1999). Research on motivation in education: Past, present, and future. In: M. L. Maehr, P. R. Pintrich & T. C. Urdan (Eds), *Advances in Motivation and Achievement: The Role of Context* (Vol. 11, pp. 1–44). Stamford: JAI Press.

Bryk, A. S., & Driscoll, M. E. (1988). *The high school as community: Contextual influences and consequences for students and teachers.* Chicago, IL: University of Chicago, Benton Center for Curriculum and Instruction.

Bryk, A. S., Lee, V. E., & Holland, P. B. (1993). *Catholic schools and the common good.* Cambridge, MA: Harvard University Press.

Bryk, A. S., Lee, V. E., & Smith, J. B. (1990). High school organization and its effects on teachers and students: An interpretive summary of the research. In: W. T. Cline, & J. F. Witte (Eds), *Choice and Control in American Education* (Vol. 1, pp. 135–226). Philadelphia, PA: Falmer Press.

Damico, S. B., & Roth, J. (1993). A different kind of responsibility: Social and academic engagement of general track high school students. In: R. Donmoyer & R. Kos (Eds), *At-risk Students: Portraits, Policies, Programs, and Practices.* Albany, NY: State University of New York Press.

De Groot, E. V. (1998, June). Patterns of perceived environment change and early adolescent functioning. Paper presented at the International Conference on the Application of Psychology to the Quality of Learning and Teaching, Hong Kong.

Eccles, J. (1983). Expectancies, values, and achievement behaviors. In: J. T. Spence (Ed.), *Achievement and Achievement Motives* (pp. 75–146). San Francisco, CA: Freeman.

Eccles, J., & Midgley, C. (1989). Stage-environment fit: Developmentally appropriate classrooms for young adolescents. In: C. Ames & R. Ames (Eds), *Research on Motivation in Education* (Vol. 3, pp. 139–186). San Diego, CA: Academic Press.

Eccles, J. S., Midgley, C., Wigfield, A., Buchanan, C. M., Rueman, D., Flanagan, C., & Mac Iver, D. (1993a). Development during adolescence: The impact of stage-environment fit on young adolescents" experiences in schools and families. *American Psychologist, 48*(2), 90–101.

Eccles, J. S., Wigfield, A., Midgley, C., Rueman, D., Mac Iver, D., & Feldlaufer, H. (1993b). Negative effects of traditional middle schools on students' motivation. *Elementary School Journal, 93*, 553–574.

Fravil, K., & De Groot, E. V. (1995, April). Early adolescents' perceptions of school reform. Paper presented at the annual meeting of the American Educational Research Association, San Francisco, CA.

Goodenow, C. (1993). Classroom belonging among early adolescent students: Relationship to motivation and achievement. *Journal of Early Adolescence, 13*, 12–43.

LeCompte, M. D., & Schensul, J. J. (1999). *Designing and conducting ethnographic research.* Walnut Creek, CA: AltaMira Press.

Lee, V. E., Bryk, A. S., & Smith, J. B. (1993). The organization of effective high schools. In: L. Darling-Hammond (Ed.), *Review of Research in Education* (Vol. 19, pp. 171–267). Washington, D.C.: American Educational Research Association.

Maehr, M. L., & Midgley, C. (1996). *Transforming school cultures.* Boulder, CO: Westview Press.

Midgley, C., Feldlaufer, H., & Eccles, J. S. (1989). Student/teacher relations and attitudes toward mathematics before and after the transition to junior high school. *Child Development, 60*, 981–992.

Midgley, C. Kaplan, A., & Middleton, M. (2001). Performance approach goals: Good for what, for whom, under what circumstances, and at what cost? *Journal of Educational Psychology, 93*, 77–86.

Miles, M. B., & Huberman, M. (1994). *Qualitative data analysis.* Thousand Oaks, CA: SAGE Publications.

Nolen, S. (1988). Reasons for studying: Motivational orientations and study strategies. *Cognition and Instruction, 5*, 269–287.

Pajares, F. (1996). Self-efficacy beliefs in academic settings. *Review of Educational Research, 66*, 543–578.

Pintrich, P. R. (2000). Educational psychology at the millennium: A look back and a look forward. *Educational Psychologist, 35*(4), 221–226.

Pintrich, P. R., & Schunk, D. H. (1996). *Motivation in education: Theory, research and applications.* Englewood Cliffs, NJ: Merrill Prentice-Hall.

Pintrich, P. R., & De Groot, E. V. (1993, April). Narrative and paradigmatic perspectives on measuring student motivation and self-regulated learning in the classroom context. In: symposium: New directions in the measurement of motivation. Paper presented at the annual meeting of the American Educational Research Association, Atlanta, GA.

Pintrich, P. R., & De Groot, E. V. (1990, April). Quantitative and qualitative perspectives on student motivational beliefs and self-regulated learning. Paper presented at the annual meeting of the American Educational Research Association, Boston, MA.

Pintrich, P. R., & De Groot, E. V. (1990). Motivational and self-regulated learning components of classroom academic performance. *Journal of Educational Psychology, 82*, 33–40.

Roeser, R., Midgley, C., & Urdan, T. (1996). Perceptions of the school psychological environment and early adolescents' psychological and behavioral functioning in school: The mediating role of goals and belonging. *Journal of Educational Psychology, 88*, 408–422.

Schensul, J. J., LeCompte, M. D., Nastasi, B. K., & Borgatti, S. P. (1999). *Enhanced ethnographic methods.* Walnut Creek, CA: AltaMira Press.

Schensul, S. L., Schensul, J. J., & LeCompte, M. D. (1999). *Essential ethnographic methods.* Walnut Creek, CA: AltaMira Press.

Seidman, I. (1998). *Interviewing as qualitative research: A guide for researchers in education and the social sciences*. New York, NY: Teachers College Press.

Weiss, R. S. (1994). *Learning from strangers: The art and method of qualitative interview studies*. New York, NY: The Free Press.

Wentzel, K. R. (1994). The relations of social goal pursuit to social acceptance, classroom behavior and perceived social support. *Journal of Educational Psychology, 86*, 173–182.

Wigfield, A., Eccles, J., & Pintrich, P. R. (1996). Development between the ages of 11 and 25. In: D. Berliner & R. Calfee (Eds), *Handbook of Educational Psychology* (pp. 148–185). New York, NY: Macmillan.

Winne, P. H., & Perry, N. E. (2000). Measuring self-regulated learning. In: M. Boekaerts, P. R. Pintrich & M. Zeidner (Eds), *Handbook of Self-regulation* (pp. 532 – 566). San Diego, CA: Academic Press.

Wolters, C., Yu, S., & Pintrich, P. R. (1996). The relation between goal orientation and students' motivational beliefs and self-regulated learning. *Learning and Individual Differences, 8*, 211–232.

Yochum, N., & De Groot, E. V. (1997, December). Making and sustaining changes in literacy instruction: Teachers as struggling learners, part II. Paper presented at the annual meeting of the National Reading Conference, Phoenix, AZ.

Yochum, N., & De Groot, E. V. (1996, December). Changing classroom instruction for children who find reading difficult: Teachers as struggling learners. Paper presented at the annual meeting of the National Reading Conference, Charleston, SC.

6. DYNAMIC ASSESSMENT AS A KEY TO UNDERSTANDING STUDENT MOTIVATION IN A CLASSROOM CONTEXT

Sanna Järvelä, Pekka Salonen and Janne Lepola

INTRODUCTION

New learning models attempt to expand learning from the traditional circles of the school by making use of more authentic learning tasks and of student participation in various cultures of expertise. Student engagement in these learning models is supported by assisting meaningful interpretation, stimulation and the self-evaluation of ideas through interaction with others and by offering tasks with multiple outcomes and multiple routes to those outcomes (Brandsford, Brown & Cocking, 2000; Brown & Campione, 1996). Participation in such pedagogical environments may contradict the configuration of the common structure in traditional instructional environments. Presumably, the cycle of instructional episodes and student engagement in these less traditional learning tasks takes different forms, for example, longer periods of motivational involvement and higher cognitive engagement (Järvelä, Lehtinen & Salonen, 2000; Järvelä & Niemivirta, 2001; Salomon, 1996). How does this interaction between student motivation and situational features take shape? How do different students cope with the demands of a situation and what is the

New Directions in Measures and Methods, Volume 12, pages 207–240.

ISBN: 0-7623-0819-2

potential provided by the features of the learning context to their motivational interpretations?

Lewin (1954) in his field-theory describes the reciprocal functional intertwinedness of an individual and environment and characterizes the person environment interaction in terms of fields of tensions. The related ideas of functional system, the structural organization of an activity and the changes in the organization of activity give a theoretical frame to develop procedures for dynamic motivation assessment. Especially the theoretical constructs of unitary versus disorganized activity are core concepts which can improve the motivation assessment in describing the fluctuation of activity and goal adaptation.

We propose that student liability to motivational changes can be investigated with dynamic motivational assessment, which is embedded in the continuous learning and performance episodes in a natural learning setting. Student's learning in a classroom environment is not determined by intrapersonal or environmental factors in a linear fashion, but presupposes the consideration of a student's motivational tendencies and the demands and the resources provided by the environment (Boekaerts, 2001). Motivational assessment, then means focusing on the actual process and assessing how a student's motivational responses change in the course of the continuous chain of learning episodes. However, there are a few models and methods to describe these changes in motivational terms even though there is evidence that individual performance differences cannot be understood simply by referring to hypothesized differences in unidimensional, static or organismic characteristics (Cole & Bruner, 1971; Endler & Magnusson, 1976).

The aim of this chapter is to discuss the dynamic assessment of motivation in a classroom context. In the first parts of the chapter previous research on motivation is discussed. We begin with a discussion of situation as a unit of motivation analysis and show that, in fact, there is a long history of viewing an interaction of a person and environment as a unit of analysis of human behavior. However, motivational assessment during the past decades has not really captured the dynamics between the learner and context. Instead, there has been a tendency to use a static type of assessment and psychometric testing. We elaborate further on dynamic assessment and introduce the theoretical models which help us to find possible patterns between student behavior and learning context. Finally, three different studies are described in order to illuminate a process-oriented methods and actual student behavior both in experimental and classroom settings. The discussion deals with issues how the methods of dynamic assessment can complete the traditional research on motivation.

HOW RESEARCH HAS DEALT WITH A SITUATION AS A UNIT OF MOTIVATION ANALYSIS

The growing interest in studying learning processes and instruction in actual classrooms rather than in laboratory settings has resulted in an understanding that student perceptions, cognitions, and actions are often contextually bound. That is, knowledge is a product of the activity, context, and culture in which it is developed and used (Alexander, 2000; De Corte, 2000). In the last decade a shift has been noticed in research on motivation from product-oriented to process-oriented models, and very recently researchers have begun to acknowledge the importance of context in motivational appraisals (e.g. Anderman & Anderman, 2000; Turner & Meyer, 2000; Volet & Järvelä, 2001).

One of the influential conceptual definitions dealing with the relationship of situation and learning has been Ford's (1992) concept of the behavior episode schema to represent coherent sequences of unitary person-in-context functioning. Ford argues that without representation of how the component processes of the person function as a unit, person variables cannot put together a whole picture of an acting person. Ford (1992, p. 31) criticizes static motivation measurements by saying that "many researchers offer person variables, but no clear set of propositions specifying how these variables operate in an organized fashion to represent the person as a whole".

The cognitive social learning theory (Mischel, 1973), instead, has called attention to the distinctive ways in which an individual's behavior varies in differing situations. Mischel and his colleagues' (Mischel & Schoda, 1995; Schoda, Mischel & Wright, 1993) extensive observation data on children ongoing behavior in various situations represents situation-behavior profiles showing how a particular individual behavior pattern in these situations differs from the normative pattern of behavior variation within them. In their model different individuals are characterized not just by average behavior tendencies, but also by their distinctive pattern of variability.

Recently, Boekaerts (1996) has followed Ford's (1992) concept of behavior episode defining it as a situation in which a person is invited, coached, or coaxed to display context-specific, goal-directed learning behavior. Her studies during the past decade (Boekaerts, 1996; 1999, see also 2001) have shown how student motivational beliefs interact with the cues present in diverse social, physical and instructional contexts in a student-situation transactional unit framework. Boekaerts' research gives evidence of the fact that what students intend to do in the classroom and what they actually do to achieve these goals depends largely on how they appraise various learning situations and their contexts.

WHY TRADITIONAL MEASURES OF MOTIVATION DO NOT CAPTURE THE DYNAMICS BETWEEN LEARNER AND CONTEXT

Conventional assessment methods used in educational-psychological research and diagnostics have been characterized as static, in the sense that a student's momentary response to a test task is viewed as an indicator of his or her position on some scale representing a certain underlying trait (Spector, 1992). New directions in educational assessment emphasize the importance of evaluating students holistically and of determining the individual routes they use to learn. A number of interactive and dynamic assessment models have been developed that can be differentiated from psychometric procedures typical in previous school assessment procedure (Lidz, 1987; Palincsar, Brown & Campione, 1991). Recent criticisms of static evaluation have pointed out several problems. Meltzer and Reid (1994) highlight problems associated with traditional methods of assessing student progress where in most cases the assessment has focused on student performance and not the qualitative processes in their learning. Static assessment procedures rely on product-based measures, yielding no direct evidence regarding the processes that underlie the performance. Therefore, such measures provide only a partial picture of student dispositions, capabilities, or learning potential and moreover, the analysis of the formation of learning skills is lacking (Brown, 1988; Campione, 1989). Since static evaluation strives for standardization of interactions between the student and the tester, and for minimization of "uncontrolled" contextual effects, the student's responsiveness to actual instruction situations cannot be assessed adequately (Campione, 1989; Gipps, 1999). Moreover, because static procedures strictly restrict all pre-test (as well as in-the-test) practice and experimenter feedback, poor test performance might reflect the students' lack of understanding of the instructions more than their task-related competency (Spector, 1992). Additionally, a student's momentary performance is not necessarily predictive of how the student will perform in the future.

The trait-type questionnaires typical in motivational assessment can provide an insight into the consistencies in student behavior and are therefore helpful and necessary to capture regularities in students' characteristic motivational beliefs. However, cautions about the validity and reliability of student questionnaire answers has been emphasized by many researchers, especially when these questionnaires are administered in a classroom setting (e.g. Brown,

1988; Nisbet & Wilson, 1977). The questionnaires consist of very general questions and student answers to such questions only give an indication of their general feelings, because the contextual and situational descriptions provided in trait questionnaires describe properties that are common to a wide range of situations. As Boekaerts (2001) remarks, the manner in which the students interpret these situations may be very different, because every student may recall or activate these descriptions in their own frame of psychological interpretations and situational experiences or they may be following different values or norms when completing the questionnaires. Students may also select their answers based on how they would like to be perceived by their teachers or classmates, rather than their actual views of themselves as learners. In other words, knowing that it is good to be task-focused and driven does not necessarily mean that one will choose to act in such way.

Questionnaires are especially problematic for young children since they are characteristically overly optimistic. Firstly, there is a risk of the compliance effect, for example, that socially desirable responses are given. Secondly, young children may have difficulty in responding to survey statements that require recalling and thinking about their typical behavior. Finally, the possible interaction between the child's motivational disposition (e.g. defensiveness) and the statements is problematic. In fact, to be an externally valid measure presupposes that the student responds to the self-report statements truthfully, which in turn seems to require a purely task-oriented motivation. However, if a child or an adult has a tendency to avoid negative matters related to him or herself, or has the tendency to please others, the responses to the items may be biased. Given these problems, the self-report measures seem to lack developmental appropriateness, specificity and validity, despite the fact that reasonable reliability values are reported (Lepola, 2000.) In order to overcome the limitations of the static type of measurement, the motivational-theoretical basis for dynamic and process-oriented approaches are outlined.

MOTIVATIONAL IMPLICATIONS OF DYNAMIC ASSESSMENT

Dynamic assessment is a general term in learning and personality research used to refer to approaches that focus on person-environment interactions and analyzes individual differences in responsiveness to progressive changes as a function of external assistance. In learning research, dynamic assessment is theoretically linked to Vygotsky's well-known notion of the Zone of Proximal Development, which points to the area just beyond the child's present capabilities on a test demanding independent performance, but within the child's capability under adult guidance or with more capable peers (Vygotsky, 1978). In dynamic assessment, the interaction of the student and his or her environment is the focus of the evaluation. The main idea is to register the changes of student motivation related to the contextual changes, for example, different episodes of classroom learning. Such assessment implies, for instance, taking into account a student's sensitivity to task difficulty cues, to time pressure factors, to obstacles and to social feedback.

Although there are different types of dynamic testing applied, for example, to assess a child's learning potential (Campione & Brown, 1987) and to evaluate the effectiveness of assisted learning in a cognitive apprenticeship (Campione, Brown, Ferrara & Bryant, 1984), the dynamic approaches are virtually lacking from the motivational research on learning. From motivational point of view dynamic assessment does not only mean focusing on a progress, that is changing the context to scaffold the student just beyond his or her capabilities as talked in terms of the zone of proximal development and assessment, but it may also refer to possible failures in interaction. The failure situations are regressive changes (e.g. cumulative failures) manifested not only on a student side as maladaptive expectations, non-task-oriented coping behavior and/or attribution pattern that is injurious to his or her self-esteem but also as teacher's failures in modeling and scaffolding students learning process (Salonen, Lehtinen & Olkinuora, 1998).

THEORETICAL GROUNDS FOR ANALYZING MOTIVATION AND ACTIVITY IN CONTEXT

In our own studies on the development of student motivational orientation on different educational levels and in a variety of pedagogical contexts, we have found motivation-dynamic differences in students with task-oriented vs. non-task-oriented motivational tendencies (e.g. Lehtinen, Vauras, Salonen, Olkinuora & Kinnunen, 1995). Based on these findings and the classical findings of Kurt Lewin's co-workers studies on aspiration level regulation (Jucknat, 1937; Sears, 1940), we assumed that during an extended performance sequence, low-achievers' vulnerability vs. high-achievers' resistance to the detrimental effects of the accumulation of failure would be reflected as differing dynamics of aspiration level regulation and emotional response patterns.

When compared to the pioneering work of the Lewin school (Lewin, 1935; Barker, Dembo & Lewin, 1941) and Luria (1932), to later Lewin-inspired research by Helm (1954) and Heckhausen (1974), or to the ethological studies by Tinbergen (Tinbergen & Tinbergen, 1983), more recent research on motivation and affect often lacks theoretical insight into the changes of the organization of an individual's activity, as well as into the functional intertwinedness of a person and environment. In a rapidly growing body of research dealing with the effects of motivational and affective factors upon academic performance, the quality of learning is almost regularly operationalized through somewhat simplistic product variables (such as frequency of errors or latency), carrying no reference to the level of the structural organization of the resulting activity.

From a Lewinian perspective (Lewin, 1954), learning and performance situations must be characterized as complex person-environment arrays, which Lewin describes with the terms "psychological field or life space". On a deeper level, Lewin's concept of a life space denotes the reciprocal functional intertwinedness of an individual and environment. Lewin, as well as Luria and Tinbergen, represents a thoroughly functionalist view claiming that no object within the environment can be defined as such, unrelated to a person's needs, motives, emotions, cognitions etc., and vice versa: no characteristic of a person can be defined without relating to the relevant elements of his or her immediate environment or psychological situation. All psychological events, such as thinking, acting, hoping, dreaming, etc., can be seen as a function of the life space, in which person and environment are intertwined into one constellation of interdependent factors.

According to Lewin (1954), an individual is in a state of an affective or motivational tension whenever a psychological need or intention exists. If a positive or negative situational goal is relevant to the individual, a tension state is created corresponding to the attracting (driving) or restraining (repulsing) motivational force. A tension may lead to activity (and need-satisfaction) on two different levels: on the level of doing (reality) or thinking (irreality). That is, a tension may lead either to actual movement toward the goal or to mere thinking (imagining, wishing, or dreaming) about this kind of activity. As the individual reaches his or her goal, tension will ease.

Motivational tension integrates the elements or modules of activity into an hierarchically organized, functional system of action that is directed toward a goal (Barker, Dembo & Lewin, 1941; Luria, 1932). In other words, a tension system arranges the multitude of single behavioral elements into an integrated activity serving some unitary adaptive goal or function, and regulates its subsystems up to the most primitive singular elements of activity, such as elementary perceptual acts and movements of single muscular fibers. Without the unifying tension system, it would be impossible to initiate and maintain any organized and systematic goal-directed activity. For instance, an individual lacking sufficient task-related motivational tension could not maintain renewed task-assimilations, elaborate task-related plans with specific subgoals, mentally reorganize and transform task-elements according to such plans, or monitor and control his or her task-related cognitive activities.

Task-approach vs. Task Avoidance

According to the ethological view (see Tinbergen & Tinbergen, 1983), a paramount major functional system is *approach.* In Lewinian terms it can be called the tension system created by positive valence or attracting motivational force. In the case of task-oriented coping, this functional system coordinates behavioral subsystems and their sub-goals, both external and internal, which contribute to moving towards the task, attending to the task, as well as exploring and manipulating the task-elements. However, for certain individuals, the most salient environmental region to be approached in an academic performance situation may not be the task, but the significant other, such as parent, teacher or experimenter (cf. Elliott, 1999; Maehr & Nicholls, 1980). If an individual, instead of attacking a given task, approaches the significant other with the purpose to appeal, to establish attachment, or to receive social rewards and acceptance, he or she is engaging in coping efforts we call social dependence. The task may not possess a significant positive motivational valence for the actor because the student expects to have better personal control on the social dimension than the task dimension (Vauras, Salonen, Lehtinen & Lepola, 2001).

Another major functional system is *avoidance*. Again, in Lewinian terms it is the tension system created by negative valence or restraining motivational force. Avoidance integrates a multitude of single activities that serve to avoid an object or a region of environment. Such activities include a variety of movements and gestures from an all-out retreat to stopping an approach, inhibiting an activity, turning away, or averting the eyes (Tinbergen & Tinbergen, 1983). Similar to approach behavior, avoidance behavior comprises not only straightforward external movements, but also internal and tentative (intended) forms of behavior. The functional system of avoidance regulates the set of coping efforts we call ego-defensive (Salonen, Lehtinen & Olkinuora, 1998). In learning and performance situations, avoidance-type coping strategies may be directed not only to the task (task-avoidance), but also to the significant other (social avoidance).

Unitary (Coherent) Activity vs. Disorganized Activity

The studies of Lewin (Barker, Dembo & Lewin, 1941), Luria (1932), Helm (1954), and Tinbergen (Tinbergen & Tinbergen, 1983) indicate that motivational-affective conflicts, especially frustrations, may lead to the situational disorganization activity. A motivational conflict may occur, for instance, between 'competing' goals or motives (i.e. between two or three different approximately equally strong attracting forces) or between two opposite goals or contrary motivational forces (i.e. simultaneous attracting and restraining forces) (Barker, Dembo & Lewin, 1941; Tinbergen & Tinbergen, 1983). A special instance of the latter conflict type is frustration, in which a barrier or obstacle prevents an individual from actualizing a certain intention or from reaching some attractive situational goal. Frustration generates a conflict-type, undischarged motivational tension that may be extended over different kinds of elements or objects of action, and from one situational context to another (Barker, Dembo & Lewin, 1941; see also Luria, 1932). For instance, a child who is prevented from reaching a candy begins to strive for another object, such as a doll. The subsequent activity, playing with the doll, is now stereotyped or diffused because of the alternated tension originating from the previous situation.

One of the original studies by Lewin and his colleagues (Barker, Dembo & Lewin, 1941) illustrates well the basic mechanism of child reactions to a situation of frustration. In their experiment, children were first allowed to play freely with highly attractive toys. After a while, they were given standard toys, and were prevented from playing with the preferred toys. When compared to the free-play phase, the constructiveness of the play activity, rated in terms of coherence, structural integration and differentiation, decreased dramatically in the frustration situation: the units of the childrens' coherent action were shorter and the continuity of consecutive units was inferior. The behavioral episodes seldom comprised unitary and coherent activities, that is, in most cases the play lacked a leading idea or task-related goal that could have coordinated the elements of activity into an integrated whole. The play had become a diffuse conglomerate of incoherent elementary trials.

As the experiment by Barker et al. (1941) shows, when frustrated, the children produced behavioral sequences within which non-task-oriented behaviors and play-activities overlapped or fluctuated rapidly. The non-task-oriented behaviors included: (1) avoidance 'flight' behaviors (e.g. coming busy with objects other than toys, efforts to leave the field, other avoidance and substitute behaviors), (2) 'barrier' behaviors (e.g. physical and social efforts to overcome the obstacle, stereotypical and 'passive' behaviors in front of the barrier, such as repeated expressions of desire), (3) simultaneously manifesting two overlapping behaviors (i.e. so called secondary play, where the child, for instance, pushes the toy-car back-and-forth while simultaneously chatting with the experimenter), (4) emotional expressions (e.g. weeping, protesting, aggressive outbursts against the experimenter or objects).

EXAMPLES OF PROCESS-ORIENTED METHODS FOR ANALYZING STUDENT MOTIVATION

As ethological research suggests, the flow of human activity is arranged by major functional systems, such as approach and avoidance, and by sets of more specific adaptive goals subsumed to these functional systems (Tinbergen & Tinbergen, 1983). Thus, it is possible to divide the flow of activity roughly into the sets of on-task (task approach) and off-task (task avoidance/social avoidance, social approach) coping behaviors (Salonen, Lepola, Vauras, Rauhanummi, Lehtinen & Kinnunen 1994). Within some periods of time, on-task behaviors dominate, then forms of off-task behaviors are shown, and so on. Each of the major functions may dominate for a longer time, or there might be very rapid fluctuations between task-approach and task-avoidance.

The model (Fig. 1) below applies a three part system of motivational orientation (i.e. task, ego-defensive and social dependence orientation) and corresponding coping strategies. In this system non-task-oriented behavior is divided into two sub-classes: ego-defensive and social dependence type of coping behavior. The model illustrates both student's motivational orientations across performance situation and the quality of cognitive performance.

A paramount indicator of the cognitive quality of performance, or high-grade hierarchical organization, is the degree of coherence or integrity of activity. An activity is termed motivationally coherent if the flow of activity is continuously guided and regulated by a single motive type, in this case the task-related mastery goal. The prerequisite of the continuous maintenance of task-related coping activities is that no competing goals arise. The behavioral sequence in Fig. 1A illustrates an extremely coherent task-oriented activity that is interrupted only by very short episodes of non-task-oriented behavior (i.e. ego-defensive and social dependence). The second sequence (Fig. 1B) represents an extremely disorganized and incoherent activity that is essentially interrupted by ego-defensive and social dependent type coping behaviors.

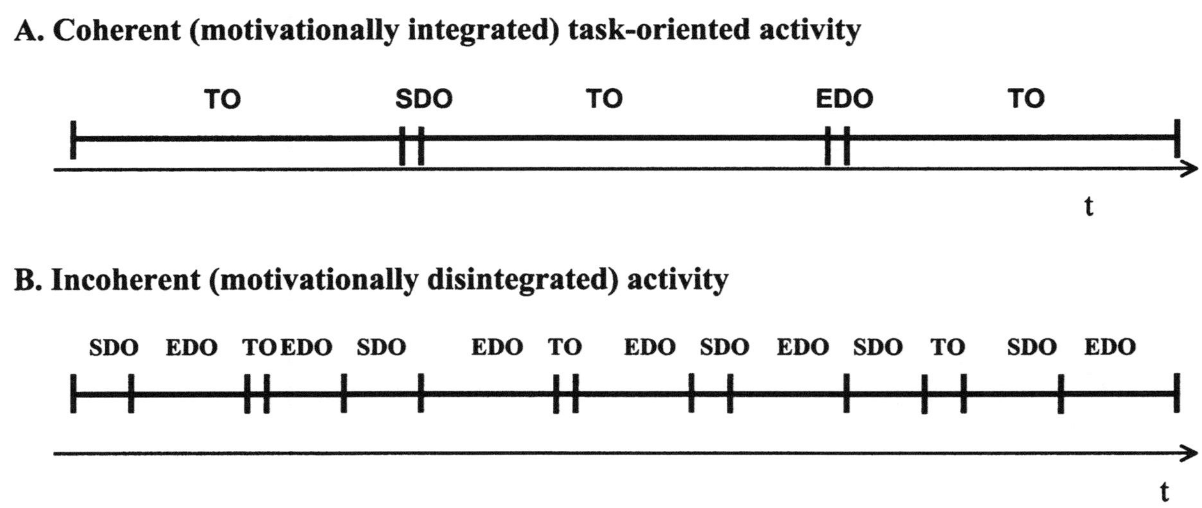

Fig. 1. Coherent vs. Incoherent Structure of Activity (TO = Task Oriented Coping Behavior, SDO = Social Dependence Oriented Coping, EDO = Ego-Defensively Oriented Coping).

A Model of Time-On-Task/Time-Off-Task Analysis

The most basic observational method to assess the motivational dynamics of activity in regard to incoherence vs. coherence, is based on the *durations of off-task and on-task episodes*. This method consists of, first, dividing a sequence of behavior into off-task and on-task types of coping strategy phases, and second, determining the proportion of time spent on off-task-/on-task coping behaviors (see Fig. 2). The grade of incoherence or disorganization of a task-oriented activity would be directly proportional to the relative amount of time spent on off-task behaviors. However, proportional total times spent on off and on-task behaviors do not necessarily adequately reflect the level of disorganization vs. organization of activity. It is possible that a sequence of activity begins with a long continuous period of non-task-oriented coping behavior (perhaps 50% of total performance time), but then the individual may succeed in gaining task (and self) control, which might yield in a long uninterrupted period of coherent task-oriented coping behavior (50% of total time). In other words, despite the unfortunate first half of the performance, the latter half may become highly organized and lead to a successful solution. Consider, then, a possible sequence, again with equal proportions of non-task- and task-oriented coping (e.g. 50%/50%), but with a totally different distribution. In this case, very short phases of non-task and task-oriented behaviors fluctuate in succession from the beginning to the end of performance, which actually indicates complete disorganization and incoherence of the task-directed activity. According to the global time-on-task assessment, both activity sequences appear equally coherent or incoherent; the essential motivation-dynamic and structural differences between these activity sequences are beyond the grasp of this quantitative method. Although global time-on-task measures can be used to roughly reflect the motivation-based qualitative differences of activity sequences, they are not well suited to describe 'microgenetic' dynamics taking place within a sequence of activity or sequences consisting of a large number of alternating short on-task and off-task episodes.

An Analysis Based On On-Task Off-Task Shifts

Another, more accurate and sophisticated, observational method of coherence-assessment is to determine the number of shifts from an on-task to an off-task type coping behavior and vice versa (see Fig. 3). For instance, a useful simple measure of incoherence would be the following quotient: frequency of shifts/total time of performance. The advantage of this method of assessment is that

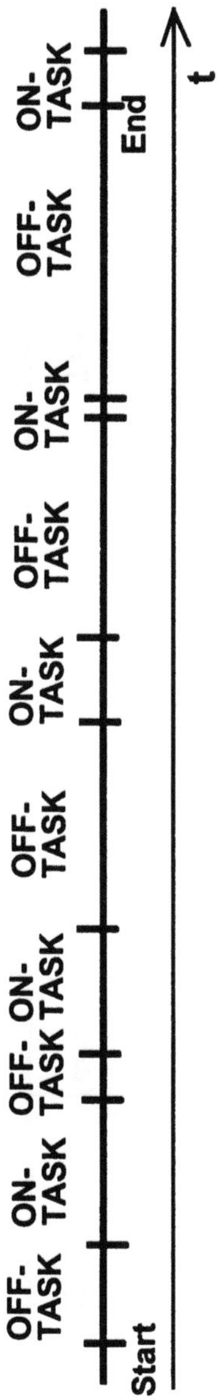

Fig. 2. Time On-Task Analysis.

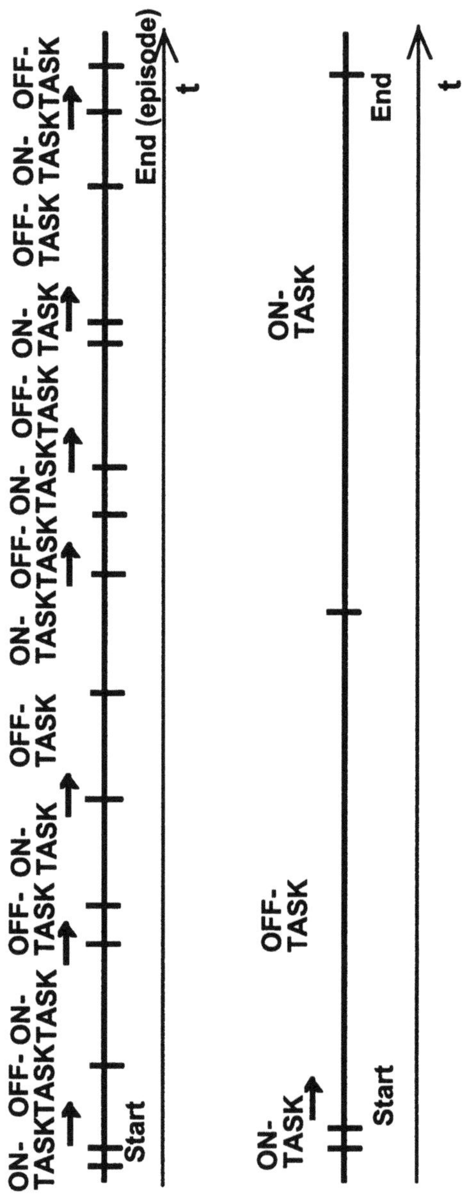

Fig. 3. Analysis Based on On-Task/Off-Task Shifts.

it reflects more adequately the motivation-dynamic and structural characteristics of sequences consisting of numerous and unevenly distributed second-to-second phase variations. This is because the frequency of shifts from a momentarily activated major functional system (goal orientation) to another, in itself, reflects an essential aspect of motivationally determined incoherence and disorganization of activity. This measure should be used to complement the time-off-task /time-on-task type of analysis.

To sum up, student's coping behavior is identified according to his or her dominating adaptive goal (goal orientation). Even if the classification to on-task or off-task coping has an exclusive nature the theoretical presumption still is that a student can have multiple rival goals and tendencies (or motivational tensions, cf. Lewin, 1954). The appearance of multiple rival goals can be seen in student's fluctuation from one coping mode to another kind of mode.

EMPIRICAL STUDIES AS EXAMPLES OF DYNAMIC ASSESSMENT

A joint focus of all the studies focusing on the dynamics of student motivation in different performance settings is student motivational responses to the variety of demands in a learning environment. That is to say, our model of dynamic assessment deals with regressive rather than progressive changes. A special emphasis in the three examples of our studies is made on demonstrating the process-oriented methods used in dynamic motivational assessment. The goals of the first study were to analyze, on the one hand, the role of school achievement on student motivational responses to cumulative failures and, on the other hand, the relationship between student motivational tendencies and emotional behavior during the task performance analogous to the classroom setting. The second example portrays the situational dynamics of coping behavior in preschool children in order to validate the link between motivational orientation constructs and child vulnerability differences reflected in actual coping with evaluative pressures. Moreover, the study indicates how children's progressive and regressive reading careers are partly motivationally based. The third study focuses on on-going student involvement and motivational responses in a more open, problem-oriented inquiry environment following the recent constructivist pedagogical principles. A student case demonstrates how the observational method and other process-oriented data collection can be used to assess student motivational dynamics in a classroom context.

The Effects of Failure on the Regulation of Aspiration Level

This study was conducted in order to find empirical evidence for the essential phenomena on which dynamic assessment is based: how does failure affect a student's motivational response to the task situation. The study was designed to examine the effects of persistent failure on setting the aspiration level and on emotional responses in students, who differ in a school-achievement and motivational orientation. Based on the classical findings of Lewin's co-workers concerning aspiration level regulation (Jucknat, 1937; Sears, 1940) as well as on studies on learned helplessness and coping with stress (Diener & Dweck, 1978), it was hypothesized that during an extended performance sequence, low achiever vulnerability vs. high-achiever resistance to the detrimental effects of accumulating failure is reflected as differing dynamics of aspiration level regulation and emotional response patterns. Corresponding motivation-dynamic differences were predicted in students with task-oriented vs. ego-defensive motivational orientation characteristics (Salonen, Lehtinen & Olkinuora, 1998).

The subjects ($N = 68$) were 43 low-achieving and 19 high-achieving students from the 4th grade. They were selected from an original sample of 417 students. The students were rated by their teachers on Likert-type scales with regard to three motivational orientation tendencies: task-orientation, social dependence orientation and ego-defensive orientation. The word-game task, in which the nonsensical arrangement of letters has to be rearranged to make a word, was employed to examine aspiration level regulation. The anagrams had either one correct solution or could not be solved at all. Task-cards were exposed to the subject in three open boxes, all of them comprising seven parallel sections. Each labeled compartment contained tasks said to belong to one of the seven difficulty-grades (from very easy to very difficult).

Each student attempted a total of 10 word-game tasks (i.e. difficulty level selections followed by the anagram solution). The occurrence of failure was "preprogrammed" as follows. For the first two trials, all of the tasks presented (box 1) were easy. For example, all the sections of the selection-box contained actually only easy tasks. For the next three trials (box 2), the selection-box contained only unsolvable anagrams, which ensured three consecutive failures. For the following three trials (box 3), the items represented the claimed difficulty levels. For the remaining two trials (again box 1), all of the items were easy.

The subjects worked individually. Each trial conformed to the following procedure: (1) The subject went to the desk and selected the difficulty-level. The first experimenter gave the task-card to the subject and asked if the subject believed she or he would find the right solution; (2) After returning to her or his place, the subject pushed the timer button which turned the timer light on and began to work. (3) After having written the answer on the sheet, the subject pushed the timer button again which turned the timer light off and went to the second experimenter to get her or his answer checked. When the time limit (50 seconds) was exceeded, the subject had to go to the second experimenter immediately. In both cases, the second experimenter first asked if the subject believed she had succeeded or failed. The second experimenter then checked the answer, said "right" or "wrong", gave corresponding mark on the answer sheet, and asked what could have caused the outcome. (4) The subject went from the second experimenter's desk to the "selection desk" for a new task-selection. All the choices and the times spent for each selection and performance were recorded. During-the-process interviews were audiotaped, and the task performance and trial selection processes were videotaped for the analysis of the subject's motivational behavior and emotional expressions. Emotional responses linked with the performance or task were classified into positive (i.e. verbal and non-verbal signs of enthusiasm, interest, or joy) and negative (i.e. verbal and non-verbal signs of depressive-inhibited moods or reactance/agitation) according to a predescribed taxonomy (Salonen et al., 1994).

The results show that highly ego-defensive and task-oriented extreme groups' initial mean levels of aspiration represented about the average on the difficulty grade scale (1–7), being, however, slightly lower in the highly ego-defensive than task-oriented group (see Fig. 4). Three successive failure experiences caused rather similar sinking patterns in both groups. As the success rate increased, task-oriented students' restored their initial levels of aspiration levels, whereas highly ego-defensive students demonstrated more marked decreasing tendency after failure.

For an analysis of emotional responses, the subjects were grouped into subgroups of low ($n = 43$) and high ($n = 19$) achievers. As Fig. 5 shows, low and high-achievers differed with regard to the dynamics of emotional responses. The most marked dynamic pattern differences could be seen on non-verbal emotional response measures. During the whole sequence, high-achievers demonstrated practically no signs of negative mood; instead, a few positive emotional responses were observed in this group through the series. Low-achievers demonstrated very few or no positive emotional responses during the sequence, whereas their negative responses increased very rapidly and remained permanently at a high level.

The main findings of the present study suggest that low-achievers' motivational vulnerability, for example, their poor rate of recovery in the face

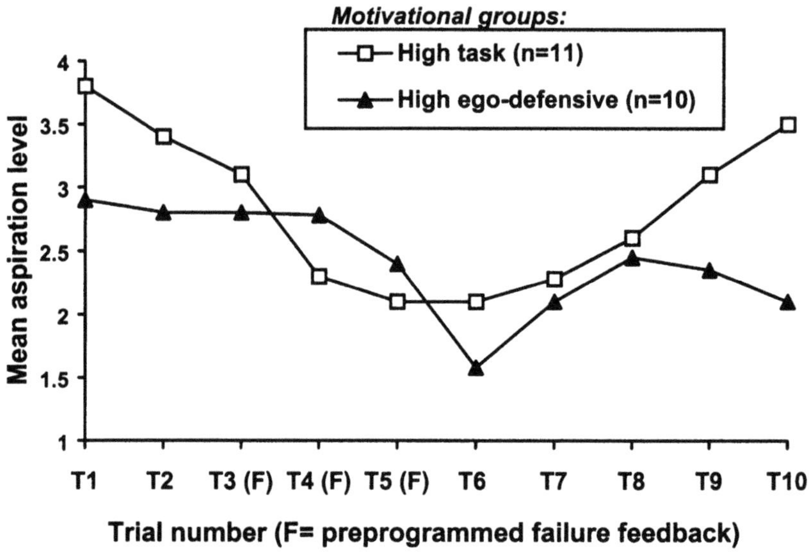

Fig. 4. Regulation of Aspiration Level in Students Rated as High Task-oriented or High Ego-defensive.

of consecutive failures, could be mediated by their tendency to become easily sensitized to situational factors (e.g. failure feedback and time pressure), inducing self-perpetuating negative moods and self-deprecatory thoughts. In larger developmental cycles, such motivational dynamics may cumulatively inhibit self-regulated challenge-formation, which seems to be an important prerequisite for the progressive growth of self-concept of attainment and cognitive skills.

Dynamic Assessment of Young Children's Motivational-emotional Vulnerability

In the study by Salonen, Lepola & Niemi (1998), the role of motivational tendencies in the formation of reading careers was examined through analyzing preschool children's coping behavior in a play-like setting. Thirty-two six-year-old preschool children participated in this study. The participants were selected from 151 kindergarten children on the basis of the preschool teacher's ratings on task, ego-defensive and social dependence orientation (see in detail Vauras, Salonen, Lehtinen & Lepola, 2001).

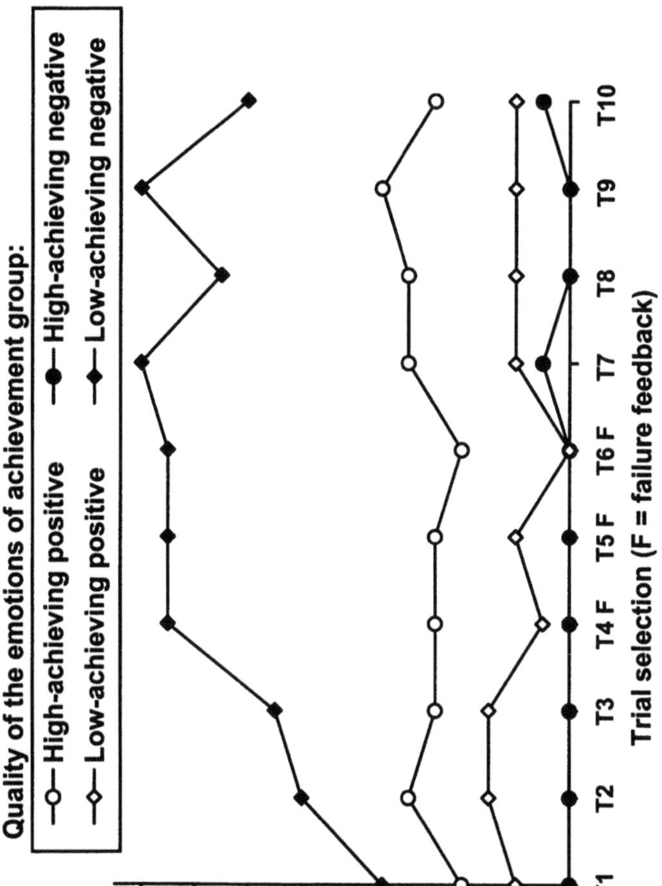

Fig. 5. Task-specific Emotional Responses Among Low and High-achieving Fourth Graders.

Children were assigned, according to their dominating motivational disposition, to one of the four motivational orientation extreme groups: (1) Task orientation (TO) ($n = 8$); (2) Social Dependence Orientation (SDO) ($n = 8$); (3) Ego-Defensive Orientation (EDO) ($n = 8$); and (4) Social Dependence plus Ego Defensive Orientation, i.e. "multiple non-task-orientation" (SEO) ($n = 8$). This grouping enabled us to analyze the validity of the orientation rating through examining the relationship between motivational orientation and coping behavior. In order to analyze children's dynamic motivational dispositions such as motivational-emotional vulnerability, the participants' coping behaviors were observed in an experimental play-like situation in day-care centers six months before the start of primary school (Salonen, Lepola & Niemi, 1998; Lepola, Salonen & Vauras, 2000). The following method illustrates one form of dynamic assessment, that is, analyzing the effects of cumulative pressures and failures on children's coping behavior.

To assess children's coping tendencies, LEGO® components were used for the construction of a castle. The participants were divided into small groups of three to four. Children were instructed to work individually, but they could observe each other's work. In the beginning, the experimenter instructed the group of children as follows, "You can build any kind of castle you like, where anyone you like could live. If you have trouble with task, you can ask for help, but I hope you try yourself!" During the play process, three pressure episodes were arranged by the experimenter: one competition and two obstacle tasks. After eight minutes of free construction, the first obstacle task was given to the children (e.g. "now your task is to build a round high tower" or in the 1st grade play "build a staircase without any supporting pillar over the castle – can you do it?"). In the beginning of each task, the experimenter demonstrated how to begin so that every child could get started. These tasks were impossible because there were only two round components available or excessively long LEGO-stairs crashed down just before the required point. After five minutes, the experimenter said: "let's leave the task. It might be too difficult" and guided the children to continue the free construction of the castle for five minutes. After this, the subjects were asked to participate in a tower-building speed competition with the experimenter. Each child was given a model and corresponding LEGO pieces. The experimenter, who was predetermined to always win, asked after the game "Who won? Who was second?" Then free construction of the castle continued again for five minutes. The second obstacle task was then induced. After five minutes with the task, the experimenter said that the children could continue working on the castle if they wanted. This last phase of free play lasted about seven minutes. The mean total performance time was 37 minutes. (Salonen, Lepola & Niemi, 1998.)

Table 1. Examples of Task-Oriented, Ego-Defensive and Social Dependence Types of Coping Behavior.

Children's behavior in play-like tasks	Coping strategy	Motivational orientation
Krista's coping behavior in pre-school:		
Instruction for a new task: Krista is immediately oriented to follow the experimenter's instruction, then glances backwards, then again follows experimenter (the instruction) and looks at her own Lego-pieces and simultaneously at the experimenter (for a 25 s).	Attending to the instructions and concentrating on the task at hand.	Task-oriented episode
Obstacle task: . . . Presses the pieces, the tower falls and then says: "Now it's broken, I cannot" and looks pleadingly at the experimenter. Then says: "I am a little baby" and smiles pleasingly in the direction of the friend and then experimenter. Then her body is pressed down and she says in a sad voice: "I can only make a square tower, not a round one" (for a 38 s).	Negative verbal expressions followed by emotional appealing and negative verbal expressions.	Ego-defensive episode
Marko's coping behavior in the first grade:		
Task instructions: Stops and follows the instructions, then asks: "How?" Then follows the instructions and the experimenter's example, places a LEGO in his castle.	Concentrating on the instructions. Task-focused questioning.	Task-oriented episode
Task performance: Takes LEGO and orientates himself on the task, says: "I'll make one like this" (in a happy, clear voice), orientates himself on the task and takes new LEGO, glances at his peer and then (for a 172 s) stops, doesn't do anything,	Positive verbal task-related emotions.	Task-oriented episode
follows his peer and then another (8 s), orientates himself anew on the task, glances at his peer and simultaneously takes LEGOs. Then	Seeking social cues.	Social dependence-oriented episode
states: "I am allowed to build a castle – that's cool". Orientates himself on the task. Compares the length of the staircase with a measuring stick! And builds the staircase (93 s).	Enthusiasm and positive task-related emotional responses.	Task-oriented episode

Table 1. Continued.

Children's behavior in play-like tasks	Coping strategy	Motivational orientation
Glances at his friend and totters: "I don't wanna do this, I'd rather build a castle", doesn't do the task, looks at his friend "I WON'T" Stops doing the task and directs himself to building the castle. (The experimenter insists that he continues the task)	Negative verbal emotional responses (e.g. frustrated self-judgements).	Ego-defensive episode
Then Marko says: "I can't, I can't" glances sideways, looks downwards "I won't!"	Anticipation of failure and avoidance intentions.	

The whole LEGO-construction process was videotaped and children's non-verbal and verbal behaviors were transcribed from the videotapes. An analysis of actual durations of behaviors with the smallest unit of a three second episode of unitary behavior was carried out. Task-oriented, ego-defensive and social dependence coping strategies were classified according to the predescribed taxonomy of coping and emotional behavior (Salonen et al, 1994). Thirty percent of transcribed construction processes were cross-checked by an independent rater. The raters agreed on more than 70 of the classified episodes, based on on-line observation. We now present the following examples of task-oriented, ego-defensive and social dependence type of coping behavior manifested in the play-like tasks of two children, Krista and Marko (see Table 1). Both of these children had low reading prerequisites and showed a regressive reading career at school.

This on-line data based on children's coping behavior allowed us to examine whether the theoretically predicted vulnerability differences between task and ego-defensively oriented preschoolers are manifested in coping with feedback and evaluative pressures. Figure 6 shows the mean percentage of ego-defensive coping behavior in total play-like situations and in three pressure tasks as a function of an extreme motivational orientation group.

We performed 4 (motivation group) $\times$ 2 (free play vs. pressure) ANOVA for ego-defensive coping. Significant main effects of motivation group $F(3, 27) = 5.07$, $p < 0.01$ and performance setting $F(1, 27) = 24.51$, $p < 0.001$, were found. In addition, a significant interaction effect of motivation group and setting emerged, $F(3, 27) = 4.92$, $p < 0.01$.

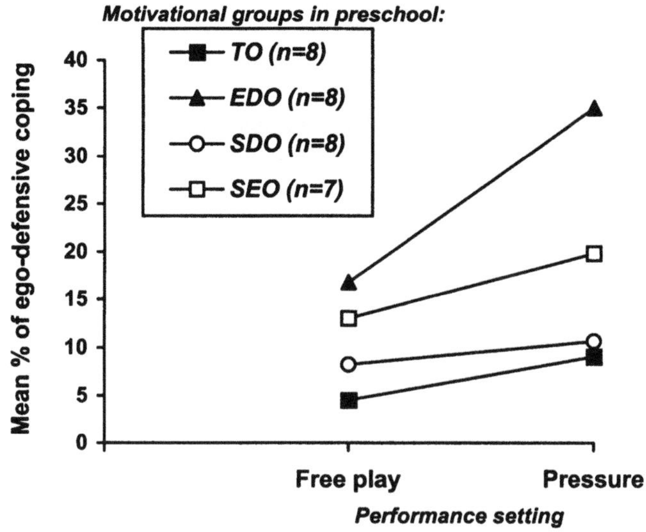

Fig. 6. The Mean Percentage of Ego-defensive Coping in Preschool as a Function of Setting and Orientation Group.

These findings indicate that those children rated high in ego-defensiveness (i.e. EDO and SEO groups) showed significantly more ego-defensive behavior in both free play and pressure situations than was observed in task-oriented children. Corresponding results (in the opposite direction) were found for task-oriented coping behavior. These findings suggest that the static type of motivational orientation rating is a valid measure in terms of task and ego-defensive orientation. Although socially dependent children showed the highest amount of dependent behavior in the various play tasks, the group differences were nonsignificant. A possible explanation could be the difficulty of distinguishing social dependence in young children through the static rating method or the assessment of social dependence is problematic in a child-guided and cognitively moderate easy play-like tasks. In fact, it has been shown that social dependence manifests itself later on with more complex task, such as text comprehension (Lehtinen, Vauras, Salonen, Olkinuora & Kinnunen, 1995).

Further analysis showed that ego-defensive coping behavior increased significantly under pressure settings in children rated as ego-defensive, but not in children rated as task-oriented. This finding underlines not only the validity of motivational orientation constructs, but also ego-defensive children's emotional vulnerability to situational pressure factors, such as evaluation, competition and failure feedback compared to task-oriented children.

Observational Method to Assess Students' Motivation in Authentic Classroom Inquiry Environment

The third study investigated students' on-going involvement and motivational responses in an authentic classroom environment where a class of 8th grade secondary school students worked with a technology supported inquiry. The purpose of this example is to demonstrate observational method based on video recording and other process-oriented data collection methods to assess motivational dynamics in a natural classroom context. Our recent case studies have focused on students' motivation and activity in technology supported inquiry environments at the primary and secondary level (Järvelä, 1998; Järvelä & Niemivirta, 2001; Järvelä, Hakkarainen, Lehtinen & Lipponen, 2001; Salovaara & Järvelä 2001; Järvelä, Lehtinen & Salonen, 2000). The results indicate that technology supported inquiry seems to foster productive task-related interactions, and to enhance student motivation in general. Similar findings on more enduring adaptive tendencies have been found in other studies on student learning in technology-based environments applying socio-constructivist pedagogical models (CTGV, 1992; Hickey, Moore & Pellegrino, 2001). Using a method of dynamic assessment has elucidated that there indeed are students who benefit from the change to a new pedagogical context, and whose situational interpretations are therefore not in line with their prior self-reported motivational tendencies (Järvelä & Niemivirta, 2001). However, it is crucial to note that there are also variances in the quality of the learning processes among the different students: some students have major difficulties in engaging in research alike working procedures and their learning processes are more regressive than progressive. We assumed that during the extended phases of inquiry, there may be certain sequences that are motivationally more demanding than the other and, thus, they may interfere with student task-focused activity.

In this study eight grade secondary students ($N = 17$) worked with a computer supported inquiry project on literacy within science fiction topic derived from a literacy curriculum. The project lasted 12 lessons, each lesson lasting 75 minutes. The student inquiries included individual and collaborative work, with and without computers. The computer supported collaborative learning environment, Knowledge Forum (Scardamalia & Bereiter, 1994), was utilized in the learning project in order to structure the inquiry process, to provide tools for inquiry and to create a forum for the knowledge construction discussion. Process-oriented data, such as on-line interviews, students' written work on the computer database and video-recording, were collected in order to investigate student motivation during the lessons.

The case of Matti is presented in order to describe the method of dynamic assessment analyzing student motivational responses in classroom inquiry activities. One case example is obviously not enough to report the results on student motivation during the classroom activities, but the case example demonstrates the type of data received not only regarding *how* a student is motivated, but also *reasons* for the emergent motivational responses.

Matti's work process was videotaped during the four lessons, yielding about 70 minutes of data per lesson except in the second lesson only 36 minutes (lesson 1 = 82 min, lesson 2 = 36 min, lesson 3 = 67 min, lesson 4 = 78 min). From the beginning of each lesson, the data was coded with the help of Noldus Observer computer program. Continuous time sampling analyses with the smallest unit of a 10 second episode of unitary behavior was categorized for on-task activity or off-task activity. If the student's behavior was impossible to code as either an on or off-task activity (for example, because of obscurity in video-tapings), it was marked as 0-orientation. The coding for on-task activity followed the categories formulated from the items in task-orientation (e.g. a student is concentrated on the task in a way that external disturbances do not interfere with his task-involvement; a student's verbal or non-verbal behavior indicates task-involvement and willingness to stay in a problem-solving situation) or non-task orientation (e.g. a student expresses unwillingness toward a task-situation, conducts imitative or superficial activities or indicates helplessness) scales (Järvelä, 1989; Salonen, Lepola & Niemi, 1998). About 30% of the ratings were cross-checked by an independent rater. The raters agreed on more than 70% of the classified episodes based on on-line observation. Figure 7 describes a coherence of Matti's on-task periods during all four lessons (1–4) and Table 2 summarizes the total time of Matti's on-task and off-task behavior during the four lessons.

The summary of Matti's coded motivational involvement and behavior during the four lessons suggested that on-task activity and learning orientation dominate across the lessons in general. His learning orientation is characterized by coherent behavioral units focused on the learning task. Additional information on his task-involvement can be obtained by focusing on one of the lessons in more detail and reading the qualitative descriptions of different episodes of task involvement that were transcribed during the data analysis (see Fig. 8). Figure 8 illustrates Matti's on-task (1), off-task (2), 0-orientation (3) or no data situations (4) during one lesson.

A phase shift analysis of Matti's task involvement during the first half of the lesson reports 30 minutes of a continuous on-task behavior. The continuous on-task episode begins with Matti's defining his research question in a topic of Science Fiction. The videotape transcription illustrates how he discussed his

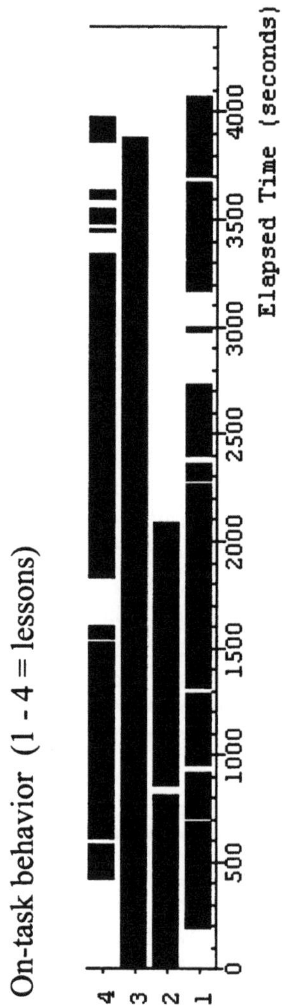

Fig. 7. Matti's On-task Behavior During the Four Lessons.

Table 2. Matti's Total Time of On-Task/Off-Task Behavior During the Four Lessons

	1st lesson	2nd lesson	3rd lesson	4th lesson
On-task	76.5%	95%	100%	70%
Off-task	0.5%	–	–	3%
0-orient.	23%	5%	–	27%
Total	100%	100%	100%	100%

Note that there are differences in amount of data available for each lesson (lesson 1 = 82 min, lesson 2 = 36 min, lesson 3 = 67 min, lesson 4 = 78 min).

topic with the other students on his topic, asked for help from the teacher and read some resource material provided by the teacher. His behavior is characterized by his intrinsic interest to master the task. Later in this episode he began working with the computer, which was to support his inquiry, since he searched for the data base and read and commented on the other student's computer notes.

The described time period is a critical indicator of Matti's approach to a challenging and open task situation, since this is one of the most challenging phases of the inquiry, in which a student is responsible to formulate his own research question on the general topic. Many students described, including Matti the phase of defining their research questions as the most difficult situation in their working process. In the interview, he says: "*Formulating my own research question was the most difficult phase of the inquiry for me*". The next example of an interview describes his own interpretation of that situation and his goals in general.

Interviewer: How did you choose your own topic then?
Matti: I kinda like outlined different alternatives.
Interviewer: What is your topic?
Matti: The planets. How they differ from the earth.
Interview: How did you discover that topic?
Matti: I spent some time thinking about it and reading the book. I also discussed it with the teacher.

(later in the interview)

Interviewer: What was your goal in this project?
Matti: To learn about Science Fiction in general, I mean what it actually is, since I don't know it very well.

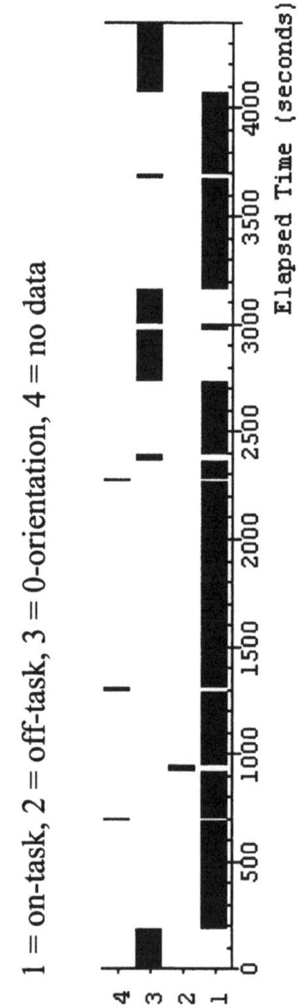

Fig. 8. Matti's On-Task/Off-Task Behavior During One Lesson.

Interviewer: Why do you have such a goal?
Matti: I would like to know more about the issue . . . what it is. If someone speaks about Science Fiction then I would know what it is.
Interviewer: What did you think about the topic of Science Fiction first?
Matti: First nothing, since I did not know anything about it and how to work with it, but finally it went very well.

Both Matti's observed behavior and his own appraisals correspond to the general motivational tendency of a learning oriented student being able to interpret the new features of the task according to his adaptive tendency to master the task (Pintrich & Schrauben, 1992). In Matti's case, an existing learning goal orientation is obvious and his task interest and self-regulation skills interacted with the features of the challenging learning situation. In general the results of this study show that there are different profiles of student motivational involvement. Frequent on-task off-task transitions report a student's difficulties in adaptation to the progressive inquiry, while long-lasting and continuous on-task sequences indicate a student's high involvement and productive process of inquiry. In summary, this case example using one form of dynamic assessment in authentic classroom learning can help in identifying students' approach and avoidance processes during an intensive working process. In a similar vein, data of students' high task-involvement or low task-involvement can describe those situational factors that are critical for the formation of a motivated learning activity in classroom.

CONCLUSIONS

In this chapter we have outlined how a dynamic assessment can be a key to understanding student motivation more profoundly in a classroom context. The theoretical advancement for research on motivation illustrated in this paper is to evidence motivation with more dynamic, interactionistic, constructs, such as motivational recovery, vulnerability and task-involvement. The aim is to capture the ways in which the learning situations are interpreted by the students and to analyze motivationally critical phases of classroom learning. The methodological triangulation carried out by using both static teacher ratings and on-line coping and aspiration level analyses aim to promote our understanding about the role of motivational processes in the development of students' progressive and regressive learning trajectories in classroom context.

Dynamic assessment has been of current interest especially in assessing student learning potential in which the methods have been concerned with identifying student strengths and weaknesses during the learning process (Lidz, 1987). Since dynamic assessment was influenced by Vygotskian (1978) theoretical tradition, its' application to motivational assessment has not been explicitly defined. From the motivational point of view, dynamic assessment contributes not only to the "progressive" aspects of learning potential assessment, but especially to discovering children's "regressive" tendencies actualizing in learning contexts. It is this regressive nature of students' interpretations which we believe to complement the motivation diagnostic. In accordance with the classical experiments of Lewin and his followers (Barker, Dembo and Lewin, 1941; Helm 1954), our dynamic diagnostic method revealed marked differences in the series of responses of high vs. low-achieving and task vs. ego-defensively-oriented students. The motivational vulnerability of low achieving students and students rated as ego-defensively orientated was shown in their tendency to respond to cumulative failures and evaluative pressures with growing negative emotional responses and increasing ego-defensive coping behavior. On the contrary, high-achieving and task-oriented students responded to cumulative failures and evaluative pressures with much stronger resiliency and motivational recovery. In sum, we see the motivational vulnerability that is manifested in an actual learning context and performance series not solely from a motivational point of view, that is, as weakening later efforts, but also as actually leading to disorganization of activity in subsequent learning situations.

An important point in dynamic assessment compared to static assessment is the possibility to take into account invariant relations of perceived learning environment and actual behavior. Consequently, dynamic assessment reveals some essentials of learning motivation that are not able to be captured in all nuances by static type of questionnaires or by paper and pencil tests, such as student motivational vulnerability and resilience. These notions are in line with the increasing amount of research that reports on findings in which students' emotion and affective experiences contribute to their task-engagement and motivation in learning (e.g. Op 't Eynde, De Corte & Verschaffel, 2001).

A critical aspect for dynamic motivational assessment in comparison with a more traditional static assessment is to design experimental settings that correspond to the typical learning and performance situations of a school context. In our studies, this has been implemented by creating tasks in which students are exposed to different motivational challenges, such as time pressure, social comparison, accumulating failure or feelings of uncertainty. It is presumed that these situations are ecologically valid to assess such social, emotional and motivational factors in learning which are not measured with static measures.

Moving from an experimental setting towards a natural classroom, the third example, which consisted of a task with open and unstructured features, illustrated the student's motivation in a classroom context. In this setting using a method of dynamic assessment elucidated that the students having different motivational tendencies can benefit from the features of the environment in different ways. Using the method of dynamic assessment can help to identify student motivational involvement, e.g. mechanisms of approach and avoidance behavior during an intensive working process. In a similar vein, the data received can describe those contextual factors, e.g. how students interpret the certain features of a pedagogical environment, which are critical for the formation of motivated learning activity in the classroom and thus, contribute to the design of more pedagogically valid learning environments.

The current educational research highlights the need to consider different aspects of human learning, such as cognitive, motivational and social (Pintrich, 2000). One of the most salient features of the current research in learning theories as well as in motivation is the importance of contextual factors and how they can facilitate or constrain student learning. Although the discussion of the interaction of context and motivation is currently lively, we can see that there is a long tradition (Lewin, 1934; Luria, 1932; see also Ford, 1992) of considering behavior as a function of the interaction of person and his or her environment.

REFERENCES

Alexander, P. A. (2000). Toward a model of academic development: Schooling and the acquisition of knowledge. *Educational Researcher, 29*, 28–33.

Anderman, L. H., & Anderman, E. M. (2000). Considering contexts in educational psychology: Introduction to the special issue. *Educational Psychologist, 35*, 67–68.

Barker, R., Dembo, T., & Lewin, K. (1941). Frustration and regression: An experiment with young children. *University of Iowa Studies in Child Welfare, 18*(1).

Boekaerts, M. (1996). Personality and the psychology of learning. *European Journal of Personality, 10*, 377–404.

Boekaerts, M. (1999). Motivated learning: studying student *situation transactional units. In: M. Boekaerts & P. Nenniger (Eds), *Advances in motivation from the European viewpoint* [Special Issue]. *European Journal of Psychology of Education, 14*, 41–55.

Boekaerts, M. (2001). Context sensitivity: activated motivational beliefs, current concerns and emotional arousal. In: S. Volet & S. Jarvela (Eds), *Motivation in Learning Contexts: Theoretical Advances and Methodological Implications* (pp. 17–31). London: Pergamon Press.

Bransford, J., Brown, A., & Cocking, R. (1999). *How people learn: brain, mind, experience, and school*. Washington, D.C.: National Academy Press.

Brown, A. L. (1988). Motivation to learn and understand: On taking charge of one's own learning. *Cognition and Instruction, 5*, 311–321.

Brown, A. L., & Campione, J. A. (1996). Psychological theory and the design of innovative learning environments. In: L. Schauble & R. Glaser (Eds), *Innovations in learning: New Environments for Education* (pp. 289–235). Mahwah, NJ: Erlbaum.

Campione, J. C. (1989). Assisted assessment: A taxonomy of approaches and an outline of strengths and weaknesses. *Journal of Learning Disabilities, 22*, 151–165.

Campione, J. C., & Brown, A. L. (1987). Linking dynamic assessment with school achievement. In: C. S. Lidz (Ed.), *Dynamic Assessment* (pp. 82–115). New York: Guilford.

Campione, J. C., Brown, A. L., Ferrara, R. A., & Bryant, N. R. (1984). The zone of proximal development: Implications for individual differences and learning. In: B. Rogoff & J. V. Wertch (Eds), *Children's Learning in the "Zone of Proximal Development"* (pp. 77–92). San Francisco: Jossey-Bass.

Cognition and Technology Group at Vanderbilt (1992). The Jasper series as an example of anchored instruction: Theory, program description, and assessment data. *Educational Psychologist, 27*, 231–315.

Cole, M., & Bruner, J. S. (1971). Cultural differences and inferences about psychological processes. *American Psychologist, 26*, 867–876.

De Corte, E. (2000). Marrying theory building and the improvement of school practice: a permanent challenge for instructional psychology. *Learning and Instruction, 10*(3), 249–266.

Diener, C., & Dweck, C. (1978). An analysis of learned helplessness: Continuous changes in performance, strategy, and achievement cognitions following failure. *Journal of Personality and Social Psychology, 36*, 451–462.

Elliot, A. J. (1999) Approach and avoidance motivation and achievement goals. *Educational Psychologist, 34*, 169–189.

Endler, N. S., & Magnusson, D. (1976). Towards an interactional psychology of personality. *Psychological Bulletin, 83*, 956–974.

Ford, M. E. (1992). *Motivating humans: Goals, emotions and personal agency beliefs*. London: SAGE.

Gipps, C. (1999). Sociocultural aspects of assessment. *Review of Research in Education, 24*, 355–392.

Heckhausen, H. (1974). *Motivationsanalysen (Motivation analyses)*. Heidelberg: Springer-Verlag.

Helm, J. (1954). Ueber den Einfluss affektiver Spannungen auf das Denkhandel [The effects of affective tension on thinking activity.] *Zeitschrift fuer Psychologie, 157*, 23–105.

Hickey, D. T., Moore, A. L., & Pellegrino, J. W. (2001). The motivational and academic consequences of two innovative mathematics environments. Do innovation and reform make a difference? *American Educational Research Journal*, in press.

Järvelä, S. (1998). Socioemotional aspects of students' learning in cognitive-apprenticeship environment. *Instructional Science, 26*, 439–471.

Järvelä, S., Hakkarainen, K., Lehtinen, E., & Lipponen, L. (2001). Creating Computer Supported Collaborative Learning (CSCL) Culture in Finnish Schools: Research Perspectives on Sociocognitive Effects. *International Journal of Continuing Engineering Education and Life-Long Learning, 11*(4/5/6), 365–374.

Järvelä, S., Lehtinen, E., & Salonen, P. (2000). Socioemotional orientation as a mediating variable in teaching learning interaction: Implications for instructional design. *Scandinavian Journal of Educational Research, 44*, 293–307.

Järvelä, S., & Niemivirta, M. (2001). Motivation in context: Challenges and possibilities in studying the role of motivation in new pedagogical cultures. In: S. Volet & S. Järvelä (Eds), *Motivation in Learning Contexts: Theoretical Advances and Methodological Implications* (pp. 105–127). London: Pergamon.

Jucknat, M. (1937). Leistung, anspruchsniveau und selbstbewusstsein. *Psychologische Forshung, 22*, 89–130.

Lehtinen, E., Vauras, M., Salonen, P., Olkinuora, E., & Kinnunen, R. (1995). Long-term development of learning activity: motivational, cognitive, and social interaction. *Educational Psychologist, 30*, 21–35.

Lepola, J. (2000). *Motivation in early school years: Developmental patterns and cognitive consequences*. Unpublished doctoral dissertation, University of Turku, Finland.

Lepola, J., Salonen, P., & Vauras, M. (2000). The development of motivational orientations as a function of divergent reading careers from pre-school to the second grade. *Learning and Instruction, 10*, 153–177.

Lewin, K. (1935). *A dynamic theory of personality*. New York: McGraw-Hill.

Lewin, K. (1954). Behavior and development as a function of the total situation. In: L. Carmichael (Ed.), *Manual of Child Psychology* (pp. 918–970). New York: Wiley.

Lidz, C. S. (Ed.) (1987). *Dynamic Assessment*. London: The Guildford Press.

Luria, A. R. (1932). *The nature of human conflicts*. New York: Liveright.

Maehr, M. L., & Nicholls, J. G. (1980). Culture and achievement motivation: a second look. In: N. Warren (Ed.), *Studies in Cross-cultural Psychology* (Vol. 2, pp. 221–268). London: Academic Press.

Meltzer. R., & Reid, D. K. (1994). New directions in the assessment of students with speacial needs: The shift toward a constructivist perspective. *Journal of Special Education, 28*, 338–356.

Mischel, W. (1973). Toward a cognitive social learning reconceptualization of personality. *Psychological Review, 80*, 252–283.

Mischel, W., & Schoda, Y. (1995). A cognitive-affective system theory of personality: Reconceptualizing situations, dispositions, dynamics, and invariance in personality structure. *Psychological Review, 102*, 246–268.

Nisbett, R. E., & Wilson, D. (1977). *Telling more than we know: Verbal reports on mental processes. Psychological Review, 84*, 231–279.

Op 't Eynde, De Corte & Verschaffel (2001). "What to learn from what we feel?" The role of students' emotions in the mathematics classroom. In: S. Volet & S. Järvelä (Eds), *Motivation in Learning Contexts: Theoretical Advances and Methodological Implications* (pp. 149–167). London: Pergamon/Elsevier.

Palincsar, A., Brown, A., & Campione, J. (1991). Dynamic assessment. In: L. Swanson (Ed.), *Handbook on the Assessment of Learning Disabilities: Theory, Research, and Practice* (pp. 75–94). Austin, TX: PRO-ED.

Pintrich, P. (2000). Educational psychology at the millennium: A look back and a look forward. *Educational Psychologist, 35* (4), 221–226.

Pintrich, P. R., & Schrauben, B. (1992). Students' motivational beliefs and their cognitive engagement on classroom tasks. In: D. H. Schunk & J. Meece (Eds), *Students Perceptions in the Classroom: Causes and Consequences* (pp. 149–183). Hillsdale, NJ: Lawrence Erlbaum Associates.

Salomon, G. (1996) Studuing novel learning environments as patterns of change. In: S. Vosniadou, E. De Corte, R. Glaser & H. Mandl (Eds), *International Perspectives on the Psychological Foundations of Technology–based Learning Environments*. Hillsdale, NJ: Erlbaum.

Salonen, P., Lehtinen, E., & Olkinuora, E. (1998). Expectations and beyond: The development of motivation and learning in a classroom context. In: J. Brophy (Ed.), *Advances in Research On Teaching. Expectations in the Classroom* (Vol. 7, pp. 111–150). Greenwich, Conn.: JAI Press.

Salonen, P., Lepola, J., & Niemi, P. (1998). The development of first graders' reading skill as a function of pre-school motivational orientation and phonemic awareness. *European Journal of Psychology of Education, 13*, 155–174.

Salonen, P., Lepola, J., Vauras, M., Rauhanummi, T, Lehtinen, E., & Kinnunen, R. (1994). *Diagnostiset testit 3: Motivaatio, metakognitio ja matematiikka* [Diagnostic tests 3: Motivation, metacognition and mathematics]. Centre for Learning Research. University of Turku.Painosalama. Turku.

Salovaara, H., & Järvelä, S. (2001). Students' strategic actions in computer supported collaborative inquiry. *Learning Environments Research*, accepted for publication.

Scardamalia, M., & Bereiter, C. (1994). Computer support for knowledge building communities. *The Journal of the Learning Sciences, 1*, 37–68.

Schoda, Y., Mischel, W., & Wright, J. C. (1993). Links between personality judgement and contextualized behavior patterns: Situation-behavior profiles of personality prototypes. *Social Cognition, 4*, 399–429.

Sears, P. S. (1940). Levels of aspiration in academically successful and unsuccessful children. *Journal of Abnormal and Social Psychology, 35*, 495–536.

Spector, J. E. (1992). Predicting progress in beginning reading: Dynamic assessment of phonemic awareness. *Journal of Educational Psychology, 84*, 353–363.

Tinbergen, N., & Tinbergen, E. (1983). *'Autistic' children: New hope for a cure*. London: Allen & Unwin.

Turner, J. C., & Meyer, D. K. (2000). Studying and understanding the instructional contexts of classrooms: Using our past to forge our future. *Educational Psychologist, 35*, 69–85.

Vauras, M., Salonen, P., Lehtinen, E., & Lepola, J. (2001). Long-term development of motivation and cognition in family and school contexts. In: S. Volet & S. Jarvela (Eds.) *Motivation in Learning Contexts: Theoretical Advances and Methodological Implications* (pp. 295–315). London: Pergamon Press.

Volet, S., & Järvelä, S. (2001) (Eds). *Motivation in learning contexts: Theoretical advances and methodological implications*. London: Pergamon Press.

Vygotsky, L. S. (1978). *Mind in society: The development of higher psychological processes*. In: M. Cole, V. John-Steiner & E. Souberman (Eds). Cambridge, MA: Harvard University Press.

7. INDIVIDUAL DIFFERENCES AND DEVELOPMENTAL TRENDS IN MOTIVATION: INTEGRATING PERSON-CENTERED AND VARIABLE-CENTERED METHODS

Markku Niemivirta

INTRODUCTION

This chapter examines the characteristics and implications of person-centered and variable-centered approaches to the study motivation. It is argued that these two approaches are not fully independent of each other, and that in many cases an integrative approach might result in a more thorough treatment of the given domain of inquiry. In the first section, the various aspects of both approaches are illustrated with the help of existing exemplary studies. Next, the possibilities and justifications for an integrative account are discussed, followed by two empirical studies utilizing such a perspective. The main goal of this chapter is thus to increase awareness of the range of methods available that can be utilized for studying individual differences and developmental trends in motivation from an integrative perspective.

New Directions in Measures and Methods, Volume 12, pages 241–275.

ISBN: 0-7623-0819-2

PERSON-CENTERED AND VARIABLE-CENTERED APPROACHES TO THE STUDY OF MOTIVATION – CHARACTERISTICS AND IMPLICATIONS

In 1968, Karabenick and Youssef reported an interesting study that examined task performance as a function of motive level and perceived difficulty (Karabenick & Youssef, 1968). Based on Atkinson's risk-taking model (Atkinson, 1957), they predicted that persons in whom the motive to achieve success is relatively stronger than the motive to avoid failure should perform better at tasks designated as being intermediately difficult than at easy or difficult tasks, and persons with the opposite motivational pattern should instead perform better at either easy or difficult tasks. Karabenick and Youssef used the Thematic Apperception Task (TAT; McClelland, Atkinson, Clark & Lowell, 1953) to measure individual differences in the strength of achievement motive and the Test Anxiety Questionnaire (TAQ; Mandler & Sarason, 1952) to assess individual differences in the strength of failure avoidance motive. Based on scores on both tasks, participants were place in four motive groups. Persons above the median on the TAT and below the median on the TAQ were classified as having high motive to achieve success and those below the median on the TAT and above the median on the TAQ were classified as having high motive to avoid failure. Participants high or low on both measures were assumed to fall between the extreme motive groups. The actual task consisted of a paired-associate learning task. Three equally difficult sets of items were designated as being either very easy or very difficult, or of intermediate difficulty. As illustrated in Fig. 1, the results of the study confirmed Karabenick and Youssef's predictions concerning the performance trends in different motive groups: the means indicated an inverted U-shaped function for the high achievement motivation group and a U-shaped function for the group of failure avoidant participants.

Three decades (and many disciplinary changes) later, Elliot, McGregor and Gable published a study that also focused on how motivational factors influence performance (Elliot, McGregor & Gable, 1999). They based their work on contemporary goal-theoretical accounts of motivation by examining the relationships between participants' achievement goals, study strategies, and exam performance. Drawing on the so-called trichotomous achievement goal framework (see Elliot, 1997), Elliot and his colleagues assumed that study-related cognitive activities – measured with self-report scales for deep processing, surface processing, disorganization, effort, and persistence, respectively – would be differently predicted by different achievement goals. Further,

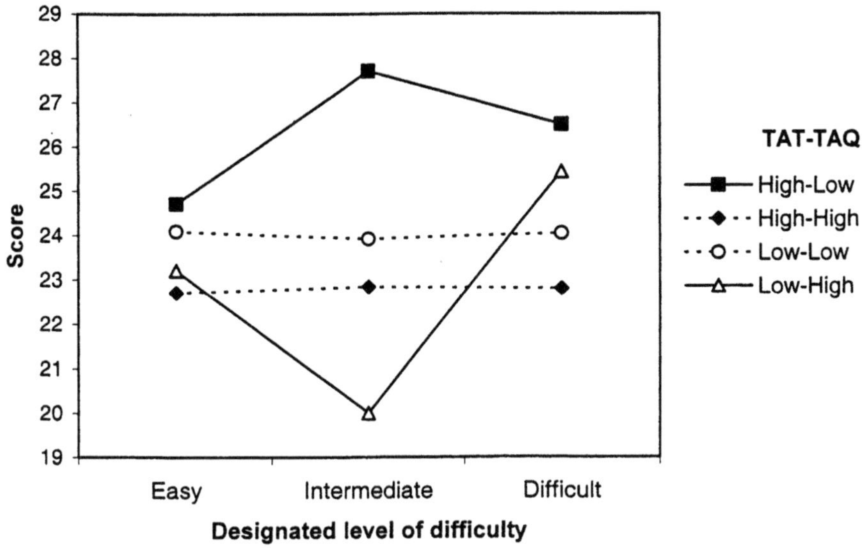

Fig. 1. Performance as a Function of Motive Level and Perceived Difficulty.
Source: Karabenick & Youssef, 1968.

study strategies were hypothesized to differently influence exam performance as well as mediate the effects of achievement goals on performance. In order to test these assumptions, Elliot et al. carried out a series of multiple regression analyses. Parts of their findings are illustrated in Fig. 2, which shows how specific study activities indeed mediated the influence of different goals on performance.

These two interesting studies – unrelated *per se* – illustrate a number of important issues relevant in current motivation research. First of all, they exemplify the historical changes in the conceptual and theoretical frameworks that have taken place in the study of motivation in recent decades. While the achievement motivation theory employed by Karabenick and Youssef (1968) considers motivational forces in terms of learned drives and describes performance situations as the battle fields between the conflicting forces of fear of failure and hope for success, the achievement goal theory advocated by Elliot et al. (1999) conceptualizes motivation in terms of the purposes and reasons that drive individuals towards action and influence the quality and intensity of their engagement. Although the differentiation of motivation as either a pulling or a pushing force is a fundamental one, these views are by no

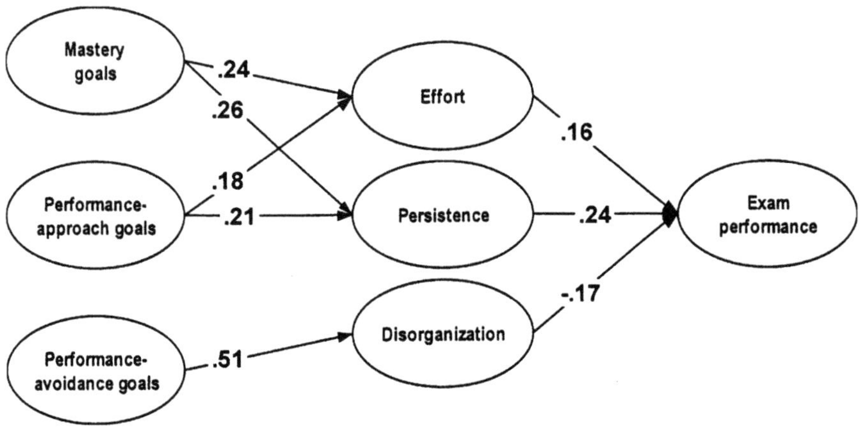

Fig. 2. A Mediational Analysis of Achievement Goals, Study Strategies, and Performance.

Source: Elliot, McGregor & Gable, 1999.

means independent of each other (e.g. Elliot, 1997; Heckhausen, 1991; see also McClelland, Koestner & Weinberger, 1989).

Despite the historical changes in the dominating paradigms of psychological and educational research (cf. Cronbach, 1957, 1975), the aforementioned theoretical standpoints do not necessarily imply different methodological approaches for studying the given phenomena. Nevertheless, this type of difference is strongly present in the above examples. The experimental study by Karabenick and Youssef (1968) is a solid example of a *person-centered* approach, while the work by Elliot, McGregor, and Gable (1999) illustrates the use of *variable-centered* methods for the study of motivation. The critical difference between these approaches is whether the analyses focus on examining relations among variables within a sample or on revealing groups of similar individuals across variables (Bergman, 1998; Magnusson, 1998). Within the person-centered approach, individuals or groups of individuals are treated as the basic units of analysis. Of specific interest are thus the individual value profiles across variables, not the variables as such. In contrast, variable-centered approaches focus on single variables or combinations of variables as well as on their interrelationships and associations with other criteria. The basic assumption – although often implicit – is that the measures of the relations among variables studied *across* individuals are valid for the relations among the variables *within* the individuals (cf. Cronbach, 1957; Magnusson, 1998).

In studies utilizing a person-centered approach, research problems and hypotheses are formulated in terms of individuals and value configurations, whereas in variable-centered analyses this is done in terms of variables and variable relations. Subsequently, the results are interpreted and generalizations made in such terms as well. In light of these remarks, let us now take another look at the example studies presented above to see how the different approaches manifest themselves in Karabenick and Youssef's and Elliot and his colleague's research designs, choices of methods, as well as in the language used.

Karabenick and Youssef (1968) formulate their hypothesis clearly in terms of different types of individuals. In line with their theoretical framework, they assume that *persons with dissimilar motivational profiles* perform differently under specific conditions. Since the study is carried out as an experiment with contextual manipulation, the design of the study concurs with the framework as well: participants are placed into different groups based on their value profiles across two central variables. Note, that the two variables in question are virtually unrelated ($r = 0.04$). Based on the results of a series of ANOVAs, Karabenick and Youssef interpret their findings in individual-oriented terms. They conclude, for example, that "an important finding of this study is that the performance of persons classified as having M_{AF} [motive to avoid failure] $> M_S$ [motive to approach success] . . . showed a relative aversion for intermediate difficulty items" (Karabenick & Youssef, 1968, p. 418).

Elliot, McGregor and Gable (1999), in contrast, formulate their assumptions in variable terms. They hypothesize that different study strategies not only influence exam performance, but also mediate the effects of various achievement goals on the outcome. All constructs – both goals and strategies – are specified by means of single variables, which in turn are based on participants' responses to self-report scales. The design of the study is purely correlational focusing on the relationships between items and variables. In practice, they first produce composite scores based on factor analyses, and then carry out a series of path analyses in order to establish predictive relationships among the sets of given variables. As pointed out earlier, being performed on the whole sample, these analyses incorporate the implicit assumption that the relations among the variables across the individuals are valid for the relations within the individuals as well. In a coherent manner, Elliot et al. then interpret their results and draw conclusions in variable terms. For example, they state that "combining deep and surface processing into an omnibus construct would have led to null results for performance-avoidance goals, thereby masking the fact that these goals were negatively related to deep processing and positively related to surface processing" (Elliot, McGregor & Gable, 1999, p. 559).

In contrast to the preceding examples, many studies cannot be categorized simply as either person-centered or variable-centered. Then again, in other cases the theoretical framework is built on such strong person- or variable-centered premises, that the valid study of the phenomenon virtually necessitates the use of corresponding methods as well (cf. Bergman, Cairns, Nilsson & Nystedt, 2000; Cairns, Bergman & Kagan, 1998). Nevertheless, it is also entirely possible that the underlying theory justifies or even invites an integrated approach for the study of the given phenomenon. In such a situation, the potential methodological eclecticism has, however, its dangers by being seriously prone to artificiality and unsound rationale. With this is mind, the main goal of the remaining part of this chapter is to illustrate with genuine research problems and real data how person- and variable-centered methods can be utilized in order to build an analytically sound design without losing its conceptual coherence.

INTEGRATING PERSON-CENTERED AND VARIABLE-CENTERED APPROACHES – EMPIRICAL EXAMPLES

Theoretical Justification for an Integrated Approach

A quick look at both the classical and contemporary models of motivation reveals, that most of them emphasize either situational or personal parameters in describing and explaining motivation (see Atkinson, 1964; McClelland, 1985; Weiner, 1986). More specifically, some models conceptualize motivational phenomena in terms of situationally induced motivational states and related behavior, whereas others treat them as dispositions – more or less stable characteristics of an individual. Many authors have, however, noted that these views need not to be alternative or competing, but rather complementary.

Niemivirta (1998a; see also Boekaerts & Niemivirta, 2000) and Pintrich (2000a) both argued that motivational dispositions could be described in terms of chronically accessible knowledge structures that become activated based on situational and environmental cues (cf. Bargh & Brandollar, 1996; Higgins, 1996). According to this position, many motivational dispositions could be defined as individuals' preferences for certain types of outcomes or as tendencies to engage in certain types of activities. A preference or a tendency is characteristic for an individual, but it may also be induced by the situations. To give an example: A competitive situation incorporates certain features and cues that make it competitive in the first place (e.g. social comparison, heightened public self-awareness). Such features serve a twofold function: on one hand, they call for the individual's attention thus activating his or her knowledge structures, and on the other hand, they are perceived and interpreted in accordance to one's prior knowledge and personal intentions. Therefore, a competitive situation should activate certain relevant knowledge structures in all people, but the better the fit between the situational setting and the individual's preferences (i.e. the applicability of chronically accessible preferences), the stronger their impact on further interpretations. Thus, people high, for example, in performance orientation should be particularly sensitive to competitiveness-related cues and hence more likely to respond accordingly to such cues.

This view implies a number of things. First of all, it suggests that we should be able to identify groups of individuals with similar types of motivational preferences or tendencies. This further implies that these groups might differ from each other in terms of, say, their situational interpretations and appraisals, but it does not, however, mean that the various situation-specific *mechanisms* that operate in their unique ways should vary between the groups. For example, the well-established fact that higher situational self-efficacy is likely to lead to better performance might well hold for all individuals (cf. Pajares, 1997).

In a sense, this line of argumentation is also in agreement with the example studies presented in the beginning. Karabenick & Youssef's (1968) study examined how groups of individuals performed under certain conditions. They assumed that the interaction between the individuals' situational interpretations (e.g. perceived difficulty) and their dispositional motivational tendencies resulted in different levels of performance. However, they did not explicitly examine the nature of this interaction and whether it operated in a similar fashion in all groups. Elliot, McGregor and Gable (1999), instead, focused on the procedural nature of individuals' performance-influencing determinants, but they did not examine whether the predictive relationships between study strategies and performance varied across individuals with different types of motivational tendencies. Their results do indicate that individuals' motivational tendencies might indeed be associated with some other individual factors, but they say nothing about the extent to which the patterning of these associations might vary across the individuals.

The first example study will focus on this particular issue. An action-theoretical view on motivation will be adopted for examining the extent to which the patterning of some relevant situation-specific personal factors varies across individuals or groups of individuals. Despite the theoretically meaningful foci, the main emphasis will be on demonstrating the use and utility of some methodological means for studying such complex questions from an integrative perspective.

Study 1: Examining the Patterning of Relationships Between Variables: Differences and Similarities Across Groups

Theoretical Framework and Research Questions

Drawing upon an action-theoretical framework, Skinner, Chapman, and Baltes (1988) proposed that children's beliefs concerning action-control are comprised of three interrelated sets of beliefs. In this tripartite view, means-ends beliefs are defined as children's expectancies about the extent to which certain causes or means produce a desired outcome or prevent an undesired one. Agency beliefs are defined as personal perceptions about the extent to which one possesses or utilizes these potential means, and control expectancy is defined as a general expectation that one can obtain a desired outcome without explicit reference to a specific means. Several empirical studies support this framework and the relative importance of these three belief systems in relation to children's academic performance is well documented (e.g. Little & Lopez, 1997; Little, Oettingen, Stetsenko & Baltes, 1995; Niemivirta, 1998b; for an overview, see Little, 1998). These studies show, for example, that self-related agency beliefs of effort and ability are strongly associated with academic performance.

Of specific interest here is the fact that basically all studies following this framework have been conducted from a variable-centered perspective. This is no surprise, though, given that the theory itself is strongly variable-oriented. However, since the core constructs represent personal beliefs – i.e. kind of dispositions – one might ask whether individuals could be classified into homogenous groups based on these presumably stable sets of beliefs. Furthermore, if that were the case, it would make sense to examine whether these groups differed from each other in relation to some other relevant factors as well.

Due to the fact that self-related agency beliefs have proven to be tightly associated with academic performance, the present study focused on them. In line with the above, the main goal was to examine: (1) whether high school students could be justly classified in terms of their agency beliefs of effort and ability; and (2) whether these potential groups of students differed from each other in relation to their performance-related situational appraisals and the actual level of performance.

Participants and Procedure

The sample comprised of 995 ninth-grade students (498 girls and 497 boys). All students participated in a test session, which consisted of a subset of tasks from a series of tests tapping various aspects of higher-order reasoning skills (Ross & Ross, 1976). Well before the test, the students completed a questionnaire tapping various domains of motivational beliefs. In the actual task situation, students were first given instructions explaining what the task was all about and what they were required to do. They were then presented an example item with the correct answer. After the instruction, but before beginning to work on the task, the students completed a short questionnaire concerning their task-related self-appraisals.

Measures

The questionnaire on students' motivational beliefs included items tapping two types of agency beliefs (see Niemivirta, 1998b). The scale for agency belief of effort (herein, "*a*Effort") included four items reflecting the students' evaluations of the extent of their school-related effort expenditure (e.g. "*I study hard in order to do well at school work*") and the scale for agency belief of ability (herein, "*a*Ability") consisted of four items assessing students' perceptions of their academic ability ("*I'm smart enough to do well at school work*"). All items were measured using a simple Likert-scale ranging from 1 ("*Does not describe me at all*") to 7 ("*Describes me perfectly*").

The pre-task questionnaire focusing on students' task-specific situational appraisals consisted of ten items concerning participants' anticipated interest (e.g. "*This test appears to be very interesting*"), claimed self-handicapping ("*I do not feel quite well now and it probably will affect my success in the next task*"), and self-efficacy (e.g. "*I believe I will do well in this task*"). All items were assessed on a seven-point Likert-scale ranging from 1 ("*Not true at all for me*") to 7 ("*Very true for me*").

Analyses and Results

Classification of participants. The first task was to categorize students based on their agency beliefs of effort and ability. Traditionally, this sort of classification has been done by means of median splits (e.g. Ames & Archer, 1988; Miller, Behrens, Greene & Newman, 1993, Pintrich, 2000b) or cluster analyses (e.g. Meece & Holt, 1993; Niemivirta, 1998b; Pintrich & Garcia, 1991). The problem with the median split method is its artificiality: it will always result in two groups, no matter whether the classification actually represents any sort of "real" taxonomy. Differences in degree (i.e. more or less of something) are not, however, the same as differences in type (see Meehl,

1992 and Waller & Meehl, 1998 for lengthy discussions on this issue). Furthermore, when there are more than one or two variables according to which the splitting procedure is performed, the solution becomes increasingly complex. For example, with three variables the number of groups would already be eight.

Cluster analytical methods, in contrast, can be considered somewhat more appropriate. In line with the principles of a person-centered approach, the goal of using cluster analysis is to organize observed data into meaningful structures (cf. Bergman, 1998; Milligan, 1981; Milligan & Cooper, 1987). However, despite its intuitively sensible logic, cluster analysis as a method has been criticized mainly because of its explorative nature (see Meehl, 1992): different algorithms easily lead to different solutions and the decision for the number of clusters is usually based on some "rules of thumb" or arbitrary criteria (for excellent discussions on how to effectively use cluster analytical methods in person-centered analyses, see Bergman, 1998; 2000).

Alternative methods for discrete data include *latent trait* and *latent class* models (Heinen, 1996; Rost & Langeheine, 1997a). They both share the assumption that the observed data structure results from a latent structure. However, with latent trait analysis (LTA) the defining unobserved structure is continuous, whereas with latent class analysis (LCA) the latent structure is nominal (cf. Table 1). Thus, latent trait refers to a continuous dimension, which all individuals are mapped on based on their response pattern on a set of categorical variables, whereas latent class refers to the categories of a latent variable that is discrete (Rost & Langeheine, 1997b).

Latent class analysis (LCA) is often called a categorical-data analogue to factors analysis (cf. McCutcheon, 1987), because it enables the description of categorical latent variables from an analysis of the structure of the relationships among several categorical observed variables. However, since LCA is more concerned with the relationships between cases than associations between variables, it seems to be more closely related to cluster analysis. An important difference between standard clustering techniques and LCA or LTA is that the

Table 1. A Simplified Typology of Latent Structure Analyses.

	Categorical latent	Continuous latent
Categorical manifest	*Latent class analysis*	*Latent trait analysis*
Continuous manifest	*Latent profile analysis*	*Factor analysis*

latter are model-based. That is, a statistical model is postulated for the population from which the sample under study is derived.

A special case of LCA is the *Mixed Rasch Model* (MR-model), which attempts to overcome some deficiencies identified with either Rasch-models or latent class models (Rost, 1990). One drawback of ordinary latent class models is the restrictive assumption that all individuals of a given class are identical with respect to their response probabilities. The idea with MR-models is that a Rasch-model describes the response behavior of all individuals *within* a latent class, but that different sets of item parameters hold for the different latent classes (Rost & von Davier, 1995). In other words, individuals sharing similar response profiles are classified into homogenous groups. The criteria for within-group similarity and between-group dissimilarity are in part dependent on the particular mixture distribution model applied (see below). Thus, another advantage with MR-modeling over, for example, cluster analysis is the possibility to test the fit of the model to the data. The present study applied the MR-model in its generalized version for polytomous ordinal responses (see Rost, 1991).

The program WINMIRA (von Davier, 2000) was used to estimate model parameters for a series of two different types of polytomous mixture models, the rating scale model (cf. Andrich, 1978) and the equidistance model (cf. Andrich, 1982), respectively, which hold slightly different presumptions about the way participants use the given response alternatives. The former assumes that the distances between (pairs of adjacent) response alternatives are constant across all items, whereas the latter assumes that the distances between different response alternatives are constant within each item.

Three items from both *a*Effort and *a*Ability were used for the analysis. The fit of different solutions for the classification was evaluated based on three typical information criteria, posterior class membership probabilities, and the results of a bootstrapping procedure (see von Davier, 1997, for details). Table 2 shows the information criteria values for different number of latent classes. For these criteria, smaller values indicate better fit of the model to the data (for a discussion on the theory and use of different types of information criteria, see Agresti, 1990). As the results show, the best fit was obtained for a three-class equidistance model.

Item parameters (location) in Table 3 illustrate the relative "attractiveness" of each item within the classes. Lower scores reflect a higher probability of agreeing with the statement. As can be inferred, the values for class 1 indicate the largest differentiation between the two sets of items. That is, the members of this group agreed more with the items referring to personal ability than with the items reflecting effort expenditure. The two other classes were mainly

Table 2. Information Criteria Values for Different Numbers of Classes.

		AIC	BIC	CAIC
2 classes	Rating scale	18106.57	18226.21	18251.21
	Equidistance scale	17737.89	17867.10	17894.10
3 classes	Rating scale	17872.47	18054.32	18092.32
	Equidistance scale	*17539.49*	*17735.70*	*17776.70*
4 classes	Rating scale	17833.40	18077.46	18128.46
	Equidistance scale	*17502.86*	17766.07	17821.07

Note: AIC = Akaike's Information Criterion (Akaike, 1987); BIC = Bayesian Information Criterion (Schwartz, 1978); CAIC = Consistent Akaike's Information Criterion (Bozdogan, 1987).

differentiated by their response sets. This becomes apparent by examining the item-specific threshold values in both groups. The index for class-specific dispersion in Table 3 shows how the category thresholds were more widely spread in class 2 than in class 3.

The quality of classification can also be determined by examining the posterior probabilities of being member of each class given the observed response pattern. Basically, the average posterior probability of belonging to one class should be clearly higher than the average posterior probability of being a member of the other classes. In Table 4, the expected class size is shown in the first column, followed by the mean of the assignment probability (maximum posterior probability). The table is completed by a list of mean posterior probabilities for all classes, given that the current class has the maximum posterior probability.

Table 3. Item Parameters for Each Class.

	Class 1		Class 2		Class 3	
Item	Location	Dispersion	Location	Dispersion	Location	Dispersion
*a*Effort 1	1.148	0.16	0.743	0.57	0.242	0.03
*a*Effort 2	0.709	0.27	0.017	0.73	−0.098	0.12
*a*Effort 3	1.025	0.31	0.496	0.75	−0.046	0.10
*a*Ability 1	−1.508	0.23	−0.729	0.54	−0.259	0.11
*a*Ability 2	−0.385	0.28	0.266	0.66	0.118	0.11
*a*Ability 3	−0.989	0.16	−0.793	0.50	0.042	0.06

Table 4. Expected Class Size and Average Posterior Probabilities for the Three-Class Solution.

	Expected class size	Avrg. post. probability	Class 1	Class 2	Class 3
Class 1	40.4%	0.85	0.85	0.07	0.08
Class 2	39.6%	0.78	0.11	0.78	0.11
Class 3	20.0%	0.84	0.07	0.10	0.84

Although the obtained solution appeared to be meaningful and sound, the sparse data table (with six items and seven categories in each, there are 117649 possible response patterns) called for further attention. The information criteria mentioned above have been considered useful in cases where the usual likelihood ratio and chi-square goodness-of-fit statistics are not appropriate (Lin & Dayton, 1997). A more robust approach for evaluating goodness-of-fit statistics is the parametric bootstrapping procedure – a simulation technique where a number of data sets are simulated based on the parameter estimates from the true data (cf. Langeheine, Pannekoek & van de Pol, 1996). Such a method is also implemented in WINMIRA. Based on von Davier's (1997) recommendations, the Pearson χ^2- and Cressie-Read –statistics were used in the present context to examine the fit of the three-class solution. The Pearson χ^2 reached a p-value of 0.15 (indicating that 15% of the simulated data sets showed worse fit than the real data set), whereas the Cressie-Read –statistic was significant ($p < 0.05$). This suggests that despite its generally acceptable level of fit, the three-class solution might exhibit some degree of instability.

As the initial intent was to form homogenous groups of students for further analysis, all participants were placed in a group based on their posterior class membership probabilities. To examine class-level differences on the aggregated measures of *a*Effort and *a*Ability, an ANOVA was performed. Figure 3 shows standardized scores for each class. The analysis showed significant overall differences among the classes for both *a*Effort ($F[2, 882] = 128.87$; $p < 0.01$) and *a*Ability ($F[2, 882] = 137.58$; $p < 0.01$), but with respect to the former, classes 2 and 3 did not differ from each other ($p > 0.05$ for a pairwise comparison with Scheffe's test). As Fig. 3 illustrates, class 1 had relatively low scores on *a*Effort, but relatively high scores on *a*Ability. Class 3 had the lowest scores on *a*Ability. It thus appeared, that class 2 represented a normative group, class 3 a low-ability group, and class 1 a low effort-high ability discrepancy group.

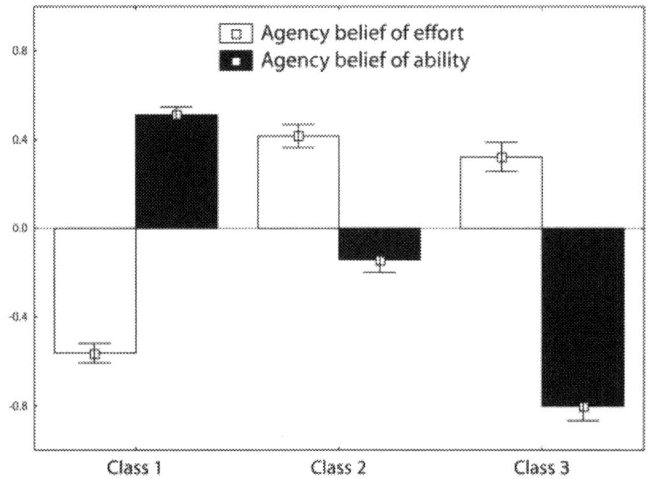

Fig. 3. Group Differences on Aggregated Measures of *a*Effort and *a*Ability.

Examining group-level differences in situational motivation and performance. The next task was to examine whether the three groups obtained in the classification phase differed from each other in terms of their situational appraisals and performance. More specifically, group-level differences and similarities across the measures were evaluated both in terms of structural properties and patterns of associations, as well as in relation to construct mean-levels. As the aim was to explore group-level differences in a predictive model, a multi-group means and covariance structure analysis (MACS) was used (e.g. Little, 1997).

MACS provides a set of powerful means for testing the comparability of both measurement and structural models, because it permits corrections for measurement error and simultaneous model fitting of hypothesized factorial and predictive structures in two or more groups, Furthermore, since in a latent variable system the construct (latent factor) is believed to have a causal influence on the observed variables, MACS allows for the estimations of disattenuated factor means, and, in the case of a multi-group analysis, tests for group-level differences (for an example, see Niemivirta, Rijavec & Yamauchi, in press). In a sense, MACS analyses are extensions of standard structural equation modeling techniques in that mean-level information is estimated along with the variance and covariance information used to reproduce the hypothesized model. Using MACS, it is therefore possible to simultaneously focus on various analytical issues. These include the examination of: (1)

construct comparability (are we measuring the same things in each group); (2) group-level differences on disattenuated means (do the groups differ with respect to latent means in contrast to just observed variables); (3) patterning of relationships between latent factors (are the correlations between latent factors similar across the groups); and (4) predictive relationships between latent factors (are the predictive relationships between dependent and independent constructs similar across the groups). A simplified illustration of the full model under investigation in the present study is given in Fig. 4. It shows the hypothesized basic model with both measurement and structural properties included. Further, even though not explicitly denoted in the graph, means and intercepts are incorporated into the model as well.

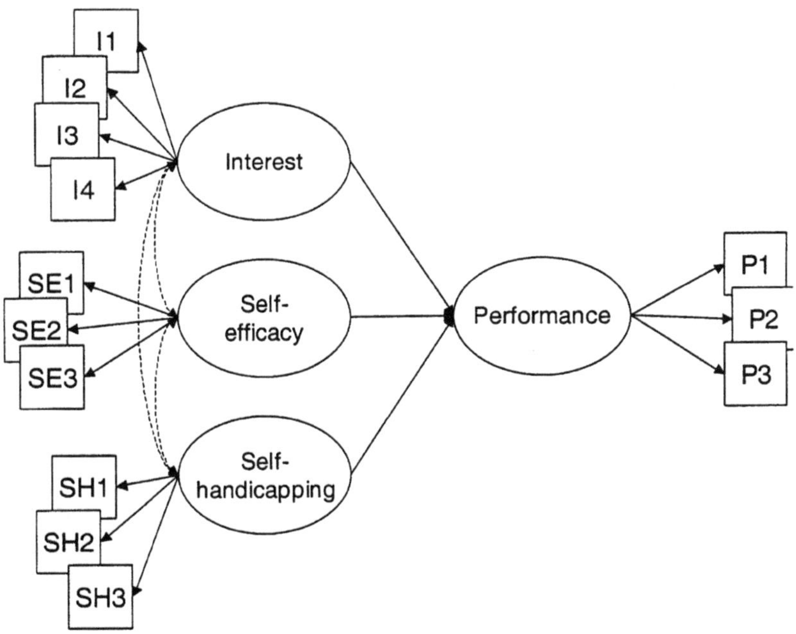

Fig. 4. The Hypothesized Model Including Both Measurement and Structural Properties.

Circles represent observed variables, rectangles represent latent variables. Solid one-headed arrows between latent variables indicate predictive effects, small solid arrows from latent variables to manifest indicators represent factor loadings. Two-headed dashed arrows represent correlations between latent factors.

If one is to compare mean levels of a given construct among two or more subgroups, the assumption of construct equivalence among those groups must be tested empirically. Measurement equivalence exists at several different levels (see Meredith, 1993). If manifest variables load on the same latent variables across groups, and if the factor loadings are not significantly different, then factorial invariance is said to exist (cf. Byrne, Shavelson & Muthén, 1989). A higher level of measurement equivalence exists if, for example, the variance-covariance matrices of the error terms are not significantly different. However, sufficient factorial invariance is the necessary condition for assessing differences in latent means and predictive relationships among the groups.

Instead of examining measurement invariance and mean differences in sequential stages, the present study employed a single-step procedure. That is, a multi-group model was specified in which all parameters (except for the error terms for manifest variables) – factor loadings, factor correlations, regression coefficients, means, and intercepts – were set invariant across the groups. More specifically, an invariance model with 12 observed variables and four latent variables was specified, in which the three correlating latent factors (i.e. anticipated interest, self-efficacy, and claimed self-handicapping, respectively) were set to predict one dependent latent factor (i.e. performance). All items were allowed to load only on the corresponding latent factor, and one item for each latent factor was fixed to 1 in order to render model identification and to provide a scale for the estimation (Jöreskog & Sörbom, 1989). The scale for latent mean comparison was achieved by fixing factor means to zero for one group (see Aiken, Stein & Bentler, 1994; Byrne et al., 1989). In other words, one group at a time was defined as a reference group against which the others were compared. Following recent recommendations (see Gerbing & Anderson, 1993), three indicators were used to examine model fit: Bentler's (1990) Comparative Fit Index (CFI); Bentler & Bonnett's (1980) Non-Normed Fit Index (NNFI); and Steiger's (1990) Root Mean Square Error of Approximation (RMSEA), respectively. In general, values close to.90 for CFI and NNFI, and values around.05 for RMSEA are considered good. The χ^2-statistic (see Jöreskog & Sörbom, 1989) was only used to assess comparative fit between alternative models due to its sensitiveness to various design- and sample-related issues. All analyses from here onward were carried out using the Mplus software (Muthén & Muthén, 1998).

The estimated model fit the data well ($\chi^2(233) = 453.61$; CFI = 0.93; NNFI = 0.92; RMSEA = 0.065, $p_{\text{RMSEA}<0.05} = 1.00$). However, an examination of modification indexes (see Jöreskog & Sörbom, 1989, p. 45) suggested a correlated error between items 5 ("I believe I will do well in this task") and 9 ("I think I won't succeed in this task"). Freeing this parameter improved the model fit significantly ($\Delta\chi^2(1) = 39.71$, $p < 0.05$). The slightly modified final model thus obtained even a better fit: ($\chi^2(232) = 413.90$; CFI = 0.94; NNFI = 0.94; RMSEA = 0.059, $p_{RMSEA<0.05} = 1.00$). Table 5 displays all the relevant parameters and their standard errors.

The fact that the invariance model fitted the data well suggests that the same measurement and structural models as well as similar mean structure held for all groups. As displayed in Fig. 5, anticipated interest correlated positively with self-efficacy and negatively with claimed self-handicapping, and self-handicapping was negatively associated with self-efficacy. The level of performance was significantly influenced only by self-efficacy.

Despite the equivalent structural and predictive relationships between the manifest and latent variables, the groups did differ from each other in relation to disattenuated latent means. As Fig. 6 demonstrates, members of groups 2 and 3 perceived the task significantly more interesting than students in group 1 did. Group 3 also had significantly higher scores on claimed self-handicapping and significantly lower scores on self-efficacy than the others did. Groups 1 and 2 did not differ from each other with respect to these appraisals. The only significant difference in the adjusted means for performance level was found

Table 5. Estimates, Residual Variances, and Intercepts for all Observed Variables.

			Residual Variances				
	Estimates	S.E.	Group 1	Group 2	Group 3	Intercepts	S.E.
I1	1.00	0.00	0.54	0.61	0.66	6.21	0.08
I2	0.83	0.05	0.33	0.27	0.40	3.50	0.13
I3	0.95	0.05	0.36	0.31	0.37	3.37	0.12
I4	0.82	0.05	0.56	0.52	0.60	4.32	0.11
SE1	1.00	0.00	0.53	0.38	0.55	5.03	0.10
SE2	1.23	0.09	0.43	0.37	0.44	3.14	0.12
SE2	1.16	0.09	0.47	0.38	0.42	3.15	0.11
SH1	1.00	0.00	0.60	0.57	0.61	5.30	0.10
SH2	0.89	0.05	0.60	0.53	0.63	3.51	0.10
SH3	0.84	0.05	0.55	0.48	0.47	3.88	0.12
P1	1.00	0.00	0.50	0.52	0.62	3.22	0.05
P2	1.12	0.10	0.53	0.55	0.56	2.89	0.06
P3	0.81	0.08	0.68	0.69	0.64	1.79	0.05

Note: I = Anticipated interest; SE = Self-efficacy; SH = Self-handicapping; P = Performance.

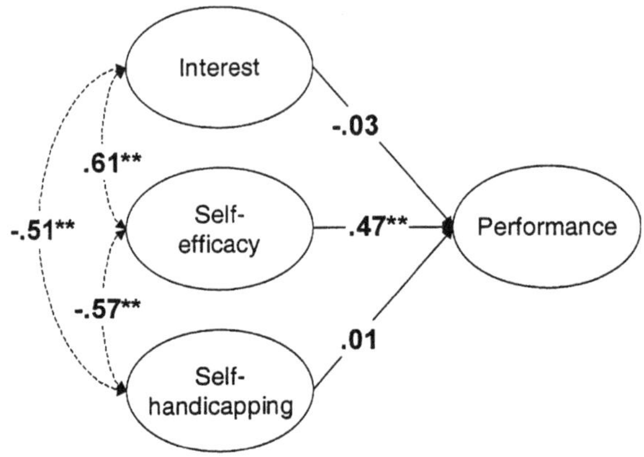

Fig. 5. Disattenuated Correlations and Predictive Relationships Among Situational Appraisals and Performance.

$** = p < 0.01$

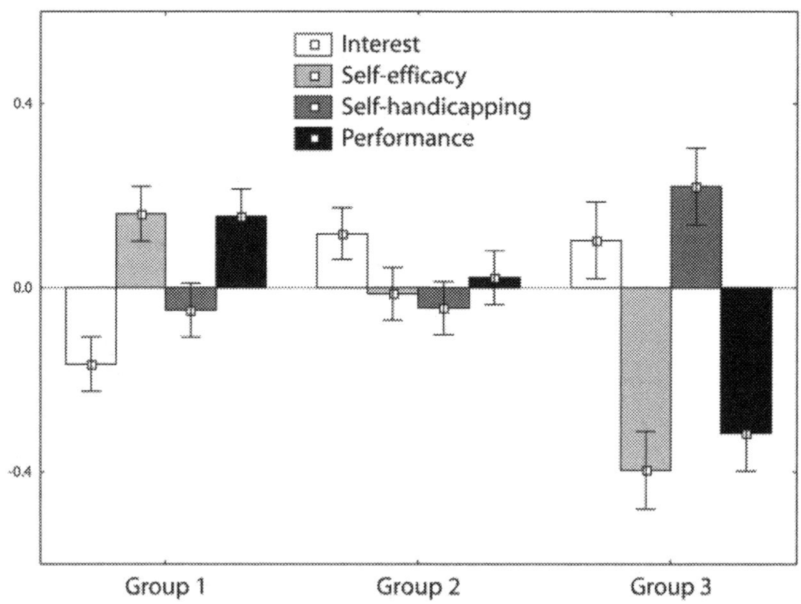

Fig. 6. Group-level Disattenuated Mean Differences (Group 1 = 0) on Situational Appraisals and Performance (non-adjusted means refer to performance scores without the influence of covariates).

between group 3 and the other two groups: students in group 3 scored lower than the others did. This result was parallel to the one obtained with non-adjusted means (i.e. with a model including correlative instead of predictive relationships).

In sum, the above findings showed how the different patterning of agency beliefs was related to differences in students' task-specific self-appraisals and performance. However, it was also found that *within each group*, the variation in task-specific self-efficacy was similarly associated with the variation in task performance. That is, relatively higher self-efficacy was related to higher level of performance in all groups. These findings imply not only that students with different type of motivational profile perceive and act in performance situations differently, but also that certain situation-specific motivational mechanisms operate similarly across all students. However, no definite conclusions can be drawn about these relationships since the participants' prior ability or performance level was not taken into account.

Discussion

The purpose of this particular study was to illustrate the utility of methodological approaches and analytical tools that might help to integrate person-centered and variable-centered aspects within one research design. In this context, the idea was basically to examine whether one homogenous group of people with one type of motivational tendencies differs from or is similar to another homogenous group of people with other type of motivational tendencies. More formally, the aim was to test the implicit assumption inherent in variable-focused approaches that the relations among variables across the individuals are valid for the relations within the individuals. This was approached by first classifying individuals in terms of their self-related agency beliefs, and then examining whether the relationships among various situation-specific constructs were similar across the resulting groups, and if so, whether any group-level mean differences existed. The first part to the scheme – classification – thus reflected a person-centered perspective, whereas the latter part – the examination of the relationships between all variables – represented a variable-centered perspective. However, since the latter focused on whether the relationships between variables were similar among different groups, it can be said to incorporate both person- and variable-based information.

This first study employed a strategy in which complementary person- and variable-focused methods were utilized in sequential stages. This was mainly due to the nature of the design: the explicit intention was to examine the degree and type of variability among groups of individuals. At times, however, it is of more interest to examine the nature of variability *within* individuals. This is the case, for example, in developmental research. Here, instead of merely looking at how people compare to each other, the focus is on how individuals compare to themselves over time – that is, the focus is on the stability and change in individuals' developmental trajectories.

The inclusion of time as one source of variation makes the task of studying individual differences progressively more complex (cf. Lerner, Lerner, Stefanis & Apfel, 2001). As Bergman (2001) recently underscored, from a methodological point of view, this complexity leads – or should lead – to the consideration of typical and atypical patterns of development, the recognition of nonlinear development and multiple interactions, and a focus on the dynamics of change. In a very limited sense, some aspects of these issues are touched upon in the second study.

Study 2: Examining Change Over Time Within and Across the Individuals: Trends and Correlates

Developmental studies in motivation research are surprisingly rare. Most of the work available has been done within the self-concept research. The debate on the developmental nature of the relationships between academic self-concept and school achievement has been especially lively (e.g. Helmke & van Aken, 1995; Skaalvik & Vålas, 1999). A quick review of the work done in this field, however, shows that: (1) virtually all studies follow a variable-centered approach; and (2) they mainly focus on the longitudinal predictive (causal) relationships between few constructs. An excellent example of such a study is that of Marsh and Yeung (1997). They carried out a longitudinal three-wave panel study on the relationships between achievement and academic self-concept in three domains, mathematics, science, and English, respectively. All the models they specified were typical autoregressive cross-lagged structural equation models, in which all time 1 variables predicted time 2 and time 3 variables, and all time 2 variables predicted all time 3 variables. With respect to results, Marsh and Yeung (1997) concluded that the study supported their reciprocal effects hypothesis. That is, prior achievement predicted later academic self-concept (i.e. the skill-development effect), and prior self-concept predicted subsequent achievement (i.e. the self-enhancement effect). However, the effects tended to be stronger from achievement to self-concept, than vice versa. It was also found, that the self-enhancement effects were stronger for mathematics than for science and English.

It is clear, that these types of analysis provide important information about the interrelationships of motivational factors influencing students' achievement. However, from a methodological standpoint, they are also amenable to a great deal of criticism (e.g. Rogosa, 1995). Three points are of particular relevance here (cf. Curran & Hussong, in press): First, an autoregressive cross-lagged model represents a fixed-effect model in that a single value is estimated for the regression parameter that holds for all individuals in the sample. Second, such a model does not take into consideration the structure of means as a function of time. Third, changes in the given construct between two measurement points is independent of the influence of earlier and later changes in the same construct. From a substantive point of view, it must also be noted that autoregressive cross-lagged models mainly focus on the stability and predictive relationships between individual variables, not on the stability and change in the configuration of these variables.

An alternative method for analyzing repeated measures over time focuses on the developmental trends or growth trajectories in the given construct rather than the predictive relationships among the variables over time. Such a method is *latent growth curve modeling* (LGCM). LGCM regards development as a continuous underlying process and fits a regression curve to a series of repeated measures taken on the same individual. With LGCM, it is possible to describe individuals' behavior in terms of initial levels and their developmental trajectories from those levels. Moreover, LGCM provides means for estimating variability across individuals in the initial levels and trajectories as well as for testing the contribution of other variables or constructs in explaining those initial levels and growth trajectories (see Curran & Hussong, in press; Duncan, Duncan, Strycker, Li & Alpert, 1999). In doing so, LGCM methods simultaneously focus on correlations over time, changes in variance, and shifts in mean values, thus using more information available in the measured variables than do traditional methods.

Figure 7 illustrates a graphical representation of four complementary types of latent growth curve models incorporated within the structural equation modeling framework: an *unconditional model* (A), which is a basic univariate growth model; a *multivariate* or *associative model* (B), which allows for the assessment of the correlational patterns among the developmental parameters for pairs of constructs; a *conditional* model (C), which includes covariates or predictors; and a *full growth model* (D), which includes both predictors and outcomes. An example study applying all these models on motivational data comes from Niemivirta (2000). Corresponding to the models described above, the research questions in that study focused on the characteristics of junior high school students' developmental trends in control expectancy and school value, their interrelationships, predictors (gender and prior GPA), and outcomes (subsequent GPA), respectively.

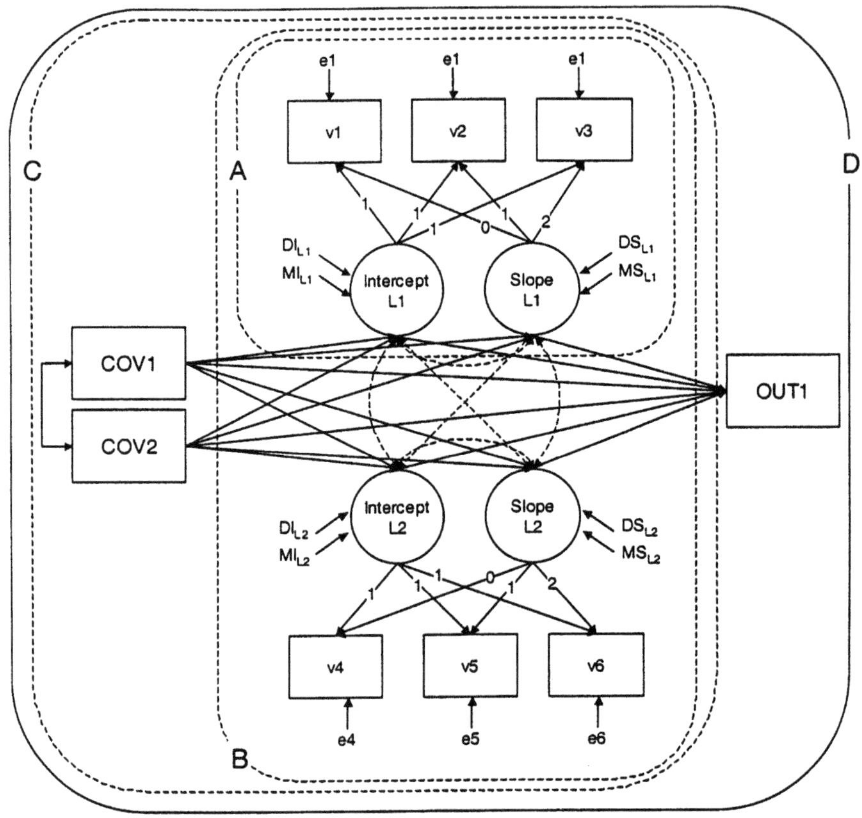

Fig. 7. A Graphical Representation of Different Types of Latent Growth Curve Models Within the Structural Equation Modeling Framework.

Note: v1 to v6 = observed variables; COV = covariate; OUT = subsequent dependent variable.

The results from separate univariate models suggested a significant increase in control expectancy and a significant decrease in school value. Furthermore, there was significant individual variability in both the initial levels and rates of change for each construct. That is, students not only reported different levels of initial control expectancy and school valuing but also differed in terms of the developmental growth trajectories. The fact that the covariance estimate between the intercept and slope factors for school value was significant indicated that students reporting higher levels of initial school value tended to report smaller rates of decrease in school value over time.

The results from the associative model showed that the initial levels of control expectancy and school valuing were significantly related. That is, students reporting higher initial levels of control expectancy also displayed higher initial levels of school value. Furthermore, the fact that the slopes for control expectancy and school value were correlated suggested that a higher rate of increase in control expectancy was associated with less decrease in school value, and vice versa. With respect to the conditional model, it was found that prior school achievement predicted the initial levels of both control expectancy and school value. Moreover, boys had significantly higher initial levels of control expectancy than girls did, but girls reported both significantly higher rates of increase in control expectancy and lower rates of decrease in school value over time than did boys. Finally, the results from the full growth model indicated that the initial level of control expectancy and the degree of growth in control expectancy had a positive influence on later achievement – even after controlling for both the prior achievement and gender differences.

This brief overview of the results from Niemivirta's (2000) study serves to illustrate the rich scope of information that can be gained from a comprehensive latent growth curve analysis. As demonstrated, the outcomes – even though relying on variable-based information – emphasize the developmental characteristics of individuals as well as the associative patterns among these characteristics, which is not the case with autoregressive cross-lagged models.

Another observation worth highlighting in the present context: in the above study, it was also found that the inclusion of prior school achievement and gender as explanatory variables *did not* significantly *reduce the variability* in both the intercept and slopes factors, thus suggesting that they were not sufficient to fully capture individual differences in growth over time. This implies, that it may not always be realistic to assume that a single-population model can account for all types of individual differences within the sample. As Muthén (2001) points out, the conventional growth model allows heterogeneity corresponding to different growth trajectories across individuals and captures that by variation in the continuous growth factors, but it cannot capture heterogeneity that corresponds to qualitatively different development. He also reminds us that while multi-group growth modeling would flexibly permit the study of qualitatively different developmental across individuals belonging to know groups (e.g. gender), the problem often is that the group membership is not known, but needs to be inferred from the data! Fortunately, the new methodology, second-generation structural equation modeling (Muthén, in press), which incorporates categorical latent variable modeling and growth curve modeling, adds to the capability of capturing heterogeneity in development (see also Muthén, 2001; Muthén & Muthén, 2000).

One type of modeling procedure incorporated into the above-mentioned framework is *growth mixture modeling* (GMM). It combines the features of conventional growth modeling (cf. Duncan, Duncan, Strycker, Li & Alpert, 1999) and latent class growth analysis (cf. Nagin, 1999). As mentioned earlier, conventional growth modeling estimates the mean growth trajectory under the assumption that individuals in the sample come from a single population. Variation around the mean growth is captured by the estimation of the growth factor variance. In contrast, latent class growth analysis estimates a mean growth trajectory for each given class, but no individual variation around the mean growth is allowed. With GMM, it is possible to estimate the mean growth trajectories for one or more latent classes as well as the trajectory variation in each class. Furthermore, GMM provides estimates of both the class probabilities and each individual's most likely class membership. The probabilities of class membership can further be related to predictor variables and the class membership can be used to predict other outcomes. A graphical representation of a full growth mixture model is given in Fig. 8.

This present example study serves as a simple illustration of growth mixture modeling with real data. In order to maintain a familiar theoretical framework, the focus will be on the developmental nature of junior high school students' agency beliefs of effort. Cross-sectional studies suggest that during the junior high school years, students appear to exhibit a steadily decreasing trend in their agency beliefs of effort (Little, Stetsenko & Maier, 1999; Niemivirta, 2001). Thus, the primary goal will be to examine the appropriateness of GMM for describing trends and variations in the aforementioned growth trajectories. Further, in case of a multi-class solution, the influence of gender and prior GPA on the slopes, initial levels, and class memberships will be examined.

Participants and Instrumentation

The sample comprised of 309 students, who completed a motivation questionnaire annually at the beginning of the 7th, 8th, and 9th grades, respectively. The scale for *a*Effort was analogous to the one presented in study 1. It included four items reflecting the degree of students' school-related effort expenditure (e.g. "*I study hard in order to do well in school*"; "*I don't put much effort into my schoolwork*"). All items were measured using a 7-point Likert-scale ranging from 1 ("*Does not describe me at all*") to 7 ("*Describes me perfectly*"). Sixth-grade GPA was used as the measure of prior school achievement.

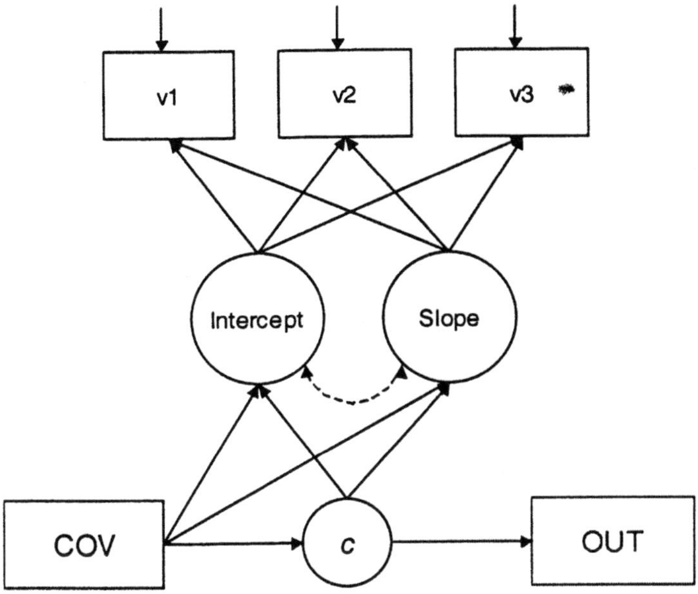

Fig. 8. A Graphical Representation of a Full Growth Mixture Model.

Note: c = class membership.

Analyses and Results

Construct equivalence over time. Since composite scores for each year were used to estimate growth models, the first task was to examine whether the measured constructs were comparable over time. This was done by means of a multi-group means and covariance analysis. An invariance model was specified in which three one-factor measurement models (one for each measurement point) were set to be equal in terms of factor loadings, factor variances, residual variances, and variable intercepts. The fit of the model was good ($\chi^2(42) = 137.67$; CFI = 0.92; NNFI = 0.93; RMSEA = 0.085), indicating that the construct was measured identically in each occasion.

Conventional latent growth curve model. The next task was to estimate a conventional linear growth model for *a*Effort with no predictors. The raw means and standard deviations (in parenthesis) for each measurement point were 4.77 (1.23), 4.46 (1.38), and 4.35 (1.39), respectively, thus suggesting a linearly decreasing general trend over time. A univariate growth model was specified accordingly (cf. model A in Fig. 7). Using the structural equation modeling framework, two latent factors were defined to represent the intercept (initial level) and slope of the growth trajectory. The factor loadings relating the three observed measures to the intercept factor were fixed to 1 in order to define the starting point of the growth trajectory. The factor loadings relating the observed measures to the slope factor were fixed to 0, 1, and 2, respectively, to capture a linear trend over three time points. The means of the two latent factors (initial level and slope) were freely estimated, but the intercepts of the observed measured were fixed to 0. Therefore, the mean structure among the repeated measures was reproduced through the latent factor means. The mean estimate of the intercept factor (*MI*) thus represents the mean initial level of the growth trajectory, and the estimate of the intercept variance (*DI*) represents the degree of individual variability in the initial levels. In a like manner, the mean estimate of the slope factor (*MS*) represents the mean slope of growth trajectory, and the slope variance (*DS*) represents individual variability in the rates of change over time.

The model fit the data well ($\chi^2(1) = 4.15$, $p > 0.01$; CFI = .99; NNFI = 0.97; RMSEA = 0.101, $p_{RMSEA<0.05} > 0.01$). Parameter estimates indicated that both the intercept means and variances ($MI = 4.76$, $t = 68.61$; $DI = 1.29$, $t = 7.96$) as well as slope means and variances ($MS = -0.21$, $t = -5.75$; $DS = 0.32$, $t = 4.68$) were significant. In other words, the students reported significant decrease in their *a*Effort over time. Further, significant individual variability in both the initial levels and rates of change existed. The fact that the estimates for intercept and mean slope correlated significantly ($r = -0.32$, $p < 0.05$) suggested that students reporting higher levels of initial effort expenditure tended to report higher rates of decrease in their subsequent effort expenditure.

Next, a conditional model was specified in which students' gender and prior GPA were included as predictors (cf. model C in Fig. 7). The aim was to see whether gender and prior GPA were related to the initial level and rate of change in effort expenditure. Again, the model fit the data well ($\chi^2(3) = 7.83$, $p > 0.01$; CFI = 0.99; NNFI = 0.96; RMSEA = 0.074, $p_{RMSEA<0.05} > 0.01$). The results showed that both gender and GPA were associated with the initial level of students' *a*Effort: when prior GPA was taken into account, boys reported significantly higher initial levels of effort expenditure than girls did. However, neither variable predicted the intercept or the rate of growth. Moreover, residual variances remained significant suggesting still considerable individual variation in the growth trajectory.

Unconditional growth mixture model. To examine whether the individual variation in the developmental trends of *a*Effort would be better captured by the inclusion of two or more latent classes with varying growth trajectories, a series of unconditional growth mixture models was specified (cf. Fig. 8). In order to define the optimal solution, models with different numbers of classes were estimated and then compared by using BIC, a standard information criterion, and examining posterior class membership probabilities (models with both fixed and free intercept and slope variances were estimated, but since the models with fixed variances obtained better fit, results on restricted models only are reported here). The BIC for the conventional growth model, which served as the baseline model, was 2838.62. For two-, three-, and four-class solutions, the corresponding indices were 2828.64, 2838.95, and 2834.30, respectively. Accordingly, the two-class solution was chosen as the best-fitting model for further examination. This was also supported by the quality of classification. Class-specific parameter estimates and class membership probabilities are displayed in Table 6. The only non-significant estimate was the slope mean for class 2.

As illustrated in Fig. 9, the first class represented a group of students with high initial levels and relatively steep decrease in their *a*Effort over time, whereas class 2 represented a group of students with average initial levels and no growth over time.

Conditional growth mixture model with covariates. In the next stage, the conditional analysis attempted to capture some of the variation in the growth factors using gender and prior school achievement as covariates. It was found, that neither gender nor prior GPA predicted growth rate in either class.

Table 6. Parameter Estimates and Class Membership Probabilities for the Two-Class Unconditional Growth Mixture Model.

	Class 1			Class 2		
	Estimate	S.E.	t-value	Estimate	S.E.	*t*-value
Initial level mean	5.62	0.09	60.32	3.64	0.11	32.90
Initial level variance	0.36	0.13	2.67	0.36	0.13	2.67
Slope mean	–0.39	0.07	–5.71	0.02	0.08	0.26
Slope variance	0.29	0.07	4.40	0.29	0.07	4.40

Average posterior probabilities for the two-class solution

	N	Class 1	Class 2
Class 1	179	0.914	0.086
Class 2	130	0.088	0.912

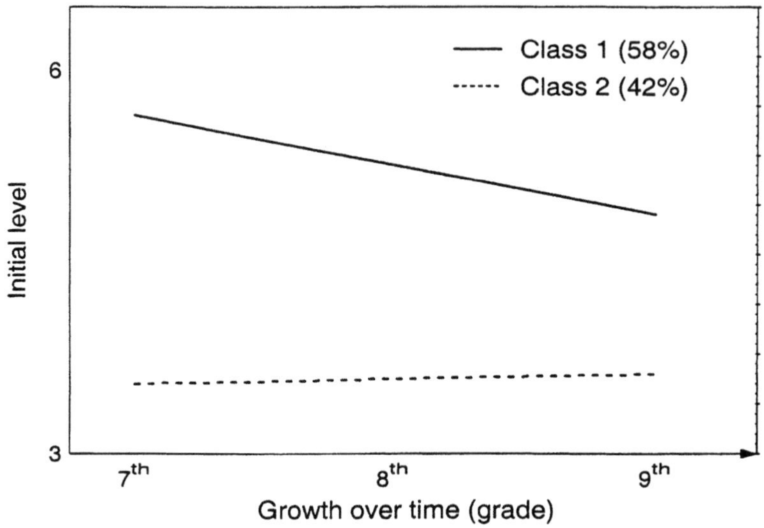

Fig. 9. Estimated Mean Curves for the Two-class Growth Mixture Model.

However, GPA did predict the initial level of effort expenditure, but only in class 2! Further, the inclusion of covariates reduced residual variance only for the initial level and only in class 1. Therefore, the corresponding findings obtained in the conventional growth analysis (see above) did not apply for all individuals. The possibility that the latent class membership was related to the covariates was examined next. As shown in Table 7, the multinomial logistic

Table 7. Predicting Class Membership: The Multinominal Logistic Regression Coefficients for Covariates.

Covariate	Estimated logit coefficients	S.E.	*t*-value
Gender	1.32	0.71	1.86
Prior GPA	1.28	0.48	2.69*

Note: $* = p < 0.05$.

regressions of class membership ("c" in Fig. 8) on gender and prior GPA indicated that GPA had a significant influence on the probability of being a member in class 1.

Discussion

The second study focused on the examination of developmental growth trajectories both within and across individuals. Moreover, examples were given on how to model qualitative differences in developmental trends and how to relate them to various antecedents and outcomes. In contrast to the first study, this one attempted to incorporate person- and variable-based analyses into a single procedure in which the classification of individuals and the estimation of their developmental characteristics were carried out simultaneously. For this task, a new modeling framework – growth mixture modeling (GMM) – was introduced (Muthén, 2001; in press). GMM goes beyond the conventional random coefficient growth modeling by using trajectory classes, which allows for heterogeneity in regard to the influence of antecedents, growth shapes, concurrent outcomes, and even later consequences (cf. Muthén & Muthén, 2000).

In this study, the flexibility and breadth of analytical possibilities GMM offers enabled the examination of qualitatively different types of developmental trends and their antecedents in junior high school students' agency beliefs of effort. The results suggested two general types of developmental trajectories – one with high initial level and steep decrease and another with average initial level and no growth – which as such were unrelated to either gender or prior school achievement. However, the probability of being a member in the high initial level-steep decrease group was associated with prior GPA. Especially noteworthy was the observation that the relationships found in conventional growth analysis between predictors and developmental parameters did not hold for all individuals in the subsequent growth mixture analysis. This points out the importance of explicitly focusing on the potential sources of systematic heterogeneity in the data.

CONCLUDING REMARKS

The purpose of this chapter was to describe and illustrate the use of methods that hitherto have been somewhat underutilized in motivation research, but which are likely to become exceedingly valuable and beneficial – if not indispensable – in future work. The starting point of the present discussion was the distinction between person-centered and variable-centered approaches to the study of motivation. Although such categorizing labels are not always explicitly attached to studies, in practice that may well be the case: the logic of a study, in terms of the core assumptions made and subsequent methodologies used, often follows one or the other perspective.

In the present context, it was argued that sometimes the theoretical framework invites or even necessitates a more eclectic methodological approach. For example, when one is to examine whether the same laws operate for different groups of people, the objects of study can be viewed from both variable- and person-centered perspectives. The two studies presented here served as examples of how to tackle with some of the difficulties associated with attempts to integrate both person- and variable-centered views. The motivating substantive example for these studies was the examination of junior high school students' agency beliefs. The first study focused on analyzing differences and similarities among groups of students with different patterning of beliefs, while the second focused on how to model developmental change in such beliefs over time.

In addition to their unique and distinctive characteristics, both studies also shared some common elements. One issue relevant in both examples was the examination of construct equivalence – a necessary but often overlooked condition for valid mean comparisons. The assessment of construct equivalence, whether across groups or over time, was carried out with the help of a means and covariance structure analysis (MACS). MACS also provided a flexible and powerful way of estimating and comparing disattenuated latent means among the different groups.

Another common issue was the problem of classification – the corner stone of almost any person-centered studies (cf. Bergman, 2000). In both studies, the complicated task of categorization was carried out within the framework of latent structure analysis. In the first case, the object of the study was the patterning of participants' responses, whereas in the second case, the classification was based on qualitatively different types of developmental trends. An important difference between these studies was the fact that in the first one, the classification served as starting point for further analyses, whereas in the latter, the trend-based classification was the analytical goal *per se*.

Despite the fact that person-centered and variable-centered approaches are often treated as separate paths into the empirical realm, which may or may not meet somewhere along the way, one cannot really exist without the other. No matter how person-centered an approach is, it must always ground on some sort of identifiable units – variables. As Horn (2000, p. 924) astutely reminds us:

"person-centered analysis must be based on variable-centered analysis, and the latter should be informed by person-centered analysis".

It is also critical to remember that statistical models – such as the ones repeatedly emphasized in the present work – are not merely instruments with which to evaluate the "empirical fit" or theoretically derived assumptions, but also tools that can be used to improve and refine our theoretical models. Even though new methods offer both flexible and powerful means with which to tackle increasingly complex problems, the advancement does not come without some dangers. As von Eye and Schuster (2001) envision, within the next few years, new paradigms will arise and statistical methods will be custom-tailored to substantive questions, but at the same time the choice between methods of analysis becomes increasingly difficult, misuse of statistics will become more frequent, and the role of the methodologist will change such that more substantive knowledge will be required. Thus, what needs to be done is to make the methods serve the theory building, not the other way around.

ACKNOWLEDGMENTS

I would like to thank the editors for thoughtful comments on an earlier draft. Thanks are also extended to my colleagues at the Centre for Educational Assessment, University of Helsinki. The preparation of this article was supported by a grant from the Emil Aaltonen foundation.

REFERENCES

Agresti, A. (1990). *Categorical data analysis*. NY: Wiley.

Aiken, L. S., Stein, J. A., & Bentler, P. M. (1994). Structural equation analyses of clinical subpopulation differences and comparative treatment outcomes: Characterizing the daily lives of drug addicts. *Journal of Consulting and Clinical Psychology*, *62*, 488–499.

Ames, C., & Archer, J. (1988). Achievement goals in the classroom: Student learning strategies and motivation processes. *Journal of Educational Psychology*, *80*, 260–267.

Andrich, D. (1978). Application of a psychometric rating model to ordered categories which are scored with successive integers. *Applied Psychological Measurement*, *2*, 581–594.

Andrich, D. (1982). An extension of the Rasch model for ratings providing both location and dispersion parameters. *Psychometrika*, *47*, 105–113.

Atkinson, J. W. (1957). Motivational determinants of risk taking behavior. *Psychological Review*, *64*, 359–372.

Bargh, J. A., & Barndollar, K. (1996). Automaticity in action. The unconscious as repository of chronic goals and motives. In: P. Gollwitzer & J. A. Bargh (Eds), *The Psychology of Action: Linking Cognition and Motivation to Behavior* (pp. 457–481). New York: Guilford.

Bentler, P. M. (1990). Fit indexes, lagrange multipliers, constraint changes and incomplete data in structural models. *Multivariate Behavioral Research*, *25*, 163–173.

Bentler, P. M., & Bonett, D. G. (1980). Significance test and goodness of fit in the analysis of covariance structures. *Psychological Bulletin*, *88*, 588–606.

Bergman, L. R. (1998). A pattern-oriented approach to studying individual development: Snapshots and processes. In: R. B. Cairns, L. R. Bergman & J. Kagan (Eds), *Methods and Models for Studying the Individual* (pp. 83–121). Thousand Oaks, CA: Sage.

Bergman, L. R. (2000). The application of a person-oriented approach: Types and clusters. In: L. R. Bergman, R. Cairns, L.-G. Nilsson & L. Nystedt (Eds), *Developmental Science and the Holistic Approach* (pp. 137–154). Mahwah, NJ: Lawrence Erlbaum.

Bergman, L. R. (2001). A Person approach in research on adolescence: Some methodological challenges. *Journal of Adolescence Research*, *16*, 28–53.

Bergman, L. R., Cairns, R. B., Nilsson, L. G., & Nystedt, L. (Eds) (2000). *Developmental science and the holistic approach*. Mahwah, NJ: Erlbaum.

Boekaerts, M., & Niemivirta, M. (2000). Self-regulation in learning: Finding a balance between learning- and ego-protective goals. In: M. Boekaerts, P. R Pintrich & M. Zeidner (Eds), *Handbook of Self-regulation* (pp. 417–450). San Diego, CA: Academic Press.

Bozdogan, H. (1987). Model selection and Akaike's Information Criterion (AIC): The general theory and its analytical extensions. *Psychometrika*, *52*, 345–370.

Byrne, B. M., Shavelson, R. J., & Muthen, B. (1989). Testing for the equivalence of factor covariance and mean structures: The issue of partial measurement invariance. *Psychological Bulletin*, *105*, 456–466.

Cairns, R. B., Bergman, L. R., & Kagan, J. (Eds) (1998). *Methods and models of studying the individual*. Thousand Oaks, CA: Sage.

Cronbach, L. J. (1957). The two disciplines of scientific psychology. *American Psychologist*, *12*(11), 671–684.

Cronbach, L. J. (1975). Beyond the two disciplines of scientific psychology. *American Psychologist*, *30*, 116–127.

Curran, P. J., & Hussong, A. M. (in press). Structural equation modeling of repeated measures data. In: D. Moskowitz & S. Hershberger (Eds), *Modeling Intra-individual Variability with Repeated Measures Data: Methods and Applications*. New York: Lawrence Erlbaum Associates.

Duncan, T. E., Duncan, S. C., Strycker, L. A., Li, F., & Alpert, A. (1999). *An Introduction to Latent Variable Growth Curve Modeling: Concepts, Issues, and Applications*. Mahwah, NJ: Lawrence Erlbaum.

Elliot, A. J. (1997). Integrating "classic" and "contemporary" approaches to achievement motivation: A hierarchical model of approach and avoidance achievement motivation. In: P. Pintrich & M. Maehr (Eds), *Advances in Motivation and Achievement* (Vol. 10, pp. 143–179). Greenwich, CT: JAI Press.

Elliot, A. J., McGregor, H. A., & Gable, S. (1999). Achievement goals, study strategies, and exam performance: A mediational analysis. *Journal of Educational Psychology*, *91*, 549–563.

Gerbing, D. W., & Anderson, J. C. (1993). Monte Carlo evaluations of goodness-of-fit indices for structural equation models. In: K. A. Bollen & J. S. Long (Eds), *Testing Structural Equation Models*. Newbury Park, CA: Sage.

Heckhausen, H. (1991). *Motivation and action*. New York: Springer.

Heinen, T. (1996). *Latent class and discrete latent trait models: Similarities and differences*. Thousand Oaks, California: Sage.

Helmke, A., & van Aken, M. A. G. (1995). The causal ordering of academic achievement and self-concept of ability during elementary school: A longitudinal study. *Journal of Educational Psychology, 87*, 624–637.

Higgins, E. T. (1996). Knowledge activation: accessibility, applicability, and salience. In: E. T. Higgins & A. W. Kruglanski (Eds), *Social Psychology: Handbook of Basic Principles* (pp. 133–169). New York: Guilford.

Jöreskog, K. G., & Sörbom, D. (1989). *LISREL 7. A guide to the Program and Applications* (2nd ed.). Chicago: SPSS Inc.

Karabenick, S. A., & Youssef, Z. I. (1968). Performance as a function of achievement motive level and perceived difficulty. *Journal of Personality and Social Psychology, 10*, 414–419.

Langeheine, R., Pannekoek, J., & van de Pol, F. (1996). Bootstrapping goodness-of-fit measures in categorical data analysis. *Sociological Methods and Research, 24*, 492–516.

Lerner, R. M., Lerner, J. V., De Stefanis, I., & Apfel, A. (2001). Understanding developmental systems in adolescence: Implications for methodological strategies, data analytic approaches, and training. *Journal of Adolescence Research, 16*, 9–27.

Lin, T. S., & Dayton, C. M. (1997). Model-selection information criteria for non-nested latent class models. *Journal of Educational and Behavioral Statistics, 22*, 249–264.

Little, T. D. (1997). Mean and covariance structures (MACS) analyses of cross-cultural data: Practical and theoretical issues. *Multivariate Behavioral Research, 32*, 53–76.

Little, T. D. (1998). Sociocultural influences on the development of children's action-control beliefs. In: J. Heckhausen & C. S. Dweck (Eds), *Motivation and Self-regulation Across the Life Span* (pp. 281–315). New York: Cambridge University Press.

Little, T. D., & Lopez, D. F. (1997). Regularities in the development of children's causality beliefs about school performance across six sociocultural contexts. *Developmental Psychology, 33*, 165–175.

Little, T. D., Oettingen, G., Stetsenko, A., & Baltes, P. B. (1995). Children's action-control beliefs and school performance: How do American children compare with German and Russian children? *Journal of Personality and Social Psychology, 69*, 686–700.

Little, T. D., Stetsenko, A., & Maier, H. (1999). Action-control beliefs and school performance: A longitudinal study of Moscow children and adolescents. *International Journal of Behavioral Development, 23*(3), 799–823.

Magnusson, D. (1998). The logic and implications of a person approach. In: R. B. Calms, L. R. Bergman & J. Kagan (Eds), *Methods and Models for Studying the Individual* (pp. 33–63). Newbury Park, CA: Sage.

Mandler G., & Sarason, S. B. (1952). A Study of Anxiety and Learning. *Journal of Abnormal Social Psychology, 47*, 166–173.

McClelland, D. C. (1985). *Human Motivation*. Cambridge, MA: Cambridge University Press.

McClelland, D. C., Atkinson, J. W., Clark, R. A., & Lowell, E. L. (1953). *The achievement motive*. New York: Appleton-Century-Crofts.

McClelland, D. C., Koestner, R., & Weinberger, J. (1989). How do self-attributed and implicit motives differ? *Psychological Review, 96*, 690–702.

McCutcheon, A. C. (1987). *Latent Class Analysis*. Beverly Hills: Sage Publications.

Meece, J. L., & Holt, K. (1993). A pattern analysis of students' achievement goals. *Journal of Educational Psychology, 85*, 582–590.

Meehl, P. E. (1992). Factors and taxa, traits and types, differences of degree and differences in kind. *Journal of Personality, 60*, 117–174.

Meredith, W. (1993). Measurement invariance, factor analysis and factorial invariance. *Psychometrika, 58*, 525–543.

Miller, R. B., Behrens, J. T., Greene, B. A., & Newman, D. (1993). Goals and perceived ability: Impact on student valuing, self-regulation and persistence. *Contemporary Educational Psychology, 18*, 2–14.
Milligan, G. E. (1981). A review of Monte Carlo tests of cluster analysis. *Multivariate Behavioral Research, 16*, 379–407.
Milligan, G. W., & Cooper, M. C. (1987). Methodology review: Clustering methods. *Applied Psychological Measurement, 11*, 329–354.
Muthén, B. (2001). Latent variable mixture modeling. In: G. A. Marcoulides & R. E. Schumacker (Eds), *Advanced Structural Equation Modeling: New Developments and Techniques* (pp. 1–33). Lawrence Erlbaum Associates.
Muthén, B. (in press). Second-generation structural equation modeling with a combination of categorical and continuous latent variables: New opportunities for latent class/latent growth modeling. In: L. M. Collins & A. Sayer (Eds), *New Methods for the Analysis of Change*. Washington, D.C.: APA.
Muthén, B., & Muthén, L. (2000). Integrating person-centered and variable-centered analysis: Growth mixture modeling with latent trajectory classes. *Alcoholism: Clinical and Experimental Research, 24*, 882–891.
Muthén, L., & Muthén, B. (1998). *Mplus User's Guide*. Los Angeles, CA: Muthén & Muthén.
Nagin, D. S. (1999). Analyzing developmental trajectories: A semi-parametric, group-based approach. *Psychological Methods, 4*, 139–157.
Niemivirta, M. J. (1998, August). Stability and change in goals and motivational beliefs: A pattern-oriented approach. Paper presented at the 24th International Congress of Applied Psychology, San Francisco, U.S.
Niemivirta, M. J. (1998b). Individual differences in motivational and cognitive factors affecting self-regulated learning – A pattern-oriented approach. In: P. Nenniger, R. S. Jäger, A. Frey & M. Wosnitza (Eds), *Advances in Motivation* (pp. 23–42). Landau: Verlag Empirische Pädagogik.
Niemivirta, M. (2000, May). Developmental trends in motivation: A longitudinal study on middle school students' control expectancy and school value. Paper presented at the 7th International Conference on Motivation, Leuven, Belgium.
Niemivirta, M. (2001). Trends and types in motivation: The case of goal orientations and action-control beliefs. Manuscript.
Niemivirta, M., Rijavec, M., & Yamauchi, H. (in press). Goal orientations and action-control beliefs: A cross-cultural comparison among Croatian, Finnish, and Japanese students. In: A. Efklides, J. Kuhl & R. Sorrentino (Eds), *Trends and Prospects in Motivation Research*. Kluwer.
Pajares, F. (1997). Current directions in self-efficacy research. In: M. Maehr & P. R. Pintrich (Eds), *Advances in Motivation and Achievement* (Vol. 10, pp. 1–49). Greenwich, CT: JAI Press.
Pintrich, P. R. (2000a). An achievement goal theory perspective on issues in motivation terminology, theory, and research. *Contemporary Educational Psychology, 25*, 92–104.
Pintrich, P. R. (2000b). Multiple goals, multiple pathways: The role of goal orientation in learning and achievement. *Journal of Educational Psychology, 92*, 544–555.
Pintrich, P. R., & Garcia, T. (1991). Student goal orientation and self-regulation in the college classroom. In: M. L. Maehr & P. R. Pintrich (Eds), *Advances in Motivation and Achievement* (Vol. 7, pp. 371–402). Greenwich, CN: JAI Press.
Rogosa, D. R. (1995). Myths and methods: "Myths about longitudinal research" plus supplemental questions. In: J. Gottman (Ed.), *The Analysis of Change* (pp. 2–65). New Jersey: Lawrence Erlbaum Associates.

Ross, J. D., & Ross, C. M. (1976). Ross test of higher cognitive processes. CA: Academic Therapy Publications.

Rost, J. (1990). Rasch models in latent classes: An integration of two approaches to item analysis. *Applied Psychological Measurement, 14*, 271–282.

Rost, J. (1991). A logistic mixture distribution model for polytomous item responses. *The British Journal of Mathematical and Statistical Psychology, 44*, 75–92.

Rost J., & Langeheine R. (Eds) (1997a). *Applications of latent trait and latent class models in the social sciences*. New York: Waxmann.

Rost, J., & Langeheine, R.(1997b). A guide through latent structure models for categorical data. In: J. Rost & R. Langeheine (Eds), *Applications of Latent Trait and Latent Class Models in the Social Sciences* (pp. 13–37). Münster: Waxmann.

Skaalvik, E. M., & Vålas, H. (1999). Relations among achievement, self-concept, and motivation in mathematics and language arts: A longitudinal study. *Journal of Experimental Education, 67*(2), 135–149.

Skinner, E. A., Chapman, M., & Baltes, P. B. (1988). Children's beliefs about control, means-ends, and agency: Developmental differences during middle childhood. *International Journal of Behavioral Development, 11*, 369–388.

Steiger, J. H. (1990). Some additional thoughts on components and factors. *Multivariate Behavioral Research, 25*, 41–45.

von Davier, M. (2000). *WINMIRA User Manual*.

Waller, N. G., & Meehl, P. E. (1998). *Multivariate taxometric procedures: Distinguishing types from continua*. Newbury Park, CA: Sage.

Weiner, B. (1986). *An attribution theory of motivation and emotion*. New York: Springer-Verlag.

Willett, J. B., & A. G. Sayer. (1994). Using covariance structure analysis to detect correlates and predictors of individual change over time. *Psychological Bulletin, 116*, 363–381.

8. THE USE OF MULTI-LEVEL MODELING TO STUDY INDIVIDUAL CHANGE AND CONTEXT EFFECTS IN ACHIEVEMENT MOTIVATION

Janis E. Jacobs and D. Wayne Osgood

Researchers studying either the developmental or the educational aspects of achievement motivation typically are interested in the changes and fluctuations in motivation that occur over time and in different contexts. How are changes in a child's performance in math related to changes in motivation to continue in math? Does an intervention related to reading affect talented students' engagement in reading in the same way as it affects average students' engagement? If intrinsic interest in soccer increases over time, how does it affect interest in school activities over the same time period? Are changes in children's engagement in school dependent on the school they attend or their classroom teacher? Although these questions differ in their emphases (e.g. group differences, context differences, relationships between constructs), they all share the goals of tracking within-individual changes in achievement motivation or of considering context effects that may impact motivation. Indeed, most of the theories of achievement motivation that have been applied to children or to educational contexts assume that changes in beliefs over time will be related to changes in achievement choices, performance, interest, or some other motivational outcome (e.g. Bandura, 1989; Eccles et al., 1983;

New Directions in Measures and Methods, Volume 12, pages 277–318.

ISBN: 0-7623-0819-2

Skinner, Wellborn & Connell, 1990; Weiner, 1985). In addition, researchers universally acknowledge that achievement is embedded within the contexts of schools, classrooms, or neighborhoods (even when they do not measure or control for the particular context).

Despite theoretical and practical interest in questions about individual change and context effects, few studies of the development of achievement motivation have actually measured either one. This has been due, in large part, to limitations imposed by the availability of statistical techniques that would allow researchers to focus their attention on these issues. The goal of this chapter is to describe potential uses of multi-level modeling to address the following three common issues in achievement motivation research: (1) differences between groups (e.g. gender) in patterns of change over time; (2) relationships between changes in one construct and changes in another (e.g. between changes in perceptions of ability and changes in how much a student likes a task); and (3) influences of context on motivation (e.g. schools, classrooms, or neighborhoods). To provide a backdrop for these analytical questions, we begin with a brief review of relevant assumptions implicit in theoretical positions about achievement motivation. We then describe the ways in which multilevel modeling can be used to address these issues when examining within-individual change and the effects of contextual variables, giving examples in each case.

ASSUMPTIONS UNDERLYING ACHIEVEMENT MOTIVATION MODELS

Assumptions Related to Within-Individual Change

The study of achievement motivation has focused on why individuals choose one achievement task over another, the reasons that they persist at that task, and the qualitative nature of achievement choices, as well as the individual's actual achievement or performance. Those interested in the *development* of motivation extend the questions to include changes in task choice, rationales, qualitative experiences, or persistence that occur with age and over time. Major theoretical models of motivation processes typically suggest that achievement beliefs of various types are important determinants of achievement outcomes. Underlying most of these models is the assumption that an individual's current experiences with a task determine expectancies and beliefs that will affect future motivation for similar tasks (e.g. Atkinson, 1957, 1966; Eccles, Futterman, Goff, Kaczala, Meece & Midgley, 1983; Feather, 1982; Bandura, 1977, 1989; Schunk, 1984). Although different theories emphasize different mechanisms (e.g. attributions, self-efficacy, expectancies, goals), all rest on the notion that, as an individual develops, earlier behaviors and beliefs related to a task will be linked to motivation to engage in the same task in the future. Thus, researchers testing these theories typically want to examine within-individual change over time.

Cognitive Models

Over the past 30 years, cognitive models have been the most prominent in the area of achievement motivation (e.g. Bandura, 1989; Covington, 1984; Kukla, 1972; Nicholls, 1984; Schunk, 1984; Weiner, 1979). In each of these models, perceptions of competence and expectations for future success have been used to explain achievement behaviors. Weiner (1979, 1985) suggested that attributions for success and failure on a particular task would make an individual more likely to either pursue or ignore the task in the future. Although Weiner's work did not focus on development, several other researchers have used parts of his theoretical framework to explain children's developing achievement choices (e.g. Nicholls, 1984; Schunk, 1984; Skinner, Wellborn & Connell, 1990). Others have focused primarily on children's perceptions of their abilities and their future expectancies as a means of maintaining motivation. Covington (1984) suggested that children attempt to maintain a sense of self-worth by maximizing attributions to ability following success and minimizing them following failure. Similarly, Nicholls and Miller (1984) gave ability perceptions a primary role as an explanation for children's achievement motivation. Other cognitive approaches have focused on the role of perceptions of efficacy as a motivational force. Children's feelings of efficacy have been related to activity choice, willingness to expend effort on a task, and persistence (e.g. Bandura, 1989; Schunk, 1983, 1984, 1990).

The goal of each of these approaches was to identify the cognitive processes (e.g. perceptions of ability, self-efficacy) underlying achievement motivation. Typically, the processes under study were isolated by using experimental methods that manipulated various conditions, allowing the researcher to compare groups of people who had received different instructions, feedback, or outcomes. Such experimental designs were ideal for testing the relationships between variables, thus providing empirical evidence for the role of cognition in achievement motivation. They did not, however, allow researchers to examine assumptions that were implicit in all of the theories regarding the within-individual relationships between variables over time. The need to examine change over time became more acute when the motivation models from the adult literature were applied to children and adolescents, who are expected to be maturing cognitively, as well as experiencing change in social and school environments as they develop. Laboratory experimentation is valuable for addressing many aspects of motivation and achievement; however, that method is not useful for studying longer term stability or enduring change, which are so central to developmental models of achievement motivation.

Multi-construct Models

As research on the development of achievement motivation has matured, the focus of many process models turned to constructs that bring together motivation and cognition as a joint influence on learning, such as self-regulated learning or metacognition (e.g. Borkowski et al., 1990; Borkowski & Muthukrisna, 1995). Others have focused on the role played by individuals' achievement goals in determining achievement behaviors (e.g. Ames & Archer, 1988; Dweck & Leggett, 1988; Maehr, 1984; Maehr & Braskamp, 1986; Wentzel, 1989). Generally, goals have been defined as the purposes children might have for engaging in a task and researchers have delineated a variety of ways to categorize such goals. For example, Nicholls (1984) defined ego involvement versus task involvement; Dweck and Elliott (1983) described performance versus learning goals; and Maehr (1984) added four types of personal incentives, ranging from intrinsic to extrinsic, including mastery, ego, social, and external reward goals (such as money). Pintrich and Schrauben (1992) developed a model that brought together components from several traditions, including concepts derived from goal theory (e.g. expectancies, values, and affect) as well as metacognitive and self-regulatory concepts. Multi-construct models go well beyond single-construct, cognitive explanations of achievement by encompassing a broader range of explanatory variables. Naturally, the emphasis in the empirical work has typically been on the relations between constructs, but researchers have not succeeded in focusing analyses on the within-person relationships that occur over time, which are implied by the theories.

Newer research also includes a central role for individuals' interests, values, or goals that first appeared in Atkinson's work (1957, 1966). He was the first to highlight the concept of values in his expectancy-value theory by developing an algorithm to describe the way in which expectancies for success and incentive values interact to produce achievement motivation for a specific task. Feather (e.g. 1988, 1992) broadened Atkinson's conceptualization by defining values as a set of stable, general beliefs about what is desirable. He integrated Rokeach's (1979) approach to values by arguing that they are a class of motives that affect behavior by influencing the attractiveness of different goals, and consequently, motivation to attain these goals. He confirmed these ideas by showing that values and expectancies are positively related for academic decisions and decisions to join political groups, suggesting that such decisions are influenced by more than the perceived difficulty of the task (Feather, 1982, 1988). His work was with college students, however, and shed little light on the origins of task values.

Eccles and her colleagues have elaborated and tested an expectancy-value model of activity choice that focuses on the social psychological influences affecting choice and persistence (e.g. Eccles, 1987; Eccles et al., 1983; Eccles, Adler & Meece, 1984; Eccles & Wigfield, 1995; Meece, Parsons, Kaczala, Goff & Futterman, 1982; Meece, Wigfield & Eccles, 1990). According to this model, the key determinants of choice will be the relative value and perceived probability of success of each available option. Expectancies and values are assumed to influence performance and task choice directly; and to be influenced by task-specific beliefs such as self-perceptions of competence; perceptions of the task demands; and the child's goals (both short- and long-term) and self-schemas. These social cognitive variables, in turn, are influenced by the child's perceptions of other people's attitudes and expectations for them, by gender roles and activity stereotypes, and by their own interpretations of their previous experiences with achievement outcomes. Finally, the child's perceptions are influenced by the greater cultural milieu, socializers' beliefs, their own aptitudes or talents, and their previous achievement-related performances.

Closely related to the work on values, is the recent research on the concept of "interest" (Alexander, Kulikovich & Jetton, 1994; Hidi, 1990; Renninger, Hidi & Krapp, 1992; Renninger & Wozniak, 1985; Schiefele, 1991; Tobias, 1994), in which researchers differentiate individual and situational interest. Individual interest is a relatively stable evaluative orientation toward certain domains; situational interest is an emotional state aroused by specific features of an activity or a task. Two aspects or components of individual interest are distinguishable (Schiefele, 1991, 1996): feeling-related and value-related valences. Feeling-related valences refer to the feelings that are associated with an object or an activity itself – feelings like involvement, stimulation, or flow (Csikszentmihalyi, 1988; 1990). Value-related valences refer to the attribution of personal significance or importance to an object.

The evidence just reviewed suggests that critical theoretical and empirical links have already been established between self beliefs and achievement motivation. Much less is known about the long-term changes in self-competence beliefs and values during childhood and adolescence, and what is already known is based primarily on cross-sectional or short-term longitudinal data. Most studies have focused on changes in the factorial structure or mean-level changes in children's competence and value beliefs. Factor analysis has been used to demonstrate that even very young children have well-differentiated beliefs in different domains (e.g. Eccles, Wigfield, Harold & Blumenfeld, 1993; Harter & Pike, 1984; Marsh & Hocevar, 1985) and across achievement constructs (e.g. Nicholls, 1978; Nicholls, Patashnick & Mettetal, 1986).

Analytic strategies that compare mean levels of competence beliefs across ages or across time generally find declines in children's self-assessments as they get older across a variety of domains (e.g. Blumenfeld, Pintrich, Meece & Wessels, 1982; Dweck & Elliott, 1983; Eccles & Midgley, 1989; Wigfield, Eccles, Mac Iver, Reuman & Midgley, 1991; Marsh, 1989). None of these studies has been able to control for within-person stability, however, potentially masking or inflating the rates of change in children's beliefs and attitudes. Small perturbations may be magnified and subtle trends may go unnoticed in cross-sectional and short-term longitudinal studies. Thus, it is critical to use methods such as multi-level modeling to chart changes across longer time periods if we want a comprehensive picture of the development of children's achievement beliefs.

Assumptions Related to Context Effects

Earlier research in both the adult and developmental literature attempted to find universal processes that would be able to explain human behavior; however, when such models failed to receive empirical support in diverse contexts, the focus shifted. In recent years, models have emphasized differences in both processes and outcomes due to context or to individual differences. Context differences have been included in the achievement motivation work in different ways. Some studies have simply demonstrated the existence of similar processes in different subject domains (e.g. math, science, sports) by analyzing data separately in each domain. Others have emphasized the power of context by including it as a moderator variable.

These studies have shown that level and trajectories of achievement beliefs vary by domain (e.g. Jacobs et al., in press; Eccles et al., 1993; Wigfield et al., 1996) and that home and school contexts make a difference. For example, a variety of studies have shown that classroom climate is important for achievement motivation (Dunkin & Biddle, 1974; Fraser & Fisher, 1982; Trickett & Moos, 1974) and that school organization and school policies affect teacher and classroom practices, which in turn affect student motivation (e.g. Bryk, Lee & Holland, 1993; Anderman & Maehr, 1992; Maehr & Midgley, 1996). Researchers have found that teachers can affect motivation by the type of material presented, the amount of work assigned, the way the work is presented, and instructional style (Ames, 1992; Pintrich et al., 1993; Stipek, 1996). School level variables that have an impact on motivation include ability grouping (e.g. Fuligni, Eccles & Barber, 1995; Pallas et al., 1994), comparative performance evaluations (e.g. Ames, 1992; Mac Iver, 1987; Rosenholtz & Rosenholtz, 1981); school culture or climate (e.g. Bryk, Lee & Holland, 1993), and grade transition points (e.g. Eccles & Midgley, 1989; Simmons & Blyth, 1987).

Theoretically, school and classroom contexts affect individual motivation because student learning is embedded or nested within a particular context (one student attends a particular school or is in a given classroom). Nevertheless, very few studies have analyzed context effects by using nested designs and the statistical techniques designed for them. This is especially true of longitudinal studies. At best, previous studies have used context as a control variable or as a grouping factor (e.g. ability grouped vs. mixed ability classes). This is due, in large part, to the fact that most studies are not large enough to use classrooms as the cases and that analysis strategies that involve nested, longitudinal designs have not been available.

Unanswered Questions

We would like to move now into a detailed discussion of the use of multi-level modeling to examine within-individual change and context effects – issues that are important to our understanding of the development of achievement motivation. Before turning to the general discussion of analysis of change; however, we would like to set the stage by previewing the research questions that we will examine in our examples at the end of the chapter.

First, how do changes over time in one group relate to changes in another group? The specific example that we will consider is how changes in girls' ability beliefs and task values are related to changes in boys' ability beliefs and task values. Do girls' and boys' beliefs change at a consistent rate or do the beliefs of one gender drop at a faster rate than those of the other? Much of the research to date has emphasized changes between groups with development (e.g. boys versus girls, high ability versus low ability). The goal of such studies is to examine whether or not group membership (e.g. gender) is related to increasing differences over time. For example, if boys are more motivated than girls to work on math and science tasks in elementary school, does the gap in achievement increase as they get older? If so, is that due to motivation? Many authors have found gender differences in self-perceptions of ability (e.g. Eccles et al., 1984; Jacobs, 1991), in task values (e.g. Eccles et al., 1993), and in attributions for success and failure (e.g. Dweck & Goetz, 1978; Stipek &

Gralinski, 1991). Also, some research has suggested that these differences are exacerbated in early adolescence due to the intensification of sex role beliefs (Eccles, 1994; Eccles et al., 1993; Harter, 1982). Nevertheless, most of this research has been done with cross-sectional data or with short-term longitudinal studies that fail to account for within-individual stability and change over time. Similar analysis issues arise in attempts to compare motivational changes between ethnic and racial groups or between groups differing by ability level (e.g. Dauber & Benbow, 1990; Graham, 1992; Hare, 1985; see Cooper & Dorr, 1995 and Graham, 1994 for reviews).

The second question we will consider is how changes over time in one motivational construct are related to changes in another. In other words, how does one set of attitudes change over time, and how does it influence the development of another? Our example is an examination of the ways in which changes in task values are affected by changes in perceptions of competence. Do children begin to value reading less as their perceptions of competence in that area declines? Do they value math more if they come to feel more competent in that arena? Most studies have not directly studied the impact of changes in one set of beliefs on changes in another set of beliefs or behaviors over time because the appropriate longitudinal data and statistical techniques have not been available.

The third question we will consider is the effect of context on motivation. As an empirical example, we will look at the effects of attending schools that differ in average parental education level on individuals' perceptions of educational opportunities. Do children who attend schools with higher average parental education levels view their educational opportunities more positively than those who attend other schools? Although we might expect the educational level of one's own parents to impact motivation, there also may be a school-level effect that operates beyond the individual level. As noted earlier, context impacts individual motivation because learning is embedded or nested within a particular setting: each student attends only one school. Nevertheless, most of the research on motivation has focused on individual-level variables while neglecting context effects.

ANALYSIS OF WITHIN-INDIVIDUAL CHANGE

Standard Approaches

The basic research design for studying within-individual change is the longitudinal panel study, in which a single sample provides data on a series of occasions extended over time. For instance, researchers might assess interest in reading each month during the third grade or self concept of math ability annually in the fourth through seventh grades.

Repeated-measures Analysis of Variance (ANOVA)

Within the experimental tradition, the standard approach to analyzing change over time is repeated-measures analysis of variance (Judd & McClelland, 1989). This statistical model provides a test of statistical significance for the differences between means on several occasions. As with all ANOVA approaches, the standard use of the repeated-measures model is the diffuse significance test for any and all differences across the several means. Even so, the general framework is also amenable to more focused comparisons (Judd & McClelland, 1989) such as tests for polynomial trends and contrasts between specified sets of occasions (e.g. before versus after an intervention). Repeated-measures ANOVA can also incorporate between-subjects factors, which allows researchers to address questions such as whether boys differ from girls in their patterns of change in motivation or achievement.

Repeated-measures ANOVA is a true analysis of within-individual change in two different senses. First, because the same individuals provide data at every wave, within-individual change is the only possible source of difference in the means over time. Second, the ANOVA significance test is built on a clear distinction between variation within people over time and stable individual differences. This is apparent in the ANOVA model of Eq. 1 (Bailey, 1971), in which each respondent, *i*, is observed on several occasions, *j*:

$$Y_{ij} = \mu + \lambda_j + (\varepsilon_{i}. + \rho_{ij}) \tag{1}$$

The term $\varepsilon_{i}.$ is the individual's mean over time (expressed as a deviation from the grand mean, μ), and it serves as a residual term capturing stable individual differences. The second residual term, ρ_{ij}, is the portion of the outcome measure, Y_{ij}, that remains after subtracting the grand mean, the mean deviation at time j, λ_j, and the individual's mean over time. This second residual term, which reflects only unexplained within-individual change over time, provides the error term for the significance test for mean differences over time.

Limiting the analysis to within-individual change is especially valuable because it eliminates a broad class of alternative explanations for the relationship of an explanatory variable to the outcome. This strategy capitalizes on the repeated assessments to use "subjects as their own controls." Because the effect takes the form of change within a person over time, it cannot be due to any stable characteristics of the person, such as most demographic characteristics, many personality factors, and any constant aspects of the individual's environment, which would include a large share of parent, school, and neighborhood effects. Only other explanatory variables that change over time remain plausible alternative explanations. Indeed, we would argue that the potential to eliminate the contribution of stable factors is the primary advantage of the longitudinal panel research design.

The fundamental limitation of repeated-measures ANOVA is its lack of flexibility. In this statistical model, every respondent provides data on the outcome measure *Y* for each value of each repeated measures factor. A special strength of tightly controlled experimental studies is the possibility of creating a data structure that meets this criterion. For instance, in a laboratory situation it is feasible to insure that each subject responds to all types of stimulus materials under each of several different instructional conditions. In that case stimulus type and mode of instruction would be orthogonal repeated-measures factors, and the data would be amenable to repeated-measures ANOVA.

Without this type of experimental control, repeated-measures ANOVA is of far less value. For the longitudinal panel design, this statistical approach is effectively limited to making comparisons between the times of assessment. Thus, its primary value is to assess developmental trends. Yet the inflexibility of the approach is problematic even for this purpose. For instance, repeated-measures ANOVA does not permit a straightforward analysis of age differences in a panel study unless respondents are uniform in age at the beginning of the study. Otherwise the age trend is buried in the interaction of the within-subjects factor of time with the between-subjects factor of initial age (e.g. Wigfield et al., 1997).

This limitation of repeated measures ANOVA precludes using the longitudinal panel research design to address the much wider range of research questions for which that design is suited. Consider our example of whether children come to place less value on an achievement domain when their perceived competence in that arena declines. A longitudinal panel study should be useful for addressing this question. Though it does not offer the experimental control necessary for certainty about causal order, it does yield sufficient information for determining whether within-individual change on one variable is associated with within-individual change on the other. Repeated-measures ANOVA is unable to capitalize on that information, however, because an explanatory variable such as perceived competence varies freely over time, rather than being constrained to a particular fixed set of values.

Longitudinal Structural Equation Models

In non-experimental research, the typical approach to analyzing data from a longitudinal panel study is structural equation models in which the outcome

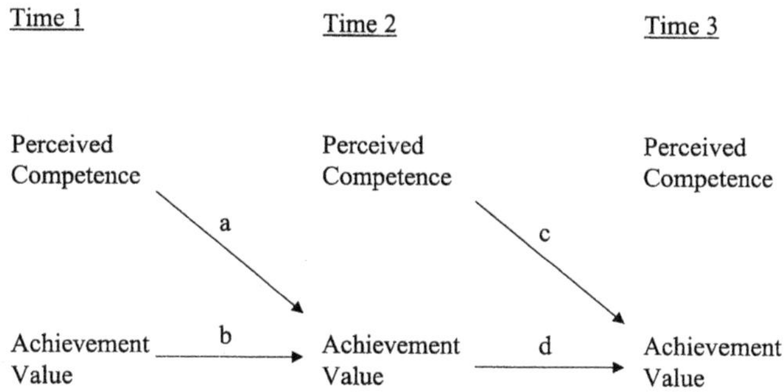

Fig. 1.

variable at each occasion is a function of explanatory variables at the preceding wave as well as the prior level of the outcome variable. Figure 1 illustrates this approach with a three wave panel study, using our example of the impact of perceived competence on value for achievement. This path model corresponds to a pair of regression equations that would provide estimates of the causal paths:

$$\begin{aligned} Value_{2i} &= a\ Competence_{1i} + b\ Value_{1i} + e_{2i} \\ Value_{3i} &= c\ Competence_{2i} + d\ Value_{2i} + e_{3i} \end{aligned} \tag{2}$$

Kessler and Greenberg (1981) provide a thorough introduction to structural equation models of this sort.

This approach overcomes the primary limitation of repeated-measures ANOVA (in this case, competence beliefs and values) because it yields an estimate of the longitudinal relationship between two uncontrolled variables. Thus, this structural equation approach focuses on precisely the kind of research question that is precluded in repeated-measures ANOVA.

Unfortunately, the strengths of repeated-measures ANOVA are the weaknesses of this type of structural equation model. The first weakness is that structural equation models of this form preclude research questions about developmental trends. The regression coefficient *a* and *c* reflect the influence of earlier competence beliefs on later values, while *b* and *c* reflect the stability of values over time. As Eq. 2 illustrates, each wave of outcome data is treated as a distinct outcome variable, and comparisons between the means of those variables play no role in the analysis. Information about development is effectively discarded. Thus, this approach fails to address the one type of research question for which repeated-measures ANOVA is well suited.

The second weakness of this structural equation approach is that estimates of longitudinal relationships are not restricted to within-individual change. This statistical model is not founded on the clear separation of within-person versus between-person variance found in repeated-measures ANOVA. Instead, Eq. 2 adjusts for the earlier measure only to the degree it is correlated with the later measure. This adjustment does not remove all stable individual differences from the analysis, and therefore it remains possible that such factors could spuriously contribute to the estimated longitudinal effects (Cronbach & Furby, 1970; Rogosa, Brandt & Zimowski, 1982).

Pooled-Wave Regression Analysis

To take full advantage of the data generated by longitudinal panel studies of motivation and achievement, we need a statistical framework that combines the strengths of repeated-measures ANOVA with those of structural equation models, as shown in Fig. 1. This framework must be capable of estimating developmental trends as well as assessing longitudinal relationships between uncontrolled variables. Furthermore, to capitalize on the strength of repeated assessments for the same sample of individuals, it should allow us to isolate within-individual change over time, eliminating the contribution of stable individual differences to estimates of longitudinal relationships.

In the following sections of this chapter we will explain how to accomplish those aims through multi-level regression models that pool several waves of data. Figure 2 illustrates how data are organized for this purpose. The upper portion of this figure shows the layout of the data for estimating the structural equation model in Fig. 1. For that analysis, each case is a person, and there is a separate variable for each time that any construct is measured. Thus, perceived competence and achievement value are each repeated as three separate variables, one for every wave of data that was collected. The lower portion of Fig. 2 shows how to reorganize the data for pooled-wave regression analysis. There are several entries for each individual, one for each wave of data. Perceived self-competence and achievement value each appear as single variables in this layout. Age is now a measured variable as well, since it varies across observations for each person. This layout is a multi-level data structure because it has a hierarchical organization in which several observations are nested within each person.

Pooled-wave regression models relate a time-varying outcome variable, such as achievement value, to both explanatory variables that vary over time, such as perceived competence, and to explanatory variables that do not, such as gender. This approach brings the full flexibility of multiple regression models (e.g.

Standard Data Layout

Respondent	Gender	Perceived Competence at age 10	Perceived Competence at age 12	Perceived Competence at age 14	Value on Achievement at age 10	Value on Achievement at age 12	Value on Achievement at age 14
1	1	4	5	6	5	5	7
2	2	7	6	5	7	5	6
3	2	2	3	4	3	5	4
.	.	.	.	.	.	.	.
.	.	.	.	.	.	.	.
.	.	.	.	.	.	.	.
N	1	3	5	3	4	5	5

Pooled-Wave Data Layout

Respondent	Age	Gender	Perceived Competence	Value on Achievement
1	10	1	4	5
1	12	1	5	5
1	14	1	6	7
2	10	2	7	7
2	12	2	6	5
2	14	2	5	6
3	10	2	2	3
3	12	2	3	5
3	14	2	4	4
.	.	.	.	.
.	.	.	.	.
.	.	.	.	.
N	10	1	3	4
N	12	1	5	5
N	14	1	3	5

Fig. 2. Organizing Data for Pooled-Wave Regression Analysis.

Judd & McClelland, 1989; McClendon, 1995) to the analysis of panel data. Longitudinal regression models of this type are widely used in a number of fields including economics (Hsaio, 1986), sociology (Peterson, 1993), political science (Stimson, 1985), and family studies (Johnson, 1995). The growth curve models that have become popular in psychology and education (Bryk & Raudenbush, 1987) fall into this class as well.

Next we discuss how regression models of this sort can be used to address the main research questions of interest in longitudinal studies of motivation and achievement, and then we turn to the task of focusing the analysis on within-individual change. Specialized multi-level regression models are a third topic we must consider because they address the inevitable dependence among the several waves of data for each person. We finish this section with an illustrative analysis.

Three Types of Models

The pooled-wave regression approach brings the full flexibility of multiple regression to the analysis of longitudinal panel data. We will next consider how this approach can be used to address three general types of research questions by highlighting changes in each model that are needed to address the specific question.

Mean-Level Change

The first and most basic model addresses the overall pattern of developmental change in mean levels of the outcome variable across values of age or time. For example, research questions related to trajectories of achievement beliefs can be answered with this model (e.g. How does self-competence change with increasing age?). Equation 3 captures developmental trends of this sort with a model that allows for a quadratic, curvilinear relationship of age to achievement value:

$$Value_{it} = \beta_0 + \beta_1 Age_{it} + \beta_2 Age_{it}^2 + \varepsilon_{it} \quad (3)$$

The subscript i is for the respondent and the subscript t is for the time or wave of the data. The βs are regression coefficients that reflect the mean difference on the outcome measure associated with a unit of difference on the explanatory variable. The model includes a residual or error term, ε_{it}, which equals the difference between the observed value on the outcome variable and the fitted or predicted value for the remainder of the equation.

The top panel of Fig. 3 shows a hypothetical quadratic trend for achievement value that could be generated by this model. Here, value decreases over time,

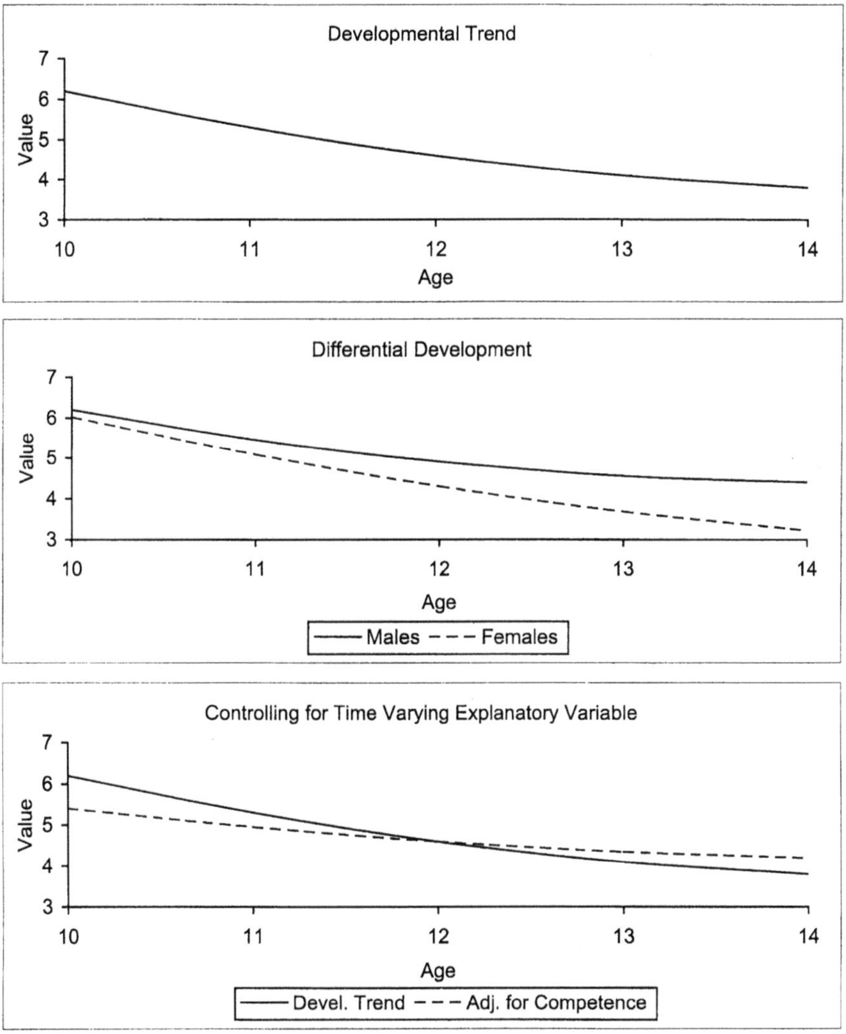

Fig. 3. Three Pooled-Wave Regression Models.

but the rate of decrease is declining and the trend leveling out toward the end of this period. Polynomial functions of this sort are a flexible and efficient means of summarizing non-linear trends, and standard regression texts explain the use of such functions to capture trends of varying levels of complexity (e.g.

Judd & McClelland, 1989; McClendon, 1995). Trends over time need not be limited to smooth, continuous patterns of change, however. The pooled-wave regression framework is also amenable to capturing discontinuous change, as might be expected for a transition from elementary to middle school or the implementation of an instructional or treatment program (see Osgood & Smith, 1995).

Group Differences in Rates of Change

The second type of model allows for differential patterns of development or change by different groups of respondents. This type of model is effective for answering questions about topics such as differences in the rates of change in achievement beliefs between girls and boys or between high and low achievers. This model elaborates the first by adding terms for a grouping or individual difference variable (i.e. sex) and its interactions with age or time:

$$Value_{it} = \beta_0 + \beta_1 Age_{it} + \beta_2 Age_{it}^2 + \beta_3 Sex_i + \beta_4 Age_{it} Sex_i + \beta_5 Age_{it}^2 Sex_i + \varepsilon_{it} \quad (4)$$

Note that *Sex* does not have the subscript *t*, which indicates that it is an attribute of the person that does not vary over time.

The middle panel of Fig. 3 shows a hypothetical example of differential development for males versus females. In this example, there is little difference between males and females in achievement value at the beginning of the study, and the value decreases with age for both sexes. The rate of decline is considerably sharper for females than males, however, so there comes to be a substantial gender gap by age 14.

The coefficients β_4 and β_5 reflect differences between the sexes in the pattern of change, while the coefficient β_3 will indicate the difference between the sexes at the age coded as zero. The data analyst can choose the age at which the difference is evaluated by simply subtracting it from the original measure of age, at which point that age becomes zero on the recoded measure. This process is called "centering" (Bryk & Raudenbush, 1992, pp. 25–29), and it must be done before computing the polynomial terms and interaction terms.

Time-varying Explanatory Variable

The third type of model incorporates time-varying explanatory variables that, unlike age, are not direct functions of time. For example, this model could be used to examine the way in which changes in one set of achievement beliefs affect changes in another set of beliefs or in achievement outcomes over time. This type of model is especially useful because it allows researchers to address the various causal processes that theorists hypothesize as underlying the development of motivation and achievement. Equation 5 illustrates this type of model with perceived competence as the time varying variable:

$$Value_{it} = \beta_0 + \beta_1 Age_{it} + \beta_2 Age^2_{it} + \beta_3 Comp_{it} + \varepsilon_{it} \quad (5)$$

The coefficient β_3 will indicate the strength of relationship between perceived competence and achievement value, expressed in terms of the mean difference in *Value* per unit of change in *Comp*, controlling for the quadratic age trends in both.

Equation 5 also provides a means for addressing a less common research question that will be of special interest to scholars interested in the development of motivation and achievement. The comparison between Eqs 3 and 5 reveals the extent to which perceived competence accounts for developmental trends in achievement value. If perceived competence is strongly related to achievement values, and if the pattern of change is similar for the two, then the addition of *Comp* to the model has the potential to account for the age trend, as indicated by the reduction of coefficients β_1 and β_2 (Hirschi & Gottfredson, 1985). This is simply the application of the standard logic of direct and indirect effects from path analysis, with self-competence serving as the mediator between age and value on achievement (McClendon, 1995). The bottom panel of Fig. 3 shows a hypothetical illustration of this pattern. After controlling for self-competence, there is much less developmental change in achievement value.

Limiting the Analysis to Within-Individual Change

Pooled-wave regression models are not inherently analyses of within-individual change. In Eq. 5, the regression coefficient for self-competence, β_3, is based on all of the observed variance of that variable. Some of that variance corresponds to stable individual differences, which arise because some respondents generally, over time, feel more competent in this domain than do other people. The remainder of the variance in perceived competence will be within-individual change over time, and this variance coincides with people feeling more competent at some points in their lives than others. If the analysis of longitudinal data is not limited to within-individual change, it has little advantage over a cross-sectional analysis. Only by focusing on within-individual change does an analysis rule out the possibility that results are attributable to unmeasured individual difference factors, such as demographic factors or stable personality traits.

Fortunately, the solution to this problem is simply to elaborate the regression model in a way that incorporates the distinction between these two types of relationship (Bryk & Raudenbush, 1992, pp. 117–123):

$$Value_{it} = \beta_0 + \beta_{betw} Comp_{i\cdot} + \beta_{within} Comp_{it} + \varepsilon_{it} \quad (6)$$

This model includes both the original score on self-competence that is specific to time *t*, $Comp_{it}$, and the individual's mean over time on that explanatory variable, $Comp_{i.}$. By the basic principles of regression analysis, the regression coefficient for any explanatory variable is entirely determined by the portion of its variance that is not shared with any other explanatory variable (Judd & McClelland, 1989). The only variance in the time-specific scores that is not shared with the individual mean is within-individual variance over time. Therefore, b_{within} will reflect the relationship of within-individual change in self competence to within-individual change in value for achievement. To obtain an analysis that is restricted to within-individual change over time, all that is needed is to control for the individual mean on that variable.

How does this distinction of within-individual versus between-individual relationships apply to age or time, variables that are in a sense controlled by the longitudinal panel research design? In a research design corresponding to Fig. 2, in which every respondent provides data at the same three ages, the mean age across time is identical for all of them. Thus, there is no between-individual variance on age so the regression coefficient for the time specific measure will automatically be restricted to within-individual change, even without including the individual mean for age or time. This would not be the case, however, if individuals differ in the mean ages for their sets of observations. Differences in mean age often do arise, either from sample attrition or as a by-product of the research design. When there is attrition, the average age of respondents who participate at all waves will be different from the average age of those who drop out of the study. In a multiple-cohort panel study, average age will correspond to initial differences in age at the beginning of the study. In both cases, the shared estimate of the relationship reflects not just within-individual change, so it is important to control for individuals' mean ages, as in Eq. 6.

Specialized Methods for Conducting Multi-level Regression Analyses

Thus far we have shown: (1) that pooled-wave regression models provide a flexible framework for answering important research questions about development and causal processes in motivation and achievement, and (2) that a simple elaboration of the basic regression model limits the analysis to within-individual change, thereby eliminating confounding with any and all stable individual differences. Next, we turn to a technical issue that will require the use of specialized statistical software for pooled-wave regression analyses. We want to emphasize, however, that this is not a substantive matter, and is has no consequence for what variables should be included in the regression equations or how the coefficients should be interpreted.

The technical problem arising for pooled-wave regression analysis is that data of this sort are almost certain to violate the standard regression assumption that all of the residuals, ε_{it}, in the entire data set are independent from one another. This assumption requires that there be no systematic pattern in which the residuals for some cases are more similar to one another than to the residuals for other cases. In longitudinal panel data, it is inevitable that we fail to explain a substantial share of the between-individual variation, which means that there will be considerable similarity among the several residuals for each person. Furthermore, there is a ubiquitous tendency for the residuals of observations closer together in time to be more highly correlated than those that are farther apart. Violating the assumption of independence does not systematically bias the estimates of the regression coefficients, but it does invalidate their significance tests, making it appear that one has more statistical power than is actually the case.

Multi-level regression models have the express purpose of addressing dependence in research designs with nested data, and they retain the full substantive flexibility of multiple regression. The key feature of these models is the addition of extra residual or error terms that capture the pattern of dependence among the residuals. Among the mostly widely known versions of these multi-level models are Bryk and Raudenbush's hierarchical linear models (HLM, 1992) and Goldstein's multi-level models (1995). Latent growth curve models (Willet & Sayer, 1994) express some of the same features within a covariance structure modeling framework.

A typical multi-level model addressing both types of dependence would be:

$$Value_{it} = \beta_0 + \beta_1 Age_{it} + \beta_2 Age_{it}^2 + (u_{0i} + u_{1i} Age_{it} + u_{2i} Age_{it}^2 + r_{it}) \qquad (7)$$

This equation divides the residual into four components, three that apply to all observations for person i (u_{0i}, u_{1i}, and u_{2i}) and one that is specific to a single wave of data t (r_{it}). This is a more elaborate version of the separation of within-individual and between-individual residual terms in repeated-measures ANOVA. u_{0i} applies to all observations for an individual, so it captures unexplained stable individual differences. The additional residual terms, u_{1i} and u_{2i}, apply to the linear and quadratic terms for age, and thus they correspond to the difference between this individual's pattern of change over time and the overall pattern of change captured by β_1 and β_2. Bryk and Raudenbush (1987) show that these additional residual terms allow for the possibility of greater correlation between observations that are closer together in time. The standard assumptions would be that the u_i terms have a multivariate normal distribution across individuals and that r_{it} is normally and independently distributed across all observations. The analysis provides estimates of the regression coefficients, the variances of both types of residuals, and the covariances among the u_i.

One often sees multi-level regression models presented in a different format that separates the time varying, or Level 1, aspects of the model from the between-individual, or Level 2, features. In this format, the Level 1 model for Eq. 7 would be:

$$Value_{it} = \pi_{0i} + \pi_{1i}Age_{it} + \pi_{2i}Age_{it}^2 + r_{it}$$

The Level 2 model for Eq. 7 is:

$$\pi_{0i} = \beta_0 + u_{0i}$$

$$\pi_{1i} = \beta_1 + u_{1i}$$

$$\pi_{2i} = \beta_2 + u_{2i}$$

Note that the π parameters of the Level 1 equation carry the subscript i, so they are the coefficients for a single individual rather than the entire sample. As the Level 2 model demonstrates, those individual coefficients are equal to the coefficients for the entire sample, β, plus the residual term reflecting the individual's deviation from the average relationship. Thus, the difference in presentation is simply a heuristic device, and this set of Level 1 and 2 equations specifies the same model as Eq. 7.

The format of separate Level 1 and 2 equations can be useful for specifying interactions between the two levels of analysis, while making clear what Level 2 residual terms would be appropriate. For instance, adding the variable sex to each of the Level 2 equations would allow for the possibility that boys and girls would differ in their pattern of change over time, comparable to Eq. 4:

$$\begin{aligned} \pi_{0i} &= \beta_{00} + \beta_{01}Sex_i + u_{0i} \\ \pi_{1i} &= \beta_{10} + \beta_{11}Sex_i + u_{1i} \\ \pi_{2i} &= \beta_{20} + \beta_{21}Sex_i + u_{2i} \end{aligned} \tag{8}$$

All of the substantive examples of pooled-wave regression are amenable to these multi-level methods, including analyses focusing on causal processes over time, such as the influence of perceived competence on achievement value in Eq. 5. Again, multi-level models add a complex error structure that addresses dependence among observations; they bring no change or limitations to the substantive model. In using these methods, it is important not to make the mistake of interpreting the separate Level 1 and Level 2 equations as implying that these models automatically make a strict separation of within-individual relationships from between-individual level relationships. Coefficients for Level 1, time-varying, explanatory variables will be shared estimates that combine the two, as we explained in the preceding section. To limit multi-level regression coefficients to within-individual relationships, which control for all stable individual differences, one must add the individual mean of the explanatory variable to the model.

Next we present two empirical examples to illustrate these methods. The first will focus on within-individual change over time and the second will focus on contextual effects.

An Example Analysis of Within-Individual Change Over Time

This example is taken from a recent study documenting gender differences in age-related trends across grades one through twelve in perceived self-competence and activity values in three achievement domains (Jacobs et al., in press).[1] All of the equations and exemplars presented in our description of multi-level analysis of individual change have used these variables. Thus, the earlier description of the analysis techniques should be readily transferred to this example. The example illustrates all three types of models described earlier – mean level change, differential rates of change between groups, and the use of a time-varying explanatory variable.

This study used a cohort-sequential design to examine within-individual changes in beliefs across childhood and adolescence, focusing on differences between girls and boys in their rates of change in task values. Based on the previous literature and our own work, we predicted that subjective task values would be highest in the first grade, with decreases across grades. Earlier work has shown that gender differences in values exist as early as first grade (Marsh, 1989; Wigfield et al., 1997), and previous reports of increases in gender differences in self beliefs in middle childhood and in adolescence (Eccles et al., 1993; Huston, 1983; Ruble & Martin, 1998) led us to expect increases in the differences between the beliefs of males and females over time. Finally, when the time-varying explanatory variable of perceived competence was added to the model, we expected declines in competence beliefs with age to explain some of the decline in values, resulting in flatter trajectories for subjective task values after controlling for competence beliefs.

In this example, we used Hierarchical Linear Modeling to implement a growth curve analysis to test our hypotheses (Bryk & Raudenbush, 1987,

1992). Although changes in mean levels of self beliefs have been tested in short-term longitudinal studies (e.g. Wigfield et al., 1997) by using repeated measures ANOVA, such an approach has the limitations that we described earlier and becomes quite unwieldy for six waves of data covering a span of twelve grade levels. Our HLM growth model improves on that approach by efficiently capturing developmental trajectories with only a few parameters and by allowing us to include all respondents, even if they did not provide data for the full set of six observations. Using HLM, we were able to implement an analysis that is strictly limited to within-individual change, controlling for all stable individual differences, while addressing the possible non-independence of residuals due to repeated measures. This approach also allowed us to take full advantage of our cohort-sequential design by determining whether individual characteristics, such as gender, are related to initial status or to change and by analyzing time-varying factors that might explain change over time in the outcome.

Sample and Measures

These data were gathered as part of the Childhood and Beyond (CAB) longitudinal project investigating the development of children's self-perceptions, task values, and activity choices. The analyses presented here will be one of the outcome variables from the Jacobs et al. (in press) study: Values for Language Arts. Data were collected between 1989–1999 from children attending 10 elementary schools in four middle class, primarily European-American school districts in the suburbs of a large Midwestern city. A cross-sequential design was employed, in which three cohorts of children were followed longitudinally across the elementary, middle, and high school years. Children were in the second, third, and fifth grades during Wave 1 of the data used in this analysis, and they were assessed again one, four, five, and six years later for a total of five waves spanning grades two to twelve. The results reported here are based on 761 students who were present at the first wave and who provided data for both sex and grade. As is necessary for pooled-wave regression analysis, the same scales were used to measure Perceived Competence and Values at each grade level. The scale for Language Arts Competence Beliefs contained five items (e.g. How good are you at reading?) and Language Arts Values were measured with a four-item scale (e.g. How useful will reading be to you in the future?). Alphas varied for each grade level, ranging between 0.73 and 0.93. The Slossen Intelligence Test – Revised (1991 edition), given to all children when they joined the study, was used as a measure of cognitive ability.

The Multi-level Model for the Analysis

The multi-level modeling framework is especially useful for our purposes because there is no assumption that the number and spacing of observations will be consistent across individuals or across time. Thus, HLM is quite compatible with the complexities of our research design, including multiple cohorts sampled in different years of school, a three-year gap in data collection, and sample attrition.

We present the model and results for this first analysis in the two level format of HLM. The Level 1 equation for our initial analysis is the following quadratic growth curve model:

$$Value_{it} = \pi_{0i} + \pi_{1i}Grade_{it} + \pi_{2i}Grade^2_{it} + r_{it}$$

This equation is identical to several pooled-wave regression models discussed above, with grade as the time index instead of age. We "centered" grade at six by subtracting this value from the original codes for grade (Bryk & Raudenbush, 1992, pp. 25–29). We do this to take advantage of the definition of the constant as the fitted value when all explanatory variables equal zero. *Grade* and *Grade*^{2} will not equal zero for the sixth grade, so the constant, π_{0i}, will characterize subjective values in the sixth grade. The rate of change in values varies over time because of the inclusion of *Grade*^{2}. As a result of centering grade, however, π_{1i} will reflect the "instantaneous" slope at the sixth grade.

The Level 2 equations for this analysis are:

$$\pi_{0i} = \beta_{00} + \beta_{01}Sex_i + \beta_{02}Ability_i + \beta_{03}Grade_{i\cdot} + \beta_{04}Grade^2_{i\cdot} + u_{0i}$$
$$\pi_{1i} = \beta_{10} + \beta_{11}Sex_i + \beta_{12}Ability_i + u_{1i}$$
$$\pi_{2i} = \beta_{20} + \beta_{21}Sex_i + \beta_{22}Ability_i$$

Here we have elaborated the basic model for differential development (Eq. 8) in two ways. First, controlling for ability insures that results for gender differences in development are not attributable to ability differences. Second, as we recommended above, the equation for the intercept, π_{0i}, also includes individual means over time for the Level 1 explanatory variables, *Grade* and *Grade*^{2}. Doing so insures that our results for trends across grades will reflect within-individual change over time rather than preexisting differences between the cohorts or between respondents who completed the study versus those who were lost in earlier waves.

We have centered all of the Level 2 explanatory variables at their sample means (i.e. subtracted the mean from the original scores) so that the Level 2 constant terms (β_{00}, β_{10}, and β_{20}) characterize the growth curves averaged across boys and girls and for students of average ability.

The coefficients for sex, β_{01}, β_{11}, and β_{21}, will indicate the difference in the growth curves for males and females, with β_{01} reflecting the mean sex difference in the sixth grade, β_{11} the difference in slope in the sixth grade, and β_{21} the difference in curvature. Because sex is a dummy variable with zero assigned to males and one to females, positive values indicate higher means, slopes, and more convex curvature (i.e. positive change in slope over time) for females than for males.[1]

To allow for dependence among the several observations for each respondent, these equations include residual terms for the Level 1 intercept, u_{0i}, and for linear change, u_{1i}. Preliminary analyses indicated that the quadratic trend, π_{2i}, did not vary significantly across respondents.

Growth Curve Results

The results for this analysis appear both as Model 1 in Table 1, which lists the regression coefficients, their statistical significance, and their standard errors, and as the solid lines in Fig. 4, which expresses their meaning by graphing the fitted values that correspond to these coefficients.

We expected subjective task values for Language Arts to decline across grades. This expectation was upheld. As can be seen in Fig. 4, initial subjective task values were high, 5.6 for boys and 5.9 for girls out of a possible score of 7.0. Though the growth curve was curvilinear, the figure shows that decline is the dominant trend for task value beliefs. In Table 1 the intercept term for linear change indicates that, at grade 6 and averaged across boys and girls, values were declining at a highly significant rate of -.12 units per year. The intercept term for grade-squared is positive. Correspondingly, Fig. 4 shows that average subjective values for language arts decline most rapidly during the elementary years, and the rate of decline slows over time.

Prior research led us to expect that females would have higher values for language arts (e.g. Eccles et al., 1993), and we expected these differences to grow larger over time due to gender role socialization. As can be seen in Table 1, tests of the Level 1 intercept for sex indicate that males and females hold significantly different task values in language arts at grade 6; females hold higher values for language arts than males. Although gender differences in the Level 1 intercept were found in language arts, no significant gender differences were found in the linear or quadratic *rate of change*. A joint test of the coefficients for sex on linear and quadratic change indicate that the overall sex differences in the pattern of change in language arts is only a statistical trend ($p = 0.12$). If it were significant, it would suggest the following: Girls initially place higher value on language arts than boys in second grade. Because girls' values decline more rapidly than boys, however, the gap narrows by late elementary school. The gap then increases again during high school as girls' value for language arts increases and boys' value levels off (see Fig. 4).

The Contribution of Perceived Competence

After describing the growth trajectories for subjective task values, we were interested in examining the potential of a time varying explanatory variable, perceived competence, to account for trajectories of change in subjective task values. As discussed above, we can determine this by adding competence beliefs as an explanatory variable in the HLM model for task values. To the

Table 1. Growth Models for Language Arts Values, With and Without Controlling for Perceived Competence.

	Model 1		Model 2	
	Coeff.	Std. Err.	Coeff.	Std. Err.
For Intercept				
Intercept	5.008*	0.042	5.095*	0.036
Sex	0.189*	0.080	–0.011	0.068
Ability Test	–0.002	0.003	–0.008*	0.002
Average Grade	0.066*	0.022	0.040*	0.019
Average Grade^2	–0.008	0.010	–0.008	0.008
Ave. Competence Beliefs			0.068	0.039
For Linear Change				
Intercept	–0.122*	0.010	–0.060*	0.009
Sex	0.002	0.018	–0.013	0.016
Ability Test	–0.0002	0.0006	–0.0006	0.0005
For Quadratic Change				
Intercept	0.017*	0.003	0.009*	0.003
Sex	0.009	0.006	0.012*	0.005
Ability Test	0.0003	0.0002	0.0004*	0.0002
For Competence Beliefs				
Intercept			0.433*	0.029

	Model 1 Var.	Model 2 Var.
Residual Variance		
For Intercept	0.320	0.155
For Linear Change	0.011	0.006
For Competence Beliefs		0.083
Within Individual	0.802	0.594

* $p < 0.05$.

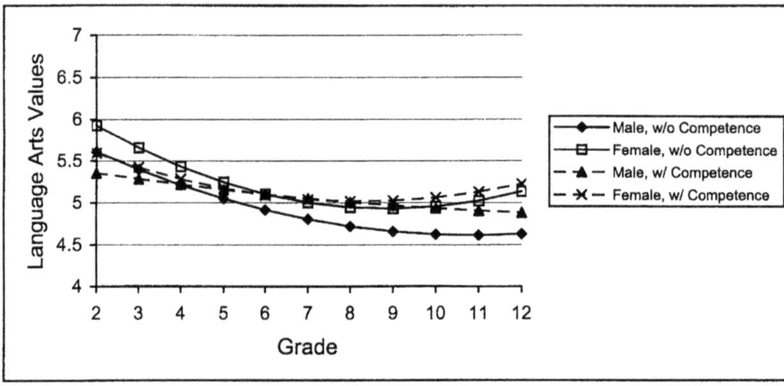

[1]Adapted from Jacobs, et al., in press.

Fig. 4. Multi-Level Model of Growth Curves for Language Arts Values with and without Controls for Language Arts Perceived Competence.[1]

extent that competence beliefs are related to trajectories of change in subjective task values, introducing that variable to the model will reduce coefficients for change over time and the trajectories will become more flat, showing less change. Also, to the extent that perceived competence is related to gender differences, the coefficients for gender will be reduced, the trajectories for males and females will be more similar in slope and shape, and their trajectories will lie closer together.

For this analysis, we modify our original HLM model by adding the time-specific measure of perceived competence to the Level 1 equation of our HLM model and the individual mean for perceived competence to the Level 2 equation for the Level 1 intercept. By including both, we insure that the Level 1 relationship is restricted to within-individual change. These results appear as Model 2 in Table 1 and as the dashed lines in Fig. 4.

Table 1 shows that respondents are much more likely to value language arts when they feel competent in that domain. The coefficient for perceived competence is both large (0.433) and highly significant. The strength of the relationship is also reflected in the variance explained by perceived competence for all of the residual terms in the analysis. Perceptions of competence explained 52% of the previously unexplained variance in stable individual differences (i.e. residual variance for intercept). Perceived Competence also explained substantial portions of the variance in change over time, in the form of both individual differences in slope (46%) and within-individual variation around the growth curves (26%). In sum, students' perceptions of competence in language arts are strongly associated with how much they value related tasks.

A time-varying explanatory variable like perceived competence has the potential to explain not only between-individual variation in trajectories of task values, but also the amount and pattern of change in the average trajectory. For this to occur, competence beliefs must be strongly associated with subjective task values, and we have just seen that they are. Furthermore, the pattern of change in perceived competence must be similar to that of task values. The extent to which perceived competence accounts for the overall trajectory will be reflected in the impact of controlling for competence beliefs upon the intercept terms for linear and quadratic change in Table 1 and in the difference in trajectories before and after controlling for perceived competence, as shown in Fig. 4.

Perceived competence is closely tied to the trajectory of values for language arts. Coefficients for both linear and quadratic change are reduced over 40% by controlling competence beliefs. Accordingly, Fig. 4 shows that the trajectories for both boys and girls are considerably flattened by taking competence beliefs into account. Other analyses (Jacobs et al., in press) indicated that self-competence in language arts declines rapidly during the elementary school years. Accordingly, Fig. 4 shows that competence beliefs account for much of the decline in language arts values during that period for both boys and girls.

Analyses reported elsewhere indicate that girls consistently feel more competent in language arts than boys do after first grade, and boys' perceived competence beliefs decline at a faster rate than those of girls (Eccles et al., 1993; Jacobs et al., under review). Figure 4 shows that perceived competence explains much of the gender difference during the middle grades, while a moderate difference remains during the earlier and later grades. Averaging across grades, controlling for competence beliefs reduces the sex difference in values by 62%, from 0.28 to 0.11. Thus, the higher perceived competence that girls experience in language arts may be an important source of the higher value they place in this domain.

ANALYSIS OF CONTEXT EFFECTS

As discussed earlier, motivation researchers all acknowledge that achievement is embedded within the context of schools, classrooms, or neighborhoods. In recent years, many models have emphasized differences in both processes and outcomes due to context or to individual differences. Despite the acknowledged importance of considering the role of context in the development of achievement motivation, researchers have seldom included true tests of context effects. We begin this section by laying out two major methodological issues that arise in studying context effects: units of analysis and separating context effects from aggregated individual effects. Fortunately, both of these issues are successfully resolved by the same multi-level regression models that we discussed above. Then, as an empirical example, we present an analysis that examines attitudes toward school achievement in relation to the contextual factor of attending a school with high or low average levels of parent education.

Methodological Issues

Unit of Analysis

In many studies of motivation and achievement, individual respondents are selected as members of larger units such as classrooms, schools, or neighborhoods. For many years researchers struggled with the question of whether individuals or aggregate units were more appropriate for analyzing such data. Suppose that 20 different teachers instructed 300 female students in a study of the effect of math teachers' gender on female students' interest in the subject. Those 300 students do not represent fully independent observations for this research question. Girls who have the same teacher share many potential influences that go well beyond their teacher's gender, such as the teacher's instructional style and skill and the quality of the classroom interaction that particular year. Therefore the data set has less information about the effect of teachers' gender than if the 300 students all had different teachers. In other words, when analyzed at the individual level, these data violate the standard statistical assumption of independence, with the consequence that significance tests are biased toward results appearing significant when they should not (Bryk & Raudenbush, 1992).

Before multi-level statistical models were available, the standard recommendation to overcome this problem of dependent observations was to conduct the analysis at the aggregate level rather than the individual level. To accomplish this, one would compute the mean of student responses for each teacher and then conduct the analysis on the 20 means rather than the 300 individual scores. This analysis solves the problem of dependence (assuming that the teachers are not further clustered, such as by school), so this analysis is legitimate. Unfortunately, the solution comes with costs. The accuracy of these means depends on the number of students in each class, so the analysis requires weighted least squares rather than ordinary regression or ANOVA (McClendon, 1995). Basing the analysis on aggregated means makes it difficult to control for individual level factors (such as gender, race, and prior achievement) that might be confounded with the aggregate variable of interest. Furthermore, limiting the analysis to means precludes the separation of individual and context effects that we discuss below.

Multi-level statistical models overcome the level of analysis problem by making use of information at both individual and aggregate levels of analysis. Here is a multi-level model for the analysis of the impact of teacher gender on students' interest in math:

$$Interest_{ij} = \beta_0 + \beta_1 TGender_j + \beta_2 Perf_{ij} + \beta_3 Race_{ij} + (u_j + r_{ij})$$

The subscript i differentiates individual student respondents and the subscript j the classrooms of which they are members. The outcome variable is interest in math, $Interest_{ij}$, which is assessed for each student. The coefficient β_1 will reflect the relationship between that outcome and the teachers' gender, $TGender_j$. Note that this variable carries the subscript j but not i because it is constant for all students in the same classroom. This model also controls for the two individual level variables of prior performance, $Perf_{ij}$, and race (such as a dummy variable for minority versus majority ethnic group). The residual term u_j allows for unexplained mean differences between classrooms, which is the main source of dependence among the observations. Thus, a multi-level regression model can simultaneously examine the relationship of an outcome to both individual level and aggregate level explanatory variables, while adjusting for any redundancy among the responses in each context.

It is also possible that the strength of an individual level relationship would vary across contexts. For instance, some teachers might be more effective than others at encouraging the interest of students who had done poorly at math in the past. If so, then the relationship of prior performance to current interest would be weaker in some classrooms than in others. To avoid an erroneous significance test, the analysis must take this variation into account. A multi-level regression model does so by adding a residual term that applies to the relevant individual level variable, such as u_{1j} in this regression equation:

$$Interest_{ij} = \beta_0 + \beta_1 TGender_j + \beta_2 Perf_{ij} + \beta_3 Race_{ij} + (u_{0j} + u_{1j} Perf_{ij} + r_{ij}) \quad (10)$$

The term u_{1j} captures the difference between the effect of prior performance in classroom j and the overall effect of classroom performance, averaged across classrooms. Texts on multi-level regression analyses (e.g. Bryk and Raudenbush, 1992; Goldstein, 1995; Kreft and deLeeuw, 1998) explain procedures for determining whether or not such a residual term is necessary for any given individual level explanatory variable.

Multi-level regression analyses can also investigate the reasons that individual level relationships vary across contexts. For instance, a researcher might want to know whether experienced teachers are more successful at eliciting greater interest among students who have done poorly at math in the past. We can capture this in a multi-level regression model by adding a variable that is the product of a measure of teacher experience and the measure of prior performance. The format of Bryk and Raudenbush's HLM program makes it quite easy to specify such interaction; one simply adds a Level 2 variable to the equation for the Level 1 variable of interest.

Significance tests for these cross-level interaction terms are sensitive to variation in the strength of the individual level relationship across contexts, just as was the case for tests of the "main effects" of Level 2 variables (described above). Fortunately, incorporating a residual term such as u_{1j} in Eq. 9 not only insures accurate significance tests of the overall relationship between prior performance and interest in math, but also insures accuracy for any interactions of prior performance with aggregate level variables, like teacher experience.

Separating Context Effects from Individual Effects

One of the most interesting reasons for studying individuals within larger units such as classrooms or neighborhoods is the possibility that the aggregate properties of these units may have emergent effects that are distinct from individual level relationships. For instance, Pong (1998) argued that student achievement is higher at schools with a larger proportion of two parent families because all students benefit from the stronger network of social relationships among adults made possible by the greater social capital of two parent families. In Pong's research, the contextual effect of the aggregate characteristic amplified the positive individual level relationship between achievement and having a two parent family. It is also possible, however, that a context effect would be in the opposite direction of an individual level effect. For example, although school achievement is positively associated with self esteem at the individual level, Felson and Reed (1986) predicted and found that the contextual effect of average school achievement is in the opposite direction. They reasoned that a high average level of achievement provides a stricter standard of social comparison that leads students to evaluate their own performance more poorly than if the average achievement were lower.

Contextual effects of this sort cannot be inferred from aggregate level analysis alone, but rather they require multi-level analysis of both individual and contextual relationships (Bryk and Raudenbush, 1992). A strictly aggregate analysis confounds individual and contextual effects. Consider the relationship of parents' level of education to students' attitudes about school, which is the research question we investigate in our empirical example of context effects below. It is likely that students will have more favorable attitudes about school achievement if their parents obtained higher levels of education. This individual level process alone is sufficient to generate more favorable mean attitudes in those schools where mean parental education is higher. This type of aggregated individual level relationship is often called a compositional or selection effect. It is conceptually distinct from a true contextual effect, in which average parents' education would impact all students, regardless of their own parents' education. This is an emergent effect of the school context rather than an individual level relationship that holds regardless of which school the student attends.

If both individual and aggregate data are available, the two types of relationship are readily separated in a multi-level regression model in this form:

$$AttSch_{ij} = \beta_0 + \beta_1 ParEd._j + \beta_2 ParEd_{ij} + (u_j + r_{ij}) \tag{9}$$

The equation specifies that the outcome variable of attitudes toward school, $AttSch_{ij}$, is a function of both the education of the individual respondents' parents, $ParEd_{ij}$, and of the mean education of all students at the school, $ParEd._j$. The coefficient β_2 will capture the individual level relationship between each student's outcome and their own parents' education. The coefficient β_1 will reflect the context effect of mean parental education on all children at the school, above and beyond the effect of their own parents' education, β_2. Thus, multi-level regression modeling provides a straightforward means of implementing this important conceptual distinction between effects at the two levels of analysis.

Note that Eq. 10 directly parallels Eq. 6, which addressed the analysis of within-individual change over time. Each of those equations includes both a Level 1 variable and its Level 2 mean. The reason for this similarity is that the two equations are designed to solve methodological problems by making a clear distinction between relationships at the two levels of analysis.

The analysis of context effects and of within-individual change are not parallel in one respect, however. The Level 1 estimate automatically controls for any and all Level 2 variables, whether measured or not. This is a considerable methodological advantage for the analysis of within-individual change because it rules out the broad class of alternative explanations having to do with stable individual differences. Unfortunately, the Level 2 coefficient only controls for the individual level factors that are included in the model. Therefore, it remains possible that any apparent context effect of mean parents' education in Eq. 10 could actually be due to other individual level factors, such as race, economic status, or family structure. Therefore, when studying context effects it is important to identify other relevant variables of this sort and include them in the analysis (Bryk & Raudenbush, 1992).

An Empirical Example

We illustrate the application of multi-level regression models to contextual data with analyses of students' attitudes about school in relation to the school context. The data for this example come from a study of 5,253 eighth grade students attending 36 different schools located in 10 different school districts widely dispersed across the U.S. The data were collected as part of an evaluation of a school-based gang prevention program (Esbensen and Osgood, 1999).[2] The sample is highly diverse, with only 44% of the respondents identifying themselves as white. It is especially useful for a contextual analysis that the schools vary widely in their population characteristics. In terms of ethnicity, these schools ranged from a low of 3% minority students to a high of 97%; in terms of family structure, they vary from a low of 9% of students living with two parents to a high of 91%; and in terms of parents' education, they varied from a low of only 39% graduating from high school or earning a GED to a high of 65% completing college.

The measure we use as our outcome variable is students' views about whether their educational opportunities are limited. This four item measure ($\alpha = 0.70$) includes questions indicating that the student feels he or she doesn't have much chance of going far in school. The explanatory variables included in the analyses are respondent's sex (1 = male, 2 = female), minority ethnic status (1 = African American or Latino, 0 = other), and parents' education (coded as the higher of two parents, 1 = less than high school, 2 = high school graduate, 3 = college graduate).

The focus of these analyses is on whether attending a school with higher or lower average parental education has a context effect on students' sense of limited educational opportunities. We would expect that individual students are more likely to see their educational prospects as limited if their parents attained a low level of education. This analysis will also address whether, in addition to this individual level relationship, students' views about these limitations are affected by attending a school where most other students come from families with higher or lower levels of parental education. In other words, is there an emergent effect whereby all students' views about educational prospects are affected by attending a school in which more or fewer families have attained higher levels of education.

To illustrate the use of multi-level regression for analyzing contextual data, we estimated three models using Raudenbush, Bryk, Cheong, and Congdon's

Table 2. Hierarchical Linear Models of Students Views that Their Educational Opportunities are Limited.

	Individual Level		School Level		Joint	
	Coeff.	S.E.	Coeff.	S.E.	Coeff.	S.E.
Individual Parents' Educ.	−0.230*	0.017			−0.220*	0.017
Mean Parents' Education			−0.567*	0.078	−0.359*	0.082
Female	−0.093*	0.020			−0.092*	0.020
Minority	0.041	0.032			−0.004	0.032
Constant	1.880*	0.019	1.914*	0.017*	1.902*	0.016
	Var.	Expl. Var.	Var.	Expl. Var.	Var.	Expl. Var.
Residual Variance						
School Mean	0.007	65.1%	0.005	73.2%	0.004	81.4%
Minority Slope	0.014				0.012	
Within School	0.500	5.5%	0.528	0.0%	0.499	5.5%

* $p < 0.05$.

(2000) HLM program. The first of these is an individual level model in the sense that all of the explanatory variables characterize the individual respondent and his or her family. As Table 2 shows, students whose parents had less education see their own educational prospects as considerably more limited. Given the coding of parents' education, students whose parents did not finish high school score an average of 0.46 lower than students whose parents graduated from college, a difference of 0.84 standard deviations. Girls saw their educational prospects as significantly less limited than boys, but there was no difference between minority and non-minority students (controlling for the other factors).

The individual level model includes three residual variance components. The first is the variance of the residual mean differences between schools (u_{0j} in the equations above), which allows for the dependence among the observations for students from the same school. There is also a residual variance component for the relationship of minority ethnicity to perceptions of limited educational opportunity, which varied significantly across schools.[3] The final residual variance component reflects differences among students within schools, and this term is most comparable to the residual variance in a standard ordinary least squares multiple regression analysis.

The variance of the residual term for school means provides a standard for gauging how well a model accounts for differences among schools in students' perceptions of limited educational opportunities. Though the first HLM model includes only individual level variables, those variables still have the potential to account for differences between schools, provided that the explanatory variable differs among schools as well. Indeed, the individual level model explains fully 65.1% of the between-school variance. This figure is computed by comparison to a "null model" which includes no explanatory variables, and it constitutes an R^2 value for the aggregate level of analysis. The proportion of the school-level variance that is explained is far larger than the 5.5% of individual level variance that is explained. It must be remembered, however, that there is far more within-school variance than between-school variance.

The second analysis in Table 2 is restricted to our school-level explanatory variable, the mean parents' education. The significant school-level relationship is more than twice as strong as the individual level relationship of parents' education to perceived limitations on educational opportunity. Does that imply that the average parents' education for an entire school has a larger impact on this outcome measure than does a student's own parents' education? The answer is "not necessarily" for two different reasons.

The larger school-level coefficient does imply that a one unit difference in a school's mean parental education makes more difference in the outcome for each student than does a one unit difference in their own parents' education. Yet the consequence of this larger coefficient is dampened by the limited variance of school means in parental education in comparison to individual level variance. Though these schools vary widely in mean parental education, a one unit difference between schools is rare while one unit difference between individuals is common. Accordingly, the school-level model explains a larger proportion of the variance between schools than does the individual level model. The school-level model can explain none of the within-school variance, however, because the explanatory variable does not differentiate among students at the same school.

Second, we cannot interpret the results of the school level model as indicating a strong effect of mean parental education on students' perceptions of limited opportunities because this coefficient does not distinguish between individual and contextual effects. Instead, it reflects the total association between means on the two variables, which combines the two sources. A model including both individual scores and school means, as in Eq. 10, is necessary to estimate the context effect.

The third HLM model in Table 2 is just such a joint model. In comparison to the previous models, the individual level relationship is essentially unchanged, while the mean level relationship is considerably smaller. In fact, the mean level relationship has been reduced by the magnitude of the individual level relationship. This is precisely what we seek as an estimate of the context effect: the relationship between the school mean for parental education level and students' views about limited educational opportunities, above and beyond the individual level relationship. Thus, the coefficient in the joint model reflects the dependence of the outcome on the overall level of parental education in a school, regardless of the student's own parents' educational levels.

In this analysis the context effect remains statistically significant and larger than the individual level effect. In combination, the individual and contextual effects account for the lion's share of variation across schools in students' views of limited educational opportunities (81.4%). As noted above, even strong context effects may account for little of the total variation in the outcome because between-school variance in the explanatory variable is typically far less than within-school variance. Even so, a finding such as this would have considerable theoretical importance for showing that students' expectations for educational success are dependent on the broader social context in which they live, rather than just their immediate family. Furthermore, such a result would point to especially pernicious effects of extreme concentration of economic disadvantage in particular neighborhoods and schools, as has been the focus of W. J. Wilson's writing (e.g. 1987). Of course, this analysis is only a simple example to illustrate these methods. The results for the context effect should not be treated as definitive without more thorough controls for other individual level factors that would provide alternative explanations (see preceding section).

CONCLUSIONS

We began this chapter by suggesting that theories and models of the development of achievement motivation rely on implicit assumptions regarding within-person change and the role of context. Researchers have not been able to test those suppositions easily in the past due to the limitations of statistical programs; thus, this chapter described potential uses of multi-level modeling to address three common issues in achievement motivation research that are based on these assumptions: (1) groups differ in their patterns of change over time; (2) changes in one motivational construct will be related to changes in another; and (3) context will affect achievement motivation.

The strength of multi-level modeling to answer the first two questions lies in its ability to take full advantage of the data generated by longitudinal panel studies of motivation and achievement by combining, in a unified statistical framework, the strengths of repeated-measures ANOVA with those of structural equation models. This framework is capable of estimating developmental trends as well as assessing longitudinal relationships between uncontrolled variables. In addition, it allows us to capitalize on repeated assessments for the same sample of individuals by isolating within-individual change over time, eliminating the contribution of stable individual differences to estimates of longitudinal relationships. A second strength of multi-level modeling over previous methods is its ability to test context effects without sacrificing individual-level data. Methods that aggregate at the school or classroom level confound individual and contextual effects. Contextual effects of this sort cannot be inferred from aggregate level analyses alone, but require multi-level analysis of both individual and contextual relationships.

It should be noted that, throughout the chapter, we have limited our discussion to two level hierarchical data, but the principles generalize to research designs with three levels or more. A three level data structure would arise, for instance, if students at a sample of schools were assessed on several occasions over time. In this case, a multi-level regression analysis would allow the investigator to study potential context effects of school variables on the patterns of within-individual change over time, while adjusting for dependence among observations within schools and within individuals. Bryk and Raudenbush (1988) provide an example of such an analysis. The HLM software is capable of estimating three level models, and Goldstein's MLWin program will handle up to ten levels!

With more than two levels of analysis, it is possible that the levels are not hierarchical, but rather "cross-nested." This would arise, for instance, if one took into account classroom changes over time, so that there were multiple classrooms per individual as well as multiple individuals per classroom (Goldstein, 1994; Raudenbush, 1995). The MLWin software can be used to conduct analyses of cross-nested data.

The goal of this chapter was to whet the reader's appetite for learning more about multi-level modeling, an analysis tool that is especially well-suited for research in achievement motivation. The emphasis here has been on the value of multi-level regression models for addressing interesting research questions that help solve important methodological problems within research on achievement motivation. There are, of course, many issues in the proper use of these methods that we have not addressed or have only mentioned briefly, such as centering variables and deciding which residual variance components to include. Readers interested in applying these methods in their own research can find useful guidance on such matters in texts by Bryk and Raudenbush (1992), Goldstein (1995), and Kreft and deLeeuw (1998). Finally, although we have focused primarily on longitudinal change and context effects, we want to emphasize the versatility of this technique – the use of multi-leveling modeling is not limited to those research designs. For example, it may be used to consider such things as within-subject relationships across items rather than across time; similarities and differences between siblings; or achievement differences between schools, nested within districts or states. In sum, we believe that this methodology has the potential to enhance our understanding of the developmental and educational aspects of achievement motivation by providing a powerful tool to test a broad array of research questions.

NOTES

1. This research was supported by Grant HD17553 from the National Institute for Child Health and Human Development to Jacquelynne S. Eccles, Allan Wigfield, Phyllis Blumenfeld, and Rena Harold. We would like to thank the principals, teachers, students, and parents of the cooperating school districts for their participation in this project.

2. The full analysis of these data also included tests of whether the growth curves varied across the three cohorts. There were no significant differences between cohorts. We do not present that aspect of the analysis here to avoid unnecessary complexity.

3. The original dataset includes 45 schools, but these analyses are limited to 36 schools for which there were at least 35 respondents.

4. All variables in this analysis were "grand mean centered," which indicates that the sample means were subtracted to give all variables a mean of zero. The value of doing so in this analysis is that the variance component for school means has a consistent interpretation across the several models (Bryk and Raudenbush, 1992).

REFERENCES

Alexander, P. A., Kulikovich, J. M., & Jetton, T. L. (1994). The role of subject-matter knowledge and interest in the processing of linear and nonlinear texts. *Review of Educational Research, 64*, 201–252.

Ames, C. (1992). Classrooms: Goals, structures, and student motivation. *Journal of Educational Psychology, 84*, 261–271.

Anderman, E. M., & Maehr, M. L. (1992).

Ames, C., & Archer, J. (1988). Achievement goals in the classroom: Students' learning strategies and motivation processes. *Journal of Educational Psychology, 80*, 260–267.

Atkinson, J. W. (1957). Motivational determinants of risk taking behavior. *Psychological Review, 64*, 359–372.

Atkinson, J. W. (1966). Motivational determinants of risk taking behavior. In: J. W. Atkinson & N. T. Feather (Eds), *A Theory of Achievement Motivation* (pp. 11–31). New York: Wiley.

Bailey, D. E. (1971). *Probability and Statistics: Models for Research*. New York: Wiley.

Bandura, (1977). Self-efficacy: Toward a unifying theory of behavioral change. *Psychological Rview, 84*, 191–215.

Bandura, (1989). Human agency in social cognitivie theory. *American Psychologist, 44*, 1175–1184.

Blumenfeld, P., Pintrich, P. R., Meece, J., & Wessels, K. (1982). The formation and role of self-perceptions of ability in elementary school classrooms. *Elementary School Journal, 82*, 401–420.

Borkowski, J. G., & Muthukrisna, N. (1995). Learning environments and skill generalization: How contexts facilitate regulatory processes and efficacy beliefs. In: F. Weinert & W. Schneider (Eds), *Recent Perspectives on Memory Development*. Hillsdale, NJ: Erlbaum.

Bryk, A. S., Lee, V. E., & Holland, P. B. (1993). *Catholic schools and the common good*. Cambridge, MA: Harvard University Press.

Bryk, A. S., & Raudenbush, S. W. (1987). Application of hierarchical linear models to assessing change. *Psychological Bulletin, 101*, 147–158.

Bryk, A. S., & Raudenbush, S. W. (1988). On heterogeneity of variance in experimental studies: A challenge to conventional interpretations. *Psychological Bulletin, 103*, 396–404.

Bryk, A. S., & Raudenbush, S. W. (1992). *Hierarchical Linear Models*. Newbury Park, CA: Sage.

Covington, M. W. (1984). The motive for self-worth. In: R. Ames & C. Ames (Eds), *Research on Motivation in Education* (Vol. 1, pp. 77–113), Academic Press, New York.

Cooper, H., & Dorr, N. (1995). Race comparisons on need for achievement: A meta-analytic alternative to Graham's narrative review. *Review of Educational Research, 65*, 483–508.

Cronbach, L. J., & Furby, L. (1970). How should we measure change – or should we? *Psychological Bulletin, 74*, 68–80.

Csikszentmihalyi, M. (1988). The flow experience and its significance for human psychology. In: M. Csikszentmihalyi & I. S. Csikszentmihalyi (Eds), *Optimal Experience* (pp. 15–35). Cambridge, MA: Cambridge University Press.

Csikszentmihalyi, M. (1990). *Flow: The psychology of optimal experience*. New York: Harper & Row.

Dauber, S. L., & Benbow, C. P. (1990). Aspects of personality and peer relations of extremely talented adolescents. *Gifted Child Quarterly, 34*, 10–15.

Dunkin, M., & Biddle, B. (1974). *The study of teaching*. Holt, Rinehart and Winston.

Dweck, C. S., & Goetz, T. E. (1978). Attributions and learned helplessness. In: J. H. Harvry, W. Ickes & R. F. Kidd (Eds), *New Directions in Attribution Research* (Vol. 2), Hillsdale, NJ: Erlbaum.

Dweck, C. S., & Elliott, E. S. (1983). Achievement motivation. In: P. H. Mussen (Ed.), *Handbook of Child Psychology* (3rd ed., Vol. 4, pp. 643–691). New York: Wiley.

Dweck, C. S. & Leggett, E. (1988). A social-cognitive approach to motivation and personality. *Psychological Review, 95*, 256–273.

Eccles (Parsons), J., Adler, T. F., Futterman, R., Goff, S. B., Kaczala, C. M., Meece, J. L. & Midgley, C. (1983). Expectancies, values, and academic behaviors. In: J. T. Spence (Ed.), *Achievement and Achievement Motivation* (pp. 75–146). San Francisco: W. H. Freeman.

Eccles, J. S., Adler, T. F., & Meece, J. L. (1984). Sex differences in achievement: A test of alternative theories. *Journal of Personality and Social Psychology, 46*, 26–43.

Eccles, J. S. (1987). Gender roles and women's achievement-related decisions. *Psychology of Women Quarterly, 11*, 135–172.

Eccles, J. S., & Midgley, C. (1989). Stage/environment fit: Developmentally appropriate classrooms for early adolescents. In: R. Ames & C. Ames (Eds), *Research on Motivation in Education* (Vol. 3, pp. 139–181). New York: Academic Press.

Eccles, J. S., Wigfield, A., Harold, R., & Blumenfeld, P. (1993). Age and gender differences in children's achivement self-perceptions during the elementary school years. *Child Development, 64*, 830–847.

Eccles, J. S., Wigfield, A., Midgley, C., Reuman, D., Mac Iver, D., & Feldlaufer, H. (1993). Are traditional middle grades schools undermining the academic motivation of early adolescents? *Elementary School J.*, *93*, 553–574.

Eccles, J. S. (1994). Understanding women's educational and occupational choices: Applying the Eccles et al. model of achievement-related choices. *Psychology of Women Quarterly*, *18*, 585–609.

Eccles, J. S. & Wigfield, A. (1995). In the mind of the achiever: The structure of adolescents' academic achievement related-beliefs and self-perceptions. *Personality and Social Psychology Bulletin*, *21*, 215–225.

Esbensen, Finn-Aage, & Osgood, D. W. (1999). Gang Resistance Education and Training (G.R.E.A.T.): Results from the National Evaluation. *Journal of Research on Crime and Delinquency*, *36*, 194–225.

Feather, N. T. (1982). Expectancy-value approaches: Present status and future directions. In: N. T. Feather (Ed.), *Expectations and actions: Expectancy-value models in psychology* (pp. 395–420). Hillsdale, NJ: Erlbaum.

Feather, N. T. (1988). Values, valences, and course enrollment: Testing the role of personal values within an expectancy-value framework. *Journal of Educational Psychology*, *80*, 381–391.

Feather, N. T. (1992). Values, valences, expectations, and actions. *Journal of Social Issues*, *48*, 109–124.

Felson, R. B., & Reed, M. D. (1986). Reference Groups and Self-Appraisals of Academic Ability and Performance. *Social Psychology Quarterly*, *49*, 103–109.

Fraser, B. J., & Fisher, D. L. (1982). Predicting students' outcomes from their perceptions of classroom psychosocial environment. *American Educational Research Journal*, *19*, 498–518.

Fuligni, A. J., Eccles, J. S., & Barber, B. L. (1995). The long-term effects of seventh-grade ability grouping n mathematics. *Journal of Early Adolescence*, *15*(1), 58–89.

Goldstein, H. (1994). Multilevel Cross-Classified Models. *Sociological Methods and Research*, *22*, 364–375.

Goldstein, H. I. (1995). *Multilevel Statistical Models* (2nd ed.). London: Arnold.

Graham, S. (1992). Most of the subjects were European American and middle class: Trends in published research on African Americans in selected APA journals 1970–1989. *American Psychologist*, *47*, 629–639.

Graham, S. (1994). Motivation in African Americans. *Review of Educational Research*, *64*, 55–117.

Hare, B. R. (1985). Stability and change in self-perceptions and achievement among African American adolescents: A longitudinal study. *Journal of African American Psychology*, *11*, 29–42.

Harter, S. (1982). The Perceived Competence Scale for Children. *Child Development*, *53*, 87–97.

Harter, S., & Pike, R. (1984). The pictorial scale of perceived competence and social acceptance for young children. *Child Development*, *55*, 1969–1982.

Hidi, S. (1990). Interest and its contributions as a mental resource for learning. *Review of Educational Research*, *60*, 549–571.

Hirschi, T., & Gottfredson, M. (1985). All wise after the fact learning theory, again: reply to Baldwin. *American Journal of Sociology*, *90*, 1330–1333.

Hsaio, C. (1986). *Analysis of panel data*. Cambridge: Cambridge University Press.

Jacobs, J. E. (1991). The influence of gender stereotypes on parent and child math attitudes: Differences across grade-levels. *Journal of Educational Psychology*, *83*, 518–527.

Jacobs, J. E., Lanza, S., Osgood, D. W., Eccles, J. S., & Wigfield, A. (in press). Longitudinal changes in self beliefs between first and twelfth grades. *Child Development*.

Johnson, D. R. (1995). Alternative methods for the quantitative analysis of panel data in family research: pooled time-series methods. *Journal of Marriage and the Family, 57*, 1065–1077.

Judd, C. M., & McClelland, G. H. (1989). *Data Analysis: A Model Comparison Approach*. San Diego, CA: Harcourt Brace Jovanovich.

Kessler, R. C., & Greenberg, D. F. (1981). *Linear Panel Analysis: Models of Quantitative Change*. New York: Academic Press.

Kreft, Ita, & Jan de Leeuw, J. (1998). *Introducing Multilevel Modeling*. London: Sage.

Kukla, A. (1972). Foundations of an attributional theory of performance. *Psychological Review, 79*, 454–470.

Maehr, M. L. (1984). Meaning and motivation. In: R. Ames & C. Ames (Eds), *Research on motivation in education* (Vol. 1, pp. 115–144). New York: Academic Press.

Maehr, M. L., & Braskamp, L. (1986). *The motivation factor: Toward a theory of personal investment*. Lexington, MA: Lexington Books.

Maehr, M. L., & Midgley, C. (1996). *Transforming school cultures*. Boulder, CO: Westview Press.

Mac Iver, D. J. (1987). Classroom factors and student characteristics predicting students' use of achievement standards during ability self-assessment. *Child Development, 58*, 1258–1271.

Marsh, H. W. (1989). Age and sex effects in multiple dimensions of self-concept: Preadolescence to early adulthood. *Journal of Educational Psychology, 81*, 417–430.

Marsh, H. W., & Hocevar, D. (1985). The application of confirmatory factory analyses to the study of self-concept: First and higher-order factor structures and their invariance across age groups. *Psychological Bulletin, 97*, 562–582.

McClendon, M. J. (1995). *Multiple Regression and Causal Analysis*. Itasca, IL: Peacock Publishers.

Meece, J. L., Eccles-Parsons, J., Kaczala, C. M., Goff, S. E., & Futterman, R. (1982). Sex differences in math achievement: Toward a model of academic choice. *Psychological Bulletin, 91*, 324–348.

Meece, J. L., Wigfield, A., & Eccles, J. S. (1990). Predictors of math anxiety and its consequences for young adolescents' course enrollment intentions and performances in mathematics. *Journal of Educational Psychology, 82*, 60–70.

Nicholls, J. G. (1978). The development of the concepts of effort and ability, perceptions of academic attainment, and the understanding that difficult tasks require more ability. *Child Development, 49*, 800–814.

Nicholls, J. G. (1984). Conceptions of ability and achievement motivation. In: R. E. Ames & C. Ames (Eds), *Motivation in Education*. New York: Academic Press.

Nicholls, J. G., & Miller, A. T. (1984). The differentiation of the concepts of difficulty and ability. *Child Development, 54*, 951–959.

Nicholls, J. G., Patashnick, M., & Mettetal, G. (1986). Conceptions of ability and intelligence. *Child Development, 57*, 636–645.

Osgood, D. W., & Smith, G. (1995). Applying hierarchical linear modeling to extended longitudinal evaluations: the Boys Town follow-up study. *Evaluation Review, 19*(1), 3–38.

Pallas, A. M., Entwisle, D. R., Alexander, K. L., & Stluka, M. F. (1994). Ability-group effects: Instructional, social, or institutional? *Sociology of Education, 67*, 27–46.

Peterson, T. (1993). Recent advances in longitudinal methodology. *Annual Review of Sociology, 19*, 425–454.

Pintrich, P. R., & Schrauben, B. (1992). Students' motivational beliefs and their cognitive engagement in classroom academic tasks. In: D. H. Schunk & J. L. Meece (Eds), *Student Perceptions in the Classroom* (pp. 149–183). Hillsdale, NJ: Erlbaum.

Pintrich, P. R., Marx, R. W., & Boyle, R. A. (1993). Beyond cold conceptual change: The role of motivational beliefs and classroom contextual factors in the process of conceptual change. *Review of Educational Research, 63*, 167–199.

Pong, S. (1998). The School Compositional Effect of Single Parenthood on 10th-Grade Achievement. *Sociology of Education, 71*, 23–42.

Raudenbush, S. W. (1995). Hierarchical linear models to study the effects of social context on development. In: J. M. Gottman, (Ed.), *The Analysis of Change* (pp. 165–201). Mahwah, New Jersey: Lawrence Erlbaum.

Raudenbush, S. W., Bryk, A. S., Cheong, Y. F., & Congdon, R. T. Jr. (2000). *HLM5: Hierarchical Linear and Nonlinear Modeling*. Chicago: Scientific Software International.

Renninger, K. A., Hidi, S. & Krapp, A. (Eds) (1992). *The role of interest in learning and development*. Hillsdale, NJ: Erlbaum.

Renninger, K. A., & Wozniak, R. H. (1985). Effect of interest on attentional shift, recognition, and recall in young children. *Developmental Psychology, 21*, 624–632.

Rogosa, D., Brandt, D., & Zimowski, M. (1982). A growth curve approach to the measurement of change. *Psychological Bulletin, 92*, 726–748.

Rokeach, M. (1979). From individual to institutional values with special references to the values of science. In: M. Rokeach (Ed.), *Understanding Human Values* (pp. 47–70). New York: Free Press.

Rosenholtz, S. R., & Rosenholtz, S. J. (1981). Classroom organization and the perception of ability. *Sociology of Education, 34*, 132–140.

Schiefele, U. (1991). Interest, learning, and motivation. *Educational Psychologist, 26*, 299–323.

Schiefele, U. (1996). Topic interest, text representation, and quality of experience. *Contemporary Educational Psychology, 21*, 3–18.

Schunk, D. H. (1983). Developing children's self-efficacy and skills: The roles of social comparative information and goal setting. *Contemporary Educational Psychology, 8*, 76–86.

Schunk, D. H. (1984). Self-efficacy perspective on achievement behavior. *Educational Psychologist, 19*, 48–58.

Schunk, D. H. (1990). Goal setting and self-efficacy during self-regulated learning. *Educational Psychologist, 25*, 71–86.

Simmons, R. G., & Blyth, D. A. (1987). *Moving into adolescence: The impact of pubertal change and school context*. Hawthorn, NY: Aldine de Gruyter.

Skinner, E. A., Wellborn, J. G., & Connell, J. P. (1990). What it takes to do well in school and whether I've got it: A process model of perceived control and children's engagement and achievement in school. *Journal of Educational Psychology, 32*, 22–32.

Stimson, J. A. (1985). Regression in space and time: a statistical essay. *American Journal of Political Science, 29*, 914–947.

Stipek, D. J. (1996). Motivation and instruction. In: R. C. Calfee & D. C. Berliner (Eds), *Handbook of Educational Psychology*. New York: Macmillan.

Stipek, D. J., & Gralinski, H. J. (1991). Gender differences in children's achievement-related beliefs and emotional responses to success and failure in mathematics. *Journal of Educational Psychology, 83*, 361–371.

Tobias, S. (1994). Interest, prior knowledge, and learning. *Review of Educational Research, 64*, 37–54.

Trickett, E. J., & Moos, R. H. (1974). Personal correlates of contrasting environments: Student satisfaction in high school classrooms. *American Journal of Community Psychology, 2*, 1–12.

Weiner, B. (1979). A theory of motivation for some classroom experiences. *Journal of Educational Psychology, 71*, 3–25.

Weiner, B. (1985). An attributional theory of achievement motivation and emotion. *Psychological Review, 92*, 548–573.

Wentzel, K. (1989). Adolescent classroom grades, standards for performance, and academic achievement: An interactionist perspective. *Journal of Educational Psychology, 81*, 131–142.

Wigfield, A., & Eccles, J. (1992). The development of achievement task values: A theoretical analysis. *Developmental Review, 12*, 265–310.

Wigfield, A., Eccles, J., Mac Iver, D. Reuman, D. & Midgley, C. (1991). Transitions at early adolescence: Changes in children's domain-specific self-perceptions and general self-esteem across the transition to junior high school. *Developmental Psychology, 27*, 552–565.

Wigfield, A., Eccles, J. S., Yoon, K. S., Harold, R. D., Arbreton, A. J. A., & Blumenfeld, P. C. (1997). Changes in children's competence beliefs and subjective task values across the elementary school years: A three-year study. *Journal of Educational Psychology, 89*, 451–469.

Willett, J. B., & Sayer, A. G. (1994). Using Covariance Structure Analysis to Detect Correlates and Predictors of Individual Change. *Psychological Bulletin, 116*, 363–381.

Wilson, W. J. (1987). *The Truly Disadvantaged: The Inner City, The Underclass, and Public Policy*. Chicago: University of Chicago Press.

9. SYSTEMATIC RESEARCH SYNTHESIS ON MOTIVATION

Jeffrey C. Valentine and Harris Cooper

Progress in any scientific field depends on the accumulation of knowledge, and the accumulation of knowledge depends greatly on the methods used to integrate individual studies into a coherent whole. Systematic integration of empirical research on human motivation has typically depended on the narrative review, in which the scholar gathers multiple studies investigating the same question, and uses those studies to arrive at a general, often impressionistic, conclusion about the causes and consequences of motivation.

Critics of the narrative review have suggested that it is fraught with difficulties. These include, but are not limited to, a lack of explicit standards of proof and a lack of precision in process and outcome (e.g. Johnson & Eagly, 2000; Rosenthal, 1984). Critics point out that narrative reviewers rarely declare in advance, or even after the fact for that matter, what pattern of results across studies will be used to accept or reject a hypothesis. Critics also note that narrative reviewers employ no scheme for weighting individual studies proportional to their size or quality, except perhaps to dismiss entirely studies with certain design flaws. Further, narrative reviewers are incapable of obtaining a sense of the overall magnitude of the relations they investigate.

In contrast to the narrative review, a systematic research synthesis employs a collection of methodological and statistical techniques designed to improve upon the integration of empirical studies. Systematic research syntheses employ literature searching strategies that are meant to minimize differences between retrieved studies and studies that could not be located. Decisions about whether to include or exclude studies based on methodological quality or other

New Directions in Measures and Methods, Volume 12, pages 319–348.

ISBN: 0-7623-0819-2

criteria are made explicit prior to their application and are applied even-handedly. The extraction of information from research reports is carried out using coding rules similar to those developed for the scientific analysis of document content. Meta-analysis, or the statistical integration of the results of studies, is conducted using open standards of proof, and is approached with the same structure and rigor as is data analysis in primary studies.

From the outset, it is important to recognize that these procedures, including meta-analysis, are not a complete solution to the problems faced by research synthesists. Indeed, meta-analysis is unsuited to addressing certain kinds of questions. For example, theoretical analyses, taxonomic studies, and qualitative research cannot be analyzed using meta-analytic techniques. A scholar interested in tracing the historical development of the concept of motivation would not find meta-analysis a useful tool. In addition, a basic premise behind the use of statistics in research synthesis is that a research body of conceptually relevant studies exists. If this assumption is not met, a quantitative research synthesis cannot be done. Further, the level of completeness and accuracy of existing primary research reports can be poor, diminishing the reliability of data used in meta-analyses. If only inaccurately and incompletely reported data are available, the value of quantitative techniques is limited. And more generally, as Wachter and Straf (1990) point out, meta-analysis is no substitute for wisdom. A statistical method cannot generate theories or hypotheses that do not already exist, nor can it tell us what topics are important to study. Even less ambitiously, a statistical method cannot point out to its user what variables should be examined as moderators of relationships. Only the human intellect can do these things.

Thus, we distinguish between two types of useful literature reviews. In a *theoretical review*, the reviewer presents theories offered to explain a particular phenomenon and compares them in terms of their breadth, internal consistency, and the nature of their predictions. Theoretical reviews will typically contain descriptions of critical experiments, assessments of which theory is most powerful and consistent with known relations, and sometimes reformulations or integrations or both of abstract notions of different theories. In contrast, a *research synthesis* focuses on empirical studies and attempts to summarize past research by drawing overall conclusions from many separate investigations that address related or identical hypotheses. The research synthesist hopes to present the state of knowledge concerning the relation(s) of interest, and to highlight important issues that research has left unresolved.

In this chapter, we describe the ways in which systematic research synthesis can be an improvement over traditional narrative reviews. Also, we will describe briefly the processes by which a systematic review is carried out. We do not aim to cover all the details of how to conduct a systematic review. For such coverage, we recommend texts by Cooper (1998), Cooper and Hedges (1994), Hedges and Olkin (in press), and Lipsey and Wilson (2001).

To illustrate our points, we will use the results of several research syntheses we have helped carry out. Particular attention will be paid to a case study examining how differences in reviewing methods can lead to different conclusions about a research literature. The case study involves a narrative review on the topic of race differences in achievement motivation (Graham, 1994). As part of her review, Graham did a vote count analysis of studies that compared Blacks and Whites on need for achievement and self-concepts of ability. Cooper and Dorr (1995) then used meta-analytic techniques to illustrate points of agreement and disagreement between the two reviewing procedures.

A BRIEF HISTORY OF SYSTEMATIC RESEARCH SYNTHESIS AND META-ANALYSIS

A century ago, Karl Pearson conducted what is believed to be the first statistical synthesis of results of independent research (Pearson, 1904). Pearson gathered data from eleven studies of the effect of a vaccine against typhoid and for each study he calculated a new statistic called the correlation coefficient. He averaged the correlations and concluded that other vaccines were more effective. Three decades later, Ronald Fisher presented a technique for combining the p-values that came from statistically independent tests of the same hypothesis (Fisher, 1932).

Early work on quantitative procedures for integrating results of independent studies was ignored for many years. However, in the mid-1970s Robert Rosenthal and Donald Rubin (1978) undertook a review of 345 studies looking at the effects of interpersonal expectations on behavior. Gene Glass and Mary Lee Smith (1979) conducted a review of the relation between class size and academic achievement and found 725 estimates of the relation, based on data from nearly 900,000 students. John Hunter, Frank Schmidt and Rhonda Hunter (1979) uncovered 866 comparisons of the differential validity of employment tests for Black and White workers. Each of these scholarly efforts led the investigators to resurrect or invent new quantitative synthesis procedures.

Glass (1976) coined the term meta-analysis to stand for "the statistical analysis of a large collection of analysis results from individual studies for purposes of integrating the findings" (p. 3). Shortly thereafter, Cooper (1979) and Cooper and Rosenthal (1980) made the empirical case for meta-analysis by showing that narrative review procedures led to inaccurate or imprecise characterizations of the cumulative research results. Glass, McGaw and Smith (1981) then proposed that meta-analysis be viewed as a new application of analysis of variance and multiple regression procedures, with the outcomes of studies, in the form of effect sizes, treated as the criterion variable and the features of studies as the predictor variables. Hunter, Schmidt and Jackson (1982) introduced an alternative meta-analytic model that: (a) compared the observed variation in study outcomes to that expected by sampling error; and (b) corrected the mean and variance of observed effect sizes for known sources of bias (e.g. measurement error, restrictions in sampled ranges). Rosenthal (1984) presented a compendium of meta-analytic methods including combining significance levels, effect size estimation, and the search for moderators of study results. Importantly, Rosenthal's procedures for testing moderators of effect sizes were not based on traditional inferential statistics, but on a new set of techniques involving assumptions tailored specifically for the analysis of study outcomes.

Simultaneous with the development of meta-analysis procedures, several attempts were undertaken to examine and place research synthesis in the context of a scientific process. In 1971, Feldman published an article entitled "Using the work of others: Some observations on reviewing and integrating" in which he wrote, "Systematically reviewing and integrating . . . the literature of a field may be considered a type of research in its own right – one using a characteristic set of research techniques and methods" (Feldman, 1971, p. 86). In the same year, Light and Smith (1971) presented a "cluster approach" to research synthesis that was meant to redress some of the deficiencies in the existing strategies. They argued that if treated properly the variation in outcomes among related studies could be a valuable source of information, rather than a source of consternation as it appeared to be when treated with traditional reviewing methods.

Two papers that appeared in the *Review of Educational Research* in the early 1980s brought the meta-analytic and review-as-research perspectives together. First, Jackson (1980) proposed six reviewing tasks "analogous to those performed during primary research" (p. 441). His paper employed a sample of 36 review articles from prestigious social science periodicals to examine the methods used in syntheses of empirical research. His conclusion was that "relatively little thought has been given to the methods for doing integrative reviews" (p. 459).

Cooper (1982) drew the analogy between research synthesis and primary research to its logical conclusion. He presented a five stage model of the review process that viewed research synthesis as a data gathering exercise and, as such, applied to it criteria similar to those employed to judge primary research. Cooper argued that, similar to primary research, a research review involves problem formulation, data collection (the literature search), data evaluation, data analysis and interpretation (the meta-analysis), and public presentation. For each stage, Cooper codified the research question, its primary function in the review, and the procedural differences that might cause variation in the conclusions of different reviews. In addition, Cooper applied the notion of threats-to-inferential-validity – introduced by Campbell and Stanley (1966; also see Cook & Campbell, 1979) for evaluating the utility of primary research designs – to research synthesis. He identified numerous threats to validity associated with reviewing procedures that might undermine the trustworthiness of a research synthesis' findings. Table 1 summarizes this approach to research synthesis.

Light and Pillemer (1984) offered a text that emphasized the use of research synthesis to inform social policy. Their approach highlighted the importance of meshing quantitative procedures and narrative descriptions in the interpretation and communication of synthesis results. Hedges and Olkin's (1985) text, titled *Statistical Procedures for Meta-Analysis*, covered a wide array of meta-analytic procedures and established the procedures' legitimacy by presenting rigorous statistical proofs.

During and after the years that the works mentioned above were appearing, the use of meta-analysis spread from psychology and education through many disciplines, especially social policy analysis (Light, 1983) and the medical sciences (see *Statistics in Medicine*, 1987, Vol. 6, No. 3). These developments led Greenberg and Folger (1988) to state that "if the current interest in meta-analysis is any indication, then meta-analysis is here to stay" (p. 191).

Since the mid-1980s, several full-text treatments have appeared on meta-analysis. Some of these treat the topic generally (e.g. Cooper, 1998; Hunter & Schmidt, 1990; Lipsey & Wilson, 2001), some treat it from the perspective of particular research design conceptualizations (e.g. Eddy, Hasselblad & Shachter, 1992; Mullen, 1989), some are tied to particular software packages (e.g. Johnson, 1989; Wang & Bushman, 1999), and some look at potential future developments in research synthesis (e.g. Wachter & Straf, 1990, Cook et al., 1992). In 1994, the first edition of Handbook of Research Synthesis was published (Cooper & Hedges, 1994). This book included 32 chapters contributed by specialists in information science, computer software, and statistics, as well as experts in the use of research synthesis for psychology, medicine, education, and public policy.

Table 1. The Integrative Review Conceptualized as a Research Project.

	Stage of Research				
Stage Characteristics	Problem Formulation	Data Collection	Data Evaluation	Analysis & Interpretation	Public Presentation
Research Question Asked	What evidence should be included in the review?	What procedures should be used to find relevant evidence?	What retrieved evidence should be included in the review?	What procedures should be used to make inferences about the literature as a whole?	What information should be included in the review report?
Primary Function in Review	Constructing definitions that distinguish relevant from irrelevant studies	Determining which sources of potentially relevant studies to examine	Applying criteria to separate "valid" from "invalid" studies	Synthesizing valid retrieved studies	Applying editorial criteria to separate important from unimportant information
Procedural Differences That Create Variation in Review Conclusions	1. Differences in included operational definitions 2. Differences in operational detail	Differences in the research contained in sources of information	1. Differences in quality criteria 2. Differences in the influence of non-quality criteria	Differences in rules of inference	Differences in guidelines for editorial judgment
Sources of Potential Invalidity in Review Conclusions	1. Narrow concepts might make review conclusions less definitive and robust 2. Superficial operational detail might obscure interacting variables	1. Accessed studies might be qualitatively different from the target population of studies 2. People sampled in accessible studies might be different from target population of people	1. Non-quality factors might cause improper weighting of study information 2. Omissions in study reports might make conclusions unreliable	1. Rules for distinguishing patterns from noise might be inappropriate 2. Review-based evidence might be used to infer causality	1. Omission of review procedures might make conclusions irreproducible 2. Omission of review findings and study procedures might make conclusions obsolete

Source: Cooper, H. (1982). Scientific guidelines for conducting integrative research reviews. *Review of Educational Research*, *52*, 291–302. Copyright 1982. American Educational Research Association, Washington, D. C. Reprinted by permission.

COMPONENTS OF SYSTEMATIC RESEARCH SYNTHESIS

As we discussed earlier, systematic research syntheses are conducted much like primary research (Cooper, 1998). A problem is formulated, data are collected, evaluated, analyzed, and interpreted, and results are presented to the public. In a sense, research synthesis may be thought of as a form of survey research, in which studies (as opposed to people) are the population of interest (Lipsey & Wilson, 2001). The "response" offered by the research report is called an effect size and the "demographics" related to the response are the characteristics of the study. An effect size is a standardized measure of the magnitude of the relationship in question. For example, a study investigating the relationship between achievement motivation and school grade point average might result in a correlation coefficient between these two variables; this correlation is the effect size. However, before the effect size is calculated, the researcher has made numerous decisions that unfold in systematic order. We will now discuss each stage of research synthesis.

Problem Formulation

In its most basic form, problem formulation involves identifying two relevant variables, specifying the anticipated relation between them, and providing a rationale for relating the variables to one another. In Graham's (1994) case, the variables were race (Whites and African Americans) and achievement motivation. The rationale for the research review was to explore whether there truly was evidence supporting the notion that Whites and Blacks differed in their level of motivation to achieve.

While the problems addressed by primary researchers are limited only by their imaginations, research synthesists have no choice but to study topics that have already appeared in the empirical literature. In fact, a topic is probably not suitable for review unless a substantial number of studies have taken it as a problem. This does not mean, however, that research synthesis is not a creative enterprise. Instead, the creativity enters when the synthesist must make sense of many related but not identical studies. More often than not, the cumulative results of studies are many times more complex than the result of any single study.

The most important issues that arise in defining the problem for research syntheses are: (a) how broadly to define the conceptual variables of interest; and (b) how to handle multiple operational definitions of the same conceptual variables. Although no two participants in any single study will be treated exactly alike, this variability within studies is small compared to the variability produced by differences in operationalizations across studies.

In motivation research, multiple operations can be a significant issue. For example, Graham (1994) anticipated multiple operations of the construct of motivation in studies that compared Whites and Blacks. She chose to focus on the specific concept of motivation to achieve. Within this conceptual definition, Graham chose to include studies that used a variety of measurement devices, including projective techniques, behavioral measures, and forced-choice questionnaire formats, among others.

Typically, a research synthesist will specify in advance the conceptual definitions of a variable covered by the review and will then assess the fit between this definition and the operations employed in any given study. In practice, it is often necessary for the synthesist to retain some flexibility in judging the relevance of a given operation of the dependent variable. Variables can be operationalized in a surprising number of ways, and it is rare to have perfect knowledge of this diversity before undertaking a search of the literature. Thus, more so than is true in primary research, problem formulation in research synthesis is an iterative process. The synthesist begins with a defined concept and known operational realizations but these two ideated sets are refined as the subsequent stages of the review proceed.

The Literature Search

For the research synthesist, the data collection stage involves gathering studies and making judgements about their relevance to the question at hand. Too often, scholars conducting a narrative research review rely on a convenience sample of studies on which to base their conclusions. For example, the reviewer might only include studies published in a few selected journals plus those that have come to their attention through informal means. Thus, the studies reviewed are neither exhaustive nor representative of all studies that have been conducted on the topic of interest.

Systematic research synthesists are advised to operate with the goal of obtaining all relevant research (Cooper, 1998; Lipsey & Wilson, 2001), regardless of whether or where it was published. Of course, whether this goal is ever obtained is unknowable. Indeed, we can be reasonably certain that the goal is often unobtainable. Setting the goal, however, does lead to the use of comprehensive searching strategies that are meant to reduce biases in the results of obtained literature. Here, bias is defined as systematic differences in the outcomes of studies that do and do not come to the attention of the synthesist.

One important question faced by research synthesists involves whether to include unpublished research. In reviewing research on race comparisons on achievement motivation Graham's (1994) employed both manual and computerized searches of psychological, educational, and sociological reference databases. In this way, she gathered a total of 133 studies, a substantial research base. However, Graham also excluded a "vast number" (Graham, 1994, p. 57) of dissertations and technical reports.

Two reasons are frequently given for excluding unpublished research reports. The first is that the research base has the potential for becoming too large and unwieldy for a narrative review. Meta-analysts solve this problem by using computers to help store, sort, and analyze study results.

The second reason given is that unpublished research is often of lesser quality than published research. We would argue that this is too simple a conclusion. For example, researchers often do not publish their results because publication is not their objective and this decision is independent of the quality of their work (see Cooper, DeNeve & Charlton, 1997). Conversely, most researchers would agree that some low quality research does get published. Suffice it to say that the quality of research, published and not, is distributed along overlapping continua.

Moreover, research is often turned down for publication for reasons other than quality (Greenwald, 1975). In particular, research failing to achieve standard levels of statistical significance are frequently left in researcher's "file drawers", a problem known as publication bias. The concern here is that studies revealing smaller effect sizes will be systematically censured from the published literature and therefore estimates of effect in the published literature may make relationships appear stronger than if all estimates were available to the synthesist. For this reason, it is now accepted practice that rigorous research syntheses will include both published and unpublished research.

An example of an exhaustive literature search strategy was presented in Cooper's synthesis of research on the effectiveness of homework (Cooper, 1989, pp. 37–39). Cooper conducted several database searches (e.g. ERIC, PsychInfo, U.S. Government Monthly Printing Catalog), and also searched reference sections of both primary research on homework and prior reviews of the homework literature. Research convention programs of the American Educational Research Association were examined for papers or symposiums that included presentations on homework. Finally, Cooper sent letters of inquiry explaining the research topic and requesting any studies that had been done to 13 active homework researchers, 25 deans of the most productive colleges of education, 53 state agencies that dealt primarily with education, and over 100 directors of research and evaluation in selected school districts across the United States. Thus, Cooper used procedures designed to generate the greatest number of studies relevant to homework, and included both published and unpublished studies.

Data Collection and Evaluation

In a typical systematic synthesis, trained personnel use standardized coding procedures to extract the desired information from research reports. The process is analogous to collecting data on a survey questionnaire or, more directly, to the content analysis of documents (Weber, 1990). The coding sheet contains information about the background characteristics of the reports (e.g. author, year of publication) as well as the specifics of the study, such as sample size and composition, research methodology, and study results. While some collected information will be the same regardless of the topic under consideration (for example, all reviewers will collect information on sample sizes), other coded study characteristics will be unique to the substantive topic of interest. For example, when the topic of interest is racial differences in achievement motivation both theoretical and practical considerations will dictate that the research synthesist collect information on how samples were obtained. This difference among studies would be of special interest because it might be predicted that samples drawn from, say, college campuses could show smaller differences in achievement motivation than samples drawn from more varied populations. However, issues of treatment strength and fidelity that might be of interest in a synthesis of studies examining interventions meant to enhance achievement motivation would be irrelevant to racial comparisons. Lipsey (1994) discusses how synthesists can go about identifying study features that might influence study outcomes.

Stock (1994) presented a detailed discussion of how to assemble a coding guide for a research synthesis. A good coding guide will facilitate complete, unambiguous, and reliable extraction of all relevant data in a research report. Among the issues Stock addressed, none is more important than the reliability of data extraction.

Reliability of Data Extraction

Traditional narrative reviewers give very little (if any) attention to the reliability of their descriptions of studies. On the other hand, systematic research reviewers pay special attention to errors that occur when extracting data from a research report. There are several sources of error in research reviews. One source of error occurs when primary researchers do not report or poorly report data that are of interest to the research synthesist. This occurs, for example, when researchers performing race comparisons on achievement motivation neglect to describe how samples were obtained. To counter this problem, the synthesist may choose to contact the study authors directly for assistance. DuBois, Holloway, Valentine and Cooper (in press) utilized this approach in a meta-analysis of the effectiveness of youth mentoring programs and had moderate success. When a research report contained missing or incomplete data, these authors attempted to contact the primary author through electronic mail. Success in both contacting study authors and retrieving data were dependent on the amount of time that had passed since original publication of the research report; we had very little success with reports that were more than 10 years old, but were able to retrieve some missing information from newer reports. While labor intensive, this approach added data to the meta-analysis that would have been otherwise unavailable, increasing the representativeness of the data set.

Also, research reviewers are not immune to making mistakes themselves. To assess the extent to which study information has been reliably extracted from research reports, most research synthesis texts suggest performing some sort of reliability assessment. This involves employing procedures akin to those used in assessing interjudge reliability in other research domains (e.g. Lipsey & Wilson, 2001; Orwin, 1994). Briefly, a reliability assessment will involve having two (or more) reviewers independently code some subset of the studies, then deriving a reliability assessment from the ratings of the reviewers. A second strategy involves having two reviewers independently code all of the studies in the review. Disagreements then may be resolved in conference or by a third reader. This procedure raises the effective reliability of codes to very high levels.

Empirical results suggest that different types of information about research are extracted from reports with different levels of reliability. For example, Stock, Okun, Haring, Miller, Kinney and Ceurvorst (1982) found that, among 27 types of information extracted from research reports describing studies of the predictors of life satisfaction, the mean reliability coefficient (uncorrected for chance), was $r = 0.88$. Eighteen of the 27 characteristics had a reliability coefficient greater than or equal to 0.90, and an additional six characteristics had a reliability coefficient of $0.80 \leq r \leq 0.90$.Two characteristics had reliabilities below 0.60, suggesting that they could not be reliably coded by the readers. One of these codes was "quality of study."

Judging Research Quality

It is a truism that a research synthesis is only as good as the studies that go into it. While multiple operationism can overcome some deficiencies in research design (see, Cook & Campbell, 1979), if only poor quality studies have been conducted on the topic of interest, one cannot expect a synthesis to yield interpretable findings. Of course, this holds true whether traditional narrative review procedures or meta-analysis are employed.

In some instances, research synthesists are interested in a variable that requires a high degree of inference on the part of the coders. Among these, the most frequent high inference codes occur because the synthesists wish to determine whether "study quality" moderates the estimated magnitude of the relationships in question. For example, do "high quality" studies reveal larger or smaller effects of a motivational intervention than "low quality" studies? Assessing whether a study is "good" or "bad" requires a complex judgement on the part of the coder, and the level of inference required may introduce error in the research review. As suggested by Stock et al. (1982), arriving at a dichotomous decision about study quality (good vs. bad) or even reducing study quality to a single continuous dimension can be difficult.

This is not to suggest that all high inference codes are unreliable. For example, Miller, Lee and Carlson (1991) had judges read a description of an experimental manipulation. Judges made inferences about the affective, cognitive, and behavioral responses of study participants. Results suggested that judges effectively inferred participant affective responses, but did not reliably infer participant behavior or attitude change.

With regard to a single index of study quality, this issue is even more problematic. For example, Jüni, Witschi, Block and Egger (1999) examined the impact of 25 quality scales on the outcome of a meta-analysis comparing the efficacy of a standard drug treatment vs. a new drug treatment on post-operative heart attack rates. Weighting results by methodological quality using 6 of the scales indicated that high quality studies showed no difference between the standard and new drug therapy, whereas low quality studies showed the new therapy to be better. Seven quality scales showed the opposite results (i.e. high quality studies suggested the new therapy was better, and low quality studies suggested no difference between the two drugs). For the remaining 12 quality scales, effect size estimates were similar for the two quality categories. Thus, the results of a meta-analysis could reverse depending on the quality criteria used.

Instead, we suggest that reviewers code study features known to vary with the strength of inferences they permit (e.g. research design, sampling frame, measurement reliability), and determine if those features actually do co-vary with effect sizes uncovered by different studies (Berlin & Rennie, 1999; Jüni et al., 1999). If so, the meta-analysts may adjust their inferences accordingly and statistically control for the presence or absence of these features when examining other substantive influence on study outcomes (cf. Lipsey & Wilson, 2000).

As an example, our meta-analysis of the effectiveness of summer school programs (Cooper, Charlton, Valentine & Muhlenbruck, 2000) revealed that studies using a one-group pretest-posttest design had a larger effect size (about one-fourth of a standard deviation separated students who went to summer school when compared to those who did not, or $d \cong 0.25$) than studies that used a nonequivalent control group design (about one-twentieth of a standard deviation difference, or $d \cong 0.05$). Studies that employed random assignment of students produced an average effect that fell between these two values. All three values were presented in our discussion of the evidence and the likely sources of bias in each estimate were examined. Based on this analysis we argued that the overall impact of summer programs likely center around a value of one-fifth of a standard deviation. However, the majority of our discussion was devoted to an examination of how these estimates of effect varied as a function of other characteristics of the summer program.

The Statistical Analysis and Interpretation Combined Study Results

In this section we discuss statistical methods that help reviewers summarize research results. Meta-analyses generally lead to more precise and reliable conclusions about a research base than does the narrative integration of research. An empirical example demonstrates this point. Cooper and Rosenthal (1980) randomly assigned 41 faculty and graduate students in a psychology department to read seven articles addressing the question of sex differences in task persistence. All participants read the same seven articles chosen to suggest that women have greater task persistence than men. Some participants were assigned to a meta-analysis condition, in which they were given detailed instructions about how to combine the study's significance levels and to obtain an overall estimate of the effect size for the seven studies. Participants assigned to the narrative review condition were simply told to use whatever procedures they typically would use to assess the literature.

After the participants completed their reviews, they were asked whether the articles they read supported the conclusion that women exhibit greater task persistence than men. Participants could respond "definitely yes", "probably yes", "can't tell", "probably no", or "definitely no." Among the narrative reviewers 73% found definitely or probably no support for the hypothesis compared with only 32% of participants using the meta-analytic technique. In fact, the combined probability that the null hypothesis was true was $p < 0.005$, indicating over twice as many inferential errors by the narrative than the quantitative reviewers. This study suggests that meta-analysis can be a superior data integration strategy.

As we mentioned in the introduction, traditional narrative reviewers are unable to generate effect sizes for the hypotheses they test, and do not employ strategies for weighting individual studies proportional to their size or quality. Rather, most narrative reviewers use, explicitly or not, a vote-count of studies. Often, this procedure leads to inferential errors.

The Vote-count

Typically, when conducting a vote count, the reviewer assigns research reports to one of three categories: either the relation between the two variables is significantly positive, significantly negative, or the null hypothesis cannot be rejected (Bushman, 1994). The number of reports in each category is counted, and a decision rule is applied to the count to determine what the research base suggests about the relation. Typically, the category with the largest number of votes wins.

The vote count is intuitively appealing. However, it has few defenders as a final data analysis strategy. Hedges and Olkin (1985) have demonstrated that vote counts have power characteristics that are inversely related to the number of studies contained in the review. That is, counterintuitively, when a real but moderate effect exists in a population of studies, the more studies that a review covers, the less likely it is that a vote count will reject the null hypothesis.

In addition, the vote counting strategy does not differentially weight studies based on sample size. This is a problem because a study with 100 participants and a study with 1,000 participants are given equal weight, even though the larger study provides the more precise and reliable estimate of the effect. Further, the effect size of the studies reviewed is not considered. A study showing small negative effects is given the same weight as a study showing large positive ones. For these reasons, vote counting is not considered a credible analytic strategy for drawing inferences (Cooper & Dorr, 1995).

We do not mean to imply that the vote count procedure has no value. For example, in our own meta-analyses (e.g. Cooper, Charlton, Valentine & Muhlenbruck, 1999) we have applied vote counting procedures to research reports from which no effect size estimate could be gleaned, using procedures outlined by Hedges and Oklin (1984) for generating a rough estimate of the population effect size using vote count procedures. We then compared the effect size estimate from the vote count to the effect size estimate generated from research. In the case of the Cooper et al. study above, the effect size estimated from the vote count largely agreed with the mean effect size estimated from more detailed research reports. However, if the two strategies disagree, the effect size estimate generated from more detailed research reports should be given interpretative priority. This strategy potentially allows the research synthesist to base conclusions on a larger, more diverse data set.

The deficiencies of relying on a vote counting procedure were evident in Graham's (1994) review, in which the approach was used to determine whether a set of studies supported a particular hypothesis. In order to demonstrate an effect, she used the rule that the hypothesis must have been supported, at the 0.05 level of statistical significance, by at least 50% of the studies included in the review. From this vote count, Graham concluded that no race differences existed in need for achievement. Cooper and Dorr's (1995) meta-analysis suggested that reliable, race differences did exist. However, we strongly advise the reader to consult Cooper and Dorr (1995) for a discussion of the complexity of relationship between need for achievement and race. Briefly, Cooper and Dorr's results suggest the relation is moderated by several factors, including the year the study was conducted, the age, education, and SES of the participants, and possibly the method of assessment. More surprising than the conclusion of no race differences in need for achievement, Graham concluded that African-Americans had a higher self-concept of ability than Whites, even though Cooper and Dorr's meta-analysis suggested that this effect size was no larger than the effect size relating race and need for achievement.

Effect Size Metrics

As an alternative to vote counting procedures, meta-analysts will: (a) calculate an effect size for the outcomes of hypothesis tests in every study; (b) average these effect sizes across hypothesis tests to estimate general magnitudes of effect; and (c) compare effect sizes to discover if variations in outcomes exist and, if so, what features of comparisons might account for them.

Cohen (1988) defined an effect size as "the degree to which the phenomenon is present in the population, or the degree to which the null hypothesis is false" (pp. 9–10). For the meta-analyst, estimates of effect size are the most crucial output of studies. Because the reporting of effect sizes in primary research is not yet universal, a meta-analyst often must estimate or calculate the effect size from other statistics present in a research report (see Rosenthal, 1984, for many of these approaches). Often, they also must adjust an effect size estimate to remove certain sampling biases (see Hedges & Olkin, in press).

Two effect size metrics are most applicable to the achievement motivation literature. The first, called the *d*-index by Cohen (1988), is a scale-free measure of the separation between two group means. Calculating the basic *d*-index for any comparison involves dividing the difference between the two group means by either their average standard deviation or the standard deviation of the control group. This results in a measure of the difference between the two group means expressed in terms of their common standard deviation. For example, a *d*-index of 0.25 indicates that one-quarter standard deviation separates the two means.

In their meta-analysis of Graham's achievement motivation research base, Cooper and Dorr (1995) found an average weighted effect size of $d = 0.21$ for the relationship between race and achievement motivation. This finding means that the average White student scored about one-fifth of a standard deviation higher on the outcome measure than did African-American students (this effect was qualified by moderator analyses, explained above).

Because the interpretation of the *d*-index is not intuitively transparent in many contexts, Cohen (1988) presented a measure associated with the *d*-index called U_3. U_3 describes the percentage of the sample with the lower mean that was exceeded by the average (or 50th percentile) score in the higher-meaned group. When $d = 0$, $U_3 = 50\%$, suggesting that half of the scores in the lower-meaned group were exceeded by the mean of the higher-scoring group. Of course, this suggests no difference between the groups. When $d = 0.50$, or when the higher-scoring group mean is one-half standard deviation above the lower-scoring group mean, $U_3 = 69\%$. This suggests that 69% of the scores in the higher-meaned group exceed the average score in the lower-meaned group. In the Cooper and Dorr (1995) meta-analysis, U_3 for $d = 0.21$ is approximately 57%, suggesting that the average achievement motivation score for White students exceeded a little more than 57% of the African-American students' scores.

Another example of how the U_3 index can be used to make the quantitative results of a meta-analysis more meaningful appeared in Cooper's (1989) synthesis of homework research. The most interesting result from these studies was the dramatic association between grade level and homework's effectiveness. Using the transformation of *d*-indexes to U_3 derived from studies that compared students who did homework with students how did not, Cooper (in press) was able to express the effect in terms of a student's rank within a class of 25. If a teacher were teaching high school students (and all else was equal) the average student in the homework class (50th percentile) would outperform 69% of the students in the no-homework class. Put differently, the student who ranked 13th in achievement in the homework class would rank 8th if he or she were shifted into the no-homework class just before the final exam. If the teacher taught in junior high school, the 13th-ranked homework-doer would rank 10th in the no-homework class. In elementary school, however, homework would not help the student surpass *any* schoolmates.

The second effect size metric well-suited to research in achievement motivation is the *r*-index, or correlation coefficient. The correlation coefficient is familiar to most researchers and students. However, interpretations of the correlation coefficient that rely on the proportion of variance explained (i.e. r^2), are frequently misinterpreted even by experienced researchers (cf. Abelson, 1985; Rosenthal & Rubin, 1982). The physicians' aspirin study (Steering Committee of the Physicians' Health Study Research Group, 1988) provides a particularly compelling example. Over a 5-year period, approximately 22,000 physicians with a history of heart attack took either 325 mg. of aspirin every other day or a placebo. The data showed that 1.7% of the placebo group and 0.09% of the aspirin group had a second heart attack during the course of the study. The correlation associated with these data was $r = 0.03$, and $r^2 = 0.0009$, a seemingly trivial relationship. However, this effect means that taking an aspirin every other day was associated with a significant reduction in the risk of having a second heart attack. In fact, risk of a second heart attack was reduced by more than one-third (Rosenthal & Rosnow, 1991). Olkin (1992), citing Chalmers (n.d.) suggests that had research synthesis techniques been applied to the efficacy of aspirin in reducing the risk of a second heart attack, sufficient evidence demonstrating the clinical benefits of aspirin existed as early as 1976, with an estimated savings of 10,000 to 20,000 lives over the next decade.

Typically, the *r*-index is used to express the relationship between two continuous variables, such as continuous measures of achievement motivation and school grades or achievement test scores. On the other hand, the *d*-index is used to relate one dichotomous variable to a continuous variable, such as comparing groups of qualitatively different students (e.g. males and females, Whites and African-Americans), on a continuous measure, such as achievement motivation. The choice of metric is determined by which fits best with the characteristics of the variables under consideration.

Identifying Independent Samples

A statistical problem arises when a single study contains multiple effect size estimates taken on the same sample of participants. There are several approaches meta-analysts use to handle such dependent effect sizes. Some treat each effect size as independent, regardless of the number that comes from the same sample of people. They assume that the effect of violating the independence assumption is not substantial. Other meta-analysts use the study as the unit of analysis. They calculate the mean effect size or take the median result and use this value to represent the study. Sophisticated statistical models also have been suggested as a solution to the problem of dependent effect size estimates (Gleser & Olkin, 1994; Raudenbush, Becker & Kalaian, 1988) but due to their complexity they are yet rarely found in practice.

In the Cooper and Dorr (1995) meta-analysis of Graham's (1994) data, a shifting unit of analysis was used (Cooper, 1998). In this procedure, each effect size is coded into the data set as if it were an independent estimate. For example, if samples of African-American and White students completed both a TAT (picture) measure and a sentence completion measure of achievement motivation, two separate *d*-indexes would be calculated for each group of students. However, for estimating the overall relation between race and achievement motivation, these two *d*-indexes would be averaged prior to entry into the analysis, so that the sample only contributed one effect size. However, in an analysis that examined the effect of measurement characteristics on effect size, each sample would contribute one estimate to the effect size for picture measures and one to the effect size for sentence-completion measures. This shifting unit of analysis approach retains as much data as possible from each study while holding to a minimum any violations of the assumption that data points are independent.

The Cooper and Dorr (1995) meta-analysis of racial differences in achievement motivation was based on 26 independent samples of students that gave rise to 36 separate comparisons. The 26 samples were described in 19 different research reports. The number of independent samples in a research report ranged from 1 to 4.

Examining Effect Size Distributions

Recently, inspecting the effect size distribution has become an important part of a complete meta-analysis. This information often includes stem-and-leaf displays and/or funnel plots (Greenhouse & Iyengar, 1994) that help convey information about the magnitude and variation in effect sizes, as well as help assess whether publication bias might exist in the sample of comparison outcomes.

Stem-and-leaf displays are a visually informative way of plotting data. Figure 1 presents the stem-and-leaf plot of overall effect sizes obtained from Cooper and Dorr's (1995) meta-analysis. The digits in the tenth's place are known as "leading digits." These leading digits form the stem, or vertical axis, of the display. The data in the one hundredths place are known as "trailing digits" and form the leaves of the display. A stem-and-leaf display gives the reader access to the raw study data presented in convenient form. Thus, Fig. 1 informs the reader that there were five effect sizes that ranged from 0.30–0.39: 0.30, 0.30, 0.34, 0.35, and 0.38. Stem-and-leaf displays are particularly useful for comparing two different distributions. An example is presented in Fig. 2, in

0.8	5
0.7	
0.6	
0.5	5
0.4	0 4 8
0.3	0 0 4 5 8
0.2	8
0.1	0 7
0.0	0 0 1 2 2 4 5
–0.0	2 2
–0.1	0 5
–0.2	
–0.3	3
–0.4	
–0.5	
–0.6	
–0.7	2

Fig. 1. Stem-and-Leaf Display of *d*-Indexes for Race Comparisons on Need for Achievement.

Note: Positive values indicate White students had higher need for achievement in the study.

which the data from Fig. 1 are categorized by whether they were published before or after 1970. As can be seen from Fig. 2, there was a significant difference in the effect size distribution depending on when the study was published.

The distribution of effects will also be examined to determine whether it contains statistical outliers (Barnett & Lewis, 1978). As with data based on primary research, if outliers are present meta-analysts then must decide how to treat them. Some synthesists remove them from the data set entirely while others will modify the outlying values so as to make them conform more closely to the general distribution of results. For either option, the meta-analysts wish both to make the distribution of effects more normal and to mitigate the effect of a few extreme values on measures of central tendency and dispersion, and on subsequent moderator analyses. Whichever option is chosen, it is important to inform the readers so they may make their own judgements about the adequacy of the strategy.

Averaging Effect Sizes and Measuring their Dispersion

The most pivotal outcomes of a meta-analysis are the average effect sizes and measures of dispersion that accompany them. Both unweighted and weighted

After 1970		Before 1970
	0.8	5
	0.7	
	0.6	
	0.5	5
	0.4	0 4 8
4 0	0.3	5 8
	0.2	8
7 0	0.1	
2 2 0	0.0	0 1 4 5
2	–0.0	2
5	–0.1	0
	–0.2	
3	–0.3	
	–0.4	
	–0.5	
	–0.6	
2	–0.7	

Fig. 2. Stem-and-Leaf Display of *d*-Indexes for Race Comparisons on Need for Achievement. Studies Conducted Before 1970 vs. Studies Conducted After 1970.

Note: Positive values indicate White students had higher need for achievement in the study.

procedures are typically used to calculate average effect sizes across comparisons. In the unweighted procedure, each effect size is given equal weight in calculating the average effect. In the weighted procedure, each independent effect size is first multiplied by the inverse of its variance and the sum of these products is then divided by the sum of the inverses.

The weighting procedure is generally preferred because it gives greater weight to effect sizes based on larger samples. Also, as noted above, confidence intervals are calculated for weighted average effects. Many texts, including Hedges and Olkin (1985), Shadish and Haddock (1994), and Lipsey and Wilson (2001) provide procedures for calculating the appropriate weights and confidence intervals. As an example, in the meta-analysis of summer school evaluations introduced above (Cooper et al., 2000) the unweighted overall estimate of effect size was $d = +0.32$. The weighted estimate of the effect size was $d = +0.26$, with a 95% confidence interval of $+0.30 > d > 0.22$.

In addition to the confidence interval as a measure of dispersion, research synthesists usually carry out a highly informative procedure called a "homogeneity analysis." A homogeneity analysis compares the amount of variance in an observed set of effect sizes with the amount of variance that would be expected by sampling error alone. If there is greater variation in effects than would be expected by chance, then the meta-analyst begins the process of examining moderators of hypothesis test outcomes. (Note also that the meta-analyst may search for moderators in the absence of a statistically significant homogeneity analysis if there are good theoretical reasons for doing so.) There are numerous statistical packages that can be used to carry out a homogeneity analysis. Cooper and Dorr (1995) conducted their homogeneity analysis using the general linear model program of the Statistical Analysis System (SAS, 1992). They found a highly significant homogeneity statistic, suggesting they reject the hypothesis that the *d*-indexes were all estimating the same underlying population value, or that sampling error alone was responsible for the variation in effects, $Q\ (1, k = 25) = 82.32$, $p < 0.001$, where Q represents the homogeneity statistic, and k represents the degrees of freedom (in this case, the number of independent samples minus 1).

Artifactual Influences of the Size of Observed Effects

There are numerous factors that influence the magnitude of an observed relation between two variables other than the "true" relationship. In particular, meta-analysts must pay attention to factors that might attenuate the magnitude of the effect size. For example, both: (a) unreliability in the instruments used to measure the dependent variable; and (b) artificially dichotomizing continuous scores on the dependent variable into groups (that is, turning a continuous measure of motivation into high and low motivated groups) will lead to smaller observed effect sizes than the "actual" effect in the population. The synthesist must decide how this attenuation should be treated. One approach is to estimate the degree to which the effect size has been attenuated due to these and other related issues. Procedures for carrying this out are described in Hunter and Schmidt (1990).

A final influence on effect sizes is the number of factors employed in a research design. If the research design includes more factors than the reviewer is interested in, the reviewer is faced with the choice of either using a standard deviation reduced by the inclusion of additional factors (inflating the estimate of the effect size), or attempting to retrieve the standard deviation that would have been obtained if all extraneous factors had been ignored. Whenever possible, this latter strategy should be employed. In practice, however, it is often difficult to retrieve this estimate. In such cases, we recommend examining whether or not the number of factors involved in the studies is correlated with effect size.

Fixed and Random Effects Models of Error

Another aspect of conducting a meta-analysis that recently has received considerable attention involves the decision about whether a fixed-effects or random-effects model of error influences the generation of study outcomes. In a fixed-effect analysis, each effect size's variance is assumed to reflect only sampling error (i.e. error solely due to participant differences) and thus can be taken into account through the procedures described previously for weighting effect sizes by sample size. When a random-effect analysis is carried out, a study-level variance component is assumed to be present as an additional source of random influence. Hedges and Vevea (1998, p. 3) state that fixed-effect models of error are most appropriate when the goal of the research is "to make inferences only about the effect size parameters in the set of studies that are observed (or a set of studies identical to the observed studies except for uncertainty associated with the sampling of subjects)." A further statistical consideration is that in the search for moderators, fixed-effect models may seriously underestimate and random-effects models seriously overestimate error variance when their assumptions are violated (Overton, 1998). In view of these competing sets of concerns, we recommend that the meta-analyst consider applying both models in all primary study analyses (e.g. Cooper et al., 2000). Specifically, all analyses could be conducted twice, once employing fixed-effect assumptions and once using random-effect assumptions. Differences in results based on which set of assumptions is used can be incorporated into the interpretation and discussion of findings. Both fixed-effect and random-effect analyses may be carried out using SAS Software in accordance with procedures described by Wang and Bushman (1999).

For example, in our meta-analysis of the effectiveness of summer school programs, the confidence interval surrounding the obtained effect size under the fixed effects assumption was ± 0.04, while under the random effects assumption it was ± 0.05. Both confidence interval values were reported in our manuscript.

Moderator Analysis

The search for why the outcomes of hypothesis tests differ is the most interesting and informative part of conducting a meta-analysis. Because effect sizes are sample statistics, they will vary somewhat even if they all estimate the same underlying population value. Homogeneity analysis allows the meta-analyst to test whether sampling error alone accounted for this variation or whether features of studies, samples, treatment designs, or outcome measures also play a role. The synthesist calculates average effect sizes for subsets of studies, comparing the average effect sizes for different methods, types of programs, outcome measures, and participants and compares these to determine if they provide incite into what influences the strength and/or direction of the relationship. In fact, the synthesist can ask questions about variables that moderate outcomes even if no individual study has included the moderator variable. For example, a meta-analyst can ask whether the relation between achievement motivation and test scores differs for students in special education programs versus students in regular education by comparing the groups' average effect sizes even if no single study has included both groups. The results of such a comparison of average effect sizes can suggest whether this student characteristic would be important to look at in future research and/or as a guide to policy.

After calculating the average effect sizes for different subgroups of comparisons, the meta-analyst statistically tests whether the group factor is reliably associated with different magnitudes of effect. Three statistical procedures for examining variation in effect sizes have appeared in the literature. The first approach applies statistical procedures typically used on primary research data, like ANOVA or multiple regression. The effect sizes serve as the dependent variable and comparison features serve as independent or predictor variables. This approach has been criticized based on the questionable tenability of the underlying assumptions (see Hedges & Olkin, in press). Most notably, traditional inferential statistics assume that the error in measurement is relatively homogeneous across data points. This assumption is often violated in meta-analytic data sets.

The second approach compares the variation in obtained effect sizes with the variation expected due to sampling error (Hunter & Schmidt, 1990). This approach involves calculating not only the observed variance in effects but also the expected variance, given that all observed effects are estimating the same population value. A formal statistical test of the difference between these two values is typically not carried out. Rather, the meta-analyst adopts a critical value for the ratio of observed-to-expected variance to use as a means for rejecting the null hypothesis. The meta-analyst might also adjust effect sizes to account for methodological artifacts such as sampling error, range restrictions, or unreliability of measurements.

The third approach involves the homogeneity statistic described above. Analogous to ANOVA, comparisons are grouped by features and the average effect sizes for these groups are tested to determine if the averages are drawn from the same population. If this hypothesis is rejected, the grouping variable remains a plausible potential moderator of effect.

It is relatively simple to carry out a homogeneity analysis using computer statistical packages. The formulas and techniques for homogeneity analysis are described in Cooper (1998), Cooper and Hedges (1994), Hedges and Olkin (in press), Lipsey and Wilson (2000), Rosenthal (1984), Wang and Bushman (1999), and Wolf (1986).

We will use an illustration to demonstrate how a search for moderators of outcomes might proceed. Recall that Cooper and Dorr (1995) found a small effect suggesting White students had higher achievement motivation than African-American students. Graham (1994) noted that the last study to find such an effect was conducted in 1969, and used this finding to infer that no relation existed between achievement and race in more recent times. Indeed, when Cooper and Dorr grouped the studies into those published prior to versus after 1970, a significant temporal effect was found. In the earlier group of studies, White students scored three-tenths of a standard deviation higher than African-American students. However, this difference disappeared almost entirely in studies conducted after 1970 ($d = 0.02$). Cooper and Dorr then examined study features to determine the cause of the difference between the two groups of studies. They found that studies conducted after 1970 used participants from higher-SES backgrounds compared to those conducted before 1970, and analyses suggested that race differences in need for achievement might be larger in lower-class than in middle-class samples. Thus, the later trend of using higher-SES samples is one possible explanation for the reduction in race differences in need for achievement over time.

In addition to SES, Cooper and Dorr (1995) also examined methodological and age differences in students that might have been associated with the effect sizes revealed by evaluations of race. For example, measurement characteristics may also affect effect size, and should be examined by the research reviewer. Cooper and Dorr's (1995) meta-analysis compared studies that used the Thematic Apperception Test to measure need for achievement with others that used nonpictorial stimuli. Using the TAT to assess need for achievement resulted in a larger effect size than nonpictorial stimuli, $Q\ (1, k = 25) = 10.59$, $p < 0.005$.

In each case, Cooper and Dorr (1995) used a homogeneity analysis to guide their conclusions. Without the aid of statistics, a narrative research reviewer would have simply grouped the comparisons by shared features, examined the statistical significance of outcomes across studies, and decided intuitively whether the feature was associated with variation in outcomes. At best, this method is imprecise. At worst, it leads to incorrect inferences, most often involving the mislabeling of reliable effects as nonexistent and the inability to detect significant moderating variables. In contrast, the meta-analyst employs a formal means for testing whether different features of studies explain variation in their outcomes. This is an extension of the same rules of inference required of primary researchers. If reliable differences do exist, the average effect sizes corresponding to these differences will take on added meaning and will help the meta-analyst make policy recommendations.

Sensitivity Analysis

An additional step in meta-analysis gaining popularity is the performance of sensitivity analyses. A sensitivity analysis is used to determine if and how the conclusions of an analysis might differ if it was conducted using different statistical procedures or assumptions. There are numerous points at which a meta-analyst might decide a sensitivity analysis is appropriate. For example, there might be a set of comparisons that fall at the edge of the conceptual definition of what constitutes an acceptably reliable measure of achievement motivation. The effects of achievement motivation might be tested with and without the inclusion of these comparisons. Or, some evaluations of the relation between achievement motivation and achievement might have missing data. These comparisons might be omitted from one analysis and included in another analysis that makes conservative assumptions about what those values might be. Lastly, the calculation of weighted, unweighted, and median effect sizes can be considered a form of sensitivity analysis. In each case, the meta-analyst is seeking to determine whether a particular finding is robust across different sets of assumptions. If the answer is "yes," then greater confidence can be placed in the conclusion.

In sum then, meta-analysts have a wide array of techniques at their disposal. Some of these techniques have been developed specifically for analysis of meta-analytic data sets and others have been adopted from other research methodologies. The specific techniques used in any meta-analysis will differ somewhat depending on the characteristics of the data set and the questions asked by the research synthesist.

Public Presentation

Research is not complete until results are shared with the scientific community (American Psychological Association, 1994). We have already touched on some of the issues related to public presentation in previous sections. For example, the research synthesist must take care to interpret and report effect sizes in such a manner as to be understandable to the intended audience. Two other potential sources of invalidity are relevant to the public presentation stage. First, leaving out evidence regarding possible moderating influences on main effects can jeopardize the trustworthiness of the conclusions presented by the research synthesist. Second, the research synthesist should ensure that the synthesis techniques employed are transparent to the reader. That is, the synthesist should provide enough information so that readers can critically assess the methods, strengths, and weaknesses of the research synthesis. Halvorsen (1994) and Light, Singer and Willett (1994) present numerous suggestions regarding effective public presentation techniques.

OTHER THREATS TO VALIDITY IN CONDUCTING RESEARCH SYNTHESIS

As we suggest above, using rigorous and systematic rules for synthesizing a literature does not ensure that the resulting inferences will be infallible. Cooper (1982) pointed to several threats to the validity of research synthesis conclusions. For example, during problem formulation threats to the validity of a synthesis could occur if the synthesist did not pay proper attention to conceptual distinctions in definitions and hypotheses that were viewed as important by others in the field. The validity of a literature search could be compromised by the use of a few selective sources of research reports or by publication bias. The validity of data evaluation can be threatened if information from research reports is missing, or if the individuals extracting information from documents are poorly trained.

Many more threats to the validity of a research synthesis can be identified (Matt & Cook, 1994). We will elaborate on two here. One obvious threat to the validity of meta-analytic conclusions involves the rules of inference employed by a synthesist. The possibility always exists that the meta-analyst has used an invalid rule for inferring a characteristic of the target population. This occurs because the target population does not conform to the assumptions underlying the analysis techniques. Of course, this is not a shortcoming unique to the use of quantitative integration techniques. In nonquantitative syntheses, rules of inference also must be used but it is difficult to gauge their appropriateness because they are not very often made explicit. For meta-analyses, the suppositions of statistical tests are generally known and some statistical biases in reviews can be removed.

Another threat to validity is that the meta-analyst might capitalize on or suffer because of the probabilitistic nature of statistical findings. First, as in primary research, the meta-analyst might conduct many statistical tests without adjusting for "synthesis-wise" error rates. Second, because of gaps in the literature, a meta-analyst might discover so few tests of a particular hypothesis that the statistical power of the meta-analysis is low. Unlike a primary researcher, the meta-analyst cannot sample more participants (or in this case, generate more studies) so as to increase the sensitivity of tests. It is possible, however, to expand the search for relevant research.

THE CONTRIBUTION OF SYSTEMATIC RESEARCH REVIEWS

Systematic research reviewing is not a perfect solution to the problems faced by social and behavioral scientists. But still, it can make important, indeed essential, contributions to the scientific enterprise. The use of proper procedures for the synthesis of multiple studies does more then simply ameliorate the problems associated with the traditional narrative review. Systematic research synthesis transforms the difficulties into strengths. Variation in the context, design, and sampling characteristics of individual studies are sources of consternation when studies are examined individually, serially, and narratively. When multiple studies, each limited in their representation of context, design, and sample, are treated as data points in a second round of scientific investigation they contribute jointly to confident, general, and properly contextualized conclusions about relationships and hypotheses.

Because of the potential value of systematic research reviews in the policy domain, both the producers and consumers of reviews now agree they must think about what distinguishes good from bad reviews. Further, they agree that without high-quality reviews, both theoreticians and practitioners will question the value of research for assisting the development of effective explanations for behavior and behavioral interventions.

REFERENCES

Abelson, R. P. (1985). A variance explanation paradox: When a little is a lot. *Psychological Bulletin*, *97*, 129–133.

Barnett, V., & Lewis, T. (1978). *Outliers in Statistical Data*. Chichester, England: Wiley.

Berlin, J. A., & Rennie, D. (1999). Measuring the quality of trials. *Journal of the American Medical Association*, *282*, 1083–1085.

Bushman, B. J. (1994). Vote-counting procedures in meta-analysis. In: H. Cooper & L. V. Hedges (Eds), *Handbook of Research Synthesis*. New York: Russell Sage.

Cohen, J. (1988). *Statistical Power Analysis in the Behavioral Sciences*. Hillsdale, NJ: Erlbaum.

Campbell, D. T., & Stanley, J. C. (1966). *Experimental and Quasi-Experimental Designs for Research*. Chicago, IL: Rand McNally.

Cook, T. D., & Campbell, D. T. (1979). *Quasi-Experimentation: Design and Analysis Issues for Field Setting*. Chicago, IL: Rand McNally.

Cook, T. D., Cooper, H. M., Cordray, D. S., Hartmann, H., Hedges, L. V., Light, R. J., Louis, T., & Mosteller, F. (1992). *Meta-Analysis for Explanation: A Casebook*. New York: Russell Sage Foundation.

Cooper, H. M. (1979). Statistically combining independent studies: A meta-analysis of sex differences in conformity research. *Journal of Personality and Social Psychology, 37*, 131–146.

Cooper, H. M. (1982). Scientific guidelines for conducting integrative research reviews. *Review of Educational Research, 52*, 291–302.

Cooper, H. (1989). *Homework*. New York: Longman.

Cooper, H. M. (1998). *Synthesizing Research: A Guide for Literature Reviews* (3rd ed.). Thousand Oaks, CA: Sage.

Cooper, H. (in press). Homework: Another lesson in moderation. *Educational Leadership*.

Cooper, H., Charlton, K., Valentine, J. V., & Muhlenbruck, L. (2000). Making the most of summer school: A meta-analytic and narrative review. *Monographs on Child Development, 65*(1). Malden, MA: Blackwell Press.

Cooper, H., DeNeve, K., & Charlton, K. (1997). Finding the missing science: The fate of studies submitted for review by a human subjects committee. *Psychological Methods, 2*, 447–452.

Cooper, H., & Dorr, N. (1995). Race comparisons on need for achievement: A meta-analytic alternative to Graham's narrative review. *Review of Educational Research, 65*, 483–508.

Cooper, H., & Hedges, L. V. (1994). *Handbook of Research Synthesis*. New York: Russell Sage.

Cooper, H. M., & Rosenthal, R. (1980). Statistical versus traditional procedures for summarizing research findings. *Psychological Bulletin, 87*, 442–449.

DuBois, D. L., Holloway, B. E., Valentine, J. C., & Cooper, H. (in press). Effectiveness of meta-analytic programs for youth: A meta-analytic review. *American Journal of Community Psychology*.

Eddy, D. M., Hassleblad, V., & Schachter, R. (1992). *Meta-Analysis by the Confidence Profile Method*. Boston: Academic Press.

Feldman, K. A. (1971). Using the work of others: Some observations on reviewing and integrating. *Sociology of Education, 4*, 86–102.

Fisher, R. A. (1932). *Statistical Methods for Research Workers*. London: Oliver & Boyd.

Glass, G. V. (1976). Primary, secondary, and meta-analysis of research. *Educational Researcher, 5*, 3–8.

Glass, G. V., McGaw, B., & Smith, M. L. (1981). *Meta-Analysis in Social Research*. Beverly Hills, CA: Sage.

Glass, G. V., & Smith, M. L. (1979). Meta-analysis of research on class size and achievement. *Educational Evaluation and Policy Analysis, 1*, 2–16.

Graham, S. (1994). Motivation in African Americans. *Review of Educational Research, 64*, 55–117.

Gleser, L. J., & Olkin, I. (1994). Stochastically dependent effect sizes. In: H. Cooper & L. V. Hedges (Eds), *Handbook of Research Synthesis*. New York: Russell Sage.

Greenberg, & Folger (1988)

Greenhouse, J. B., & Iyengar, S. (1994). Sensitivity analysis and diagnostics. In: H. Cooper & L. V. Hedges (Eds), *Handbook of Research Synthesis* (pp. 383–398). New York: Russell Sage.

Greenwald, A. (1975). Consequences of prejudice against the null hypothesis. *Psychological Bulletin, 82*, 1–20.

Halvorsen, K. T. (1994). The reporting format. In: H. Cooper & L. V. Hedges (Eds), *Handbook of Research Synthesis* (pp. 425–438). New York: Russell Sage.

Hedges, L. V., & Olkin, I. (1985). *Statistical methods for meta-analysis*. Orlando, FL: Academic Press.

Hedges, L. V., & Olkin, I. (in press). *Statistical methods for meta-analysis* (2nd ed.). Orlando, FL: Academic Press.

Hedges, L. V., & Vevea, J. L. (1998). Fixed and random effects models in meta-analysis. *Psychological Methods*, *3*, 486–504.

Hunter, J. E., & Schmidt, F. L. (1990). *Methods of Meta-Analysis: Correcting Error and Bias in Research Findings*. Beverly Hills, CA: Sage.

Hunter, J. E., Schmidt, F. L., & Hunter, R. (1979). Differential validity of employment tests by race: A comprehensive review and analysis. *Psychological Bulletin*, *86*, 721–735.

Hunter, J. E., Schmidt, F. L., & Jackson, G. B. (1982). *Meta-Analysis: Cumulating Research Findings Across Studies*. Beverly Hills, CA: Sage.

Jackson, G. B. (1980). Methods for integrative reviews. *Review of Educational Research*, *50*, 438–460.

Johnson, B. T. (1989). *DSTAT: Software for the Meta-Analytic Review of Research Literatures*. Hillsdale, NJ: Erlbaum.

Johnson, B. T., & Eagly, A. H. (2000). Quantitative synthesis of social psychological research. In: H. T. Reis & C. M. Judd (Eds), *Handbook of Research Methods in Social and Personality Psychology* (pp. 496–528). New York: Cambridge University Press.

Jüni, P., Witschi, A., Bloch, R., & Egger, M. (1999). The hazards of scoring the quality of clinical trials for meta-analysis. *Journal of the American Medical Association*, *282*, 1054–1060.

Light, R. J. (Ed.) (1983). *Evaluation Studies Review Annual* (Vol. 8). Beverly Hills, CA: Russell Sage.

Light, R. J., & Pillemer, D. B. (1984). *Summing Up: The Science of Research Reviewing*. Cambridge, MA: Harvard University Press.

Light, R. J., Singer, J. D., & Willett, J. B. (1994). The visual presentation and interpretation of meta-analyses. In: H. Cooper & L. V. Hedges (Eds), *Handbook of Research Synthesis* (pp. 439–453). New York: Russell Sage.

Light, R. J., & Smith, P. V. (1971). Accumulating evidence: Procedures for resolving contradictions among research studies. *Harvard Educational Review*, *41*, 429–471.

Lipsey, M. W., & Wilson, D. B. (2001). *Practical meta-analysis*. Thousand Oaks, CA: Sage Publications.

Matt, G. E., & Cook, T. D.(1994). Threats to the validity of research syntheses. In: H. Cooper & L. V. Hedges (Eds), *Handbook of Research Synthesis* (pp. 503–520). New York: Russell Sage.

Miller, N., Lee, J., & Carlson, M. (1991). The validity of inferential judgements when used in theory-testing meta-analysis. *Personality and Social Psychology Bulletin*, *17*, 335–343.

Mullen, B. (1989). *Advanced BASIC Meta-Analysis*. Hillsdale, NJ: Erlbaum.

Olkin, I. (1992). Reconcilable differences: Gleaning insight from conflicting scientific studies. *The Sciences*, 30–36.

Orwin, R. G. (1994). Evaluating coding decisions. In: H. Cooper & L. V. Hedges (Eds), *Handbook of Research Synthesis* (pp. 139–162). New York: Russell Sage.

Overton, R. C. (1998). A comparison of fixed-effects and mixed (random-effects) models for meta-analysis tests of moderator variable effects. *Psychological Methods*, *3*, 354–379.

Pearson, K. (1904). Report on certain enteric fever inoculation statistics. *British Medical Journal*, *3*, 1243–1246.

Raudenbush, S. W., Becker, B. J., & Kalaian, H. (1988). Modeling multivariate effect sizes. *Psychological Bulletin*, *103*, 111–120.

Rosenthal, R. (1984). *Meta-Analytic Procedures for Social Research*. Beverly Hills, CA: Sage.

Rosenthal, R., & Rosnow, R. L. (1991). *Essentials of Behavioral Research: Methods and Data Analysis* (2nd ed.). New York: McGraw Hill.

Rosenthal, R., & Rubin, D. (1978). Interpersonal expectancy effects: The first 345 studies. *Behavioral and Brain Sciences*, *3*, 377–415.

Rosenthal, R., & Rubin, D. (1982). Comparing effect sizes of independent studies. *Psychological Bulletin*, *92*, 500–504.

SAS Institute. (1992). *SAS User's Guide: Statistics* (Version 6). Cary, NC: Author.

Shadish, W. R., & Haddock, C. K. (1994). Combining estimates of effect size. In: H. Cooper & L. V. Hedges (Eds), *Handbook of Research Synthesis* (pp. 261–282). New York: Russell Sage.

Statistics in Medicine (1987).

Steering Committee of the Physicians' Health Study Research Group (1988). Preliminary report: Findings from the aspirin component of the ongoing physicians' health study. *New England Journal of Medicine*, *318*, 262–264.

Stock, W. A. (1994). Systematic coding for research synthesis. In: H. Cooper & L. V. Hedges (Eds), *Handbook of Research Synthesis* (pp. 125–138). New York: Russell Sage.

Stock, W. A., Okun, M. A., Haring, M. J., Miller, W., Kinney, C., & Ceurvorst, R. W. (1982). Rigor in data synthesis: A case study of reliability in meta-analysis. *Educational Researcher*, *11*(6), 10–14, 20.

Wachter, K. W., & Straf, M. L. (Eds) (1990). *The Future of Meta-Analysis*. New York, NY: Russell Sage Foundation.

Wang, M. C., & Bushman, B. J. (1999). *Integrating results through meta-analytic review using SAS software*. Cary, NC: SAS Institute.

Weber, R. P. (1990). *Basic content analysis* (2nd ed.). Thousand Oaks, CA: Sage.

Wolf, F. W. (1986). *Meta-analysis: Quantitative Methods for Research Synthesis*. Beverly Hills, CA: Sage.

10. ISSUES IN THE ASSESSMENT OF MOTIVATION IN STUDENTS FROM ETHNIC MINORITY POPULATIONS

Shirley L. Yu and Christopher A. Wolters

In recent years, there has been an increasing awareness of the need to study culture and ethnicity in educational and psychological research, although there is still a tendency for these topics to be considered a secondary concern of mainstream American research. In order to obtain a complete understanding of human learning and development, researchers must pay attention to ethnicity and culture (Portes, 1996). In particular, the study of motivation is an important area of investigation that can help researchers and educators understand the academic functioning of students from ethnic minority populations. However, conducting research assessing motivation in non-Caucasian, non-middle class populations is not a simple enterprise. The purpose of this chapter is to examine issues in the assessment of motivation in students from ethnic minority populations.

In order to examine these assessment issues Messick's (1989, 1995a, b), and Pintrich, Wolters and Baxter's (2000) conceptualization of validity is utilized as an organizing framework. This framework is viewed as an appropriate organizing system because the assumption that the assessment process is valid for all participants underpins any research and seems especially relevant for research involving participants from different ethnic minority groups. That is, if the assessment of motivation is to be valid for all participants, then

New Directions in Measures and Methods, Volume 12, pages 349–380.

ISBN: 0-7623-0819-2

researchers must be mindful of validity issues relevant to the assessment of participants who may differ from the middle-class Caucasian samples typically studied. Hence, the overall goal of this chapter is to highlight a set of issues relevant to motivational research in ethnic minority populations and evaluate how these issues may threaten the validity of the research in this area. Some of these research issues obviously apply to psychological and educational research in general, but examples from the motivation literature are utilized to illustrate the specific ways in which these issues may be pertinent to the study of motivation. Because of the number of motivational constructs and measurement instruments available, the aim is not to be exhaustive; rather, it is hoped that this chapter will raise some important issues for researchers to consider in the assessment process.

The chapter begins with a brief overview of the current status of ethnic minority students in the United States, including numbers and achievement differences. The main portion of the chapter discusses Messick's (1989, 1995a, b) conceptualization of validity, using examples from the motivation literature and motivation research with ethnic minority samples, specifically, to highlight the validity issues. The chapter closes with several recommendations for researchers in this area.

Increasing Numbers of Students Identified as Members of Ethnic Minority Groups

The need to study motivation among students identified as ethnic minorities is highlighted by the great rise in their numbers over the last couple decades. In some areas of the country, the term "minority" has become a misnomer. Recent figures indicate that 38% of elementary and secondary public school students in 1999 were minorities, an increase of 16 percentage points from 1972 (U.S. Department of Education, National Center for Education Statistics [NCES], 2001). While there was an increase in the number of students from all racial-ethnic groups, the growth of proportions of minority students was attributable mostly to growth in the number of Hispanic students, and to a lesser degree, Black students. Specifically, Hispanic and Black students each accounted for 16% of students enrolled in public school in 1999, an increase of 10 and 2 percentage points, respectively, from 1972. At this time, students with Hispanic background are the fastest growing group of the population of public elementary and secondary school students (NCES, 2001).

Growth in minority populations has been recorded at the postsecondary level as well. In fall 1995, 26% of the students enrolled in our nation's colleges and universities were members of minority groups (not including those with nonresident alien status), an increase of 9 percentage points from 1976. Asian/Pacific Islander and Hispanic students contributed the most to this rise in minority enrollments, with both groups increasing enrollments about 4 percentage points from 1976 to 1995. In 1995, students of Asian/Pacific Island and Hispanic background accounted for 8 and 6% of all post-secondary students, respectively, increasing from 5 and 2% in 1976, respectively. Enrollment of both Black and American Indian/Alaskan Native students has remained about the same from 1976 to 1995, representing about 10 and 1% of post-secondary students, respectively (NCES, 2001). These statistics alone suggest that research directed at understanding the academic functioning and motivation, more specifically, of students from ethnic minority backgrounds should also be increasing.

Concerns About Ethnic Minority Students' Achievement, Motivation, and Theory-building

At the same time that the number of students who are members of ethnic minority groups has been increasing, achievement differences between these groups continue to be documented. It has been well-established that across all age groups, on average, the achievement levels of African American and Hispanic students lag behind that of their Caucasian classmates, while many Asian American students (although not all subgroups) achieve at higher levels, both in scores and level of education completed (NCES, 2001). Because of its influence on learning and achievement, motivation has been investigated as one explanation for the differences in performance observed between ethnic minority and Caucasian students. For example, motivational processes have been investigated to understand low levels of achievement often seen in African American students (Graham, 1994). At the same time, motivational variables have been used as one explanation for the high achievement levels often found in Asian American student populations (Chen & Stevenson, 1995). However, while achievement differences between students of different ethnic background have been well-documented, the motivational factors that may contribute to these differences still remain as a gap in the literature, despite repeated recognition over the past decade that these factors have not been well-established (Henderson & Dweck, 1990; Pintrich & Schunk, 1996).

A final reason for the need to examine motivation among ethnic minority groups concerns theory building more generally. Even when not specifically investigating motivation among minority students, researchers often want their results to generalize to diverse populations that include students from different racial and ethnic backgrounds. Therefore, participants from various racial and ethnic backgrounds may be included in different research endeavors. However, researchers utilizing diverse samples must face the increasing concern that motivational constructs, processes, and the relations among them and with important outcomes may vary across ethnic or racial groups. These concerns suggest that more general models of motivation and its impact on learning and achievement must account for the possible differences in the assessment of motivation between and among ethnic groups. An understanding of Messick's (1989, 1995a, b) conceptualization of six aspects of validity and identification of examples of these issues in the study of motivation in ethnic minority populations may help researchers working toward that end.

IDENTIFYING THE RELEVANT ASPECTS OF VALIDITY

Traditionally, at least three related forms of validity have been discussed as relevant to any form of assessment, including content validity, construct validity, and criterion validity. In this chapter, however, we rely on Messick's (1989, 1995a, b) characterization of construct validity as a unifying concept that incorporates all other forms of validity. From this perspective, construct validity is the overarching concern, and other aspects of validity can be understood as impacting or subsumed under this general framework. Different "types" of validity such as content validity are not distinct but rather describe different forms of evidence or components that can be emphasized to support the overall validity of an assessment. In particular, Messick identifies six types of evidence that can be used to generate support for the overall construct validity of an assessment, including content relevance, substantive, structural, external, generalizability, and consequential components. These facets of validity are not mutually exclusive; indeed, a particular assessment issue may be conceptualized as impacting multiple components of validity. Because the six aspects of construct validity are interdependent, it can be difficult to draw sharp distinctions between them; nonetheless, they can be discussed separately to highlight particular issues important for the overall and unified concept of construct validity.

Also emphasized by Messick (1989, 1995a, b) is the belief that validity is not related to a single test, instrument, or procedure, but rather is a broader concern related to any assessment process. That is, validity is a function of test scores, not of a test itself, and scores are a function of the test, the individuals being tested, and the context or social situation of the testing process. Hence, what is to be validated is an interpretation of data arising from a specified procedure for a particular group of individuals (Cronbach, 1971). Although the terms test or assessment are generally used to describe this procedure in this chapter, the components of validity and the issues evaluated can be more broadly understood as applying to any process in which motivation is evaluated. Specifically, using research instruments to assess forms of motivation and using the data produced to build theories or models of motivation and how it interacts with other educational factors is dependent, at a very basic level, on the validity and interpretation of the data produced. These different forms of assessment encompass a variety of data, including quantitative data such as those produced from surveys, questionnaires, and experiments, as well as qualitative data such as those produced from ethnographies or participant observations. In the remainder of this section, each of Messick's aspects of validity is explained in more detail, using examples from the motivation literature, and then particular concerns in the assessment of motivation among ethnic minority groups are described. More specifically, explanation of how these issues can be understood as threatening the overall construct validity of the assessment process is provided. The issues presented are not intended to be exhaustive of every concern with motivational research among ethnic minority groups, but they do represent many of the most pressing concerns in the assessment of motivation among these populations.

CONTENT RELEVANCE COMPONENT

The content relevance component of construct validity is concerned with the representativeness of the content coverage of an assessment in relation to the theoretical domain of interest (Messick, 1989). One important threat to this aspect of construct validity is construct under-representation, which can occur when an instrument fails to sample some theoretically important behavior or dimension of the underlying target construct. For example, some attempts to assess academic self-concept have been criticized for assessing students' beliefs about their academic abilities but failing to account for their beliefs regarding their affective response to those abilities (Bong & Clarke, 1999). Because this affective response is commonly understood to be an essential theoretical component of self-concept, instruments that do not tap into these beliefs can be viewed as lacking in the content relevance component of construct validity. That is, such self-concept instruments fail to provide evidence that the assessment process adequately samples the relevant domain and that the scores assigned to individuals accurately reflect the target construct.

Even when an assessment includes all aspects of a construct, it may lack validity because it does not reflect the relative theoretical importance or emphases presumed within the construct. For example, a mastery or learning goal orientation has been described as including students' focus on goals based on accomplishing a challenging task, improving their competence, increasing their feelings of autonomy or satisfying other intrinsic forms of motivation (Ames, 1992; Elliot, 1999; Pintrich, 2000). A measure of mastery goal orientation could be faulted because it does not adequately sample each of these aspects of the underlying construct to an appropriate degree or because it does not sample these different aspects in the correct balance. Too much of an emphasis on one aspect or another (e.g. accomplishing a challenging task) reduces the validity with which one can use the subsequent scores as a measure of students' overall mastery goal orientation. These problems serve as threats to construct validity in that the scores or conclusions based on such an assessment presume to reflect the total or actual underlying construct when in fact it only provides information about a subset of that construct. In other words, the issue here is that an assessment does not adequately sample all aspects that are theoretically subsumed within a single construct or does so in a balance that does not accurately reflect theoretical assumptions (Pintrich et al., 2000).

Another way in which an assessment may suffer from construct under-representation is when it fails to adequately sample the content domain that it purports to cover. This issue is particularly relevant for motivational constructs that are theoretically tied to a particular domain, topic, or subject area. Perceived self-efficacy is an example of how this type of content-related evidence can be important for establishing the overall construct validity of an assessment. From a theoretical perspective, it is assumed that an individual's self-efficacy may vary across domains and topics, or even tasks within a domain (Bandura, 1997; Pajares, 1996; Schunk, 1991). For instance, within the domain of mathematics, a student may express a high sense of self-efficacy for algebra, but a low level of self-efficacy for calculus. At the same time, a student's view of his/her ability to solve mathematics problems may be quite different with regard to one task (e.g. solving equations for unknowns) versus another (e.g. managing exponents) within a particular topic area (e.g. algebra). Assessments of self-efficacy for a particular domain or subject area (e.g. algebra) must therefore sample enough of the skills and do so specifically enough so that one can reasonably assume that students who express self-efficacy on the tested items (e.g. solving equations) would also express efficacy on other relevant items (i.e. managing exponents). A measure that claims to indicate students' self-efficacy for algebra, but which taps into students' self-efficacy for only a small subset of the skills important for algebra fails to demonstrate this aspect of construct validity. Hence, an assessment of motivation must be examined with regard to its coverage of the underlying subject area, topic or task to determine whether it adequately represents that content domain.

Content Relevance Component and the Assessment of Motivation in Ethnic Minority Groups

With regard to assessing motivation among ethnic minority samples, the main construct validity issue in terms of content relevance seems to amount to the basic question of whether a particular construct has the same meaning for all groups or whether a particular construct even exists for all groups. Typically, psychologists are concerned with universal descriptions of human behavior and social phenomena, utilizing concepts that are either pancultural or culture-free. This level of analysis is described as an *etic* approach and can be contrasted with an *emic* approach, which is focused on creating an accurate description of phenomena by studying behavior within one culture only (Pike, 1954/1966, as cited in Berry, 1980; Triandis, 1972). In cross-cultural psychology, both etics and emics are considered necessary levels of analysis, as the etics provide a frame, and the emics provide the substance.

As an example, Sue and Sue (2000) describe that good decision making may be exemplified in Western cultures by the "ability to make a personal decision without being unduly influenced by others" (p. 3), while in Asian cultures it may be the "ability to make a decision that is the best for the group" (p. 3). Decision making can be described as an etic, while both personal and group-referenced decision making would be considered emics. Similarly, if a particular motivational belief is defined differently for Caucasian students and members of an ethnic minority, then research on this motivation etic must take into account the culture-specific emics.

However, etics may often be assumed and not truly tested; in this case, they are deemed pseudo etics or imposed etics (Berry, 1980). These etics are usually Euro-American etics that are imposed blindly or ethnocentrically in other cultural systems. In this situation, content relevance is compromised because the assessment may fail to sample the dimension of the underlying target construct that is theoretically important for members of different ethnic minority groups.

Berry (1969, as cited in Berry, 1980) describes a strategy for addressing the problem of pseudo etics or imposed etics that is conceptually aligned with a strategy proposed by Sue and Sue (1987) called the parallel research design. Basically, the strategy involves a recursive research process in which the investigator begins with an imposed etic view but recognizes the cultural limitations of it and remains willing to incorporate new, perhaps contradictory evidence in modifying the target behavioral system. Thus, the imposed etic or potentially universal concept or process serves as a starting point and can be progressively altered or defined in ways appropriate to a culture from the perspective of insiders until a true emic is achieved. If the beginning etic categories can then be understood with respect to both the original behavioral system as well as the new, emically-described one, this derived etic can then be considered a valid framework for comparing behavior across settings. Similarities and differences both within and across cultural groups with respect to these concepts and processes, as well as factors contributing to within-group variance are then determined.

In summary, the content relevance component of construct validity refers to how well the assessment process represents the theoretical domain of interest. Content relevance may be threatened when the assessment under-represents or disproportionately represents dimensions or domains of the target construct. This aspect of validity is germane when assessing a construct such as motivation in students from ethnic minority populations because the basic question of whether the construct exists or has equivalent meanings across ethnic groups is a core issue impacting every aspect of the entire research process.

SUBSTANTIVE COMPONENT

Closely related to the content component, the substantive component of construct validity emphasizes two types of evidence needed to support the validity of a test. First, Messick (1989) notes that items on the test as well as individuals' responses to these items should exemplify only the construct being measured and not other constructs. Second, other items that ostensibly measure a different construct should not be related to the test items of the target construct. This general issue with substantive evidence is illustrated when scores vary because some extraneous or theoretically distinct factor is erroneously included in the assessment of some motivational construct. For example, an instrument designed to assess students' self-efficacy for a domain may be affected by the social desirability of some pattern of responses. If students are more inclined to report higher levels of self-efficacy because this is the socially desired response, this would introduce extraneous information into the scores and dilute the validity of the instrument for indicating students' actual self-efficacy. In other words, rather than reflecting only students' perceived self-efficacy for doing a task, scores on the instrument reflect students' relative tendency to report socially desired responses. In a similar fashion, poorly worded items, ambiguous or complex directions, or excessive amounts of reading (when assessing reading is not the purpose of the test), can introduce randomness or error that reduces the overall construct validity of the assessment (Messick, 1989).

As a way of establishing evidence for this aspect of construct validity, Messick (1989) describes the need to establish that the content or processes used within an assessment reflect the actual processes used in the motivational process. Typically, items on an assessment are designed based on expert opinion as to what processes or content will reflect the motivational process being considered. Messick, however, argues that empirical evidence must eventually be provided to establish this connection. For example, the items used to tap into students' various goal orientations might originally be constructed by researchers familiar with the theoretical understanding of these goal orientations. However, the substantitive aspect of construct validity requires that empirical evidence be accumulated that shows that students who report a focus on mastery goals on a particular instrument actually adopt mastery related goals when engaged in academic tasks. The emphasis here is for evidence that an assessment actually taps into the construct or processes that it purports to assess. For example, empirical evidence would be needed to demonstrate that self-report surveys of self-efficacy are related to students' actual beliefs about their ability to complete a task, and that these beliefs really do operate in ways that are consistent with theoretical models of this construct.

Substantive Component and the Assessment of Motivation in Ethnic Minority Groups

One important way in which substantive evidence for the validity of an assessment can be threatened concerns the tendency of researchers to confound race or ethnicity with other important factors that might be related to motivation. Simple classification by race is often used without taking into account socioeconomic status, level of acculturation, immigrant status, or ethnic identity. For example, because minority status and social class are confounded, with minorities overrepresented in the lower socioeconomic levels in American society, researchers often focus on racial differences when differences based on social class may fit better with theory. This confound poses a problem to research on minority populations because phenomena have been ascribed to ethnicity when in fact social class has been a better explanation (Spencer & Dornbusch, 1990). In violating the assumption that the race variable is not measuring a variety of other constructs related to race, the substantive component of the validity of the assessment is at risk.

Another way in which this component of validity may be threatened in research examining motivation among minority students concerns the often-cited need to match the ethnicity of a researcher to the participant's race or ethnicity. It is frequently noted that when making assessments with participants who are members of ethnic minority groups, the researcher and participant should be matched on ethnicity. This type of researcher/participant matching, for example, is commonly accepted as necessary in studies involving interviews or studies in which researchers visit participants in their homes. The accepted logic is that participants may feel more comfortable, more willing to discuss sensitive topics, or less anxious when interacting with someone of their own race or ethnicity. To the extent that this is true, not matching interviewers to participants on ethnic or racial group may degrade the substantive aspect of the assessment's construct validity.

On the one hand, this type of matching may work to increase the substantive evidence for construct validity. When not matched, interviews that are intended to measure a respondent's value, interest or other motivational construct may instead be tapping into noise introduced by social desirability. For example, for interviews in the home, African-American researchers may be more comfortable than Caucasians entering neighborhoods that are predominantly African American (Cauce, Ryan & Grove, 1998). It is commonly believed that a researcher who is of the same ethnicity as the participant will be able to establish rapport better than someone of a different ethnicity. This could also be an issue when individuals are observing in classrooms.

On the other hand, simple matching of interviewer and interviewee by race or ethnicity may not alleviate this problem. As Cauce et al. (1998) point out, the purpose of matching interviewers' ethnicity to participants is to be more culturally sensitive, including gaining participants' trust and knowing that African-Americans may be more comfortable than Caucasians entering neighborhoods that are predominantly African American. However, cultural sensitivity is "not a product of simple ethnicity" (Cauce et al., 1998, p. 163). As an example, they describe knowing a number of college and graduate students of color who were raised in predominantly Caucasian neighborhoods and schools who were sent to low SES minority communities without training or supervision. Rather than being culturally sensitive, this type of simple ethnic-matching is actually insensitive, as well as potentially dangerous. Cauce et al. (1998) assert that research teams need to include individuals familiar with the participants' culture by way of birth and personal history or specific experience and training. Given individual differences in background, education, and other characteristics, the researcher and participant may have little in common beyond belonging to the same general racial or ethnic category, which does not necessarily result in special insight or good rapport. Further, according to Doucette-Gates, Brooks-Gunn, and Chase-Lansdale (1998) and Guerra and Jagers (1998), there is actually very little data reported in the existing literature that documents the effect of researcher characteristics, specifically race, on outcomes of respondents.

Despite this apprehension or cautions, there is reason to consider this issue when designing and completing motivational research. That is, the general issue remains important to consider because motivational assessments that inadvertently include variance due to lack of rapport, cultural understanding, or trust reduce the construct validity of the assessment.

An additional threat to this aspect of validity concerns the possibility that measures are tapping into culturally defined response styles and not the actual target construct. Culturally defined response styles are characteristic ways of responding that are not directly related to the content of assessment but to how items are worded (Guerra & Jagers, 1998). For example, "si-ismo" exists in Latino culture, which is a tendency to say "yes" or "si" as an indication of agreement with others (especially authority figures), regardless of actual beliefs (Guerra & Jagers, 1998). "Si-ismo" is an example of "yea-saying," a widely known response style or response set in which respondents show a tendency to agree with questionnaire or test items, independent of content (Bachman & O'Malley, 1984). One suggestion to counteract this possible problem is to include both positively and negatively worded items within an interview or survey. However, items that include double negatives can be difficult for younger children to understand.

Another culturally defined response style is the extreme response style, in which respondents over-select the extreme ends of the categories in Likert-scaled questionnaire items. There is evidence that African-American children are more likely than Caucasians to use extreme response categories in Likert-type questionnaires (Bachman & O'Malley, 1984). These response styles threaten the substantive validity of an assessment because they suggest that an instrument is not measuring its intended target construct but instead is reflecting some culturally defined understanding of how to respond to particular types of questions.

A final way in which the substantive component of validity may be compromised is when participants' language and meaning differ from the researchers developing the measures. Researchers may think they are eliciting the information they are seeking with measures, but if issues in language proficiency or differences in meaning exist, the data provided for a construct may actually contain irrelevant information. For example, Guerra and Jagers (1998) identify that participants need to be tested in their primary language, although there is remarkable inconsistency in actual practice, and Sue and Sue (2000) advocate the use of tests that can be understood linguistically.

According to Vygotsky's (1986) sociocultural theory, language serves as a tool to guide one's thinking. Individuals internalize language, which is shared externally by members of a culture in social situations, such that the individual can learn the mental structures necessary for understanding the surrounding world. Garcia (1994) asserts that when the classroom negates students' native language, they lose the tools they use to construct basic cognitive frameworks. Educational practices that ignore or negatively view a students' native language when it is not English may have negative effects on the student's cognitive development. Similarly, it is very likely that motivational assessment practices that do not consider native language may provide an inaccurate portrayal of the motivational processes at work in language minority students.

Testing participants in their native language requires the use of translations that are equivalent in meaning. The back-translation method, where the instrument is translated into the second language and then subsequently translated back to English by independent translators to check for equivalence, has been advocated as preferred over standard, one-way translation methods. However, back-translation is still not a perfect solution, as bilingual translators may still be of different culture or status as respondents, yielding a measure that is difficult for respondents to understand (van de Vijver & Leung, 1997).

Concerns with the substantive component of validity similarly apply to any situations where respondents' meanings of language may vary systematically from that of researchers. For example, in common usage, the word "bad" can be used to mean "good" (Guerra & Jagers, 1998). Researchers not familiar with the vernacular of the participants may inadvertently ascribe erroneous information on a motivational construct when language is not shared.

To summarize, the substantive component of validity concerns the need to ensure that assessments are tapping into a target construct and not some ancillary factor. Particular threats to this component of validity occur when researchers confound ethnicity with factors that might vary by ethnicity such as social class, language, rapport with others of a particular ethnicity, or response style.

STRUCTURAL COMPONENT

The structural component of construct validity concerns the relations between the scoring system and the theoretical model of the construct. Messick (1989) points out that the relations between items on a test, including how items are scored and then summed, combined, or kept separate, should reflect the same relations as those expressed in the theoretical model of the construct. Here the relevant issue is whether the data produced from an assessment accurately reflect the theoretical nature of the underlying construct being assessed (Pintrich et al., 2000). For instance, an instrument that produces a single total score from a test implies that the construct is unitary, whereas an instrument that produces a number of different subscales or scores implies a differentiated construct. Some prior research on students' values could be criticized for failing to maintain this aspect of validity. For instance, theoretical accounts of value often differentiate two, three, or even four distinct types of value that students might have with regard to academic work (Eccles et al., 1983; Wigfield, 1994; Wigfield & Eccles, 1992). However, measures of value used in research often lump together items that tap into these various forms of value to create a single indicator for value (e.g. Wigfield et al., 1997) implying that value is a unitary construct or that the theoretical distinctions are unnecessary or unimportant. This aspect of construct validity is also at risk when theoretical constructs viewed as continuous are measured and used in analyses as dichotomous variables. As an example, theoretical accounts of goal theory typically view particular goal orientations (e.g. mastery goal orientation) as continuous constructs in which students can fall anywhere along a range from a strong focus on a particular type of goal to a complete absence of any concern with this type of goal. Despite this theoretical understanding of students' goal orientations, prior studies in this area often created dichotomous indicators for these goal orientations (e.g. Schraw, Horn, Thorndike-Christ & Bruning, 1995), implying that students either are or are not focused on each type of goal and that there is a qualitative difference between these groups.

Structural Component and the Assessment of Motivation in Ethnic Minority Groups

One threat to this aspect of construct validity often present in research on ethnic minorities concerns the need to establish that the structural configuration of a construct is similar across different groups of individuals. In other words, do the internal relations and emphases proposed by theory and used in analyses remain consistent across ethnic groups or when considering mixed ethnic samples? One strategy that researchers can employ in order to provide this type of evidence is to conduct separate factor analyses on survey items according to ethnicity of the respondents to see if the factor structure holds across groups. For example, using goal theory, Middleton and Midgley (1997) examined performance-avoidance goals as an extension of task and performance-approach goals. They conducted exploratory factor analysis on sixth graders' responses to Likert-scaled survey items, then conducted several more exploratory factor analyses for girls, boys, African Americans, and European Americans separately. Items for the three goal orientations formed separate factors with high Cronbach's alpha coefficients when the samples were split by gender and race. This type of structural evidence supports the overall construct validity of the assessment by providing evidence for the structural component of validity across different groups of students.

Perhaps a more general, pressing concern with the structural component is presented when researchers use a particular assessment in their research with ethnic minority students in absence of a clearly identified or articulated theoretical framework. As identified by Graham (1994), research on minority samples can be plagued by an atheoretical focus. Using convenience samples, researchers may administer various instruments and collect data on ethnic minorities, but without a theoretical framework guiding the research process, including formulation of the research questions and hypotheses and selection of data collection procedures. In doing so, the structural component of validity is compromised. There is no way to assess the extent to which data are accurately reflecting the underlying theoretical construct without an understanding of those theories.

Another potential problem arises when researchers fail to consider whether the experimental manipulations they use work the same for students from different ethnic or cultural groups. When exposed to particular experimental manipulations (or lack thereof) students are often expected to show a different pattern of relations among their data or are expected to display a different structural pattern. In effect, the motivational construct is "assessed" by exposing particular individuals to the experimental manipulation. For example, research on goal orientation sometimes relies on instilling either a performance or mastery goal orientation in students and then examining differences among the groups of students with respect to particular outcomes of interest (Elliot & Harackiewicz, 1996). If these manipulations do not affect students of different ethnic groups similarly, then the structural pattern presumed to be present in all students may be lacking for some. This absence threatens the overall validity of the asssessment especially when checks on the effect of an experimental manipulation are not included in the design of a study.

To review, the structural aspect of validity entails a need to provide evidence for congruence between how an assessment is scored and the theoretical model that provides the basis for that assessment. This aspect of validity is lacking when research fails to provide evidence that this congruence is present across ethnic groups, when assessments completely lack a theoretical basis, or when checks on experimental manipulations are neglected.

EXTERNAL COMPONENT

The external component of construct validity concerns the relation between one particular measure of a construct and another measure of the same construct, as well as the relation between one particular measure of a construct and those of different constructs. Supportive evidence for this aspect of validity comes when a particular measure of a construct relates highly to other methods that purport to measure the same construct, but fails to relate as highly to theoretically distinct constructs assessed using the same methodology.

For example, assessing individual interest using a self-report measure should be related positively to measures of the same interest based on observational data, think-alouds, event sampling, or other more direct measures of that individual interest (Alexander & Jetton, 1996; Schiefele, Krapp & Winteler, 1992). Failure to find the expected pattern of relations (i.e. high inter-correlations) suggests that scores on one or more of the measures does not actually reflect a student's individual interest but rather something else, such as another type of interest, knowledge, or the response format. At the same time, the self-report measure of individual interest should be related to a much lesser extent to self-report measures of other motivational constructs such as self-efficacy and self-concept that are theoretically distinct. Observed empirical relations among distinct constructs assessed with the same methodology indicate that students' scores are strongly influenced by some superfluous factor related to the methodology (e.g. social desirability, response bias) rather than by the respective underlying constructs.

The need for evidence of this type of validity is one justification for undertaking multi-trait multi-method studies in which theoretically distinct constructs are evaluated using two or more forms of assessment (e.g. Howard-Rose & Winne, 1993). Similarly, the need to accumulate this type of evidence regarding the construct validity of an assessment can be used to argue that a field should not rely too heavily on any single form of assessment procedure because an emphasis on one form of data reduces the opportunities to establish this aspect of validity.

External Component and the Assessment of Motivation in Ethnic Minority Groups

Establishing evidence for the external component of validity can present a challenge for motivation researchers studying individuals from ethnic minority groups for several reasons. Over reliance on particular methods of data collection is always problematic for this aspect of validity, but it may be even more problematic when considering research with students from minority populations. More specifically, the over use of a single method of data collection may magnify any problems associated with using this form of data collection with a particular minority population. For example, consistently using surveys to assess and understand students' self-beliefs may highlight or intensify issues arising from language or reading difficulties experienced by students whose native language is not English. Similarly, research based exclusively on interview methods may be problematic for groups or sub-groups of minority populations that are interviewed in a fashion that inadvertently produces distrust, fear, anxiety, shyness, or evasive responses.

Another problem in generating evidence for the external aspect of validity is that a construct may "work" differently across ethnic groups in terms of the relations of that construct to other variables. For example, most of the dominant motivational theories include an expectancy for success component as an important variable that is positively related to achievement and achievement strivings. Relatedly, self-concept of ability is another motivational variable that has been examined widely in motivation research. The relation between variables is bi-directional, such that students who have high expectancies or self-concept tend to perform well, and those who perform well tend to have high expectancies or self-concept. However, research suggests that this relation does not hold for African Americans. Specifically, Graham's (1994) review of motivation research with African Americans found consistent evidence that these students did not have low expectancies or self-concept of ability relative to their actual achievement levels or relative to their higher-achieving Caucasian classmates. Even in the face of failure, African Americans continue to report high levels of expectancy for success or self-concept. One interpretation of these counterintuitive findings that has been suggested is that these students are unrealistic, perhaps even delusional, in their appraisals, while another interpretation is that these students do remarkably well in maintaining optimism in negative situations. The fact that the appraisals and the actual outcomes are miscalibrated calls to question the external aspect of validity in motivation research.

In addition, the external issue may prove to complicate motivation research with ethnic minority samples with respect to the effect of racial or ethnic identity on the relations between variables. For example, following the Multidimensional Model of Racial Identity (Sellers, Rowley, Chavous, Shelton & Smith, 1997; Sellers, Smith, Shelton, Rowley & Chavous, 1998), researchers have found a moderating effect of identification with race for African American high school and college students on the relation between racial beliefs and motivational and academic outcomes. Specifically, for African Americans with high levels of racial centrality, or view of race as a central component of one's self-definition, positive feelings toward African Americans in general were positively related to personal self-esteem. This relation was not found for students with low levels of racial centrality (Rowley, Sellers, Chavous & Smith, 1998). Likewise, for high centrality African American college students, several racial ideology variables were related to college GPA, but there were no relations for low centrality students (Sellers, Chavous & Cooke, 1998). This type of moderator effect presents complexity to the study of motivation among ethnic minority students and can be construed as an issue of the external component of construct validity.

To summarize, the external component of validity refers to the relations between measures of a particular construct and different measures of the same construct, in addition to the relations between measures of a target construct to other constructs. Th external component of the construct validity of research with ethnic minority populations may be threatened with over-reliance on a single type of assessment procedure. More problematic is the possibility that a construct may relate differently to other variables or may be moderated by variables such as racial identity when looking across ethnic groups.

GENERALIZABILITY COMPONENT

Another important form of support for the overall construct validity of an assessment comes from evidence that, when expected based on theoretical models, the scores produced are generalizable across different domains, tasks, situations, times or groups (see Linn, Baker & Dunbar, 1991). Unlike the content representativeness issue discussed earlier, generalizability does not concern whether a particular motivational construct (e.g. task value, achievement motive) adequately covers the particular domain that it purports to represent. Instead generalizability concerns whether there is evidence that an assessment of a construct within a particular domain can be used as an indicator of the same construct in other contexts, times, or within other groups. The issue of task generalizability is less of an concern for some assessments because they are designed to tap into motivational constructs that are presumed to vary across situations, domains, or time (e.g. task value, situational interest). For instance, theoretical accounts suggest that a student's situational interest (Alexander & Jetton, 1996; Krapp, Hidi & Renninger, 1992) for academic material may vary across situations or time within the same situation and so an assessment that reflects students' situational interest for a particular context (e.g. algebra class) may not correlate highly with one that reflects students' situational interest for another context (e.g. science class). In contrast, measures of motivational constructs that are viewed as more stable or traitlike would need to demonstrate evidence of their generalizability across tasks or situations in order to establish their overall construct validity. For example, some theoretical accounts of motivation have relied on traitlike achievement motives to explain an individual's behavior and motivation across contexts (Atkinson, 1964; Harackiewicz, Barron, Elliot, Carter & Lehto, 1997; McClelland, 1961). Assessments of this type of construct need to provide evidence demonstrating a higher level of generalizability across situations or contexts to support their overall validity. Similarly, in terms of temporal generalizability, for the same tasks in the same domain, there should be some consistency across time in individuals' scores, at least within a restricted range of time where development or learning opportunities are minimal. In short, issues of domain, task, and time generalizability are more or less critical depending on the theoretical stance adopted regarding the stability and situated nature of the motivational construct under consideration. If the conceptual model assumes that the motivational construct is always and mainly situated (e.g. situational interest), then there is no expectation that there will be much consistency across domains, tasks, or times. At the other end of the continuum, if the conceptual model assumes that a motivational construct is more of a stable personal trait of the individual (e.g. achievement motives), then there should be a fairly high level of consistency across these facets and deviations from consistency are viewed as problematic for validity.

Generalizability Component and the Assessment of Motivation in Ethnic Minority Groups

Most relevant for the current discussion is evidence that the data produced from a particular assessment can be scored and interpreted in a similar fashion across different ethnic or racial groups. The question here is whether an assessment provides similar results or similar findings when used to assess the construct in populations of minority students as it does in majority populations. Despite their situational nature, most motivational constructs are assumed to operate similarly among different groups of students (e.g. gifted, learning disabled, gender), including students from different ethnic groups. Specific evidence supporting these assumptions, however, is often lacking. One clear threat to this facet of an assessment's overall validity occurs when general models of motivation are developed using non-diverse populations. It can be argued that one goal of psychological research is to uncover commonalities in processes and phenomena across human beings, that is, general psychological laws of behavior. However, when studies are conducted repeatedly using a single demographic segment of the population (e.g. introductory psychology students who are mainly middle class and Caucasian) the generalizability of findings to other populations is called to question.

A related problem that also puts the generalizability of results at risk is when research does include ethnic minorities but does not select a representative group of ethnic students. As noted previously, there is often as much variance within an ethnic group as between groups. The very process of grouping many different people with different countries of ancestral origin and years and generations of living in the United States under one umbrella group such as "Asian American" or "Hispanic" tends to obscure the fact that there are different subgroups who may show different patterns of motivation and achievement. For example, the term "Hispanic" is a convenience label used to describe individuals living in the United States who were born in or who have ancestry to a Spanish-speaking Latin American country or Spain (Marín & Marín, 1991). This means that an individual born in the United States who is a descendent of Spanish settlers but does not speak Spanish would be considered to be a member of the same category (e.g. Hispanic) as an individual who has just arrived to the United States from Mexico. Similarly, if research is conducted that focuses on a particular sub-group (e.g. low income African Americans) results may not generalize to members that do not fall into this subgroup (e.g. high income African Americans).

With respect to contexts, research on motivation among ethnic minority students is limited in that it tends to examine motivated functioning without much consideration for context. Consistent with psychological research that measures attitudes, beliefs, and the like without simultaneously measuring aspects of the surrounding cultural environment, motivational research on ethnic minorities has been similarly myopic. This is not the case with all motivation research that includes ethnic minority participants. In some motivation research, context is given a greater role and is a central focus of the study; however, it tends to focus on only one context in which students develop, such as school or home, but not both. This issue of the context specificity of behavior and constructs may be particularly important for students from ethnic minority groups whose home and community contexts may be disparate from that of school.

Okagaki's (2001) triarchic model of minority children's school achievement provides a good description of a research model that addresses this contextual concern of generalizability. In this model, three factors are considered as contributing to minority children's school achievement: "the form and perceived function of school, the family's cultural norms and beliefs about education and development, and the characteristics of the child" (Okagaki, 2001, p. 9). Researchers need to examine the impact of multiple contexts such as family, peers, school, neighborhood, media, and the larger society on children's academic functioning. By examining the simultaneous roles and interplay among influences from multiple contexts, researchers should advance theories about these students' school experiences (Wong & Rowley, 2001). Examining the multiple contexts that may initiate or sustain motivated behaviors should help address Messick's (1989) issue of generalizability.

In sum, the generalizability component of construct validity refers to the extent to which results from an assessment can be applied to different contexts, times, or groups. This issue is relevant to research with ethnic minority populations when limited groups of ethnic minorities are included as participants or contexts are not taken account in the research process.

CONSEQUENTIAL COMPONENT

Messick (1989) emphasizes that the overall construct validity of a test is also affected by how it is interpreted and used in practice or applied settings. That is, the meaning, relevance, and utility of a measure for the reasons or purposes for which it is actually used (as opposed to only those uses for which it was intended) must be evaluated because these also affect the validity of the assessment. Hence, evidence regarding how particular tests are used or the purposes for which they are used bears on the validity of that instrument. As an example with regard to motivation more generally, an important distinction in purpose concerns whether tests are used for research or for instructional purposes including intervention or remediation. For example, a survey such as the Learning and Study Strategies Inventory (Weinstein, Palmer & Schulte, 1987), which is designed to be used as a tool for diagnosis and intervention, may not be valid when used to measure motivation for theory building purposes. Similarly, the Self Descriptive Questionnaire (Marsh & O'Neil, 1984) or other self-concept measures that are intended to research and build theoretical understandings of students' self-concept may lack validity if used to diagnose deficits in a particular individual's self-concept or as a basis for intervention.

Consequential evidence includes the importance of an assessment having validity with respect to the social consequences or actions it precipitates through its uses or misuses (Messick, 1989). The idea here is that conclusions about whether a test does what it is intended to do or serves the function it is intended to serve requires that one evaluate the intended as well as unintended social consequences of the assessment. As Messick (1989) notes, the key issue with this aspect of validity is whether a test or assessment can be used for its intended purpose if it is also used for an unintended and perhaps unwanted purpose as well. For instance, the Patterns of Adaptive Learning Survey (Midgley et al., 1998) includes scales that tap into classroom goal structures for theory building and research purposes. However, it is also possible for principals or other school personnel to use feedback from these scales as a basis for judging the effectiveness of an individual teacher or as a basis for general school reform (Maehr & Midgley, 1991). Hence, using the assessment may have intentional as well as unintentional social consequences that must be evaluated and used to judge the overall validity of the instrument.

Consequential Component and the Assessment of Motivation in Ethnic Minority Groups

The need to understand and evaluate social consequences is an important concern when assessing motivation among minority groups. In the majority of research on ethnic minority populations, including motivation research, the prevalent design involves comparing mean level differences in various constructs between Caucasian and non-Caucasian participants. For example, in Graham's (1994) review of 133 studies on motivation in African Americans from the 1960s to 1990, 103 studies, or 77%, were classified as race comparative. In other words, the majority of motivation research published in those decades focused on documenting mean level differences and similarities between Blacks and Whites on motivational constructs such as need for achievement, locus of control, causal attributions, expectancy level, and ability self-concept. Research within this framework has been described as a comparative racial approach (Graham, 1992, 1994), between group general process model (Phinney & Landin, 1998), and deficit model (McLoyd, 1991; Spencer & Dornbusch, 1990). According to Spencer and Dornbusch (1990), research in this tradition sets out to document what non-Caucasian participants are missing, or deficient in, compared to Caucasians, hence leading to the term deficit model. With respect to studying adolescents, they explain that because most of the data upon which general conclusions have been drawn have come from middle-class white families, it is not surprising to see that social scientists have viewed the mainstream white behaviors as the norm. According to the deficit model "minority youth perform poorly in school and later on the job because their family background is deprived, deficient, or deviant compared with white middle-class norms" (Spencer & Dornbusch, 1990, p. 126).

Use of the comparative research design or deficit model is a common way of explicitly making negative comparisons between Whites and ethnic minorities and represents a form of cultural bias (Wong & Rowley, 2001). These mistaken assumptions can create exactly the type of unintended consequences that would seem to violate the consequential validity of the entire assessment process. In particular, this research paradigm often carries with it an implied assumption that White or mainstream means or processes are "normal" or preferred while any differences from these norms is deviant or abnormal. Over time and through repeated use this form of assessment, therefore, can highlight ethnic differences, downplay ethnic similarities, and mask the impact of other important constructs and create unintended, unfounded, or erroneous implications for educational research and practice.

As noted by Messick (1989), the solution is not simply to halt all research that examines group differences but to rely on designs that avoid these unintended consequences. For example, Phinney and Landin (1998) offer models of how research on ethnic groups should proceed. In particular, these authors suggest that rather than examine group differences as an end, research designs should allow for an exploration of why group differences may exist. Thus, correlates of group membership that might be used to interpret group differences or the actual socio-cultural or ethnic factors that might be important in understanding the topic under study should be assessed. For instance, one could assess cultural norms, values, or attitudes assumed to be associated with outcomes of interest and then examine their relations to the outcomes. More specifically, one could address degree of acculturation, level of collectivism, degree of racial identity, socioeconomic status or other factors that may be more directly related to group differences. Measuring these factors is an improvement over research that may assume differences on these variables among ethnic groups but fails to establish them empirically. As an example, traditional or historical justification is often used to characterize students from Asian cultures as more collectivist or focused on social obligations. However, these assumed characteristics may or may not be present in any particular population of Asian students, and even if they are present may not be responsible any observed differences. The extent of these problems cannot be explored unless specific data is collected on the factor that is presumed to drive group differences (e.g. level of collectivism).

In sum, an assessment's overall validity cannot be firmly established without considering the consequences of how the assessment is used in actual practice. Included in these consequences must be the direct as well as indirect or unintentional results of using a particular assessment.

CONCLUSION

The purpose of this chapter was to present a set of issues relevant to the validity of the assessment of motivation in students from ethnic minority populations. Utilizing Messick's (1989) conceptualization of the components of construct validity as a framework, examples from motivation research in general and with ethnic minority samples specifically were discussed. The final section of the chapter is intended to provide a set of recommendations for motivation researchers based upon a synthesis of these construct validity issues. These recommendations also reflect a synthesis of the guidelines presented by the American Psychological Association's Council of National Psychological Associations for the Advancement of Ethnic Minority Interests (2000). As such, the recommendations should apply not only to motivation researchers, but also to those in education and psychology more generally.

1. Include the Study of Ethnic Minority Students in Motivation Research

This first recommendation, to include the study of ethnic minority students in motivation research, is a basic one directed toward all researchers, even if they are not specifically interested in focusing on ethnic minority issues or populations. When deciding what participants to include in their studies, researchers are encouraged to consider using ethnically diverse samples and not just white, middle-class ones (Graham, 1992). This ethnic diversity should include individuals from not only different racial and ethnic backgrounds, but also varying socioeconomic levels. To the extent that there is access to populations of ethnic minorities, whether in community, university, primary or secondary school settings, researchers should try to recruit and retain these individuals in their motivation studies.

According to Cauce et al. (1998), for survey studies, the response rate for ethnic minorities seems to be about the same as Caucasians, but retention of ethnic minorities in longitudinal studies, particularly individuals who are poor, may be more difficult. Cauce et al. offer several suggestions for recruiting and tracking ethnic minority participants, including offering payment for involvement, getting an endorsement from respected individuals in the school or community (e.g. principals of schools, leaders of community ethnic minority organizations), contacting families frequently to maintain current addresses, and making the research activity as enjoyable as possible. However, the main barrier in developing a research base on ethnic minorities seems not to be with recruitment and retention but at the initial phase of participant selection.

Thus, in order to advance our understanding of student learning, motivation researchers must make a concerted effort to include the study of a growing percentage of the student population, those from ethnic minority groups across different socioeconomic levels. It is imperative that motivational theories and practices not be based upon a collection of studies that fail to adequately represent the students in today's classrooms. It would be regrettable to look at the motivation research base a decade from now and be able to criticize the work as focused mostly on Caucasian students from middle class suburban schools, or if ethnic minority students are included, only those from a narrow cross-section of social class.

Along with the basic recommendation to include ethnic minorities in motivation studies, researchers should collect information on the ethnicity of their participants and report those data in the write-up of their research. In terms of collecting data on ethnic group membership, researchers should know their population and the distinctions that are likely to be made within it and allow for this variation. For example, in Florida it may be especially important to include separate response categories for individuals of Cuban, Jamaican or other Caribbean island descent, and in a Californian community, it may be pertinent to identify different Asian-American subgroups such as Philippino, Chinese, Korean, or Vietnamese. Further, as the rate of inter-cultural and inter-racial marriages and adoptions increase (Brodzinsky, Lang & Smith, 1995) and children develop in increasingly multi-cultural contexts, participants should be permitted to self-identify in more than one ethnic category. The census now allows multiple ethnic categories to be selected, and this level of description should also be standard within research. The need to include more specific distinctions in ethnicity reported will of course also depend on the heterogeneity of the particular sample and the purpose of the study.

2. Establish the Meaningfulness of Constructs and Methods Used to Assess Motivation in Ethnic Minority Groups

Including participants who are ethnic minorities in motivation studies will not alone advance the understanding of these individuals. Researchers need to be sensitive to the possibility that the constructs studied in motivation research may have different meanings for members of ethnic minority groups and that methods may tap into extraneous factors due to things such as language differences or response bias. The overall thrust of this recommendation is to consider the ways in which ethnicity may impact methodology and take steps to ensure that the research process taps into the target constructs and not other constructs or other extraneous factors. This recommendation is not a trivial one, and accordingly, reviewing all the strategies addressing this issue is beyond the scope of this chapter. However, there are several key ideas that researchers may want to bear in mind in light of this recommendation.

One necessary approach toward establishing the meaningfulness of constructs for different ethnic groups is being mindful that one may inadvertently be working with pseudo etics or imposed etics (Berry, 1980). The development of emics and true etics, for example, by following research strategies suggested by Berry (1969, as cited in Berry, 1980) and Sue and Sue (1987), is an important endeavor in order to decrease the Eurocentrism of motivation research. Focus groups and expert consultation with individuals familiar with the culture of interest may provide crucial information necessary to understand, modify, or create new theoretical constructs or research directions in the study of motivation.

A related implication of this recommendation is that researchers need to establish the integrity of existing methods vis a vis ethnic minority participants and to use methods that have been made culturally relevant. For example, for self-report surveys of motivation, researchers can utilize confirmatory factor analytic procedures separately by ethnic group to determine if the factor structure remains consistent across groups. Researchers can also help reduce the possibility that the research method is tapping into irrelevant processes by incorporating strategies such as having participants complete the assessment in their native language or with a researcher of similar ethnicity and background, keeping in mind the issues discussed in considering these options. In addition, the use of multi-trait, multi-methods can help provide convergence onto an understanding of motivation in different populations.

The overall focus of this suggestion is that researchers should revisit existing instruments and methods and work to improve their validity across different ethnic minority populations. Researchers should strive to use research instruments and procedures that have been established as valid with diverse populations. This selection will not only increase the validity of the research for those participants who are members of ethnic minority groups, but also improve the generalizability of the results to ethnic minority populations. If methods have not been established as culturally relevant, then interpretation of results and any consequential actions or policies should be made very cautiously with respect to ethnic minorities.

3. Decrease the Reliance on Race Comparative Studies and Instead Develop and Test Theoretical Models to Understand Motivation Within Ethnic Minorities

Another recommendation for motivation researchers is to decrease the reliance on race comparative studies that report simple mean-level differences on a host of variables and constructs across ethnic groups defined according to simple classification schemes. In line with Azibo (1992), race comparative research can serve some useful purposes, but it tends to be misused and over-used. As an example of a proper usage, comparative figures on levels of academic attainment or employment rates can help depict the current status of ethnic minorities and highlight areas of both adaptive functioning and areas where there is room for improvement in the condition of members of these populations. Although this type of research may provide a starting point for understanding motivation or another facet of functioning, it is not sufficient to understand the ethnic minority experience.

The preponderance of race comparative studies ultimately results in a collection of studies that highlights group differences but fails to account for why group differences may occur. Especially when one considers that it is not likely that the cultural meaningfulness of constructs and methods utilized has been established, the race comparative framework has limited usefulness. If a construct that is not meaningful in an ethnic minority culture is measured and compared to the majority culture, the results will erroneously be interpreted to indicate that the minority culture is deficient or deprived in some manner.

Instead, the basic recommendation is that researchers turn their focus toward including measures of specific cultural or ethnicity-related factors that one wants to explore theoretically in relation to motivation. In other words, research must move beyond investigating and documenting that there are differences between Caucasian and non- Caucasian populations and instead should focus on the mechanisms that drive or produce these differences. It should no longer be sufficient to uncover group differences and attribute them to some culturally assumed difference between groups (e.g. assuming Asians are different than Caucasians on Variable A because they have a more collectivist sense of self). Rather, researchers should strive actually to assess those presumed cultural mechanisms that affect motivation and investigate whether they can be used to explain differences in group outcomes (e.g. by measuring how sense of self is defined in Asian and Caucasian participants and relating it to the motivational construct of concern).

The recommendation to develop and test theoretical models to understand motivation in ethnic minorities goes hand in hand with a decreasing reliance on simple race comparative studies. Research that unpacks the meaning of being a member of an ethnic minority group should serve more useful in understanding these students than identifying basic mean-level differences according to group membership. Researchers interested in working on culturally-relevant theoretical models will likely need to consider carefully the sociocultural contexts in which ethnic minorities develop, including complexities in variables such as acculturation, ethnic identity, reception by American society, and feelings of obligation to family (Fuligni, 1998). Researchers should avoid the fallacy of homogeneity or monolithic identity in ethnic minorities (Stanfield, 1993) by consciously taking into account the heterogeneity within ethnic groups, for example, by examining variations in motivated functioning within a single ethnic group.

4. Increase the Participation of Ethnic Minorities in Mainstream Motivation Research

This last recommendation is two-fold and refers both to including individuals who are members of ethnic minorities on research teams as well as increasing the acceptance of ethnic minority motivation studies in mainstream journals. With respect to the former, individuals who are themselves members of ethnic minority groups may be particularly important as principal investigators, key informants, or consultants on research projects investigating motivation in these populations by way of their specific background and experiences as members of that group. This strategy is suggested with the caveat that simply being a member of an ethnic minority group does not make an individual an expert or spokesperson for that group. Again, there is great variation in individuals who are considered ethnic minorities, so it should not be presumed that an individual belonging to a particular group will have any special insight into that culture. However, to the extent that these individuals have had personal and professional experiences that may be relevant to the research endeavor, their participation and knowledge should be sought.

In terms of the latter suggestion, individuals involved in the publication of mainstream motivation research should strive to increase the number of well-executed studies published on ethnic minority issues. This recommendation is directed toward editors, peer reviewers, and researchers themselves. Too often, studies involving ethnic minority samples have been relegated to specialty journals devoted solely to ethnic or cross-cultural studies, such as *Journal of Black Psychology*, or to the occasional special issue of mainstream journals. Although the existence of entire journals or issues of journals targeted to understanding ethnic minorities is laudable, a major consequence seems to be that researchers who do not seek out these publication outlets are not aware of the research findings pertaining to these populations, and the study of the functioning of members of these populations continues to be viewed as separate from the study of psychological processes in general. Further, the fact that there are not many ethnic minority studies published in the mainstream journals overall sends an implicit message that this type of work is not as rigorous, important, or necessary. Research on motivation in ethnic minority populations should be viewed as a crucial step toward a complete understanding of motivation, and publication of such research should reflect that importance.

In closing, it is important to acknowledge that the issues and recommendations outlined in this chapter certainly do not address all concerns in research with ethnic minorities, and that researchers will need to determine which issues are especially important for their particular studies. Studying motivation in order to understand the educational and psychological functioning of students from ethnic minority populations is not an easy enterprise. Researchers should remember that competence in studies with ethnic minority samples is a skill that must be developed through education, supervised training, and professional experience. This chapter represents one step toward improving the field of motivational research so that researchers can conduct valid studies and make sound recommendations for policy or practice. Over 10 years ago, Henderson and Dweck (1990) identified that the motivational functioning of students from ethnic minority populations was not well known or researched, and the state of current knowledge is not remarkably better. It is hoped that in the next decade of motivation research on ethnic minority populations, advances will be made and help improve the lives of these students, because doing so will ultimately improve the condition of all students.

REFERENCES

Alexander, P., & Jetton, T. (1996). The role of importance and interest in the processing of text. *Educational Psychology Review, 8*, 89–121.

Ames, C. (1992). Classrooms: Goals, structures, and student motivation. *Journal of Educational Psychology, 84*, 261–271.

Atkinson, J. (1964). *An introduction to motivation*. Princeton, NJ: Van Nostrand.

Azibo, D. A. Y. (1992). Understanding the proper and improper usage of the comparative research framework. In: A. K. H. Burlew, W. C. Banks, H. P. McAdoo, & D. A. Y. Azibo (Eds), *African American Psychology: Theory, Research, and Practice* (pp. 18–27). Newbury Park, CA: Sage Publications.

Bachman, J. G., & O'Malley, P. M. (1984). Yea-saying, nay-saying, and going to extremes: Black-White differences in response styles. *Public Opinion Quarterly, 48*, 491–509.

Bandura, A. (1997). *Self-efficacy: The exercise of control*. New York: W. H. Freeman.

Berry, J. W. (1980). Introduction to *Methodology*. In: H. C. Triandis & J. W. Berry (Eds), *Handbook of Cross-cultural Psychology* (Vol. 2: Methodology, pp. 1–28). Boston: Allyn and Bacon.

Bong, M., & Clark, R. (1999). Comparison between self-concept and self-efficacy in academic motivation research. *Educational Psychologist*, *34*, 139–153.

Brodzinsky, D. M., Lang, R., & Smith, D. W. (1995). Parenting adopted children. In: M. H. Bornstein (Ed.), *Handbook of Parenting* (Vol. 3: Status and social conditions of parenting. pp. 209–232). Hillsdale, NJ: Erlbaum.

Cauce., A. M., Ryan, K. D., & Grove, K. (1998). Children and adolescents of color, Where are you? Participation, selection, recruitment, and retention in developmental research. In: V. C. McLoyd & L. Steinberg (Eds), *Studying Minority Adolescents: Conceptual, Methodological, and Theoretical Issues* (pp. 147–166). Mahwah, NJ: Lawrence Erlbaum Associates.

Chen, C., & Stevenson, H. W. (1995). Motivation and mathematics achievement: A comparative study of Asian-American, Caucasian-American, and East Asian high school students. *Child Development*, *66*, 1215–1234.

Council of National Psychological Associations for the Advancement of Ethnic Minority Interests (2000). *Guidelines for research in ethnic minority communities*. Washington, D.C.: American Psychological Association.

Cronbach, L. J. (1971). Test validation. In: R. L. Thorndike (Ed.), *Educational Measurement* (2nd ed., pp. 443–507). Washington, D.C.: American Council on Education.

Doucette-Gates, A., Brooks-Gunn, J., & Chase-Lansdale, P. L. (1998). The role of bias and equivalence in the study of race, class, and ethnicity. In: V. C. McLoyd & L. Steinberg (Eds), *Studying Minority Adolescents: Conceptual, Methodological, and Theoretical Issues* (pp. 211–236). Mahwah, NJ: Lawrence Erlbaum Associates.

Eccles, J., Adler, T., Futterman, R., Goff, S., Kaczala, C., Meece, J., & Midgley, C. (1983). Expectancies, values and academic behaviors. In: J. T.. Spence (Ed.), *Achievement and Achievement Motives* (pp. 75–146). San Francisco: W. H. Freeman.

Elliott, A. (1999). Approach and avoidance motivation and achievement goals. *Educational Psychologist*, *34*, 169–189.

Elliott, A., & Harackiewicz, J. (1996). Approach and avoidance achievement goals and intrinsic motivation: A mediational analysis. *Journal of Personality and Social Psychology*, *70*, 461–475.

Fuligni, A. J. (1998). Adolescents from immigrant families. In: V. C. McLoyd & L. Steinberg (Eds), *Studying Minority Adolescents: Conceptual, Methodological, and Theoretical Issues* (pp. 127–143). Mahwah, NJ: Lawrence Erlbaum Associates.

Garcia, E. (1994). *Understanding and meeting the challenge of student cultural diversity*. Boston: Houghton Mifflin Company.

Graham, S. (1992). "Most of the subjects were white and middle class": Trends in reported research on African Americans in selected APA journals, 1970–1989. *American Psychologist*, *47*, 629–639.

Graham, S. (1994). Motivation in African Americans. *Review of Educational Research*, *64*(1), 55–117.

Guerra, N. G., & Jagers, R. (1998). The importance of culture in the assessment of children and youth. In: V. C. McLoyd & L. Steinberg (Eds), *Studying Minority Adolescents: Conceptual, Methodological, and Theoretical Issues* (pp. 167–181). Mahwah, NJ: Lawrence Erlbaum Associates.

Harackiewicz, J., Barron, K., Elliot, A., Carter, S., & Lehto, A. (1997). Predictors and consequences of achievement goals in the college classroom: Maintaining interest and making the grade. *Journal of Personality and Social Psychology, 73*, 1284–1295.

Henderson, V. L., & Dweck, C. S. (1990). Motivation and achievement. In: S. S. Feldman & G. R. Elliot (Eds), *At the Threshold: The Developing Adolescent* (pp. 308–329). Cambridge: Harvard University Press.

Howard-Rose, D., & Winne, P. (1993). Measuring component and sets of cognitive processes in self-regulated learning. *Journal of Educational Psychology, 85*, 591–604.

Krapp, A., Hidi, S., & Renninger, K. (1992). Interest, learning, and development. In: K. Renninger, S. Hidi & A. Krapp (Eds), *The Role of Interest in Learning and Development* (pp. 1–26). Hillsdale, NJ: Lawrence Elrbaum Associates.

Linn, R., Baker, E., & Dunbar, S. (1991). Complex, performance-based assessment: Expectations and validation criteria. *Educational Researcher, 17*, 15–21.

Maehr, M., & Midgley, C. (1991). Enhancing student motivation: A schoolwide approach. *Educational Psychologist, 26*, 399–427.

Marín, G., & Marín, B. V. (1991). *Research with Hispanic populations*. Newbury Park, CA: Sage Publications.

Marsh, H., & O'Neil, R. (1984). Self-Description Questionnaire III: The construct validity of multidimensional self-concept ratings by late adolescents. *Journal of Educational Psychology, 21*, 153–174.

McClelland, D. (1961). *The achieving society*. Princeton, NJ: Van Nostrand.

McLoyd, V. C. (1991). What is the study of African American children the study of? The conduct, publication, and changing nature of research on African American children. In: R. L. Jones (Ed.), *Black Psychology* (3rd ed., pp. 419–440). Berkeley, CA: Cobb and Henry Publishers.

Messick, S. (1989). Validity. In: R. L. Linn (Ed.), *Educational Measurement* (3rd ed., pp. 13–104). New York: Macmillan.

Messick, S. (1995a). Standards of validity and the validity of standards in performance assessment. *Educational Measurement: Issues and Practice, 14*, 5–8.

Messick, S. (1995b). Validity of psychological assessment: Validation of inferences from person's responses and performances as scientific inquiry into score meaning. *American Psychologist, 50*, 741–749.

Middleton, M. J., & Midgley, C. (1997). Avoiding the demonstration of lack of ability: An underexplored aspect of goal theory. *Journal of Educational Psychology, 89*(4), 710–718.

Midgley, C., Kaplan, A., Middleton, M., Maehr, M., Urdan, T., Anderman, L., Anderman, E., & Roeser, R. (1998). The development and validation of scales assessing students' achievement goal orientations. *Contemporary Educational Psychology, 23*, 113–131.

Okagaki, L. (2001). Triarchic model of minority children's school achievement. *Educational Psychologist, 36*(1), 9–20.

Pajares, F. (1996). Self-efficacy beliefs in academic settings. *Review of Educational Research, 66*, 543–578.

Phinney, J. S., & Landin, J. (1998). Research paradigms for studying ethnic minority families within and across groups. In: V. C. McLoyd & L. Steinberg (Eds), *Studying Minority Adolescents: Conceptual, Methodological, and Theoretical Issues* (pp. 89–109). Mahwah, NJ: Lawrence Erlbaum Associates.

Pintrich, P. (2000). Multiple goals, multiple pathways: The role of goal orientation in learning and achievement. *Journal of Educational Psychology, 92*, 544–555.

Pintrich, P. R., & Schunk, D. H. (1996). *Motivation in education: Theory, research, and application*. Englewood Cliffs, NJ: Merrill Prentice Hall.

Pintrich, P. R., Wolters, C. A., & Baxter, G. (2000). Assessing metacognition and self-regulated learning. In: G. Schraw & J. Impara (Eds), *Issues in the Measurement of Metacognition* (pp. 43–97). Lincoln, NE: The University of Nebraska Press.

Portes, P. R. (1996). Ethnicity and culture in educational psychology. In: D. C. Berliner & R. C. Calfee (Eds), *Handbook of Educational Psychology* (pp. 331–357). New York: Simon and Schuster Macmillan.

Rowley, S. J., Sellers, R. M., Chavous, T. M., & Smith, M. A. (1998). The relationship between racial identity and self-esteem in African American college and high school students. *Journal of Personality and Social Psychology, 74*(3), 715–724.

Schiefele, U., Krapp, A., & Winteler, A. (1992). Interest as a predictor of academic achievement: A meta-analysis of research. In: K. Renninger, S. Hidi, & A. Krapp (Eds), *The Role of Interest in Learning and Development* (pp. 183–212). Hillsdale, NJ: Erlbaum.

Schraw, G., Horn, C., Thorndike-Christ, T., & Bruning, R. (1995). Academic goal orientations and student classroom achievement. *Contemporary Educational Psychology, 20*, 359–368.

Schunk, D. (1991). Self-efficacy and academic motivation. *Educational Psychologist, 26*, 207–231.

Sellers, R. M., Chavous, T. M., & Cooke, D. Y. (1998). Racial ideology and racial centrality as predictors of African American college students' academic performance. *Journal of Black Psychology, 24*(1), 8–27.

Sellers, R. M., Rowley, S. A. J., Chavous, T. M., Shelton, J. N., & Smith, M. A. (1997). Multidimensional Inventory of Black Identity: A preliminary investigation of reliability and construct validity. *Journal of Personality and Social Psychology, 73*(4), 805–815.

Sellers, R. M., Smith, M. A., Shelton, J. N., Rowley, S. A. J., & Chavous, T. M. (1998). Multidimensional model of racial identity: A reconceptualization of African American racial identity. *Personality and Social Psychology Review, 2*(1), 18–39.

Spencer, M. B., & Dornbusch, S. M. (1990). Challenges in studying minority youth. In: S. S. Feldman & G. R. Elliot (Eds), *At the Threshold: The Developing Adolescent* (pp. 123–146). Cambridge: Harvard University Press.

Stanfield, J. H. II. (1993). Epistemological considerations. In: J. H. Stanfield II & R. M. Dennis (Eds), *Race and Ethnicity in Research Methods* (pp. 16–36). Newbury Park, CA: Sage Publications.

Sue, D., & Sue, S. (1987). Cultural factors in the clinical assessment of Asian Americans. *Journal of Consulting and Clinical Psychology, 55*, 479–487.

Sue, S., & Sue, D. W. (2000). Conducting psychological research with the Asian American/Pacific Islander population. In: Council of National Psychological Associations for the Advancement of Ethnic Minority Interests, *Guidelines for Research in Ethnic Minority Communities* (pp. 2–4). Washington, D.C.: American Psychological Association.

Triandis, H. C. (1972). *The analysis of subjective culture*. New York: Wiley-Interscience.

U.S. Department of Education, National Center for Education Statistics (2001). *The Condition of Education 2001* [NCES 2000–602]. Washington, D.C.: U.S. Government Printing Office. [Available online: http://nces.ed.gov/edstats/]

van de Vijver, F., & Leung, K. (1997). *Methods and data analysis for cross-cultural research*. Thousand Oaks, CA: Sage.

Vygotsky, L. (1986). *Thought and language*. Cambridge: The MIT Press.

Weinstein, C., Palmer, D., & Schulte, A. (1987). *Learning and Study Strategies Inventory*. Clearwater, FL: H&H Publishing Company, Inc.

Wigfield, A. (1994). Expectancy-Value theory of achievement motivation: A developmental perspective. *Educational Psychology Review*, *6*, 49–78.

Wigfield, A., & Eccles, J. (1992). The development of achievement task values: A theoretical analysis. *Developmental Review*, *12*, 265–310.

Wigfield, A., Eccles, J., Suk Yoon, K., Harold, R., Arbreton, A., Freedman-Doan, C., & Blumenfeld, P. (1997). Change in children's competence beliefs and subjective task values across the elementary school years: A 3-year study. *Journal of Educational Psychology*, *89*, 451–469.

Wong, C. A., & Rowley, S. J. (2001). The schooling of ethnic minority children: Commentary. *Educational Psychologist*, *36*(1), 57–66.

SUBJECT INDEX

www.ingramcontent.com/pod-product-compliance
Ingram Content Group UK Ltd.
Pitfield, Milton Keynes, MK11 3LW, UK
UKHW020846290926
15470UKWH00004B/1573

9 780762 308194